THE GAME

THE GAME

THE HARVARD-YALE FOOTBALL RIVALRY, 1875–1983

THOMAS G. BERGIN   **FOREWORD BY WILL CLONEY**

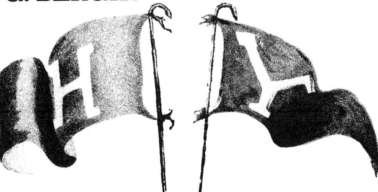

YALE UNIVERSITY PRESS   NEW HAVEN AND LONDON

Designed by Sally Harris
and set in Melior type by The Saybrook Press, Inc.
Printed in the United States of America by
The Murray Printing Company, Westford, Mass.

Library of Congress Cataloging in Publication Data

Bergin, Thomas Goddard, 1904–
  The Game: the Harvard-Yale football rivalry, 1875–1983.
  Bibliography: p.
  Includes index.
  1. Harvard University—Football—History.   2. Yale
University—Football—History.   I. Title.
GV958.H3B47   1984   796.332'72   84-40189
ISBN 0-300-03267-6

The paper in this book meets the guidelines for
permanence and durability of the Committee on
Production Guidelines for Book Longevity
of the Council on Library Resources.

10 9 8 7 6 5 4 3 2 1

To the enduring presence of
Walter Camp
and
Percy Haughton

CONTENTS

LIST OF ILLUSTRATIONS

FOREWORD

The history of intercollegiate football is encapsulated in Professor Bergin's chronicle of one hundred years of Harvard–Yale gridiron rivalry. This carefully researched and documented book presents the complete picture of the sport, from the uncontrolled viciousness of the early years to the more scientific, cerebral approach to the game today.

Harvard and Yale were the Adam and Eve of college football (assign the gender as your loyalties dictate). Over the years most of their original sins have been erased—but any true follower of the sport should at least know what those sins were.

This book reveals them, just as it brings to life the great names of the past. Walking through the huge arched portal called the Walter Camp Memorial Gateway to the Yale Bowl will take on a new significance when you get to know this fabulous figure intimately. Harvard men should remember him for a little realized fact: the long string of early Yale victories was directly attributable to his lengthy tenure as player, coach, and adviser in the era when Harvard had only an informal coach, usually a different one each year.

A visit to the Ray Tompkins House will be more meaningful when the visitor realizes it was named after the famous captain of the 1882 Yale team. And Frank Hinkey? I've always pictured this legendary character as a hulking brute, so it was a surprise to learn that he was a 165-pound "disembodied spirit" who made up in fury for his lack of size.

These and other bits of nineteenth-century gridiron lore appear to have a distinctly Blue tinge. The reason might appear obvious: ask a loyal Yale man to write a sports history and the deep cerulean hue is inevitable. Not so in this case. Professor Bergin is a scholar and author first, an Eli second, and this book is scrupulously objective, colored from era to era only by the facts, not by sentimental attachment.

In addition to being given due credit for its numerous victories through the years, Harvard is hailed as a pioneer in many innovations: spring practice (how the present coaches wish it were still allowed in the Ivy League!), the tackling dummy, slippery leather uniforms, the Stadium, shelters for half-time intermission, and many more.

The book is a football historian's delight, yet it escapes the dullness of a mere reportorial account of each annual game by the clever introduction of background material on contemporary political and economic affairs. The anecdotes of the students' mores, from the days when New York bars were besieged by pigskin celebrants to the handkerchief waving and dirges of the present, also lend color to the story of the famous rivalry.

That rivalry deserves a book such as this. In 1897, an editorial in the Harvard *Crimson* welcomed Yale "as Harvard's nearest and dearest foe." So it has been for the last hundred years; so may it be for the next hundred.

Will Cloney
Harvard 1933

ACKNOWLEDGMENTS

In the making of this book I have had many helpers. In my task of collecting material the assistance of Frank Ryan, director of athletics at Yale, and his staff has been invaluable. Mark Curran of Yale Sports Information has been a comrade-in-arms throughout the enterprise. I was fortunate, too, in securing the services of Neal Pease, who did much laborious research for me. I am grateful for the typing expertise of Jean Conklin, Linda Nelson, and Daphne Foreman. On the Harvard side Robert A. Pickett of the Harvard Varsity Club, John Bethel of the *Harvard Magazine*, and Ed Markey of Harvard Sports Information gave ready assistance. I am also grateful for the contributions made by the staffs of the Yale and Harvard Archives and the Scranton Library of Madison, by Mrs. Arline S. Morton of the City Library of Springfield, Massachusetts, and by Robin McElheny of the Harvard Archives, whose extraordinary labors turned up many of the photographs that appear in this book.

Bob Barton of the *New Haven Register* consented to read my first draft, graciously putting at my disposal both his editorial expertise and his vast knowledge of Yale football. My book has profited greatly by his scrupulous, one might say merciless reading. Other readers of the first version include Will Cloney (Cantabrigian guide and counselor throughout the enterprise), Madison Sayles, and John Yovicsin; all have been helpful and likewise encouraging. Others who have given help along the road, either by supplying information, offering suggestions, or in other ways are Malcolm P. Aldrich, Mrs. William Henry Barnum, Richard Birdsall, John Chamberlain, Thomas Darling, Jr., Pierre Demarque, Stanley Flink, Robert A. Hall, Mrs. Drayton Heard, Fenno Heath, Jr., Ralph Horween, Donald E. Jaekle, the late Samuel M. S. Lanham, Richard Lowry, Paul Morgan, David M. Nelson, John H. Norton, George Vaill, G. Harold Welch, Harold B. Whiteman, Jr., and Mrs. David P. Williams; and I want to say a special thank you to John Ellsworth, who not only read the first draft and the galleys of the final version but also gave generous help and guidance in many matters of detail.

There is another area of indebtedness to be acknowledged. My book, like all of similar nature, is of necessity cannibalistic, feeding itself on the substance of its predecessors. I have, in my notes, recognized my many specific debts to the works of Bealle, Cohane, Parke H. Davis, the *H Book of Harvard Athletics*, and the like. But probably I owe them even more than I realize; I suspect they may have sharpened my perceptions and clarified my judgment in ways that are not easily documentable. In any event, I am happy to acknowledge my debt.

The cradle years of American intercollegiate football coincide with a remarkably exuberant period in our national history. Samuel Eliot Morison, in opening chapter 14 of his *Three Centuries of Harvard*, provides a perceptive sketch of those brash and self-confident years:

In the year 1869, America was in the midst of the most roaring, spectacular material development that she had ever known. Exploitation and expansion were the order of the day. A golden spike forged the last link in the railway chain from Atlantic to Pacific. The mining empire in the Rocky Mountains, the cattle kingdom on the Great Plains, and the westward-striding army of homesteaders were wiping out the frontier. Steel mills in Pittsburgh were running full-blast; cotton and woollen mills in New England were hanging up new annual records of production. In the rapidly growing cities of the East, politicians and financiers, railroad barons and merchant princes, were stepping wide, high, and handsome. Even the prostrate South was beginning to look up again and call the land her own. Ulysses S. Grant was inaugurated President of the United States in 1869, and the Knights of Labor were organized. Everyone was making money and expecting to make more; the inevitable post-war depression was not even suspected; the clank of machinery and the clink of dollars silenced religion, letters, and the arts.[1]

A few additional details may be added to supplement Morison's deft summary. Expansion is perhaps the chief characteristic of the early post-bellum decades. Between 1870 and 1890 the population of the United States, fed by wave upon wave of immigration, swelled from approximately 40 million to 63 million, and it would reach 76 million by the turn of the century. The country needed more room; it would be provided by the "winning of the West," a conquest vigorously pursued through the rest of the century and beyond, adding eight stars to the flag in the course of the eighth and ninth decades, giving breathing room to the teeming East, and adding its own quotient of wealth to the national coffers—to say nothing of making "The Chisholm Trail" a national favorite. Technological innovations were another feature of the times. Within the decade of the seventies alone Remington patented the first typewriter (1873), the first electrically powered cars rumbled over New York streets in 1874, the first telephone exchange was inaugurated—in New Haven—in 1877, the fertile-minded Thomas Edison patented his talking machine in 1878 and his incandescent bulb a year later. Political historians would add to expansion and innovation corruption in public and business affairs as also characteristic of the Brownstone era; the plunderings of Boss Tweed were on such an imposing scale as to send him to prison, but they were a poor second to the piracy of the princes of industry and finance—who remained at large. In 1876, historians concur, the national election was "stolen," robbing an honest Yale man of the presidency. Yet the country was organically healthy and survived and prospered through it all.

And if venality and corruption were rife and materialism the order of the day it is only fair to remark that the Gilded Age gave appreciative audience to Mark Twain and Henry James. Nor was the era inhospitable to higher education: Johns Hopkins opened its doors in 1876, Leland Stanford Junior University in 1885; Cornell (1868) and the University of Chicago (1892), although their inaugural years fall a little outside the brackets of the gaslit decades, are products of the same cultural climate. For that matter it was in this era that Harvard's president Charles Eliot achieved national recognition as an educator. Nor can one feel ungrateful to a decade that has bequeathed to us "Home on the Range," "White Winds," and "Wait till the Clouds Roll By."

Eighteen sixty-nine, properly celebrated by Morison for the installation of Eliot and the driving of the golden spike, is also significant for our chronicle; it was the year of the first intercollegiate football match, played between Princeton and Rutgers, the tiny seed from which luxuriant foliage would very quickly sprout. It is probably fair to see in the genesis and growth of the game a natural by-product of the times, aggressive, combative, and competitive; times that also, incidentally, provided a large segment of the population with leisure and means to satisfy the abiding taste for colorful and animated spectacles, which is a constant of the human psyche.

If we think of American football as a great tree, waxing ever more lofty through the years, we may properly see in the Harvard–Yale rivalry one of its most robust and impressive branches. The rivalry was natural and predictable; Crimson and Blue had already a tradition of competition in crew dating back to 1852, in baseball to a few years later. But it was not until six years after the planting of the seed in New Jersey that the great pigskin rivalry began, in New Haven, in the waning years of Grant's administration, while the Old Fence still stood and Noah Porter directed the destinies of Yale.

Aside from its historic importance as the first link in a golden chain, the game of 1875 had some unique features. It was not the first season for either the Blue or the Crimson. Yale had played its first intercollegiate match in 1872 against Columbia; Harvard had begun its pigskin parade with two games with McGill in 1874. Neither Harvard nor Yale had played what Americans now call football: Yale's opener with Columbia and all subsequent encounters until 1875 were in effect soccer (with varying numbers on a side; the Columbia game had featured "picked twenties"); Harvard, tutored by McGill, had played Canadian rugby. So when Captain Nathaniel Curtis of Harvard challenged Captain William Arnold of Yale to meet on the field of battle, preliminary negotiations were necessary to agree on the style of play to be followed. The game of 1875 was therefore known as the "concessionary game."

There is still some uncertainty about the nature of the rules agreed upon. According to Allison Danzig, "the game they played was largely Rugby. Harvard agreed to certain changes on the side of soccer [Danzig does not specify which], and Yale conceded to play fifteen men on a side . . . instead of the eleven it advocated. The Rugby principle of running with the ball and tackling was permitted. Harvard agreed that touchdowns, as in British Rugby, would affect the score only by permitting a try for goal."[2] The ball, which, incidentally, collapsed in the course of the contest and had to be reinflated on the field, was a rugby ball but somewhat larger and more rounded than the one in use today. Rugby is a game of running and passing (laterally), while in soccer, the game with which Yale was familiar, the ball cannot be touched by hands but must be advanced by kicking only, with an occasional header. It is hardly surprising that the Crimson came out on top. More significantly for the future of the sport, the Harvards won an ideological victory, too, for, although the wearers of the Blue did not enjoy their humiliation, they found the Cambridge game much more to their taste than soccer. Two Princetonian observers were also enthralled by the new style of play, and the following year Old Nassau joined her sisters and adopted Cantabrigian rugby.

As for the game itself, the account in the *Harvard Crimson* contains some memorable details, evocative of the blithe air of the early dawn of the sport.

About 150 Harvard men accompanied the football team to New Haven. Special cars were provided and arrangements had been made at New Haven so that all found ample accommodations at the New Haven House. . . . Saturday morning the Yale men kindly drove the team about New Haven, showing them the objects of interest in-

cluding the college buildings and the new boat-house of the Yale Navy, which is one of the most complete structures of the kind and one of which Yale may feel justly proud. The game was called at 2:30 p.m. in the presence of a large number of spectators and paying fifty cents each; many of the quality coming by carriage.[3] An enclosure at Hamilton Park had been roped off, leaving a field of perfect smoothness. The Harvard students formed in a group and encouraged the players, lavishing their applause on Yale or Harvard, as the occasion required it. . . . The adopted rules were not fully understood by either team, and the Yale men said they differed from theirs more than from Harvard's. The Yale men wore dark trousers, blue shirts, yellow caps; and Harvard the usual crimson shirts and stockings with knee britches.[4]

Hamilton Park, New Haven, ca. 1890, scene of the first Harvard–Yale game in 1875. Photo The New Haven Colony Historical Society.

Spectators watching game from carriage, 1880s.

All accounts agree that the weather was good, slightly overcast but no wind. The game was divided into three half-hour periods. In the first half-hour Leeds and Seamans scored goals for Harvard (the former also made a touchdown); in the second half-hour Blanchard kicked another Crimson goal and Cushing made another touchdown; the last half-hour Blanchard made the last Harvard touchdown and Tower the last Crimson goal. The official record, crediting Blanchard with a second touchdown, scores the game as four goals and four touchdowns for Harvard with nothing for Yale; the *Crimson*, counting three touchdowns as equal to a goal, declared Harvard the winner by five goals to nothing.

Wetherbe
Tower

The 1875 Harvard team, captained by Nathaniel Curtis *(far right)*.

1875 FOOTBALL TEAM

	Seamans		Herrick							Thayer	
Cushing		Hall		Blanchard	Keys		Faucon	Leeds			Cate
		Bacon		Morse							Curtis

The epoch-making event was ignored by the *New York Times*, but the *New Haven Register* was on hand and supplies a few picturesque details:

The first two goals were won by Harvard with an ease almost ludicrous, the Yale men, from their utter ignorance of the game, doing very little, except to look on. As the game went on, however, and the blues became better acquainted with its nature the play became more exciting, and the spectators were entertained by many really fine points. The running of the Harvard men was very fine, that point, together with their bodying and throwing, being the most noticeable incidents in their game. Yale was outplayed at every point except that of kicking, and as in this game kicking was not of the slightest use, that availed them nothing. . . . The Harvard men were remarkable for the accuracy with which they threw the ball into each other's hands, even under circumstances the most embarrassing. They had eight rushers and, wherever the ball was, there one was sure to see half a dozen of the crimsons surrounding and taking possession of it generally. The Yale men, on the other hand, threw the ball in that direction which seemed most convenient to them, and failed altogether to follow up the ball. . . . The uniform worn by the Harvard team was remarkably pretty, and useful withal, as the brilliancy of its color was such that its wearers knew intuitively almost where to throw the ball. The Yale team on the other hand was dressed so plainly that they really seemed to be fewer in number than their adversaries. . . . We would recommend the adoption of white trousers as part of the costume, and "shoot the caps."[5]

The *Crimson*, understandably, found the game "was beautifully played throughout and Harvard may feel well pleased with her team." It seems to have thrilled the spectators, too, for the *Crimson* reports that in the final moments of combat many "rushed over the rope into the enclosure and cheered on the respective parties." The same source indicates that it was a festive night in New Haven: "In the evening the teams were entertained at supper and representatives of the two colleges sang in the college yard."[6] The *Register* adds the information: "Seven Harvard students were arrested in this city Saturday night for creating disturbances by hooting and singing in the public streets. They all gave fictitious names and deposited their watches and other articles of jewelry as security for a fine of $5.29 in each case."[7]

We may regard the original Yale–Harvard game as the fertilization of the game we know as American football. The hatching process proceeded apace. The Princeton witnesses of the first battle of Hamilton Park not only persuaded the young Tigers to turn from soccer to the rugby style, but suggested a meeting with the ambassadors of Yale, Harvard, and Columbia to codify the rules of the new pattern of combat. This historic convention took place on November 26, 1876, in the Massasoit House of Springfield, Massachusetts; the representatives denominated themselves the Intercollegiate Football Association and for the first time formalized rules to apply to all games in the future (previously, ad hoc specification had been the common practice between prospective contending parties). In general, the new association adopted the Rugby Union code (not a very ancient design itself, for the Rugby Union dated back only to 1872; it is interesting to note that the first Oxford–Cambridge match took place only three years before the first Harvard–Yale duello). Dimensions of the field were fixed at 140 by 70 yards, playing time was to be ninety minutes—two forty-minute halves with an interval of ten minutes between them. Scoring and the size of the team proved to be very controversial matters; it was finally voted that "a match shall be decided by a majority of touchdowns. A goal shall be equal to four touchdowns but in the case of a tie a goal shall take precedence over four touchdowns," and further, "a team shall consist of 15 players." To both of these decisions Yale objected, arguing for counting only goals in the scoring and for fielding a team of only eleven men. Failing to prevail, Yale refused to join the association until 1879 but continued to send representatives to the annual meeting and in fact abided by the rules (with occasional exceptions, as we shall see). All agreed that henceforth the rugby ball would be the official ball of the game.

The association's design for play lasted only until 1880, when Yale's persistence paid off, and the New Haven delegation, headed by Walter Camp, recently graduated but still a member of the Yale team, won concessions on all its points of disagreement. The team complement was changed to eleven, and the dimensions of the field were reduced to 110 by 53 yards. But even more important in the hatching of the new chick was the change from scrum to scrimmage. In a rugby match play is continuous; when a runner is downed the ball is fed immediately into the scrum, which, depending on chance and the skill of the forwards, feeds it back to one side or the other to be put in play by the back. Camp believed that a team having possession deserved the right to keep the ball and put it in play without abandoning it to the caprice of the scrum. This concept meant a pause in the action after a runner was brought down, with opportunity for both offense and defense to deploy their forces. The center of the possessing team then put the ball in play (at first by heeling it; not until a decade later did the hand come into the operation), and a scrimmage resulted. More than any one innovation it was the invention of the scrimmage—Walter Camp's idea—that marked the distinction of American football from its parent, rugby. The new system had one defect. There was no provision for making the possessing team give up the ball. Failing to gain or losing ground could do you no harm; even if you were pushed behind your goal line you had nothing to lose, for a safety did not count in the scoring. This weakness was dramatically illustrated in the Princeton–Yale game of 1881 (the infamous "block" game), in which Princeton kept the ball all the first half and Yale, receiving the second-half kickoff, followed the same tactic—all to the immense disgust of the spectators. It was clear that henceforth, unless the scrimmage was abandoned or some remedy found, all games would end in ties and probably scoreless ties at that. In 1882 Camp came to the rescue of his own innovation and conceived the notion of *downs*; it was ruled that a team holding the ball must either gain five yards or lose ten in three attempts or give up the ball. This change has been called "the very heart of the modern game" and had its effect on the appearance of the field and, in course of time, on the terminology of the game. In order to measure the yardage necessary for a first down the field had to be marked with transverse stripes, and thus the term *gridiron* came into being. Furthermore, the new arrangement of the players necessitated by the ground game presently brought about a new vocabulary, descriptive of the functions of the members of the team. Up to this time the players had been divided into *rushes* and *tends*—linemen and backs, as we would style them. The innovation of the controlled scrimmage resulted in more precise terminology. Players at either end of the rush line were naturally called *ends*; since the style of line play (even as today) centered on the space between the end men and the next player, it normally fell to the latter to make most of the tackles, and the name of the function was assigned to the player. *Guards* were thought of as guarding the center, as indeed they did—particularly before the neutral zone between offensive and defensive lines was ordained in 1906 after long and persistent prodding by Camp. The absence of that no-man's-land gave the old game a special sector of violence that may have contributed to its bad reputation among the squeamish. For before the scrimmage began by

Walter Camp, '80.

the center passing the ball to his back (usually with his foot), the opposing lines stood nose to nose, taunting each other and "slugging it out," man to man, as often as the referee's eye was fixed elsewhere. Backs were given special designations—quarter, half, full—based on their deployment behind the scrimmage line.

Having, as it were, invented the game, Camp, in 1883, proceeded to make the ticklish business of scoring much easier to manage, giving numerical values to touchdowns, goals, and safeties. Subsequent valuations have given more weight to the touchdown and less to the field goal. One other feature of the American game, distinctive from rugby, is blocking, or interference. The association made no rules on this practice; it seems to have grown up quietly (first scientifically or at least deliberately used, it is said, by the Princeton team of 1884) and won tacit toleration. Blocking is illegal in rugby.

Let us return now to the chronicle of battle. The second Yale–Harvard engagement took place, again in Hamilton Park, on November 18, 1876—the year that Crazy Horse slaughtered the gallant Custer and his troopers. This game, too, might be called concessionary, for Harvard consented to play with an eleven-man team, as Yale firmly requested. And again it was agreed that touchdowns would not count in the scoring, although this time kick-outs were permitted. Playing conditions were not ideal; the *Harvard Advocate*, while granting that the bright new uniforms of the teams were pleasing to the eye, reported that "pieces of

clothesline supplied the places of crossbars on two very short goal posts" and that the touchlines were so poorly marked as to be invisible.[8] The Harvard delegation was strong, having already won two victories; for Yale the engagement with the Crimson was the season's opener (for the only time in the history of the series). Besides, Yale was still unfamiliar with the rugby game and did not even possess a rugby ball to practice with until, a few days before the encounter, Harvard chivalrously supplied one. However, the Blue prevailed, thanks to the nature of the rules. Harvard power scored four touchdowns but no goal followed. Yale won on a kick by Oliver Thompson, '79, who, by chance, found the ball lying in front of him and propelled it a lusty thirty-five yards over the crossbar. The *Crimson* reports of the match: "The weather was rather cold and the grounds were a little slippery; the game was called at three o'clock and played in two heats of three quarters of an hour each." Noting that the Elis played a much better game than they had the previous year, the *Crimson* added that "the Yale team, though undoubtedly very strong, was so ignorant of the rules that they persisted in a course of play which throughout the game was very productive of 'fouls.'"[9] The crowd followed the action with enthusiasm. A report in *Field and Stream* discloses that, following Thompson's kick, "the crowd, which at no time during the game kept the proper limits, broke in upon the field and used up twenty minutes of valuable time by carrying the Yale men around on their shoulders."[10] One paladin thus enthroned was young Walter Camp, a freshman making his first appearance in the Blue lineup.

Harvard must have felt she had been sadly used; she had graciously consented to play with eleven men, had lent Yale a practice ball—and then had to see her four touchdowns go for naught. One can understand her refusal to play the game of 1877 under the same conditions; Yale, on her part, was adamant and again insisted on an eleven-man team. Neither party yielding, no game was played in 1877.

Action was resumed in 1878, the meeting, for the first time, taking place on Harvard's home field—on this occasion the Boston baseball grounds. It was a soggy field that day and the Yale fifteen had more success in dealing with the wet leather than the Crimson, winning by the margin of Thompson's goal, the only score of the game.

Parke H. Davis relates that "a moment of happy diversion for the spectators occurred when the ball rolled off the field into a deep pool of water, into which players on both sides flung them-selves."[11] After some competitive wallowing Camp emerged with the ball, soaked but triumphant.

The *Advocate* records the victory as follows: "The ball rose high in the air and went straight for our goal, and passing over the bar was caught by our end. It was a goal for Yale and the Yale men ran about the field congratulating one anoth-er." Stars of the game, it is reported, were Cushing for Harvard and Camp for Yale; the latter very narrowly missed a goal from fifty yards out. Re-grettably, according to the *Advocate* at least, the Yale style of play was ungentlemanly. It was the unseemly practice of the Blue players, the *Advo-cate* noted, to run into the Harvard ballcarriers,

"knocking them down after they had caught the ball on the fly and were entitled to a fair kick. This was done four or five times in 15 minutes. Their only object was to disable the Harvard players."[12]

On her visit to New Haven on November 8, 1879, Harvard fared somewhat better; the game ended in a scoreless tie; each team made more safeties than goals or touchdowns (a defensive battle, we should call it nowadays), but safeties didn't count in the scoring. The *New York Times* estimated the attendance at 1,500 and found the teams so evenly matched that there was little to choose between them, though Yale was superior in skill. Camp kicked the only field goal of the game, but since the ball had been touched by Cushing of Harvard the kick was ruled invalid (such was the bylaw of the times). It was Camp's second year as captain; his team was undefeated and unscored on but had to settle for ties with both Harvard and Princeton. (Camp had the rare opportunity for a Yale captain to referee the Harvard–Princeton game a week later, played in Hoboken and won by the Tigers; although the *Crimson* commented that he fulfilled his task in a way "highly satisfactory to both parties," it could not refrain from remarking gratuitously that in the match "the utmost good feeling was displayed on either side—an agreeable contrast to the treat-ment experienced by our teams at New Haven.")[13] Apparently Yale's behavior was continuing to eli-cit the usual reproaches from Harvard men. For the '79 game it would seem only fair to give the Yale point of view. A staff member of the *Yale Daily News* commented (November 20) that

It may be interesting to know what Harvard was doing when Yale was so shamefully abusing her. The first disturbance that we saw, and we watched the game very closely, was caused by a Harvard player throttling one of our men. This man was so openly unfair in his playing that [Harvard's] Captain Bacon [who would become in the fullness of time assistant secretary of state and ambassador to France] was compelled to reprimand him. We saw another Harvard man strike an opponent in the face with closed fist. Twice we saw a Harvard man rush into Captain Camp when the latter was preparing to kick the ball, thereby endangering the limbs of our captain. . . . Once, during an altercation in the field, the Harvard men who were witnessing the game ran swearing and in a threatening manner on the field, thereby almost precipitating a row. . . . It is worthy of note that at this moment not a Yale man crossed the ropes.

Pictorial evidence of the vigorous action in those primordial years may be found in the illustrations of Frederic Remington, himself one of Camp's warriors in 1879.

"A Day with the Yale Team," drawings by Frederic Remington published in *Harper's Weekly*.

Drawing by Frederic Remington published in *Harper's Weekly*.

The 1880 Yale team. Captain R. W. Watson, '80, is holding the ball. Walter Camp is to Watson's left.

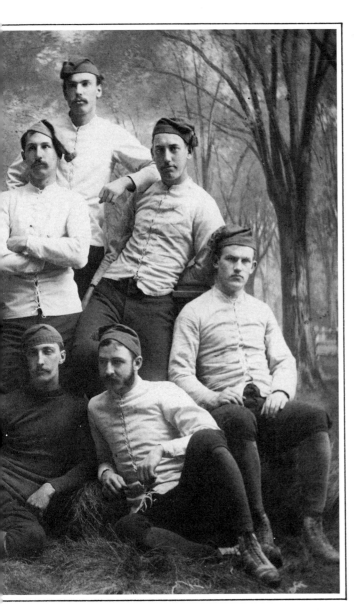

The engagement of 1880, fought out on the Boston baseball ground on November 20, was played under the new rules that Camp had argued for: eleven men to a side and the replacement of the scrum by the scrimmage. It was therefore only fitting that Camp should score the one goal of the game, played with fire and dedication on both sides. "The Yale 'roughs,'" the Harvard historian Morris A. Bealle affirms (and Yale men should feel grateful for the quotation marks),

had no easy time in ekeing out a victory by a goal and a touchdown. . . . Edmands blocked a Yale score early in the game. Good work by Foster then pushed the ball close to the Yale goal, much to the delight of the home rooters, but Edmands missed a drop kick by inches. Yale then worked the ball into Harvard territory where three attempts by Walter Camp to drop-kick were blocked by the Harvard rushers. Yale missed a score early in the second period when the ball carrier slipped just before he reached the Harvard goal line. Play continued with several fierce exchanges with no side holding the advantage, when suddenly Camp booted a long drop kick from Harvard's 42-yard line for the only score of the game.[14]

Toward the end of the game, Bealle adds, after a Harvard kick, "the Yale captain, R. W. Watson, ran the ball 100 yards for a touchdown. The try for goal was not permitted, as time had run out." Watson's run still stands as a record for the game. It is pleasant to read (*Yale Daily News*, November 22) that "the Harvard team gave ours an excellent spread in the evening at Young's."

The following year Harvard brought a strong team to New Haven, having gone undefeated in six games—including a win over Michigan, the first intersectional clash recorded by the Ivies. It was, as usual, a sturdy Yale squad, too, destined to go unvanquished through the season, though suffering a tie with Princeton, in the "block" game alluded to earlier. Ivy Leaguers may be pleased to note that in that happy year both Yale and Harvard defeated Michigan. Harvard was a little unlucky in her timing; in 1880 the game with Yale would have been a draw, but the rules for 1881 laid it down that when there was no other scoring, victory would go to the team having the fewer safeties scored against it. Harvard made four safeties (one involuntarily, the others by choice) and Yale only two. So it was another Blue triumph, but only, one might say, technically speaking. The *New York Times* counted 1,500 spectators (310 Harvard students had come by special train) and remarked that the "game was played in a drenching rain. . . . Each team was heartily supported by encouraging cheers. Both sides played with great skill and without any block game business. Good feeling prevailed."[15] The *Harvard Advocate* seemed to feel that the Crimson had scored a moral victory, particularly since the muddy field worked to the advantage of the Elis: "We owe our defeat to the superiority of the Yale team in weight and strength, especially to that of her rushers, to the brilliant playing of Camp and to the slipperiness of the ground and the ball. If it had been dry, the strong points of our eleven could have been more easily shown. . . . The Yale men appeared like giants. . . . But in spite of her superiority in size and strength [and in spite of the fact that the referee was "decidedly in favor of Harvard," in the view of the *New Haven Register* (November 13)], Yale won by the smallest possible score." The *Advocate* then tries, not entirely successfully, to come to terms with Yale's football manners:

It has been the custom since the beginning of football contests between Yale and Harvard for Harvard men to accuse Yale men of uncalled-for brutality, of a desire to win by maiming our men, and at an early stage of this game it looked as though we should have to chronicle a continuance of this old roughness. When Edmands was lying on the ball outside the line there was no reason for a heavy Yale man's throwing himself upon Edmands with over 200 pounds of weight.

But later in the game the roughness disappeared. Yale did not try to maim our men as much as she usually does, and the second inning was to all appearances gentlemanly throughout. . . . It is felt by nearly all Harvard men that Yale plays more violently than is necessary or in good taste, but we must remember that she plays no more roughly against us than she does against other teams, and against her own men when they appear on the field too.

However, the writer concludes with a cryptic sentence: "Still there can be no excuse for the use of teeth in football."[16] What *was* the Bulldog up to that soggy afternoon? Yale readers of the *Advocate's* observations may find some comfort in Bealle's comment on the scoreless tie with Princeton that closed the Harvard season: "The contest was marked by rough play, and resulted in bitter feelings."[17]

As we have noted, 1882 might truly be said to mark the beginning of American football, since Camp's notion of downs had come into force and given the field the familiar gridiron appearance. In this year, too, spoken signals were first used. It was a good year for both Yale and Harvard; under the leadership of Ray Tompkins the Bulldogs came through an eight-game schedule undefeated

The 1882 Yale team. *Front row, l. to r.:* H. W. Slocum, W. Terry, E. L. Richards, H. B. Twombly, A. L. Farwell. *Back row:* C. S. Beck, B. W. Bacon, L. K. Hull, H. Knapp, Captain R. Tompkins, F. G. Peters, W. Camp, W. H. Hyndman.

and untied—the first time such immaculate perfection had been achieved since 1876 (and Baker's
team that year had played only three games). Harvard also had a series of seven victories under her
belt (including a triumph over Dartmouth, the
first meeting in that long rivalry) when Yale came
up to Holmes Field on November 25 to spoil it all.
As in the previous year, the Blue margin was
scanty; the Bulldogs made three touchdowns but
converted only one, so the score reads one goal to
nothing. For the second year in a row a very promising Crimson team (the '82 club had even beaten
Princeton) had suffered frustration—this time in
the presence of 2,500 spectators, most of them
Harvard supporters. Not surprisingly, the behavior of the visiting Elis came in for some disparag-
ing comment; the *Advocate* summed up the combat as follows:

*We have met the enemy and we are theirs. We
had hopes of victory but the Fates decreed otherwise. The Yale eleven played a fine—almost a
perfect game. Its play was violent as it usually is,
and she very often wantonly broke the rules of the
game. . . . Our men, seemingly awed by the brutality of their opponents, with the exception of a few
men, did little. . . . It must be evident to Harvard
men that if we are at any time to beat Yale at
football, our style of play must be radically
changed. We must adapt ourselves to the Yale
game.*[18]

The '83 game had several features of interest.
Played on the Polo Grounds in New York on November 29, the match attracted 10,000 spectators,
a record crowd for an athletic contest of any sort
(according to Bealle) up to that time.[19] Also, for
the first time Camp's suggestion of numerical scoring was put into effect. A touchdown counted two
points, a goal after touchdown four points, a goal
from the field five points, and a safety one point.
Yale took the game rather easily 23 to 2. In the
first half Yale blocked a kick by Harvard's excellent punter, Henry, and recovered for a safety; just
before the half ended Wyllys Terry kicked a goal
from the field. Yale opened the second half with
a touchdown and conversion. Henry of Harvard
set up a Crimson touchdown with an electrifying
run, but the conversion kick hit the goalpost. Yale
retorted with a touchdown by Farwell, converted
by Terry, who ended the scoring with another
long field goal. The *Crimson* handsomely comments that "the Yale team played an almost perfect game throughout and several rushes of Terry's
were the finest we have seen this season. Twombly
[the Yale quarterback and future mayor of Summit,
New Jersey] stood up to his work manfully, for
his aggressive playing called forth considerable
rough handling. Tompkins and Farwell worked
hard for their side. For Harvard Henry's half
back play was universally acknowledged as the
best work of the day." Yale's manners were gradually improving, it would seem, for the same journal goes on to remark: "The game throughout was
the fairest ever played with Yale, and were it not
for the deliberate fouling the Yale rushers showed
in their tackling of Henry their playing seemed
very straightforward."[20] But if Yale was learning,
perhaps, on the other and darker side of the coin,

Harvard was, too. The "aggressive" Twombly reported:

The ball was kicked to me and I stood ready to catch it, when somehow or other I was struck in the mouth by a Harvard knee. The ball that time wasn't caught! They tried it again later on, but instead of my mouth it was the mouths of two charging rushers which pushed themselves against my extended fists. I was never bothered that way again in the game, though I came out of the game with two black eyes, a bloody nose and two swollen lips.[21]

The *New York Times's* (November 30) account of the game, all but lyric in tone, carries over the years the flavor of the Gilded Age. The "assembly of about ten thousand people" the *Times* informs us,

filled the grand stand and the general stands, packed coaches, hacks and other vehicles, and lined the rail on the south and east sides of the field, and the rope that was stretched along two sides of the rectangular field and hundreds who couldn't find a specially desirable spot roamed aimlessly about. A Broadway omnibus was pressed into service by a horde of Yale men, covered with blue cambric and decorated with Yale flags of silk.

Long before the elevens put in an appearance the students . . . made things lively with their good natured banter, and filled the air with their peculiar cheers, the tooting of horns and the music of their buglers. Gay balloons of red and blue were floated by Harvard and Yale men respectively, and these novel decorations attracted much attention.

The Yale team . . . wore dirty white jerseys, fustian knickerbockers and blue stockings and caps.

Harvard's stalwarts, also wearing dirty white jerseys, had brown knickerbockers, with stockings, shirt-sleeves, and caps of crimson. "The halfbacks and backs wore crimson shirts over their jerseys and the Yale occupants of the same positions wore blue jackets." The *Times's* reporter spotted Harvard's illustrious professor Charles E. Norton "watching over his 'lambs' from the grand stand and saw them tumbled about considerably. He also saw them act on the aggressive in the rough work of the game, and perhaps noticed with chagrin that none of the 'lambs' were ordered off the field for interference or rough play. It must have been the cause of more chagrin that one of the Yale 'bullies' were ordered off the field. His feelings were somewhat allayed probably when the Harvard lambs succeeded in laying out Richards of Yale just at the close of the first half." At the end of the game, "the field was filled with wearers of the blue. . . . They cheered the team collectively and individually. Then they cheered Harvard, Yale, themselves, and everything else they could think of."

For the '84 season the scoring values were reassessed; henceforth (until 1898) a touchdown would count as four points, the goal from touchdown two; safeties went up to two points, the field

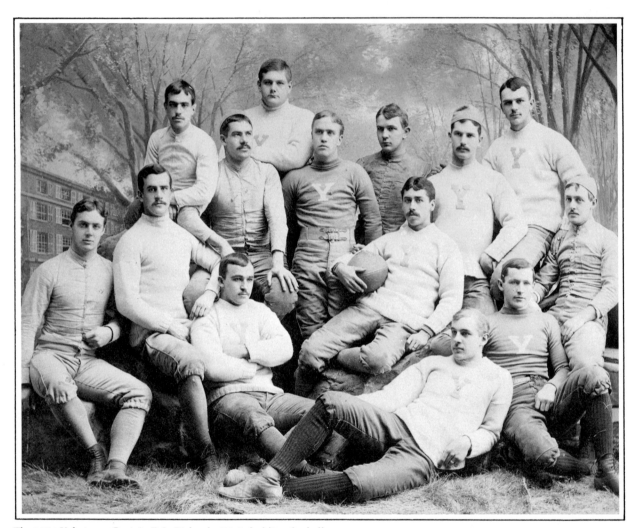

The 1884 Yale team. Captain E. L. Richards, '85, is holding the ball.

goal stayed at five. Richards's powerful Yale squad would have fared well under any system; it turned out to be one of the Blue's strongest teams up to that time, totaling 495 points (of which 113 were harvested in the first Bulldog encounter with Dartmouth) to opponents' 10. A tie with Princeton spoiled an otherwise perfect season. For Harvard, on the other hand, '84 was a somewhat disappointing year; the Crimson came to New Haven with three defeats already on her record, having lost to Pennsylvania, Princeton, and—shockingly—to Wesleyan (in a game played in Hartford and no doubt still remembered in Middletown). For the first time in the history of the rivalry (though not the last) the spectators saw two sadly mismatched teams. Yale ran away with the game, scoring 24 points in the first half and as much again after the interval. Nine touchdowns and six goals after touchdown were scored; in today's system the total would come out to 60 points. But 48 was quite enough to stand as a record for seventy-three years.* Yale stars were Coxe, Richards, and Bayne at quarterback. Bayne, a sophomore at the time, showed unusual promise, but his extracurricular activities outside the playing field eventually resulted in his leaving Yale. He later coached Tulane and Louisiana State. For

*There remains still some uncertainty about the score. Both the Harvard and Yale information guides, published annually, give the score 52–0. Bealle and *The H Book of Harvard Athletics* record 48–0. The *New Haven Register* (November 23, 1884) states the score is "variously recorded as 52–0 and 48–0; we say 48, and so do several members of the Yale team."

Amos Alonzo Stagg, '85.

once the Harvard *Crimson*, perhaps dazed by the debacle, found little to complain of in the Yale style of play, noting only that "Yale's passing and blocking were good and the men got down on the ball in good shape. They had little tackling to do." The account adds somewhat sourly that "the perfection of [Yale's] team play was not quite up to the Princeton standard."[22]

The meeting in 1884 was the first to take place on the new Yale Field, more spacious and better equipped for accommodating the ever-growing crowds than Hamilton Park. Yale Field, a mile or so south of Hamilton Park, was situated on the Derby Turnpike, roughly opposite to where the Bowl now stands, approached on that day "over a rickety wooden bridge." (*New Haven Register*, November 23) The *Yale Daily News*, understandably, could not refrain from comment on "the initiatory game at the new ground. . . . Surely," ran the lyric editorial (November 24),

it was a grand day for the new grounds. Broad and level with the grand stand over looking them, they lay stretched out, smiled upon by one of the most perfect days that ever a lover of the sport could wish for. With no associations of the past, no grand old victories to be proud of . . . they seemed to lie waiting for their christening. In the hands of our eleven rested this task and never was a more glorious christening given to any field than that bestowed on our College grounds, Saturday. . . . Carriages lined the south side and eastern end of the field and about two thousand persons were ranged on each side. Harvard was the first

to appear and she presented a team of fine appearance and strong physique. Yale sent her best team onto the field and though not presenting so fine an appearance, each dirty canvas jacket and mud-stained trousers told of good work done by the owner.

Strictly speaking the true "christening" had taken place a few weeks earlier; to Yale's ever-obliging sparring partner, Wesleyan, belongs the honor of inaugurating the new arena. The reference to a "grand stand" may be a little misleading; it accommodated only 600, as Stagg remembers it.[23] Not until 1897 could spectators (aside from those in carriages and tallyhos) watch the game without freezing their feet on the hard and sometimes muddy ground. Stands for 15,000 were put up that year; the number was periodically increased to 29,000 in 1903, 32,000 in 1905, and finally to 35,000 in 1908. There was never, in the life of the old field, an unoccupied seat for a major contest.

In 1885 there was no game. This hiatus was occasioned by the decision of the Harvard faculty, in whose eyes football had become a dangerous and degrading pastime. The faculty ukase was the result of a special report of the athletic committee, drawn up December 2, 1884, and submitted to the faculty on January 6, 1885. It reads, in part, as follows:

To the Faculty of Harvard College
Gentlemen:—

On the 22 of November 1883 the Committee on Athletics, believing that the game of football had

Harvard student spectators watching football game from their carriage, 1887.

begun to degenerate into a brutal and dangerous contest, informed the Captain of the Harvard eleven that the team could not be allowed to take part in further intercollegiate match games until substantial changes in the rules had been made. According to the rules then existing a player could hack, throttle, butt, trip, tackle below the hips, or strike an opponent with closed fist three times before he was sent from the field.

Changes in the rules were made immediately, and they were subsequently adopted by the Intercollegiate Association. In June of the present year the Committee said to the captain of the Harvard team for 1884, that the eleven would be allowed to play during the following season, on the understanding that the game should be regarded as a test whether or not the changes of rules had resulted in substantial change of the character of the game.

At the beginning of this season your Committee decided to attend the games of the Intercollegiate series, and to observe them carefully in order to learn the precise nature of the game as played by college teams under the revised rules. . . .

In every one of these games there was brutal fighting with the fists where the men had to be separated by other players, or by the judges and referee, or by the by-standers and the police. We saw one such case in the Harvard–Princeton game, two in the Harvard–Yale game, three in the Yale–Princeton game, and three in the Wesleyan–Pennsylvania game.

In addition to these fights there were numerous instances where a single blow was struck. A man was felled by a blow in the face in the Harvard–

Princeton game. In the Wesleyan–Pennsylvania game, a man was thrown unfairly, out of bounds, by an opposing player. Then, as he was rising, but before he was on his feet, his antagonist turned, struck him in the face and knocked him down, and returned in triumph with the ball.

In all of the games the manifestation of gentlemanly spirit was lacking—the spirit that scorned to take an unfair advantage of an opponent. Unfair play, often premeditated and sometimes concerted, was a permanent feature in all of the games, and although not always successful was rarely punished. Intentional offside play, and unlawful interference with opponents who were not running with the ball, were the rule rather than the exception; and tackling below the hips, tripping, butting, tackling in-touch (all of which are prohibited by the rules) were common and deliberate.

The game is demoralizing to the spectators, mainly through its brutality; unfair play they usually fail to recognize. We often heard cries of "kill him," "break his neck," "slug him," "hit him" and "knock him down" from those around us. . . .

After deliberate investigation we have become convinced that the game of football, as at present played by college teams, is brutal, demoralizing to teams and spectators, and extremely dangerous. We do not believe that, at the present time, and with the prevailing spirit, any revision of the rules made by the Intercollegiate Association would be effective in removing these objectionable features.

We therefore recommend that all games of foot-

ball be prohibited to students of the College, except those played by our men, on our own grounds, and that these shall be allowed only in case it shall prove possible to eliminate all objectionable features from the game. We believe that football, played in the proper spirit, under proper conditions, may be made one of the most valuable of college sports, and we should deprecate its permanent loss.[24]

The faculty, unanimously approving the committee's recommendation, decreed that "intercollegiate football is prohibited for the future." Yet the statement of that august body went on to enumerate a number of suggestions made by "a New York graduate" which might, if implemented, redeem the game. The suggestions included doing away with the partisan judges (hitherto it had been the practice for each team to select one such arbiter of its own color to "assist the referee"), imposing severe penalties for objectionable play, and instituting a rather complicated design for scrimmage that would put ten yards between the teams at the time of the snapback. The faculty's publication of these proposals was a tolerably clear indication that "for the future" was not quite as final as it might seem.

We may take advantage of the armistice of 1885 to cast a retrospective glance over the course of the sport and The Game in their formative years. The former was no longer a toddler; it was a robust adolescent with features clearly delineated and character firmly formed. It was not soccer or rugby; it was American football. The years would bring modifications and growth, but the essential structure would not change. The building of Yale Field was a vote of confidence in its future. The Game, too, had come to stay; it had won a wide following and was already a kind of tradition in the making. In the year of its tenth birthday (which was also the year of the *Mikado*, the election of a Democrat to the Presidency, and the invention of a strange internal combustion machine by one Karl Benz) The Game might well feel it had much to look forward to. Like Karl Benz's machine.

THE BLUE EXPRESS TO THE NINETIES VIA SPRINGFIELD

Harvard poster, ca. 1890.

In the fall of 1886 Harvard observed with considerable pomp her two hundred and fiftieth birthday. "The anniversary was celebrated on four days, November 5−8," Morison writes.

[There was] great preparation, especially in the matter of academic gowns, which for the first time were formally adopted for members of all faculties. About twenty-two hundred alumni, and three hundred other guests, including President and Mrs. Cleveland, attended. Forty-two honorary degrees were conferred but President Cleveland resolutely refused to accept the LL.D. that had been voted by the Governing Boards, on the ground that his education had been scanty, and he could not figure as an eminent lawyer. . . . Oliver Wendell Holmes read one of the last of his occasional poems, including the lines:

> *As once of old from Ida's lofty height*
> *The flaming signal flashed across the night,*
> *So Harvard's beacon sheds its unspent rays*
> *Till every watch-tower shows its kindling blaze.*
> *Caught from a spark and fanned by every gale,*
> *A brighter radiance gilds the roofs of Yale;*
> *Amherst and Williams bid their flambeaus shine,*
> *And Bowdoin answers through her groves of pine;*
> *O'er Princeton's sands the far reflections steal,*
> *Where mighty Edwards stamped his iron heel. . .*

President McCosh of Princeton took offense at this and went home early; but that was the only untoward incident.

Morison notes further: "President Dwight brought

the greetings of Yale; Mark Hopkins, those of Williams. President Angell represented the University of Michigan [Yalies would hope he brought his son Jim with him] and for Johns Hopkins, Professor Gildersleeve graciously acknowledged, 'We measure everything today by the standard of Harvard' "[1] [which might fairly have given Timothy Dwight, who knew his football, better reason than McCosh to leave early]. The football match which was a part of that festive weekend was played between the varsity and a team of graduates, the former winning handily. On the subject of Cantabrigian chronicles it is to be noted that beginning in the fall of that anniversary year attendance at prayers was no longer required of Harvard undergraduates. This "godless" emancipation shocked the educational world; forty years passed before Yale followed the Cambridge example. It is surprising that the austere McCosh turned up for the ceremonies.

Eighteen eighty-six has its place in Eli annals, too. Timothy Dwight was inaugurated in July of that year. His administration would extend until 1899; he, like Eliot, fostered the growth of the graduate schools and gave Yale farsighted and able direction. For many years, however, the alumni regarded him with anything but affection; he rebuilt the old campus in such a way as to make of it an enclosed quandrangle; no longer would Yalies, as for generations of yore, sit on the fence at twilight exchanging witticisms and profundities and watching the comely daughters of the burghers as they passed along College and Chapel streets. Osborn Hall, built in 1888, took the largest bite out of the sacred palisade; its Romanesque architecture was in painful conflict with the simple lines of the old brick row; the irate graduates dubbed it "the squatting toad."

Inspired no doubt by the pageantry, respectively, of commemoration and inauguration, the warriors of the Crimson and the Blue renewed hostilities that November. The Harvard faculty, finding the revised rules of combat acceptable, had lifted their ban. Severe penalties for misconduct had been prescribed; the partisan "judges" were gone forever; the game, in fact, was in the hands of one impartial referee—Walter Camp. The choice of the quintessential Yalie for this demanding post was a great tribute to Camp, nor were there any complaints about his handling of the game. The honor, though exceptional, was not unique. Camp had three years earlier refereed a Princeton–Yale game and shown admirable restraint in not tripping up Old Nassau's Lamar as he ran along the sidelines eighty yards and more for the winning Tiger touchdown. (Camp later admitted he had been sorely tempted.)

The Harvard delegation, welcoming their New Haven friends to Jarvis Field that year, was the highest scoring team in Crimson history. It also had the longest schedule of any Cantab club, playing fourteen games. Against all opponents Captain Brooks's cohorts, powered by speedsters like Joe Sears and Charley Porter, ran up 765 points, 77 more than "Pa" Corbin's juggernaut of '88, which holds the Blue record. An impressive total, even though 244 points were garnered in contests with Exeter and Andover; yet sadly and strangely the

R. N. Corwin, '87, captain of Yale's 1886 team.

Crimson was frustrated in the only two games that counted, losing to Princeton by a score of 12 to 0 and to Yale by the margin of 25 points (29 to 4). To be sure, Captain Corwin's battalion of Elis was another one in the sequence of Blue powerhouses; his team went unbeaten through nine games, totaling 687 points (admittedly, 273 were at the expense of Wesleyan, who obligingly took on the Blue in three matches) against 4. (The Blue season was spoiled, as happened not infrequently in the heroic age, by a scoreless tie with Princeton.) The Game of 1886 was Yale's from the beginning, Beecher, the Bulldog's sprightly quarterback, scoring on the fifth play of the game. Yale made three more touchdowns, another by Beecher and one each by Morrison and Gill. Watkinson kicked all the points after touchdown and added a field goal of his own; Harvard's Holden had at least the solace of knowing that his touchdown was the only score made against Yale in that season. The game, though one-sided, was hard-fought; Bealle records that Charley Fletcher, the Crimson quarterback, had his collarbone broken in the second half, but since he had replaced the starting quarterback and no third man was available, he played out the game, "although unable to lift his arm above his shoulder."[2]

Blue blood flowed freely that day, too; Stagg's memory of the fracas indicates that the Cantabrigian lambs were learning to take care of themselves; he writes:

In all my playing days I was never slugged but I escaped narrowly in 1886. . . . Before the Harvard

game, Corwin told me that right tackle lay be-
tween Eddie Burke . . . and me. Burke won out.
Harvard was outclassed and roughed the Blue
eleven up to offset the 29 to 4 score. George Wood-
ruff brought home a broken nose from Cambridge;
George Carter, guard, came out of the game with
a cut over the eye needing eight stitches; and
Burke, who had beaten me out for right tackle,
was a campus curiosity for several days. Both his
eyes were closed and his lips were mangled and
hideously swollen. He had had the bad luck to
play opposite Remington, the Harvard champion
heavyweight boxer.[3]

There were giants in those days—or at least *rudes
encaisseurs*, as the French have it. Substitutions,
incidentally, were rare in the golden age; in the
last five years of the eighties Harvard had a total
of seven and Yale five.

The Harvard '87 contingent was one of the best
yet fielded by the Crimson; 660 points were scored
against 23 for opponents. Harding, Porter, and
Boydon were talented ballcarriers, and the line
was unusually strong: when the moment of truth
with Yale came in the Polo Grounds on November 24 (with 18,000 excited spectators on hand),
only 6 points had been scored against the stalwarts from Cambridge. The *New York Times* (November 25) notes that the day was gray and cold,
but the stands were a blaze of color— especially
the ladies. "They all wore ribbons and the wearers
of the blue glared at the wearers of the crimson as
if the Amazonian War of the roses were to be revived." But again Harvard's timing was bad.

Strong as they were, the Cantabrigians ran head-
on into yet another Yale bulldozer, victor over all
comers (this time including Princeton) when the
whistle blew for the climactic clash. It was only
the third time that both squads had come to the
duello with unblemished records. It was a hard-
fought battle, beginning with a punting duel between Yale's Billy Bull and Harvard's Joe Sears,
the latter having the better of it. Profiting by his
skill and good rushing, Harvard found herself on
the Blue 30-yard line when Yale recovered a fumble. Here Yale's great center, Pa Corbin, showed
inventive ingenuity; instead of passing the ball to
a back, he kicked it forward, dodged around his
amazed counterpart, picked it up himself (a legal
though rarely used tactic in those days), and ran
deep into Crimson territory before the surprised
Cantabs knew what was happening. The result
was a field goal by Bull, followed later by a touchdown by Corbin. (It was a great era for centers.)
Harvard fought back: a kick blocked by Parry
Trafford resulted in a Yale safety, and a brilliant
run by Charley Porter made the score 11−8. In
the dying moments of the game Yale's Wurtenburg turned Harvard's left end for the final score,
17−8. It was a brave battle on Harvard's part, especially since the Crimson captain, Holden, was
unable to play. But what team could have prevailed against a Blue squad which included not
only Pa Corbin and Billy Bull, but also such immortals as Charley Gill, G. W. Woodruff, and of
course Beecher himself?

Yale's undefeated 1887 juggernaut. *Front row, l. to r.:* W. C.
Wurtenberg, Captain H. Beecher, W. P. Graves. *Back row:*
F. C. Pratt, S. M. Cross, G. W. Woodruff, W. H. Corbin, G. R.
Carter, C. O. Gill, F. W. Wallace, W. T. Bull.

H. Beecher, '88, captain of Yale's 1887 team.

For Eli followers it was a happy night in New York. The *New Haven Register* (November 25) reports, with obvious empathy:

Harvard men took their ill luck much to heart, and after the game went straight to their hotel. After dinner they seemed to throw aside their misery, and flocked to the theaters along with the rest of the world. Yale men thronged the Fifth Avenue and Hoffman House and blue reigned supreme. Almost all the orchestra stalls at the Bijou were occupied by Yale students, who made Rome howl. They cheered, applauded and groaned in turn. Two of the comedians of the burlesque took occasion to compliment the audience by interpolating the familiar song that often shakes the walls in Moriarty's quaint little taproom in New Haven:

> *Here's to good old Yale,*
> *Drink it down, Drink it down. . . .*

Similar episodes astonished the ordinary patrons of other comedy houses. Every now and then for no apparent reason a body of men would suddenly rise in their places and send a thundering volley of college cheers echoing through the theater. Then they would quietly sit down again or else go out to see somebody who sold cloves.

In '88 the Crimson may have been lucky. The Game had been scheduled again for the Polo Grounds, but the Harvard faculty (faculties could be difficult in the Brownstone era) refused to let the team play that far from home. Yale, no doubt with happy memories of the Bijou, refused to play elsewhere, and there was no game. The officiousness of the faculty saved the Johnnies—as they were affectionately called by their New Haven friends—from an encounter with the highest-scoring machine in Bulldog history; under the guidance of Pa Corbin, the Elis went through a thirteen-game season unbeaten. Yet, it was a good Harvard team that year, too, the Crimson winning twelve games and losing only to Princeton. They were a high-scoring lot, with a total of 635 points (Pa Corbin rolled up 698 points, not counting the 6 acquired by Harvard's forfeit). Comparative scores against Amherst must have given Harvard hearts grounds for hope: the Crimson crushed the Lord Jeffs 102 to 0; Yale played Amherst twice, winning 39–0 the first time and 70–0 the second. (Sabrina must have used up a lot of liniment in '88.)

The season of 1888, aside from producing Corbin's invincibles, marked the beginning of an all but revolutionary change in the tactics of American football. Walter Camp, whose word was still law in such matters, was responsible for what seemed at first sight a slight and hardly significant modification in the rules. On his suggestion, tackling below the waist was for the first time made legal. Camp's reasoning was that the offense had had things too much its own way (the high-scoring machines of the early eighties could be cited in evidence) and that the time had come to make life a little easier for the defense. The effect on high-scoring rampages was not immediately apparent; as noted, Corbin's team holds the Yale record, even though all of its games were played

W. H. "Pa" Corbin, '89, captain of Yale's 1888 team.

Though it did not play Harvard, Yale's undefeated team of 1888 scored 698 points to opponents' 0. *Front row, l. to r.:* W. C. Wurtenberg, W. Graves. *Middle row:* A. A. Stagg, Lee "Bum" McClung, Captain W. H. "Pa" Corbin. *Back row:* G. W. Woodruff, W. W. "Pudge" Heffelfinger, C. O. Gill (captain of the '89 team), F. W. Wallace, W. T. Bull.

under the new rules, but in course of time, save for sporadic "rabbit hunting," the astronomical totals began to wither. But Camp's new regulation had broader results, which may even have surprised him. Tim Cohane summarizes economically and perceptively the effect of the new tackling permissiveness:

Camp did not realize he was opening Pandora's box. When tackling was prohibited below the waist, the runner found it comparatively easy to twist loose from open-field tackling. That made individual rushing profitable. The rush line and the backs deployed loosely across the field, and the defense spread out similarly to meet them. But with tackling lowered to the knees, the back found it much harder to break away in the open. The wide-open game no longer paid such rich dividends.

Instead, the offense discovered more profit in having the rush line deploy shoulder to shoulder and the backs line up in close order for concentrated smashes at one point. . . . All types of mass and momentum-mass plays came chugging into the picture. Wedges. The guard-back, the tackle-back. Open field playing was reduced to a minimum. It got to be pull-and-haul football. Strain-and-groan football. Injuries, death, public hue and cry. Yet, eventually, this grinding mass football would force by its inequities the advent of the forward pass and the beginnings of modern football.[4]

To which one may only add that the rule calling for seven men in the line at the time of putting the ball in play was no less effective than the forward pass in unclogging some of the massive, bruising formations of the game of the eighties and nineties—with the corollary that in spite of such modifications, a good running game even today demands a certain amount of mass-momentum charging through center or off tackle, and without a reasonably good running game a passing team finds victory hard to come by.

Camp's ruling (originally permitting tackling only as far down as the knees but later generously enlarging the area of vulnerability pretty much from head to toe) left a lasting mark on the game. First of all, it put a premium on poundage. Although all football teams down at least to World War I were light by the standards of today, there was a notable increment of weight, particularly in linemen, after the new rule took effect. In the Harvard—Yale contest of 1887, for example, the Crimson forwards averaged 168 pounds; ten years later the average stood at 188. Further, since mass plays give scant scope for breakaway running, low-scoring games became the rule. In the four Harvard—Yale matches before the new rules, the point total for both teams averaged out at 32; in the four seasons following the new dispensation the figure dropped to 10. Finally, the innovation occasioned a demand for heavy armor. Previously only very light padding had been necessary to protect the athletes. The new, bone-crushing style changed all that. By the end of the century nose guards, shin guards, helmets (apparently introduced by Princeton in 1895), and pants heavily reinforced with reed or cane had come into use.

For those who scorned headgear (and many did down through the twenties), long hair, by the turn of the century a traditional mark of the football player, was an acceptable substitute. It took the homicidal ingenuity of our own century to bring in plastic helmets, precious to the wearer but potentially lethal to a tackler. These headpieces were soon provided with masks, behind which the eyes of the wearer peer out as from a cage; these are the contemporary equivalents of the ancient nose guard. This piece of armament has the distinction of putting two further penalties in the book: "spearing" for the wearer and "face mask violation" for the inept or vengeful tackler.[5] On the subject of penalties, loss of yardage for misbehavior came into the rule book a year after Camp's revolutionary change. Previously, one assumes, it had been dealt with by admonition or ejection. But beginning in 1889 "throttling, butting or tripping" would cost your team twenty-five yards. Over the years many offenses, minor and major, have been added to the list.

Historians of the sport old enough to remember the early open style unanimously deplored its passing. Harford Powel, Jr., in his biography of Walter Camp, speaks for many. "For several years," he writes, "the teams on the offensive had usually been placed in a far flung line across the playing field and the ball was tossed laterally by the quarterback to put the play in motion. This was the open game so much enjoyed at the time and so vociferously regretted when, by mischance, it was sacrificed." Sadly acknowledging Camp's responsibility in the matter, Powel goes on to note the

sorry result: "there began the mass plays, the heaps of players, the close, confusing tactics which remained an unattractive character of football until the 1905 upheaval forced a change."[6] Indeed, taking the broad view, one may say that all of the modifications adopted in the sport since the lapse of '88 have evidenced a yearning for the unfettered, free, lost Eden of old. It apparently occurred to no one that paradise could be regained simply by reinstating the prohibition against tackling below the waist. But perhaps such obtuseness was providential in bringing about the invention of the forward pass—making it possible to enjoy the best of both worlds, the freedom of the open game and the impressive power of close-order thrusts through the line.

For both of the old rivals the season of 1889 was similar in pattern to that of 1887. Yale had another very strong aggregation, led by Captain Charley Gill, who played on five varsity teams and never missed a game or called for a substitute— an endurance record unique in the chronicles of the Bulldog. On the eve of the encounter with the Crimson, his company had run up fourteen straight victories with a point total, second only to Pa Corbin's delegation, of 659 points to opponents' 16. The Elis of '89 were the first to play a sixteen-game schedule and the first to encounter Cornell. (In fact, two games were played with the Ithacans: the first, on the Blue's home ground, was won by Yale by a score of 60–6. Ashamed of being scored on, the Elis suggested a return match. This was played in Ithaca and won by Gill's stalwarts with

C. O. Gill, captain of Yale's 1889 team.

a more satisfying score of 70–0. Yet it was a good Cornell team for those days, victor over Michigan among other triumphs.) In short if the squad of '89 cannot be numbered among the true elite in the Blue succession it is only because the last game on the schedule was lost to Princeton by a 6–0 margin.

As in '87, the Harvard task force that came to the trial with the Bulldog was rugged, with nine victories and only one loss—to Princeton, of course. It was a grand year for the Tiger, whose champions included immortals Hector Cowan, Old Nassau's outstanding divinity student, Ed-

gär Allan Poe (who did not write "The Raven"), "Snake" Ames, T. H. Channing, and W. G. George—all named to Camp's first All-American team. (Eighty-nine marked the beginning of such honor rolls; it is still debated whether or not the notion was originally Camp's, but it was Camp who made the first selection and did so regularly henceforth until 1924. His '89 choices were all from the Big Three, with Yale's "Pudge" Heffelfinger, Gill, and Stagg and Harvard's Captain Art Cumnock, Jack Cranston, and Jim Lee joining the five glittering Tigers.) The '89 season has other features worthy of note: that year the zealous Cumnock introduced spring practice at Harvard; the notion soon spread through the pigskin world. And in the tactical sector, the device of pulling a guard out of line to join the interference for the runner was introduced by Heffelfinger. This year for the first time the scene of combat was Springfield, Massachusetts, chosen perhaps because of the Harvard faculty's reluctance to let their charges go as far afield as the Polo Grounds—and Springfield's Hampden Park Field could accommodate as many as 18,000 spectators.

Crimson and Blue had not been so evenly matched since the scoreless ties of a decade past. Both sides presented heroes of legendary stature; aside from Gill and his fellow theology student Stagg, Heffelfinger, playing his first Harvard game and weighing in at 190, the heaviest man on the team, and "Bum" McClung reinforced the Bulldog outfit; for Harvard, in addition to the All-Americans cited, the young Bernie Trafford, for whom destiny had great things in store, was in the lineup. The battle was ferocious and bitter. Yale won 6−0 on the strength of a touchdown scored by McClung, who was pushed and pulled over the goal line by the whole Yale team. McClung also made the point after. "No better or closer game had ever been played between the two [rivals]," in the view of the Harvard historian Bealle, writing in 1946.[7] Yet, today's observers might have found the '89 meeting rather dull. It was an excellent example of the mass and mayhem tactics that had evolved from Camp's new permissive tackling rule. Years later Heffelfinger remembered the first battle of Springfield as the roughest in his career. John McCallum quotes from his conversation with the Old Eli great:

It was some bloodbath. We went out there and murdered one another for sixty minutes and after the game we all agreed that there had been no slugging by either side. The slaughter had been so fierce that it was a wonder any of us came out alive. One of the Harvards suffered a broken collarbone, and a Yale teammate had one eye nearly blinded. Practically all of us were bleeding from cuts or from kicks or smashes. Another one of our players was unconscious for five hours afterward in a Springfield hospital. I don't remember now exactly who it was but I can still see him being carried off the field, dead to the world. They just dumped him on a pile of blankets, covered him up and then turned to look at the game again.[8]

Pudge also speaks of McClung's prowess. "In those days," he recalls, "you had to kick the goal from a point in front of where the touchdown had gone over the line [only in 1920 was the ball spotted directly in front of the goalposts, making the point after touchdown almost a certainty]. We had scored our touchdown over at one side of the field and I am telling you that William Tell couldn't have shot an arrow through the goalposts from that angle but Bum McClung made it just the same."

With regard to the casualties suffered in combat, Pudge's memory may be at fault. Accounts of the game record only four substitutions, two for each side. And the language of Baker's scrapbook strongly suggests that none was a result of an injury. For Harvard, Hallowell replaced Hutchinson at the beginning of the second half; the two Yalies who needed replacements were "disqualified," and Harvard's Stickney, Baker states baldly, "was ruled off for slugging."[9] It is pleasant to observe that as Harvard had accepted Camp as referee in '87 so this time Yale was content with Harvard's C. A. Porter, veteran of the Crimson '87 squad. E. C. Peace of Princeton served as umpire with the special duty of watching out for slugging. According to Heffelfinger a capacity crowd of 18,000 was on hand; Bealle puts it at 12,000. The *Yale Daily News* noted that "six grand stands ranged completely around the field and the crowd, pressing within the rope, occasioned no trouble whatever."[10]

Yale readers at least and perhaps not a few indulgent members of the Cambridge clan would find us remiss if we were to leave 1889 without noting two events which, quite aside from the change of venue to Springfield, make the year of

W. W. "Pudge" Heffelfinger (left) and T. L. "Bum" McClung. The latter was captain of the 1891 team.

"Down Went McGinty" memorable for the Blue. For it was the year in which Handsome Dan, a brindled bulldog picked up in a blacksmith shop by a strolling undergraduate (one Andrew D. Graves, '92S), became the mascot and symbol of the Blue armed forces.[11] Henceforth they would cheerfully and proudly accept the designation of Bulldogs. Handsome Dan I was a worthy head of a distinguished line. He reigned over six successive football seasons, victorious more often than not; he won a prize at a kennel show in his own right, and it is said that he never failed to bark joyously whenever a Yale runner scored a touchdown or a Yale batter made a hit. And 1889 was also the year in which Walter Camp was first recorded as Yale's football coach. De facto he had fulfilled that function for some time.

Coaching, both at Yale and Harvard, had over the early years of the game spontaneously evolved into an important element in the sport. In New Haven the first coach was the captain; when Yale played her first game in 1872—in effect a soccer game—no one on campus except Captain Schaff knew anything about the British sport. His double function is possibly the source of the great authority subsequently given to all Yale captains; down almost to World War I the football captain was not only the leader on the field but the chief executive and organizer of the pigskin enterprise. Assuredly through most of his playing years Camp, three times captain, was coach. After a year in medical school (1880–81) he spent another year in New York, returning to New Haven in 1882. He never lost touch with the game or with the

Blue warrior class. Very soon in the early years the custom arose of inviting veteran players back to advise and instruct: Camp was always one of them and the most respected among them. His appointment in 1889 merely gave official recognition to his services, incidentally unpaid. Formally his years of service came to an end in 1892. From that time on, it was customary for the captain to appoint a "field coach," frequently the captain of the previous year's delegation. But Camp remained as "graduate advisor" in effective if unobtrusive charge of operations, strategic or tactical. His regular meetings with the captain and the field coach—for years in rooms of the old New Haven House—assured efficient cooperation. During all his period of service as coach or graduate advisor Camp was employed by the New Haven Clock Company; his duties there frequently made it impossible for him to attend practice, but he had an invaluable assistant in the person of his wife, Allie, daughter of Yale's great William Graham Sumner; there were many who thought that Allie was as shrewd a tactician as Walter himself. Camp's domination of the instructional area of Yale football lasted from his undergraduate years until 1910, when he formally abdicated. Yale did not have a professional coach until Howard Jones was appointed in 1912.

Generally speaking the Harvard system was not unlike the Yale one, with the captain in charge and empowered to appoint field coaches. But Harvard records seem to indicate that such appointments were only sporadic; captains assumed coaching duties themselves or called in alumni for occasional consultation. In fact, Thomas C. Thacher states categorically that "until the fall of 1881 there were no coaches and no coaching by anyone but the captain."[12] In 1890 formal coaching was instituted, and for the next decade and beyond Harvard had some very able mentors for her youth: George A. Steward (1890–93), W. Cameron Forbes (1897–98), Benjamin H. Dibblee (1889– 1900), William T. Reid in 1901 and again in 1905 and 1906. But their terms were short, like those of Yale's field coaches, and until the coming of Haughton, Harvard never had that invaluable asset of continuity provided in New Haven by the enduring presence of Camp. That circumstance is, to a large degree, the explanation of the long Blue predominance in the sport. (Although in the early days Harvard also had recruiting problems. Thacher complains that there was a lack of "big men"; for a while crew was reluctant to let any oarsmen take part in football.)

The second battle of Springfield, in the last year of the ninth decade and the first year of the Gay Nineties, was a memorable event for the wearers of the Crimson, who after fifteen years and encounters of frustration finally brought down the Blue. As in '89 both teams came onto the field unbeaten and untied (the first Harvard team to have that distinction since the four-game season of 1875–76), and both rosters contained names that still shine brightly in the chronicles of American football: Heffelfinger, Billy Rhodes, and McClung for Yale and Art Cumnock, Bernie Trafford, Dudley Dean, and Everit Lake (later governor of Connecticut) for Harvard. The battle was worthy of

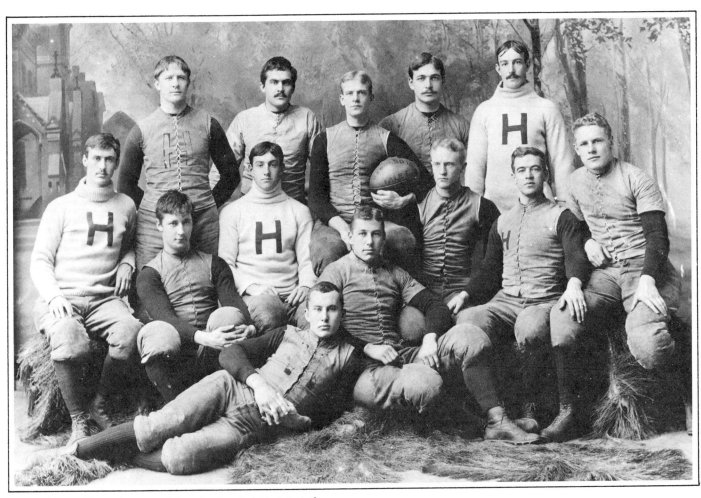

The 1890 Harvard team, undefeated and untied. Captain Arthur
Cumnock is holding the ball.

W. C. Rhodes, captain of Yale's 1890 team *(left)*, and T. L. "Bum" McClung.

the Titans who waged it. Harvard had the better of the first half, but a fumble spoiled her one scoring opportunity. Early in the second half Lee, replacing the injured Lake at right halfback, ran sixty yards for the Crimson's first score, giving Harvard a lead over Yale for the first time in many years, as Bealle notes.[13] Trafford kicked the goal. Another run around right end, this time by Dean, gave Harvard a second touchdown; Trafford's second conversion made the score 12–0. At last the Elis rallied and McClung went over for a touchdown and, as he had in '89, kicked the extra point. Time was too short for any further action; the final score was 12–6, Harvard.

As in all the skirmishes on Hampden Field no quarter was asked or given. The warriors battered each other with a kind of high-spirited ferocity, yet, it would seem, with no real ill will. On this engagement too we have available the vivid commentary of Yale's articulate Pudge Heffelfinger. "We have been ordered," he recalls,

to scowl at our Harvard opponents and act tough, but Francis Barbour burst out laughing when he saw his old Exeter roommate John Cranston across the scrimmage line. They had a great time kidding each other.

Still and all, this Cranston was no laughing matter for us. Lewis our substitute center couldn't handle him alone. This spoiled our running guard play because I didn't dare drop out of line while Cranston was on the rampage. To make things worse, Ham Wallis, our tackle, couldn't keep Harvard's Newell from crashing through. Newell

Marshall Newell, a member of Harvard's 1890 team, weighed only 166 pounds, but he had "the leg drive of a mule and the heart of a lion," according to Yale's Pudge Heffelfinger.

weighed only 166 pounds but he had the leg drive of a mule and the heart of a lion, a stubby, thickset chap, with unbreakable willpower. They called him "Ma" because he mothered lonely freshmen and stood up for the weaklings. Whoever wrote "the greatest are the bravest" might have had Newell in mind.

All through the game Captain Arthur Cumnock of Harvard kept kidding Captain Rhodes of Yale. "It's a beautiful day, Bill," he'd say. This got on Rhodes's nerves. Along about 4 o'clock he didn't think so much of the day. Cumnock was a born leader. He had coached his own team for two seasons, had made them do conditioning exercises both winter and summer, and had set his heart to beating Yale. Well, they did it thanks to two long runs that caught us napping.[14]

The meeting of two Exeter roommates across the battle line is a reminder of the role played by private schools in the heroic years. On this occasion, of the twenty-five players who took part in the game nine had prepared at Exeter, including Yale's McClung and Harvard's plucky Newell.

It was a day on which, as the Harvard song puts it, the sun truly set in Crimson. (In point of fact it had set before the warfare ended; the moon came up to witness Yale's desperate counterthrust.) Bealle reports that "every Harvard man who could raise the trainfare to Springfield went down to see the Yale game."[15] The *Boston Globe's* comment on the triumph is dithyrambic:

All hail, Harvard! . . . For the first time in the memory of men Harvard has won a football game from Yale. [This is a little hard on the concessionary team.] She has won it, not on a fluke, not on a unfortunate combination of circumstances, but on the cleanest kind of football ever seen on a field. . . . Yale had this year the finest team she had ever sent out. Captain Rhodes was an ideal Yale captain: aggressive, a hard fighter and a fierce man to lead an uphill attack. Walter Camp, Corbin, Knapp and the whole Yale coterie spread their intelligence over the Yale team and there was no question that the Yale eleven of 1890 knew more football and was better drilled than any eleven that represented the hard fighting of the Elm City. This only serves to emphasize Harvard's victory. The Cambridge lads have beaten the best team Yale ever produced.[16]

As the *Globe* observes, it was an unusually clean game; each team made but one substitution, both for minor injuries. Both referees were Princetonians—which may have had something to do with it.

Major credit for the Crimson breakthrough on that memorable day must go to Captain Cumnock. His name stands high on the Harvard honor roll and not only for his prowess on the field. As we have noted, it was he who introduced spring practice and he also who invented the first tackling dummy ever used at Cambridge. (Stagg had anticipated him by a year, according to the latter's statement in *Touchdown!*) Thacher describes it as a crude and rather fearful engine which, however, undoubtedly taught the men to tackle low, although it was so heavy and so hard that a good

many men were injured, some even breaking their collarbones in tackling practice. Finally, Thacher recalls another Harvard innovation of 1890— though not apparently of Cumnock's devising. The credit must go to the team's Doctor Conant. He had constructed just outside the stands in Hampden Park "a very crude board shack. When the first half was over the Harvard players raced off the fields into this rough building, where they rested stretched on mattresses. Some were rubbed down, bruises were fixed up, and when the call for the second half came Harvard's players went on the field thoroughly refreshed and eager to play. Meanwhile the Yale team, dumbfounded at Harvard's departure from previous custom, sat huddled in an old barge in which they had driven to the field."[17] The supremacy of Harvard in the second half suggests that Conant's notion had merit.

The 1891 affair, Bealle admits, was a disappointment to Harvard supporters, who saw no good reason why the fair beginning of 1890 should not be followed up. A sturdy Crimson delegation, too, came into Hampden Park on November 21, with 25,000 gathered to witness the fray. Cumnock had gone, but the redoubtable Bernie Trafford, now captain, was back, as were Lake and Corbett in the backfield and Frank Hallowell and Newell in the line. The Crimson had run up 588 points to opponents' 16 in the course of its all-victorious campaign. Yale's scoring total was modest by comparison, a mere 549 points; on the other hand, she had allowed the opposition no points at all. The Blue too had stalwart veterans

The 1891 Yale team.

returning: Captain McClung, Laurie Bliss, Vance McCormick, and Barbour as ballcarriers, with Morrison and Heffelfinger, now a graduate student, up front. The Elis also had a pair of sensational recruits: at center stood the freshman "townie" Foster Sanford, admired for his prowess if not for his lifestyle, and, weighing in at 147 pounds, another freshman, all but peerless in the Bulldog Hall of Fame.

There has never been anyone quite like Frank Hinkey, even in the overcrowded pantheon of Blue immortals. He had taken the place of an injured regular in midseason—from that time on he never missed a game or a tackle. "No man ever went around Hinkey's end." He scorned "dirty" playing, but his tackles were so violent that ballcarriers were shaken and stunned; he liked to whipsaw a runner before bringing him to the ground. Short, slight, unimpressive in appearance, Hinkey was almost pathologically reserved; he was not given to conversation. His face was pale, giving the appearance of an invalid: there was, as his teammates testify, something a little fey about him. He lived only for football; he seems to have had no pleasures in life save for the joy of sweeping aside the interference and rattling the bones of the adversary's running backs. Camp, marveling at his ability to drift through the blocking and nail the runner, called him the disembodied spirit. Harvard soon learned of his prowess on that chill autumn afternoon of 1891. Bealle writes: "Yale's first touchdown was set up by Captain Lee McClung, who made a brilliant 40-yard dash around Frank Hallowell's end, after the great Harvard

Frank Hinkey, Yale's "disembodied spirit," was short and slight, but no opposing runner ever succeeded in going around his end.

wingman had been suddenly taken out of the play by an unheralded blue-clad freshman, weighing every bit of 135 pounds (the program says 147) named Frank Hinkey. It was this one man who would be the key figure in Yale's victories over Harvard for the next four years." (In his four years of playing Hinkey was on the losing side only once—never against Harvard.) Bealle continues: "Three plays later Yale mass plays had carried the ball over the Harvard goal four minutes after the game started and without the Elis once having surrendered the ball. McClung missed the goal but newspaper speculation was that he had done so intentionally. Under the rules then in effect Harvard put the ball in play on her own twenty yard line after a missed conversion. Had the two points been made Harvard would have put the ball in play in the center of the field."[18] There was no further scoring in the first half (it was forty-five minutes long). Harvard counterattacked strongly in the early moments of the second half but was stopped at the Blue twenty. Shortly after, Harvard, getting the ball at midfield, sent Corbett around Hinkey's end; the disembodied spirit tackled with such violence that the ball was shaken from Corbett's grasp and picked up in the air by Yale's Laurie Bliss, who carried it over the Crimson goal line. McClung converted, making the count 10–0, Yale; there was no further scoring. Neither team used a substitute. The *Boston Globe* offered the following crisp analysis: "It was Harvard beef against Yale science, Harvard muscle against Yale agility. Science and agility won." The *Globe's* concluding lines have a poetic coloring that makes quotation irresistible; let the reader savor this charged prose:

What a scene there was when the game ended! Fighting with the grim tenacity of bulldogs, Harvard was hammered back into their last ditch— the fatal 25 yard line. Here, with clenched teeth and white faces they held the Yale giants in a grip of death. Then above the long barking roll of the Yale cheer, came the sound of the shrill penny whistle in the mouth of the referee. Bernie Trafford, who was the first man on his feet, heard it and held up his war-battered hand. Slowly the scrimmage untangled, and slowly the Harvard men understood they were beaten.[19]

The long barking roll of the Yale cheer undoubtedly refers to the old "Brek eke kek, coax, coax," ingeniously plundered by undergraduates from Aristophanes and used first in 1884 by an eating group to serenade an admired professor.

McClung's delegation concluded its season with a victory over Princeton the following week—and remained unscored on. It was assuredly one of the best of all Yale teams and, incidentally, the most widely traveled. Of the thirteen games, six were played away from home; there was even— unique in the Blue annals—a meeting with Williams in Albany, New York. Yale teams of the golden year traveled much more readily than Harvard's representatives. Yet in the fullness of time the long-distance record would go to Harvard, with two visits to California: one for the triumph of the Rose Bowl in 1919 and another thirty years later for a less happy rendezvous with Stanford.

Yale has never been further west than Madison, Wisconsin.

In 1892, the year of the founding of the Populist party and the reelection of Grover Cleveland (an event no doubt pleasing to Yale's Captain Vance McCormick, who was one of that rare species, a Yale Democrat: he would be in later life the party's candidate for governor of Pennsylvania), Hampden Park was the scene of yet another hard-fought engagement. The Blue came onto the field unbeaten and unscored on. Bernie Trafford, for the second time captain of the Crimson forces, led an equally formidable troop, also unvanquished in ten previous encounters. Old hands were back on both sides of the scrimmage line: Hallowell, Newell, and Lake for Harvard, Bliss and Hinkey for Yale. Recruits such as Charley Brewer, a gifted kicker for the Crimson, and "Wild Bill" Hickok and Frank Butterworth for the Elis were notable additions. Again the attendance (20,000) was impressive, the weather good, and again Yale won—this time by the margin of a single touchdown. But the game has its special niche in pigskin history because of the Crimson's awesome tactical contribution. Tim Cohane describes it with his wonted vividness, as follows:

At the beginning of the second half [the first had been scoreless] a ripple of expectancy flowed through the stands. Harvard was up to something. She was not lining up in the orthodox starting wedge. Instead, Captain Bernie Trafford stood with the ball alone at the 55-yard midfield stripe halfway between the sidelines. The other ten

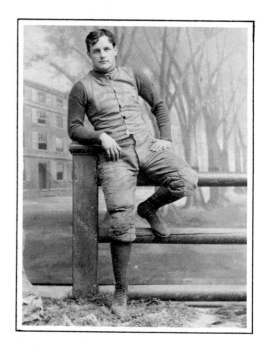

Vance McCormick, captain of Yale's 1892 team.
"Wild Bill" Hickok, a member of Yale's 1892 team.

players were split up into two slanting files of five each. Each side was well to either side of Trafford and behind him. The lead man in each was posted at the 40-yard line. Heavier men were at the front of each file, lighter men to the rear.

As this strange alignment was drawn up, Captain Vance McCormick walked up and down the Yale line.

"Boys," he said, "this is something new but play the game as you have been taught. Keep your eyes open and do not let them draw you in."

Trafford gave a signal. The two Harvard files began running. They were moving at top speed as they passed Trafford and converged to a V in front of him. At that instant, Trafford touched the ball down, handed it to Charlie Brewer, the fullback, who was in the moving mass and then joined it himself. . . . The rolling mass moved on, reaching the Yale 25-yard line before McCormick, Hinkey and the rest could fight their way through it and bring Brewer down.[20]

This was the famous, or infamous, flying wedge, conceived in the mind of Lorin F. Deland, a Harvard man; Deland was no football player but a chess expert who knew how to get there fastest with the mostest. The play, in effect, added momentum to mass and had it endured its homicidal

Harvard's flying wedge, 1892.

Yale team in wedge formation, 1893.

effect would probably have led to the banning of football. Happily for the game, the wedge was outlawed at the end of the '93 season, though momentum plays, in which blockers start before the ball is snapped, lingered on until 1897. The concept dies hard and at various times attempts have been made to make use of the principle. The famous Minnesota shift (excogitated by Harry Williams, Yale, '91, inventive and successful coach at Minnesota from 1900 to 1921) is one later example, and I have myself seen, in the late twenties, a Princeton team use a modified momentum play to good effect. In 1926 against Harvard the Tiger forwards lined up a yard or so behind the scrimmage line and, at a signal, lunged forward to their normal positions and with the briefest of pauses the ball was snapped and the line charged. This tactic demolished Harvard that year; Yale, having had a week to ponder the problem, solved it by placing their defensive linemen a yard or so back, meeting the Tiger preliminary charge with their own and so equalizing what momentum had been generated in the byplay. The legacy of the wedge is perceptible in the austere rules of today's game, by which a "man in motion" can run away from the line laterally, but if he takes a step forward before the ball is snapped his team is penalized. Offensive linemen must not move a muscle or even turn their heads before the snap. Sometimes an involuntary movement will result in a penalty, which may seem unfair, but momentum plays must be very carefully guarded against. The offense has a fractional momentum inbuilt, as it were, in the nature of the game, and any further concession would ruin the defense—not merely in the abstract sense of the verb.

The wedge did not win for Harvard; Yale held at the twenty-five and yet again after a blocked kick and, finally, following a thirty-five-yard run by Bliss and plunges by him and Butterworth, the former scooted around end from the 2-yard line for the only score, giving Yale a 6–0 win. In spite of the widely advertised savagery of the play, only two substitutes were used by Harvard (their presence at end and tackle was occasioned by Hinkey's vigorous assaults; of the starters, he "hit them so hard," Bealle reports, "that they were carried off the field"[21]—their involuntary defection was a notable help to the Blue cause). The Yale starting eleven survived intact; the only Blue casualty was Pudge Heffelfinger, now a graduate and a spectator. Carried away by empathy for his erstwhile comrades, he vaulted the fence surrounding the field and was promptly though not easily subdued by three policemen.

That busy afternoon in Springfield witnessed, in addition to the wedge, another and happier innovation in the annual rite. According to Baker the partisans of Handsome Dan introduced on that occasion the practice of singing tribal songs during the progress of action on the field. They had chosen the popular tune "Hold the Fort," to which they had supplied their own words. We may quote the first verse and the chorus here:

> *Harvard thinks she'll win because*
> *We've lost McClung and Heff;*
> *But when they run against the line*
> *They'll find there's something left.*

> *Hold the ball, McCormick's coming;*
> *He will signal still;*
> *We have always beaten Harvard;*
> *Win we must and will.*[22]

This melodious initiative proved to be very successful. It is hard nowadays to think of The Game (or any college game) without a musical accompaniment. Wedges come and go; song remains.

Strong delegations were again fielded by Blue and Crimson alike in 1893. At the end of the season Harvard's record was twelve wins against one defeat; Yale's, ten victories against a sole loss— that to Princeton, Hinkey's only defeat in his four years on the Bulldog team. In the course of the season's play Yale, captained by Hinkey, scored 336 points to opponents' 12, Harvard 418 to opponents' 15, figures that suggest that the Crimson had greater scoring power than the sons of Eli: but, as often in the case of Harvard, a substantial contribution to her total (114 points) was made by Andover and Exeter. On the eve of the Springfield rendezvous both squads were unbeaten. Harvard was a slight favorite in the betting, partly because Morris, Yale's veteran quarterback,

Harvard in action, 1893.

had been injured in the Penn game and would be replaced by the inexperienced Adee. But, once again, in a gruelling, hard-fought war of wedges and mass formations, Yale came out ahead, by the margin of one touchdown scored by Frank Butterworth early in the first half, with a conversion by Wild Bill Hickok. Hinkey called the signals and his generalship was a significant factor. Twenty-five thousand spectators looked on in awe as the match lived up to its predecessors' level of violent contact. Yet Harvard used only one substitute and Yale none. James L. Knox reports that "the game was far from interesting to the average spectator because of the uninterrupted use of mass formations,"[23] but it is memorable for yet another

Cantabrigian innovation. (Parenthetically we may note that in the Springfield series, although Yale was usually the winner, it was Harvard that produced the greater number of surprises.) To the amazement of the public and the consternation of the Elis, Harvard's team appeared on the field clad, not in the canvas jackets and moleskins that had become conventional, but in leather. Ostensibly this radical sartorial innovation (canvas had yielded to moleskins in 1887) was intended to insure that weight would not be absorbed in case of rain, as happened with cloth. Captain Waters of Harvard, however, openly revealed that the purpose was to enable the runner to shake off Eli tacklers. He said later, "I do not think that the suits surprised or dismayed Yale at all. I was informed that the Yale team procured some resin which they used on their hands so that they could hold on to the Harvard players when they tackled them"[24] He adds that the suits were made by the fashionable tailor Sommers of Park Street and cost $125.00 each—a tidy sum in the days of the five-cent cigar and the free lunch. Against Waters's statement one may only adduce that Hinkey debated long and vigorously with the referee before game time, arguing that such costumes were illegal. But the referee, of course, could find nothing in the rule book. (Perhaps Hinkey's demurral provided time for the Bulldogs to arm themselves with resin.) In any event Crimson ingenuity or perfidy availed them naught, though again adding spice to the homely Springfield sauce.

As the ever-increasing throngs of spectators attest, The Game, entering its third decade, was rapidly becoming a national event, of social as well as athletic significance. The coverage given to the '93 encounter may illustrate the new status, as well as, incidentally, bring to us something of the joyous flavor of the carefree decade of the nineties. The *New York Times* of November 19, the Sunday before the game, devotes a full page and a half to the prospective lineup of the gladiators on both sides, with individual sketches and biographical summaries. It describes as well the last days of intensive and secret practice. Harvard men, unlike the Yalies, the *Times* noted, are in the best of condition, cheered by the fact that Pennsylvania, though vanquished, scored a touchdown on the Blue, whose stalwarts are practicing

"with heroic desperation." "Tricks galore have been learned and defensive play enough has been mastered to win any championship, but there still remain the fatal weakness in the centre, and nobody here disputes Harvard's claim that it will be easy enough to score two couple [*sic*] of touchdowns from the middle of the field on sharp work during the game next Saturday." The *Times* of the 24th, the morning of the game, reported that the Bulldogs were practicing to the bitter end in order to give Adee a chance to accustom himself to his role, and that the absence of Morris from the lineup had caused Yale to omit half of her repertoire of plays. Shifting his focus from this discouraging topic, the correspondent continues:

A new feature is to be added to the picturesque scene. . . . Nearly 1,000 Yale students will be together in the grandstands on the Yale side and during the intermission will sing football songs composed for the occasion. The Yale Glee Club will sit in the centre of the cluster and will lead the colossal male chorus.

One of the songs, which will be sung to the tune of "Marching through Georgia," will be:

Harvard men from Boston come with hearts
  that quail
When they see the blue upon the sons of Eli
  Yale
When they hit the line, their tricks will be of
  no avail,
Down with the crimson forever.

Chorus

Hurray! Hurray then for the blue!
Hurray! Hurray! Hurray for Capt. Hinkey too!
We'll triumph over Harvard in the way we always do:
Down with the Crimson forever.

"This and other martial airs have been distributed," the *Times* tells us, "to the Yale undergraduates, who have been practicing them nightly gathered around the Fence."

A dispatch from Springfield on the same page graphically paints the color of the eve of battle: "Harvard is a slight favorite; Yale money is scarce; Hampden Park has been sold out; unfortunately there is some uncertainty about the seating arrangements. . . . The game is expected to yield $40,000 to its promoters." The arrival of the two teams is described; the contrast is interesting:

The Yale team arrived here in a special train of two cars. . . . Adee, senior [father of the Bulldog quarterback] was one of the few present to give the Yale boys a hearty welcome. . . . The New-Haven collegians went right to their quarters and were not seen after that. . . . The Harvard train was to arrive at 6:30 o'clock but it was nearly an hour later when the monster special rolled slowly into the station. . . . But when Captain Waters's men finally got here the cold feet and chilled nose and lips were forgotten in the rousing welcome thundered forth.

It was with great difficulty that the team worked its way through to their carriages, while the "Rah, rah, rah, rah, rah, rah, rah, rah, Harvard!" of the collegians and the "Hooray for Harvard" of the plebeians, together with the encouraging cries of the Springfield beauties—and they have them by the hundreds in the little town— rolled across the tracks . . . and the flutter of hundreds of crimson banners and flags made the scene inspiring.

While the tumult was at its greatest three passengers on a train on another track hurriedly raised windows and, gazing delightedly at the forest of colors, drew suspicious-looking bandanas from their pockets and with stentorian voices joined in the noise.

"Hoch die Anarchie! Hoch die Anarchie!" rang out their cries and the trained pulled out with the Germans gesticulating wildly and evidently wondering what socialistic paradise they had struck.

Elsewhere in the same section there is a detailed account of the six special trains run from New York to Springfield on Saturday morning and of the sleeping cars, with names of prominent occupants, departing Friday night. A special car was reserved for the Princeton team, destined to face the Bulldogs the following week. They took scouting seriously in those days.

Aside from covering the action of the game with its usual competence, the *Times* for Sunday the 26th reported a few interesting ancillary details. Governor Russell and Governor-elect McKinley took their seats on the Harvard side and were roundly applauded. At the end of the game the Princeton captain was sure the Tigers would

Yale boosters on their way to the Princeton game at the Polo
Grounds, New York City, 1893.

beat Yale on Thanksgiving Day. (He was right.) The Pennsylvania captain felt equally sure that Harvard would be easy meat for his team on the same festive date. (He was wrong.) The *Times* even noted the appearance of Handsome Dan on the field. "Some Harvard humorist," the account adds, "got a big dog of red cloth, stuffed with rags. . . . He was displayed with this placard: 'Where's Dan?' After the game the Yale dog tore the dummy to pieces and evidently relished the job."

In 1894, when "East Side, West Side" became the unofficial anthem of New York, Crimson and Blue came again to Springfield unbeaten, as was the rule in those days. Harvard could claim twelve victories, with a scant 16 points scored by opponents (12 by upstart Cornell). Yale's performance had been even more impressive: fourteen wins— and only 5 points in the adversarys' column, scored by a stubborn Army team. Hinkey was once more leader of the Elis; his henchmen included the All-Americans Phil Stillwell, George Adee, and Frank Butterworth. Harvard, as in the previous year entering the game a slight favorite, captained by R. D. Wrenn, could boast of Bert Waters, also All-American, Norm Cabot, and the able kicker Charley Brewer as well as Wrightington, a formidable competitor.

It was an ideal day for football, clear, dry, and with little wind. This year both bands of rooters were in voice. A favorite Yale song ran as follows:

Though Harvard has blue-stocking girls,
*   Yale has blue-stocking men;*
We've done fair Harvard up before,
*   We'll do her up again.*
And although the Harvard football team
*   May try what they can do,*
They can never on their tintype
*   Beat the grand old blue.*

To which Harvard voices replied (to the tune of "Rally round the flag"):

The Crimson forever,
Hurray boys hurrah,
Down with Pa Hinkey
Up with our Ma
And we'll sing a song of victory
As we cheer our players brave,
Waving the grand old banner Crimson.

The *Times* found the tunes "trite," and in truth the better melodic efforts of the rivals were still in the future. Diversions preliminary to the game were provided by Harvard's "Orange John" (well-known campus pedlar of soft drinks) parading along the sidelines in a red cape wearing a white hat with a large crimson band, and "to offset the effect of this, the Yale men liberated a big rooster, decorated with bright blue ribbon," whose arrogant strutting greatly delighted the crowd. The teams of Princeton and Pennsylvania were among the spectators, the former cheering for Yale, the latter for Harvard. A large force of Boston police, the *Times* notes, had been imported to help the local constabulary keep order in the vast crowd of 25,000, but the behavior of the throng was exemplary. So much could not be said of the players: "It has been suggested," says the *Times*, "that New York City be called on to furnish an ambulance corps and a body of surgeons"[25] for the encounter next year.

Once more, when twilight fell and the smoke of battle cleared, Yale stood triumphant—this time by a score of 12 to 4. And once more it was the loser who came up with the novelties. To Harvard goes the distinction of trying the first onside kick in the series (it worked, too) and the first "end around" that the annals of the game have recorded. It was good for sixteen yards, as Fairchild, loafing behind the Crimson left end, took a pass from Wrightington, who was charging as if to turn the Blue flank, and sped toward the Eli goal. Hinkey caught him on the Yale 4-yard line with "one of the most vicious tackles" he ever made.[26] The game, witnessed by 23,000 awed spectators, was closer than the score would suggest; it was really two touchdowns to one, with Harvard missing the conversion on a bit of bad luck. In those days the ball was not moved to the center of the field for the convenience of the kicker but had to be punted out from the point on the goal line where the runner had gone over. (The "puntout" endured until 1919.) What's more, the punt had to be caught and, from the point of the catch, a placekick was made for the extra point. The Harvard back, however, dropped the punt, and the attempt at conversion could not be made. Harvard's touchdown followed Yale's first score, made by Stillman, who blocked a kick and fell on the ball behind the Harvard goal, Hickok converting. Yale's second touchdown was scored in similar fashion: a kick hurried by the Yale charge fell short on the Harvard 4-yard line, and Thorne on three attempts bulled over. Harvard had a right to feel abused by Fortune; both Blue touchdowns came as a result of poor Cantab kicks, and these misplays were undoubtedly due to the circumstances that Harvard's excellent punter, Charley Brewer, could not use his skills, having twisted his ankle in a scrimmage prior to the game. Indeed, he had to be replaced by Whittemore in the course of the fray. Save for those mischances the Crimson more than held its own and even achieved a unique distinction: the Harvard touchdown was scored when Hayes, Whittemore's replacement, turned Frank Hinkey's end, the only time that happened in four years of the silent man's defense of his outpost. Perhaps the Crimson could claim a moral victory.

However, the combat of '94 is regrettably memorable for another reason. It was the roughest game in the history of the series. Each side was obliged to use four substitutes, a large number for those Spartan days. The Harvard historian James L. Knox is content merely to note that "the outstanding feature of the struggle was the roughness of the play."[27] The *Times* is more explicit and censorious: "It was a game in which an unusual amount of bad blood and foul playing was shown. . . . Charles Brewer of the Harvard team had his leg broken, Wrightington had a collarbone broken and Hallowell goes back to Cambridge with a broken nose. As for Yale, there was a rumor abroad in the night that Murphy, Yale's massive tackle, had died in the Springfield Hospital." The *Times* found out, however, that he was suffering merely from "contusion of the brain." Jerrems and Butterworth of Yale also suffered head injuries. (Incredibly, they were all, even Murphy, in the lineup against Princeton six days later.) The *Times* singles out Hinkey for special dishonorable mention: "It seemed to be Hinkey's main object to disable the best players of Harvard," and concludes its account with the prophetic remark: "Even the most enthusiastic devotee of football admitted that the play today will do much to injure the game, and may call for interference by the college authorities."[28]

Shocked by the carnage at Springfield, the public—or at least the journalists, for the crowds kept coming—reacted so strongly as to threaten the existence of the game. Alarming statistics were compiled enumerating the number of young men killed or wounded in the pursuit of the savage sport. Camp had his own census made and was able to report that the numbers of the casualties were greatly exaggerated, and Alonzo Stagg later said that he had never known of anyone to be seriously injured in a college game, but the outcry would not be stilled. Editorials thundered, pundits shook their heads in horror. The "massacre" itself achieved international notoriety. Parke Davis quotes with relish a report from the *Münchener Nachrichten*:

The football tournament between the teams of Harvard and Yale, recently held in America, had terrible results. It turned into an awful butchery. Of twenty-two participants seven were so severely injured that they had to be carried from the field in a dying condition. One player had his back broken, another lost an eye, and a third lost a leg. Both teams appeared upon the field with a crowd of ambulances, surgeons and nurses. Many ladies fainted at the awful cries of the injured players. The indignation of the spectators was powerful, but they were so terrorized that they were afraid to leave the field.[29]

There was swift reaction in the football world, too. As if suspecting that play on alien fields were provocative of brutality, the secretaries of War and Navy ruled that service teams should play only home games. Cornell followed suit. In March 1895 the representatives of Harvard, Yale, Princeton, Pennsylvania, and Cornell met to consider their strategy. Yale and Princeton favored the outlawing of mass momentum plays, but the other schools (having more effective means of implementing such tactics) demurred. For a few years conflicting regulations made each game a matter of compromise and ad hoc agreements.

Although, as we have noted, casualties were evenly divided on the lists at Springfield it was Yale that was more severely censured. Hinkey in particular was singled out as an example of the most brutal and insensitive kind of gladiator. "Brute" and "thug" were epithets regularly applied to him. The *Yale Alumni Weekly* for December 4, 1894, quoted from the *New York Post* a comment on the dark side of the sport: "One of its bad signs is the kind of men who, as general rule, are chosen as 'captains' of their teams. They are apt to be of the Hinkey type, brutal fellows, born sluggers, without the smallest pretension to gentlemanhood.'' The Harvard players made no complaints, but in the view of Brinck Thorne, Yale's captain-elect, they were at fault for not speaking up publicly to exonerate the silent man. After some correspondence between Thorne and Brewer of Harvard such a statement was in fact elicited from the Crimson. But by that time (the spring of 1895) exacerbation had reached such a point that the authorities deemed it wise to suspend the rivalry. Harvard and Yale did not meet in any sport in the season of 1895–96, and football relations were not resumed until 1897. Nor did the rivals ever again meet on the neutral and bloody ground of Hampden Park.

Press pass, 1890s.

A NEW CENTURY, A NEW GAME

Cover of *The Yale Record*, November 22, 1902.

While our moleskin express interrupts for a brief interval its journey through the years we may descend and take a look at the landscape, which has been constantly if unobtrusively changing as we have been borne along. Our station stop comes at the peak of the nineties, a decade which has lingered in the national memory with enduring fragrance for nearly a century. It is, in truth, a happy time to remember. In some respects, to be sure, it was not unlike the previous decade in the annals of our country; both were characterized by territorial expansion and technological innovation. But in the last years of the century expansion accelerated; the conquest of the West was pressed with increasing vigor and, geographically speaking, the American domain was extended even beyond the confines of the continent. The conclusion of a war fought to save poor little Cuba from Spanish oppression found us somehow in possession not only of Cuba but also of Puerto Rico and the remote Philippines. All but unobtrusively Hawaii had come under the Stars and Stripes. The nation had become an empire. At home, two more golden spikes had been driven to facilitate communication between the shores of the Atlantic and the Pacific. The population center was moving west; cities such as Chicago, Cleveland, Milwaukee, and St. Louis were beginning to catch up—both in population and prosperity—with the older centers of the East. It was a happy era for capitalism; fortunes were made, the rich got steadily richer, as yet unhampered by the income tax or antitrust regulations (it was in 1895 that J. P. Morgan's bank could bail out the Treasury with an infusion of $62 million, and in gold, too), and thanks to the emergence of combative labor unions even the working class was gradually improving its lot.

The pace of technological development—at least in practical matters affecting the life style of the ordinary citizen—had also accelerated. By the mid-nineties electric street lighting had replaced the gas lamps of the earlier decade in all the major cities; electric trolley cars had succeeded horse cars and stage service to suburbs. The safety bicycle, invented in the seventies, had, thanks to Dunlop's pneumatic tire (patented in 1889), facilitated the joyous mobility of millions of happy riders; bicycles built for two—or even more—careered blithely over the roads, not yet made perilous by the motor car, although a portent of things to come was evident in 1895, when Duryea put the first American-made, gas-propelled buggy on the market. Movies began with the "peep show" in 1894. Even wider horizons were sighted before the century ended; Marconi gave us wireless telegraphy in 1895, and Count Zeppelin initiated the conquest of the air, sending up his first lighter-than-air vehicle in 1900, as the incredibly inventive century came to an end.

But if the nineties were in these respects a prolongation of the eighties, they were at the same time very different in cultural attitudes and in flavor. Perhaps one could say that in the American eighties people knew how to make money and in the nineties they were learning how to spend it. The rich went in for yachting and horse racing; they bought yet statelier mansions in Newport and lodges in the Adirondacks; they wined and dined at Rectors and Delmonicos; in increasing numbers they married their daughters into the English peerage. Those not so rich yet managed to find many devices to brighten the drabness of life. Harrigan and Hart were followed by Weber and Fields. Tunes of melodious operettas filled the air. How could weddings have taken place, one wonders, before De Koven's "O Promise Me" had become available? Nor should we forget that the nineties bequeathed to us to have and to hold such precious items as "Sweet Adeline," "After the Ball," and "On the Banks of the Wabash." These are the years, too, of Whistler, Sargent, and Winslow Homer, to say nothing of James Whitcomb Riley and Richard Harding Davis. Where the eighties had been purposeful, the nineties were blithe and carefree. In such documentation changes of fashion are eloquent: in the last decade bustles had departed, and the clean silhouettes of the Gibson girls were coming in to delight the eye (admittedly the underpinnings of those slim waists must have been restrictive). Beards were no longer considered an essential feature of the male visage, though mustaches lingered on.

The aroma of the nineties knew no chronological barrier; it carried over into the next decade, which gave us the self-confident leadership of rough-riding Teddy, the stories of O. Henry, and the first World Series (1905). Throughout both decades the country enjoyed a sense of self-assurance and confidence. Things had a stability which was taken for granted and which we have never really known since. The dollar stood firm; *inflation*

Harvard . . .

was not yet a household word. Steadfast and sober Republicans, pillars of the Establishment (though some plutocrats came to have their doubts about "trust-busting" Teddy and his successor), dwelt in the White House. As for affairs abroad, no one gave them a thought. Great liners bore off the rich for grand tours in Europe and came back loaded with immigrants (mostly Italians and Slavs now, thus boosting the Irish up a notch on the totem pole)—which proved that America was God's country.

In the microcosm of the Crimson and the Blue, the last decade of the century presented its own novelties. Morison's chapter "The Harvest Season," which covers three years of Eliot's imaginative administration, informs us that "by the dawn of the twentieth century the 'pure' elective system seemed to be as firmly established as the trivium and quadrivium of the Middle Ages. Every large college or university in the country had adopted it except Yale. The idea had been sold to the American public. Eliot had outlived most of his earlier critics; success had silenced others."[1] Enrollment increased during the nineties at a 90 percent rate; Harvard had never enjoyed greater prestige. In 1894 the Society for the Collegiate Instruction for Women, founded in the eighties, became Radcliffe College. Harvard, though it would be years before she would admit it, had become coeducational, as the sons of Eli were quick to point out in the previously cited gridiron lyric: "Though Harvard has blue-stocking girls, Yale has blue-stocking men."

Things were going on at Yale, too, though at a

different pace and in different fields. In 1887 Timothy Dwight succeeded in getting the name of the institution changed from Yale College to Yale University, a move indicative of his intention to build up the professional schools. In 1894 the Connecticut legislature, uneasy about the failure of the Sheffield Scientific School to provide practical guidance for nutmegger farmers, terminated land grants to Yale and created an agricultural school at Storrs (with ultimate implications for the Bulldog warrior class). Perhaps because of its rigid requirements, Yale's enrollment was static during this period. But change would come. Arthur Twining Hadley, who succeeded Timothy Dwight in 1899, was the first president of Yale who was not a clergyman. (He was also fond of sports, especially football, and in 1900 appointed Walter Camp to the post of athletic advisor, adumbrating the director of athletics function yet to come.) In 1903 the requirement of Greek for the B.A. was scrapped, sixteen years after Harvard had licensed Attic illiteracy. But if through these years Harvard led the way, yet the stragglers had virtues of their own. George Santayana, on a visit to New Haven in 1892, found much to admire in the Yale ethos.[2] But the time has come now to board our express once more. A long and exciting journey lies ahead of us.

In February of 1897 Walter Camp for Yale and W. A. Brooks for Harvard negotiated a resumption of athletic relations between the two schools. Both parties were delighted; Baker quotes the lyric conclusion of the *Crimson* editorial on the accord:

and Yale fans.

W. Cameron Forbes, Harvard coach in 1897 and 1898.

(RIGHT) Charlie DeSaulles quarterbacked the 1897 Yale team, which played Harvard to a scoreless tie.

"Forgetting the past and resolving a generous, open-handed rivalry for the future, Harvard joins hands with Yale and welcomes her heartily and joyfully to her old place as Harvard's nearest and dearest foe."[3] Amicable hostilities on the gridiron resumed on November 13 of that year. In the interim the rules had been changed to require at least six men on the offensive scrimmage line, thus somewhat mitigating the menace of the mass plays of the era. And in the same year Yale initiated the direct pass from center to kicker.

On the evidence of the results of the encounters in the fading nineties one would have to say that the Crimson had profited more from the armistice than the Blue. The Bulldog was still strong but not quite as formidable as Hinkey had left him; the Cantabs, on the other hand, had reached an impressive peak. On form the Redshirts should have won all the games from 1897 through 1899—and probably would have save for a little bad luck and some Blue deviousness. Historians tend to attribute Harvard's edge to coaching: in New Haven Camp's advice was not so eagerly sought nor so readily followed as it had been, while the Cantabrigians rejoiced in a succession of very able mentors: Cameron Forbes in '97 and '98 and Ben Dibblee in 1899. Perhaps a change in venue had something to do with the shift of power: Springfield (where Yale had got used to winning) was abandoned forever and The Game returned to its campus background. In '97 the scene of battle was Soldiers Field, which had become Harvard's home field in 1894; it was destined to be the site of the new stadium to be erected six years in the future.

Yale came undefeated to Cambridge that year, and her lineup included some distinguished names: Charlie DeSaulles at quarterback, the freshman Gordon Brown (he would be a four-year All-American choice), and Art McBride, a talented punter. Yet the team performance was not quite up to the standard of McCormick or Hinkey; the record was marred by a tie with Army and a very close call with Brown. Captain Jim Rodgers's club had scored, on the eve of the Harvard game, a · mere 170 points to opponents' 35. Harvard had ten victories and no ties on her record and had scored 233 points to a minuscule 5 for the opposition. The Crimson had beaten Army 10–0; her roster included the fleet Dibblee, the All-American center Doucette, and a kicker of prowess called Percy Haughton. The Crimson was favored but had to settle for a scoreless tie. Twenty thousand spectators witnessed what seems to have been a rather unexciting game. Bealle writes, "For almost two hours [an exaggeration, for the new regulations prescribed two thirty-five-minute halves; conceivably it seemed much longer to a spectator] there had been incessant collision of bone and muscle, but no man had become famous for brilliant dashes, great runs or clever stratagems."[4] It was, however, a notable punting duel between Haughton and McBride; statistically, honors were even but perhaps McBride should be given the prize; most of his kicks were made against the wind and all under great pressure from a strong and well-coached line that blocked no fewer than five of his efforts. Yale had her chance in the first half but lost it by a fumble on the Harvard 13-yard

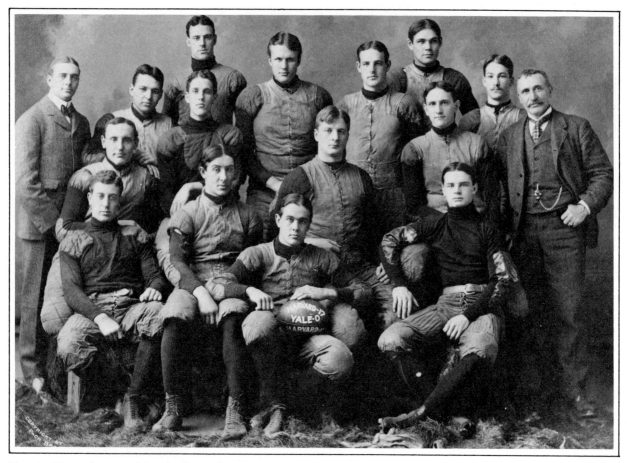

The 1898 Harvard team, unbeaten and untied. Captain Benjamin Dibblee holds the ball.

line. In the second half it was Harvard's turn; following a short kick by McBride she had the ball deep in Blue territory and powered her way to a first down on the Yale five. At this point Yale put on one of those goal line stands for which the Bulldog would be famed—this was the first to receive acclaim in the press. Harvard was turned away. The Elis used no subs; Harvard called on four; the unrestrained violence of earlier days was absent, however, and there were no serious injuries. The Harvard team in frustration vowed they would not accept their H's unless they redeemed themselves against Penn the following week. The Quakers, a power in the nineties, won, and no varsity letters were given in Cambridge that year.

Eighteen ninety-eight was a different story and

a happier one for Harvard. (It was a war year, but the fighting was conveniently over by the time the football season came around.) Again Forbes was in charge of the Crimson forces and this time his pupils went through the season unbeaten and untied. This year the Crimson had disposed of Penn and came to New Haven with a cast of confident stalwarts including not only Dibblee, now captain, and Haughton but also a pair of brilliant sophomore backs, Bill Reid and Charlie Daly. It was another Forbes-coached team, disciplined, aggressive, and smart. It possessed, too, a rare though invisible asset, a lighthearted blitheness of spirit, very different from the dour earnestness that is the normal characteristic of a winning squad. Knox's anecdote illustrates its cheerful *jemenfichisme*:

If you had been at Meriden, Connecticut on the night of November 18, 1898, with the Harvard football squad, you would have realized that a great transformation had been brought about. Parading the streets to the great amusement of the natives were the great big-hearted giant, Percy Jaffray, '99, and little Charlie Daly, '01. Percy had found a hat that accentuated his great height and Charlie another in which his active brain was lost. Percy led Charlie by the hand through the public streets, Charlie walking bowlegged to diminish his size so that the picture was, for all the world, like an organ grinder and his monkey. And that carefree by-play was on the eve of a Yale game.[5]

Although the Crimson was, as it had been in

'97, the favorite in the betting, Yale followers had hopes. Coached by Frank Butterworth and captained by Burr Chamberlin, the Bulldog had had an undefeated season. (One could not have known, on the dawning of that November Saturday, that it would be the first Yale team in history to lose to both Harvard and Princeton, although uneasy partisans of the Blue could not fail to note, looking at the record, that their point total [146] was the lowest since numerical scoring had come in.) Blue illusions were soon shattered. It was the first Harvard game played on Yale Field since 1884; accommodations had been expanded in the interim. The stands could now hold 14,000 spectators; it is said that all seats were taken and another 4,000 stood to watch the action. Rain fell throughout the contest, but it did not dampen the ardor or impair the efficiency of the debonair visitors from Cambridge. Dibblee ran brilliantly, Reid plunged effectively; the former made one touchdown, the latter two. Haughton missed one conversion. (This year the point values had been changed: a touchdown counted five points, a conversion one.) 17–0. There was no Yale counterattack. It was the best day the Crimson had spent in New Haven since 1875.

The Harvard machine should have done as well or even better in 1899, but a combination of Blue chicanery and sheer bad luck brought about yet another scoreless tie, spoiling an otherwise immaculate Crimson record. The Bulldogs of '99, like their immediate predecessors, were not quite up to the standards of old; they had suffered— *incredibile dictu*—a defeat at the hands of Colum-

Harvard poster, 1898.

bia earlier in the season. Still, the squad was by no means untalented, with Gordon Brown in the line, Al Sharpe in the backfield, and the very able punter McBride, who now captained the team. It was possible for Blue partisans to hope.

As it turned out, the Bulldogs never did get a chance to score, but they played, as they had two years earlier, valiantly on defense. And on this occasion they took advantage of a rule (no longer in effect) that permitted the ball-holding team failing to make five yards in three downs to re-tain possession and put the ball in play twenty yards behind the scrimmage line. This stratagem, combined with McBride's kicking, kept the Can-tabs at a safe distance—most of the time. Even so Harvard would have won save for a freakish acci-dent. The Crimson's Daly, the star of the game, engineered an irresistible drive which brought the ball to the Blue 1-yard line. Daly handed off to Ellis, his fullback, who with lowered head plunged straight into the arms of McBride, who was braced against the goalpost. (Twenty-eight years would pass before it would occur to the rule makers that it might be advisable to put the posts back from the goal line.) Harvard never got another chance at a touchdown, but had, in the waning minutes of the game, two opportunities for a field goal. Both were missed. A bitter outcome indeed for a team that was clearly superior. But when were the pigskin gods ever fair? The game was witnessed by 36,000 spectators, including Gover-nor Theodore Roosevelt of New York and Gover-nor Roger Walcott of Massachusetts, both Harvard graduates. It is said that Teddy evinced great dis-

appointment when Ellis was turned back by the perfidious goalpost. Yale used no subs; Harvard needed four, but, to quote the *Post*, "no Harvard player was hurt in a serious way. There were no bandages."[6]

The old century went out in a blaze of glory; 1900 is the year of *Tosca* and *Lord Jim*, to say nothing of the cakewalk and the launching of the hamburger sandwich, first served in Louis' Lunch in New Haven. In the last meeting of the century, played on Yale Field November 24, 1900, the Blue had no need of either good luck or guileful tactics to score an impressive victory. The 1900 team, captained by the intense and dedicated Grotonian Gordon Brown (wearer of a Phi Beta Kappa key as well as winner of four successive major Y's), was among the three or four best—if not perhaps *the* best—of all Yale teams. The roll call of the starting eleven is rich in hallowed names. Beau Olcott, center, Ralph Bloomer and George Still-man, tackles, Bill Fincke, rated the best quar-terback in the country, George Chadwick, half-back, and Perry Hale, fullback: all were named on Walter Camp's All-America first team. Three other members were selected for the second All-America and one for the third. (Such a distinction was no novelty to Gordon Brown: he was one of only three four-time, first-team All-Americans, Frank Hinkey and Truxtun Hare of Penn being the others.) About half the personnel of Brown's com-pany were veterans of the rather unsatisfactory '99 season, but they had an additional year of ex-perience and were strengthened by the presence of new recruits and inspired by the magnetic leadership of their captain. Baker affirms that "with this team there was a feeling that was almost spiritual. Brown represented Yale idealism."[7] Brown was on better terms with Camp than some recent leaders had been; he and McBride, now field coach, faithfully followed the strategic counsel offered by the wily Walter in his "fireside chats." Among his suggestions was the famous tackleback tandem, a pattern for mass mayhem originally conceived by Harry Williams, Yale '91, but quietly adopted and improved by Camp. Many historians credit the skilled and patient attentions of Mike Murphy, Yale's beloved trainer, who had returned from a sojourn at Penn, for the consistently sharp condition of the team. Theoretically the squad had one weakness; no talented kicker was available to take the place of McBride. But in practice the weakness was irrelevant; Gordon Brown's team never had to depend on kicking. The squad had developed slowly, winning the early games by modest margins and fighting off Columbia in a real squeaker. But a smashing victory over Princeton the week before the Harvard engagement indicated that a truly formidable combination would be ready for the Crimson. Twenty-two thousand came to see.

Yet it was a sturdy Crimson delegation, too, coming to Yale Field undefeated and untied in ten games (including an easy victory over Army), coached by Dibblee and with many veterans of the '99 team, which had been clearly superior to the Blue. Cambridge hopes were high, particularly as the injured Charlie Daly, now captain, was healed and ready to face the Bulldogs. Bealle com-

Gordon Brown was a four-time All-American at Yale.

ments somewhat wryly that Daly's presence may have proved costly to Harvard; he made a grave mental error in accepting a penalty when declining it would have given Harvard possession of the

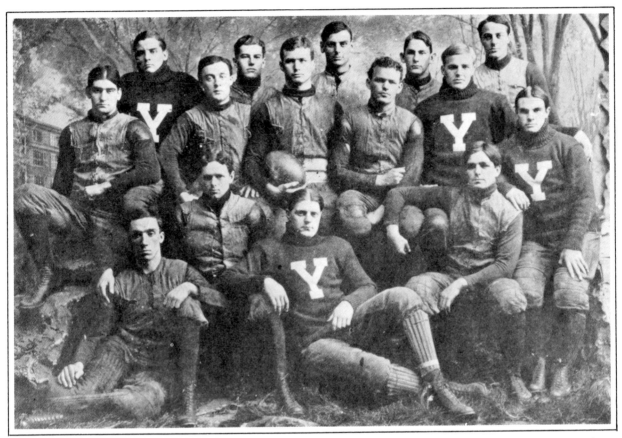

The 1900 Yale team, perhaps the best of all time, won all thirteen of its games and was unscored on. *Front row, l. to r.:* C. D. Rafferty, C. Dupee, J. R. Bloomer, H. P. Okott. *Middle row:* H. C. Holt, C. Gould, Captain F. G. Brown, P. T. Hale, G. S. Stillman, G. B. Chadwick. *Back row:* J. H. Wear, S. L. Coy, R. Sheldon, A. H. Sharpe, W. N. Fincke.

ball.[8] But it would be unfair to blame the gallant and usually resourceful Charlie for the day's debacle; Brown's team, at its peak of perfection, was simply too much for the Crimson to handle. Harvard's coach Dibblee said, with truth, that "such a line as that of the Yale team of 1900 has hardly ever been seen on the gridiron,"[9] and Knox felt that, looking back on Brown's team, "we may congratulate our representatives in doing as well as they did."[10] The action may be briefly resumed: Yale's first touchdown was scored by Bloomer on the tackle-back play of Camp's arsenal; later in the half Fincke ran back a punt for the Blue's second score. Hale's conversions gave Yale a twelve-point lead at halftime. In the second half Chadwick bulled his way over center sixteen yards for the score, Hale converting again. Finally Sherman Coy recovered a fumbled pass in the Harvard backfield and ran fifty yards for the fourth touchdown. Yale used one substitute; Harvard called on nine—not because of injuries but in a desperate attempt to contain the Yale power by the use of fresh troops. For the first time in the history of The Game the mocking strains of the "undertaker song" were heard rising from the Yale stands. Tradition permits its lugubrious chanting only in the last moments of a game when victory is certain. (I can recall a few premature renderings over the years.) Nineteen hundred, incidentally, was a good year for Yale songs: "Boola Boola" made its tuneful debut, as did the sacred "Bright College Years," first sung at Princeton a week before the game we have chronicled. And assuredly the Team of the Century was most deserving of musical tribute. Harvard, shocked and shaken, could only "wait till next year." Which, in fact, would bring her considerable solace.

In the first year of the new century Yale celebrated her 200th anniversary. The ceremonial rites included a torchlight procession, two exhibition football games on the campus, and a climactic convocation, which was held in the Hyperion

Theater since the new auditorium, which Hadley had declared a necessity, was not yet ready. On this occasion, which took place on October 23, sixty-two honorary degrees were given—one to Harvard's most prestigious alumnus, Theodore Roosevelt, recently installed as president of the United States. The historian Brooks Kelley reports: "Roosevelt, the only recipient to speak, said of Yale what it most liked to hear: 'I have never worked at a task worth doing that I did not find myself working shoulder to shoulder with some son of Yale. I have never yet been in any struggle for righteousness or decency, that there were not men of Yale to aid me and give me strength and courage.'"[11] Thus reassured, Yale could enter her third century with pride and confidence.

In pigskin terms, however, things were a little different. The old century had departed in an appropriately Blue afterglow, but the new one dawned in a resplendent Crimson as Campbell's powerful and resourceful clan gave Gould's Bulldogs a sound licking. (In retrospect, we can see that the rosy dawn was indeed prophetic. Of the games played in the nineteenth century, Yale had won fifteen, tied three, and lost only three. So far in our century the Blue has a lead, but it is a very slight one compared to the older figures: thirty-nine wins, thirty-five defeats, and five ties. Harvard has been catching up.)

The Cambridge task force of 1901 was certainly one of the best to trot out onto Soldiers Field for the annual joust. It went undefeated through a twelve-game season and placed no fewer than five team members on Walter Camp's All-America, including Captain Campbell at end and the controversial Ollie Cutts (of whom more presently) at tackle. Of the Yale team of 1901 only Holt at center was Camp's choice for his first team. It must be admitted, however, that the Elis faced their now ancient rivals with a *dossier* commanding respect. The Bulldog, too, had been undefeated; only a tie with Army blotted his record. If it was not quite up to the quality of the Team of the Century, well, who could hope to be? The record-breaking crowd of 40,000 expected an even battle.

In fact, it turned out to be a walkaway for the Crimson; their great tackle Cutts smashed the Yale defense apart with his rushes; he carried the ball twenty times and carried the Eli line along with the ball. Harvard made 327 yards to the Blue's 38. What's more, they did it with no substitutes. Touchdowns were made by Blagden, Ristine, and Graydon; Cutts made two conversions. Yale never seriously threatened.

The Crimson may have had an unfair advantage that afternoon. On the eve of The Game the Har-

Dave Campbell, captain of Harvard's 1901 team, played left end for three years. Here he is shown practicing at halfback.

vard team received the following message: "White House, Washington, November 21—Regret more than I can say. Utterly impossible to come. Will you personally give my good wishes to the team, and I am sure they can win and that I count upon their playing without a letup from the first to the last—Theodore Roosevelt."[12] What hope could the underprivileged Bulldog entertain in the face of this authoritative benediction?

The game of 1901 had been preceded by arguments concerning eligibility. Late in the season Harvard ferreted out the deplorable fact that Yale's Glass—a puissant lineman whom many connoisseurs regard as the peer of Heffelfinger—had played for Syracuse before entering the Sheffield Scientific School: thus, by Yale's own rules, he should be ineligible for his first year of residence in New Haven. Yale conceded the justice of the argument, and the redoubtable Glass did not play in either the Princeton or Harvard games. But in her turn Yale protested the eligibility of Harvard's Cutts, pointing out that he had been employed by the Haverford College Grammar School as an instructor in mathematics and physical education

Crowd and trolley cars outside Yale Field, 1901.

and that Harvard's rules stated that no one should be eligible to play on a Harvard team who had taught "in any athletic exercise or sport as a means of livelihood." An affidavit being produced from the headmaster of the institution (a Harvard graduate, as it happened) affirming that Cutts had in fact never taught physical education at the school, Cutts was permitted to fulfill his destiny and demolish the sons of Eli. After the season was over Cutts remembered that he *had* taught physical education for one term at the Haverford school. Harvard offered an apology. But the score stands.[13]

Between 1889 and 1911 Harvard played no football games with Princeton; her most dangerous rival next to Yale was Pennsylvania, who was not on the Bulldog schedule. The calculation of superiority by comparative scores was commonly based on the results of the game with Army, which regularly took on both the Blue and the Crimson. In 1902 Harvard beat the soldiers 14−6 while the Elis could manage only a tie at West Point. For this reason Harvard's unbeaten warriors of 1902 (captained by Bob Kernan, a good runner, with the smart quarterback Carl Marshall and a pair of rugged linemen to help out) might have felt a certain measure of confidence as they entrained for their visit to New Haven. (Extra seats were constructed at the last minute to accommodate a crowd of 30,000.) The visitors from Cambridge could not know at the time that they were facing another Blue squad that would rank very close to Gordon Brown's cast of Bulldog immortals, but by sunset of that day of battle they were much wiser. Yale won (23−0) with the greatest of

Advertisement for "The Students' Train," 1902.

Kickoff of Harvard–Yale game,
November 22, 1902, Yale Field.
Thirty thousand spectators watched
the contest, which Yale won 23−0.

ease, scoring two touchdowns in the first half, one
on a seventy-three-yard run from scrimmage by
Metcalf (the longest in the rivalry until Harvard's
DeMars capped it seventy years later). The Blue
added two more in the second half; three conversions were made to round out the 23. Harvard
once reached the Blue 8-yard line but was unable
to score; it was a disappointing day for the Crimson. The margin of victory was probably not indicative of the real difference between the competitors; Harvard on the record was a better team
than she seemed to be on that day: "tackles were
missed, backfield men couldn't get started and
Yale continued to score," Bealle comments.[14] But
though the score might have been lower the result
would assuredly have been the same; it was a
truly great Yale team with power to spare. Captained by the blond and boyish George Chadwick,
the Bulldog roster presented a galaxy of stars.
Glass, eligible this year, was back at guard; his
running mate at left guard was G. A. Goss; Kinney
and the sophomore Jim Hogan held down the
tackle spots, and Rafferty and the freshman Tom
Shevlin rounded out what would go down in
Bulldog annals as "the Irish line." Foster Rockwell at quarterback—another freshman—was considered for years to be peerless among Yale signal callers; Metcalf and Chadwick were talented
runners, as was Bowman at fullback. As in Gordon Brown's year, seven of Yale's starters made
Camp's first All-America (Chadwick, Glass, Holt,
Hogan, Kinney, Rockwell, and Shevlin); Bowman,
Goss, and Metcalf were put on his second team.

Freshman Tom Shevlin made Camp's All-American team in
1902 and later captained the 1905 Yale team.

The 1902 Yale team, captained by George Chadwick (holding ball).

Cohane comments, "Why Rif Rafferty failed to make end even on the third team was known only to Camp and to God, not necessarily in that order."[15]

As in the case of Brown's squad, so too with Chadwick: the captain worked very closely with Camp, who this year came up with a variation of the tackle back (it may not have been original with him) which was in effect a kind of misdirection play. The tackle could be set behind the lines, with two blockers in front of him, as if set to carry the ball (still legal in those days) through the opposing tackle and end. This would draw the defense to the flank; the quarterback would then hand off to the halfback, who would charge straight ahead through a gap made by the center and guard and be well on his way before the opponent's secondary could recover. As Cohane points out, this innovation of Camp's was noteworthy because it was designed not merely to pick up a few yards (the purpose of most mass formations) but to break a runner into a clear field for a score. It was used first against Princeton, with Chadwick going fifty-five yards for the score; Metcalf's run, already mentioned, came out of the same formation. While pulling the tackle back is no longer legal, football today has many variations of this technique, which works of course only when you have a guard like Goss and a center like Holt, who can be counted on to provide the essential blocking in the line.

The public's distaste for the violence characteristic of the wedge and mass style of play became increasingly apparent in the early years of the century. Parke H. Davis writes: "Although the season of 1902 had been fraught with no excessive number of accidents nor with any personal mishap of a severe and sensational character, the long dormant football reformer awoke. He found ready support in that portion of the football public which saw in the agitation an opportunity to use roughness as a weapon with which to force the return of open play." Accordingly, the rules committee, hoping to encourage "openness," ruled that henceforth (beginning with the season of 1903) the player (usually the quarterback) who received the ball directly from the snapper back would be permitted to run with the ball; hitherto his function had been limited to handing off to a teammate. "Cautious, however, in their radicalness," Davis continues, "the legislators of the game imposed a condition that such a run must cross the line of scrimmage five yards distant from the point where the ball was put in play. . . . The imposition of this five-yard restriction brought in the autumn of 1903 the lengthwise stripes of the playing field, thereby changing its countenance from the classic gridiron to a checkerboard."[16]

However, for the old rivals, the inauguration of the checkerboard was not the only novelty of the year. In 1903 the great Harvard Stadium was built, designed to accommodate 40,000 spectators (subsequently enlarged to contain 55,000); it was the largest edifice of its kind and certainly a striking monument to the status achieved by the sport invented less than thirty years earlier. The Stadium erected on Soldiers Field was—and is—an impressive architectural specimen; its somewhat

Harvard Stadium, built in 1903, was designed to accommodate 40,000 spectators.

imperial design suggests the Colosseum of Rome. In a way it is surprising that Harvard should have preceded Yale in this tangible recognition of the prestige of the pigskin; at the time of its construction, Yale loomed larger than her rival in the context of the game. But Harvard got the money first— and made spectacular use of it. The 1903 season was also the year of the notorious hidden ball trick of the wily Carlisle Indians, whose ruse in tucking the spheroid under the jersey brought them within one point of beating the Crimson. It was a year, too, of an unusually unpredictable Harvard team (Marshall was back as captain, flanked by the

spirited Don Hurley and featuring the All-American Don Knowlton at tackle), which vanquished both Army and Pennsylvania and lost (for the only time in history) to Amherst and (for the first time in history) to Dartmouth, who helped their hosts inaugurate the new stadium. Imposing though the edifice was, it must have seemed to contemporary Cantabrigians to be anything but lucky for the home team.

A week after the dedication game with Dartmouth, Yale, headed by "Rif" Rafferty, came to town and walked off with a solid victory over the Cantabs. Goss, who had seemed the most likely candidate to succeed Chadwick, had fallen victim to a new Yale ruling that limited eligibility to four years—and Goss had played two years for Syracuse before coming to Yale. It was, to be sure, another strong Bulldog delegation, losing only (in a last-minute desperation play) to Princeton. Of the Irish line of 1902 only Hogan, Shevlin, and Rafferty were left, but the sprightly Rockwell was back at quarterback, and Harold Metcalf, now a senior and fleeter than ever, sparkled at halfback. Hogan of course was a major asset. The score was 17–0, but it not an easy triumph for the Blue. Harvard had the ball five times inside the Yale 30-yard line and twice got as far as the seven, but a stalwart Blue defense fought off the Redshirts. Yale scored once in the first half—a touchdown by Kinney set up by a long run by Metcalf; in the second half two blocked kicks were downed by the redoubtable Hogan behind the Crimson goal line. Bealle remarks of the contest that Harvard "played its best game of the year and had no apologies to offer for the loss."[17] Yale men thought the new stadium was a fine place to play. A decade would pass before they had cause for second thoughts. For what it is worth we may note that, although occasionally after a run of losses for the Blue one hears talk of "the Stadium jinx," Yale has to date won eighteen and tied three of the thirty-seven battles in the great red amphitheater.

Captained by the All-American Dan Hurley at right half, Harvard, though a young and inexperienced delegation, was off to a good start in 1904, running through its first six games undefeated, bagging Army and the always dangerous Carlisle

Indians among others. As in 1902 the victory over Army was especially encouraging, since the cadets that year for the first time in history eked out a victory over Yale. This moment of exultation, however, was followed by a surprising licking at the hands of Penn, which for the past six years had been an obliging and docile sparring partner. (It turned out to be an undefeated year for Penn.) The setback by the Quakers seemed to have a demoralizing effect on the Cantabs; in successive weeks Dartmouth held them to a scoreless tie and Holy Cross (a newcomer to Soldiers Field) had the temerity to score a touchdown on them. The reverse at West Point seemed to have, on the other hand, a tonic effect on the Yale squad, captained by Jim Hogan, the second of the Irish line to be entrusted with leadership. It is recorded that Hogan, shaken to the point of tears by the loss to the cadets, had congratulated Army in the simple words, "You fellows don't realize it but you have beaten the champions," and then proceeded with homely eloquence to inspire his comrades to greater effort in the future.[18] And in fact the remaining opponents, Columbia, Brown, Princeton, and Harvard, did not so much as score a point on Jim Hogan's lads. Perhaps the song "Down the Field," composed by Stanley Friedman, '05, the student bandmaster, and first sung at the Princeton game, was a morale builder. It still lives in the Blue repertoire. But probably no incentive was needed; the Elis of '04 were a doughty crew, with stalwarts such as Shevlin, Bloomer, and Roraback up front along with Hogan; Rockwell was back at quarterback, and the sophomore Sammy Morse was an adequate replacement for Metcalf at right half. Roraback, a massive and talented center, was the heaviest man yet to wear the Blue, weighing in at 236 pounds. His opposite number, the freshman Bartol Parker, was no lightweight either, carrying 227 pounds. In which connection we may note that pigskin chasers were beginning to put on weight: this year each side fielded four linemen of 200 pounds or more, which was something of a record. The Crimson line averaged 191 pounds per man; the Yale forwards, thanks to Roraback's contribution, 196.5. Ten years earlier the respective averages had been 186.5 and 186. But it must be admitted that the delegations of '04 were unusually ponderous; many teams in later years would field lines of lesser displacement. The impressive poundage we see today came in only after World War II.

The game attracted 35,000 spectators. The *New York Times* reports: "Out of the Grand Central Station the New York, New Haven and Hartford Railroad ran six special trains, carrying 54 private cars to New Haven, and among the owners, T. H. Gillespie came in his 'Caligula,' O. H. P. Belmont in his 'Twilight,' J. P. Morgan in his 'Connecticut,' and T. H. Shevlin in his 'Elysian.'" The *Times* man described the weather as "an autumnal dream" and the crowd as "one which nothing could ruffle. Refinement, culture, and an easy disposition were written on its face."[19] Harvard's Theodore Roosevelt did not attend, but his daughter Alice Lee Roosevelt (later Mrs. Nicholas Longworth) did, as did Charles Warren Fairbanks of Indianapolis, his running mate in his successful presidential campaign just ended. Fairbanks's son Richard was a Yale senior.

As for the action on the field, the Blue came out on top by a score of 12−0. Yale's Morse scored the first touchdown at the end of a long march; the second came as a result of a Harvard kick blocked by Tripp and carried over the Harvard goal line by Flinn. Conversions were made by Hoyt. Throughout the game Harvard put up a very stubborn defense; their new crouching stance proved effective in containing the Blue attack, and a slippery field (it had rained the preceding day) made it difficult for either side to mount an effective attack. Yale used no substitutions; Harvard used eight reserves in an attempt to hold off the persistent Bulldog. There were no injuries.

One incident of the rather unexciting afternoon's exercise is worthy of note. Harvard's reserves included one W. C. Matthews, a black. Baker reports that in the second half Matthews, coming down under a punt, tackled Rockwell so hard that both men were shaken up, Matthews more than Rockwell. The story spread that Matthews had been deliberately singled out for assault. In a letter to the *Yale Alumni Weekly*, however, Matthews blamed his injuries on his failure to wear padding on his shoulders and on his own hard tackling, adding: "I do not believe any Yale man tried to use me unfairly. When I entered the game, Captain Hogan, Bloomer, Sammy Morse and Shevlin greeted me and several Yale men on the sidelines expressed pleasure on seeing me in. I had played with and against most of the men on the Yale team while at Andover and I felt confi-

Jim Hogan, captain of Yale's 1904 team, was not only three times All-American but also an honor student.

dent that they had nothing but good wishes for me."[20] The statement is not only reassuring with regard to the Bulldog's behavior but instructive as shedding light on the exclusive nature of the pool from which both institutions drew their recruits.

Yet the same match presented in the person of Yale's captain evidence that The Game, even though it might draw its levees largely from the prep schools, was no longer restricted to old American stock. The Irish had emerged, and in Hogan they had found a symbol not only of recognition but of prestige. Hogan was Irish-born; his father was a stonemason and his mother a laundress. He had come to Yale late (he would graduate at the age of twenty-eight) because he had had to work and save for his education. By all accounts of contemporaries he was an unusual man: not only three times All-American but an honor student as well and an inspirational leader. "Barrel chested, with great tree trunk legs and a lantern jaw, he even looked like a Bulldog."[21] He enjoyed the admiring respect of his classmates and was elected to Skull and Bones. He was not the first Celt to appear in the Blue lineup (nor in Harvard's either, for that matter), but his prestige was a clear indication that the Irish had arrived. To be sure, they had for some time enjoyed prominence in politics. They had long been a power to be reckoned with in New York, but at the turn of the century they had extended their domain to the Yankee towns of New England; both Cambridge and New Haven had seen Irish mayors take over their city halls. A Cambridge historian remarks that they would continue to dominate Cambridge politics for nearly four decades—a statement that would, in general, hold for New Haven as well.[22] On the gridiron the process of integration was not, of course, limited to Yale and Harvard, but the high esteem in which both institutions were held, both academically and socially, gave special significance to the phenomenon. For the social historian J. C. Furnas, "The most constructive thing done by intercollegiate football was to open opportunities for ethnic minorities."[23] Coming back to our own game, we may note that the prominence of Hogan should not make us overlook that Harvard fielded a sturdy Celtic captain, too, in the person of Dan Hurley, "a team in himself," in the words of the *Boston Globe*. A Harvard–Yale game with Hibernian leadership on both sides and featuring a black surely has a place in American social history.

The 1905 season, although players and public did not realize it, marked the end of an era—or perhaps a sub-era. It was the last year that games were played with no forward passing; it was the last year for Yale and Harvard (and most other schools, for that matter) that graduate students were allowed to play. Things would be different in 1906, and the goings on in the Stadium in 1905 would have something to do with the changes. Harvard had brought back the vivacious and articulate Bill Reid, who had coached the '01 team; the valiant Hurley, now in law school, was re-elected captain; injuries kept him out of most games, including the contest with Yale, but the veteran Knowlton and Jack Wendell were dependable backs. In the line were two All-Americans:

Beaton Squires at tackle and the freshman "Hooks" Burr at guard. It was not, however, the best of seasons for Harvard; although they beat the Army by a touchdown, the Crimson warriors lost to a resurgent Penn and suffered a tie with Dartmouth. It would be the last game with the Quakers for many a year; a dispute over eligibility and the treachery of the Red and Blue in icing the field before the game brought about a rancorous rupture. So when the Bulldog came to Cambridge with an imposing record, no defeats and easy wins over Army and Princeton (the latter being the only team to score against the Elis and that a mere field goal), even the most loyal Harvard fans feared a debacle. Once more the Blue was led by a Celt, the flamboyant, lighthearted Tom Shevlin (very different in temperament from the puritanical Hogan, who was not happy to see Tom succeed him). Among his more prominent assistants were the sophomore Lucius Biglow at tackle, Sammy Morse at right half, and the freshman Tad Jones, a surprise starter at quarterback. However, when the smoke had cleared it revealed another Blue victory to be sure, but won by a single touchdown and characterized by the roughest play since the Springfield era. The most spectacular act of illegal violence was Yale's mauling of Harvard's Burr, whose signal for a fair catch was ignored by Shevlin, who tackled him low, and Quill, who managed to break his nose. (Quill, not denying his fault, claimed after the game that he had been bitten by Harvard's Brill, which understandably made him resentful.) But the flagrant felony of the Blue was made even more intolerable to Harvard by the fact that the referee,

1905 Harvard–Yale
football program.

Paul Dashiell, saw no reason to call a penalty.
The short-fused Reid, justifiably annoyed, protested vigorously, and the Harvard stands were in
full sympathy. Major Higginbotham (who gave
Soldiers Field to Harvard) sent a note to Reid ad-
vising him to take his team from the field. But
Reid decided to go on, and the first half ended in
a scoreless deadlock. (Before the Burr incident
Yale's Morse had been ejected from the game for
slugging Jack Wendell, who he claimed had
been repeatedly holding him and had gone un-
punished by Dashiell. It was a hard day for the
arbiter. Reid saw to it that he would never again
be permitted to referee a Harvard game.) In the
second half the Bulldogs fought off a savage Crimson advance; finally a Cantab fumble recovered

by Forbes on the Harvard 30-yard line gave the Blue its chance. LeVine and Forbes alternated in smashes, the latter, dragged by the former, finally going over for the game's only touchdown. This year the playing time was cut to two thirty-minute halves, but the shorter periods sufficed to include a high quotient of mayhem.

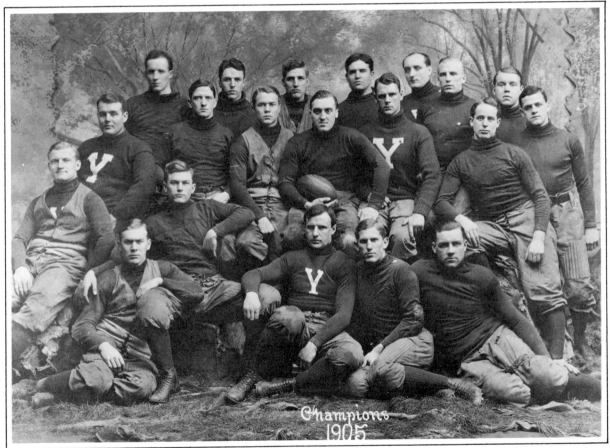

(LEFT) Bill Reid coached Harvard in 1901 and again in 1905 and 1906.

The 1905 Yale team. *First row, l. to r.:* P. L. Veeder, J. N. Levine, H. Jones, R. B. Forbes. *Second row:* H. L. Roome, T. A. D. Jones. *Third row:* P. C. Smith, A. R. Flinn, S. F. B. Morse, Captain T. L. Shevlin, R. B. Tripp, J. M. Cates, W. F. Knox. *Fourth row:* L. Hoyt, L. H. Bigelow, C. Flanders, A. G. Erwin, J. J. Quill, G. Hutchinson, C. W. Hockenberger.

The roughness of the combat was characteristic of the season of 1905. Stagg quotes a *Chicago Tribune* compilation of the casualties of the year: 18 deaths and 159 serious injuries.[24] Public criticism of the game was mounting (as in 1895) and the general concern was reflected in very high quarters; early in the 1905 season President Roosevelt had called to the White House representatives of Harvard, Yale, and other schools and urged them to take proper measures to curb the brutal style of play; he seemed more concerned with foul play than with changes in the rules. His counsel had little effect on the season under way; criticism of the game mounted to new heights at the close of the season; some institutions took drastic action: Columbia abandoned football and California and Stanford reverted to rugby. The most eloquent philippic against the game was voiced by Harvard's president, who, in his report to the Board of Overseers for the academic year 1904–05, affirmed,

The American game of football as now played, is unfit for colleges and schools. It causes an unreasonable number of serious injuries and deaths. . . . Acts of brutality are constantly committed, partly as results of the passions naturally aroused in fighting, but often on well-grounded calculations of profit toward victory. . . . As a spectacle football is more brutalizing than prize-fighting, cockfighting or bull fighting. . . . It is clearly the duty of the colleges, which have permitted these monstrous evils to grow up and to become intense, to purge themselves of such immoralities and to do what they can to help the secondary schools purge themselves likewise.

The exasperated president prevailed on the Board of Overseers to forbid further playing of the game by Harvard men: however, before the decision could be promulgated, Coach Reid, the resourceful master of Machiavellian tactics, affecting ignorance of the overseers' ruling, published an open letter to the secretary of the Harvard Athletic Association, expressing his own conviction of the kind of reforms needed if the game was to go on.[25] Reid's notions and those of others of like mind were presented at the convocation summoned by Chancellor Henry M. MacCracken of New York University and attended by sixty delegates representing twenty-six institutions. This was the first meeting of the Intercollegiate Football Conference, which was the seed of the National Collegiate Athletic Association (NCAA). Deliberations went on from late December to mid-January and from them a "new" or at least a more open game emerged. The most significant innovations, in order of public impact if not perhaps of effectiveness in achieving the purpose of the reformers, were the legalizing of the forward pass, the requirement of at least six men in the line when the ball is put in play, imposition on the team in possession to make ten yards instead of five in three downs (to encourage end runs and passes), and the establishment of a neutral zone between offensive and defensive linemen (a change Camp had been seeking for years). "Hurdling" was banned. Reid played a considerable role in getting the conference to adopt the new rules.

In the course of a few years some of these rulings would be modified as a result of experience with them. Later, the offense would be obliged to put seven men in the line, and in successive years the restrictions on the forward pass would be eased. When first legalized, a pass could be thrown only from an area five yards behind and five yards either side of the center, and an incomplete pass signified loss of possession, since a dropped pass counted as a fumble and could be recovered by the defenders. But as they stood, the reforms of 1905 were radical enough to satisfy the critics—at least for a while—and to introduce a new direction if not a basically different game. Thanks to these innovations American football survived. Historians of the sport credit the intervention of President Roosevelt with "saving the game," and the importance of his demarche should not be underestimated; yet on reflection I am not sure that, if the game was really "saved" at that point, it is not rather Harvard's Bill Reid who should be recognized as the true savior.

Today's aficionado may well be grateful to the committee of 1905 for bringing in the forward pass and adding a new and exciting element to the game. But how effective the new regulations were in cutting down on deaths and injuries is, on the record, hard to determine. As it happened, neither Yale nor Harvard had played a game up to that time in which anyone was killed. But in the new era each one has been involved in a fatality on the field (Harvard in 1909, Yale in 1932). I am not even sure that the "open game" is less lethal than the old mass formations. Anyone today who has seen a clash between a receiver and a safety knows how disastrous for one or the other party such contacts can be. Perhaps the public of 1906 was content with the reforms as much because they provided a more exciting pattern of combat as because they seemed to be less brutal.

But to resume our narrative. As the 1906 season came on, Bill Reid confesses he felt considerable resentment against a new change—not in the style of warfare but in the eligibility rules. For, as the 1906 encounter would be the first with a legalized forward pass, so too it would be the first in which all combatants would be required to be undergraduates. (Yale, Harvard, and Princeton also agreed not to play freshmen, which must have been a blow to Ham Fish and Ted Coy, waiting in the wings, as it were, at St. Marks and Hotchkiss, respectively.) This ruling was made, Reid writes, without his knowledge, although Professor White, the chairman of the Harvard Athletic Committee, had consulted with Camp. Reid did not object in principle but thought in fairness to all a year's notice should have been given. "As a result of the graduate rule," he writes, "I lost, as I recall it, seven H men with one or two of them All-American grade. . . . I had at least six men all lined up for 1906 who were twenty-five or thirty years old, hard fighters, and who loved the game. . . . Meanwhile Yale lost only one man, Carl Flanders, center, and he was not outstanding. Thus did Walter Camp outmaneuver Mr. White."[26] Reid's feelings are understandable, but in fairness to Walter Camp, admittedly not without his own share of wiliness, it must be recalled that he had been pressing for such a ruling for many years, often when he too had useful veterans waiting in the wings.

As it turned out, Reid had no need to apologize for his 1906 delegation. With Captain Hatheby

Yale takes to the air. Veeder to Forbes, 1906.

Foster and Jack Wendell as running backs, Mort Newhall as signal caller, and forwards like Parker, Burr, and Von Hersberg it lacked neither strength nor talent. It came onto Yale Field November 24 undefeated and with wins over Army and Dartmouth on its record. In fact, Harvard entered the combat a slight favorite (I am not sure on what basis) and fought a valiant battle against a strong Yale outfit captained by Morse and featuring the talented Tad Jones at quarterback. Only a scoreless tie with Princeton marred a record of perfection. The game has its niche in history as being the first Yale–Harvard game won by a forward pass, from Paul Veeder to Clarence Alcott, a substitute end. The ball was thrown thirty yards through the air to the Crimson 4-yard line, from which Howard Roome, substitute right half, carried it over in two smashes at the grim Cantab wall, giving the Blue (inspired by the new song "Fight, Fight for Yale," apparently more potent than "Yo ho, the Good Ship Harvard," launched the same year) a 6–0 victory. Bealle comments:

"The thousands of Harvard supporters . . . called it a great battle, even though their side lost."[27] And so it was. Oddly, Bealle does not mention a detail which the Crimson might be proud of. Veeder's pass was not the first in the game; he had tossed another to Alcott, which was dropped, but before that, in the first quarter, Harvard had completed a pass, Newhall to Starr, good for twenty yards. So the Crimson has the distinction of being the first to employ the new weapon in The Game. (Incidentally, in spite of their early start neither Harvard nor Yale would field "passing teams" for many years to come.)

The public was pleased with the "new" game. The *Nation* (November 29, p. 455) commented that "football was much improved by the new rules that emphasize brain over brawn", but could not refrain from expressing agreement with Eliot that "intercollegiate sport is an unnecessary distraction of students from their studies." The *New York Times* (November 25, pp. 1–2), reporting an attendance of 32,000, in its cover story is impressed by the number of "autos in evidence: the grounds were simply black with machines parked together in such a hopeless mass as to make it seem impossible for one ever to find his own once more," and continues with the first recorded evidence of the now ritualistic tailgate preliminaries, commenting on the "small parties of automobilists eating tempting viands that had been brought in hampers spread out in picnic fashion on a table cloth laid upon the ground."

Reid, who had left his mark on the game and had served Harvard well in his two-year stint as coach, left at the end of the 1906 season. The squad of 1907 came too late to profit by his direction and a year too soon to take lessons from Percy Haughton. Joshua Crane, who served in this interim year, was not very successful; some critics accused him of being too easygoing. Assuredly the material was good. Parker, now captain, and Burr

Francis Burr, captain of the 1908 Harvard team.

were seasoned linemen and Ham Fish had arrived to help them. Newhall and Wendell were veteran ballcarriers. Yet for some reason the Crimson fell a little below the level of performance of the Reid years. In the weeks immediately preceding the encounter with Yale the team succumbed successively to the Carlisle Indians and to Dartmouth— and had barely squeaked through to a 6–5 win over Brown before those losses. Yale, as usual, captained by Lucius Biglow with Tad Jones at quarterback and the rugged sophomore Ted Coy at fullback, was formidable, undefeated (though tied by the Army in midseason), and of course favored. On the field the Harvards didn't do too badly. Yale won 12–0 on two touchdowns by Coy, one in each half; but it was a dogged battle all the way, and at the end of the game Harvard had brought the ball to the Yale six-inch line, the closest thing to a Crimson touchdown since 1901. It was agreed by all observers that the performance of Jack Wendell had brought honor to the Crimson, and many felt that Newhall showed himself a better quarterback in all respects than Yale's famous Tad. If the Cantabs of '07 were foredoomed, they went down gamely; Harvard men were, on the whole, not depressed by the outcome. Perhaps they could sense better things were ahead.

The eleven years we have chronicled in this chapter are rich in spirited engagement and memorable figures in the parade of Crimson and Blue immortals. The totals show two ties, two wins for Harvard, and seven for Yale; the period ends with five successive Bulldog victories, the longest sequence since the mid-eighties. A little mischie-vously James L. Knox reports: "At a banquet of Princeton Alumni held in Boston November 1907, 'Pa' Corbin '89, the famous old Eli player and coach said, 'I hope that Harvard will get a system and method that will make her really formidable in football, but until she does we must count Princeton as our dearest foe.' " To which Knox adds: " 'Pa' got his wish."[28]

WITH CRIMSON IN TRIUMPH FLASHING

Harvard poster, 1914.

The year 1908 marked the most important event in the history of Harvard football." With this estimate of the contribution of Percy Haughton, '99, Bealle opens his tenth chapter;[1] it is hardly an overstatement. In his nine years of guiding the Crimson's destinies, Haughton teams, out of eighty-three games played, had a record of seventy-one wins, five ties, and only seven defeats, and scored a total of 1,427 points against opponents' 206. Against Yale, which is what matters most to any right-thinking Harvard man, the record was 5−2−2, with the Crimson scoring 119 points to the Blue's 19. But to measure the contribution of "P.D." to the Harvard cause one has properly to think beyond the results of those nine years. The Haughton momentum carried over to his disciple, Bob Fisher, whose seven-year record against Yale was 4−2−1. From 1910, when Haughton really got his system in gear, until 1923 Yale won only one game; from his first year at the helm in 1908 until "Ducky" Pond of the Blue '23 squad lumbered through the mud of the Stadium across the soggy goal line, incredibly only one Yale touchdown was scored against Harvard. Further, I think it is quite possible to claim that the influence of Haughton still lives; he changed the character of the competition for years to come. To quote a final and eloquent item of statistical nature: before Haughton, Yale had won twenty-one of the twenty-eight games played; since the inaugural Haughton year the Blue has won thirty-three of the seventy-two combats. Before Haughton a Yale victory was normal; the Blue had that precious asset, "the habit of victory." The Haughton years gave Harvard that habit; today, happily for the health of the rivalry, neither side can count on tradition to bring home the bacon. In short, in terms of The Game, Haughton was Harvard's Walter Camp.

The two paladins have much in common. Like Camp, Haughton was a versatile athlete; he captained the Harvard baseball nine in his senior year; he also excelled at racquets. A classmate of Ben Dibblee, he came to Harvard from Groton, where he had distinguished himself in both major sports. It may be noted that in Dibblee's demolition of Yale in 1898 P.D. played directly across the line from the Bulldog's Gordon Brown, another muscular Grotonian. Perhaps between buffets they exchanged reminiscences. Haughton's record with the Cantabs as well as two successful years of coaching at Cornell made him a natural choice to succeed Crane. Up to that point the Harvard habit had been to give a coach a two-year term, but it would have been folly to release the designer of the puissant Crimson machines of '08 and '09; P.D. would stay on, with ever-increasing prestige, until 1917, when he entered the service of his country.

Haughton could not claim to be, as Camp was, an architect of the sport; he came too late for that. But as a coach he was not inferior to the great Walter. He designed or perfected such tactical devices as the mousetrap play (which he had learned from his imaginative coach at Groton), the unbalanced backfield formation, regrouping the traditional T formation by a flexible tandem, giving

Percy Haughton, Harvard coach from 1908 to 1916.

scope for the deft and mystifying ball handling for which his teams were famous, and the "roving center," who gave defensive signals, an invaluable asset on defense. But in fact Haughton's genius lay less in the area of invention than in his systematic and perfectionist attention to fundamentals. His charges were drilled long and hard, and their minds as well as their muscles were trained by their demanding mentor. He expected his players to know the rules and avoid penalties. He insisted on perfect conditioning (here he had the help of "Pooch" Donovan, a skilled and beloved trainer who joined the staff the same year that Haughton did). P.D.'s assistants were given precise, individual assignments; Haughton in effect brought to Harvard football the "system and method" which Pa Corbin had so thoughtfully prescribed.[2] Furthermore Haughton was a practical psychologist; having brought his charges to fighting pitch it was his custom to relieve their tension by sundry acts of clowning and horseplay on the eve of their important matches. His teams regularly came on the field in superb physical condition, confident, alert—and relaxed. To be sure, P.D. had his foibles: his secret practices were carefully guarded; even President Lowell respected their privacy, and to the end of his career Haughton refused to allow his players to be numbered—as suggested though not required in his day.[3]

Appropriately, his very first team was unbeaten and a winner over the Bulldog. (Parenthetically, the legend that Haughton tore a living bulldog apart in the presence of his squad has been au-

thoritatively refuted;[4] it contains, however, a poetic truth.) It was a sturdy canine that year, too, coming to the final tryst unvanquished, though tied by Brown, a club, incidentally, that Haughton's pupils had found hard to handle, winning by a scant 6–2. For once, comparative scores hit it on the nail; Harvard beat Yale by four points. The battle that afternoon was bruising, with Yale threatening more often than Harvard. But one play was decisive. Early in the first half Harvard moved the ball to the Yale 15-yard line, where the Bulldog stopped the advance. On fourth down, very daringly, Haughton substituted Vic Kennard for Ver Wiebe at fullback. (By the rules of those days a player once removed could not return to the game, and Ver Wiebe was, overall, a better fullback than Kennard.) But Kennard could kick and Haughton's instinct told him the moment had come. Kennard's successful dropkick has a special place in the annals of the game. It was not a particularly long kick, but the circumstances give it a historical resonance. The Yale line was grimly determined to block the effort (and blocked kicks were not infrequent in the early part of our century); however, by previous arrangement with Nourse, the Harvard center, the ball was snapped back at once, before the Elis could get set for the Redshirt charge. Bealle adds the further detail that Kennard was a left-footed kicker; the innocent Bulldogs exerted their blocking efforts on the wrong flank.[5] (This may well be true, but if so Yale scouting has much to answer for: this was not Kennard's first kick.) For the rest of the game honors were even; 4–0 was the final score, and

Kennard's famous kick, 1908.

after seven starved years the Cantabs had a victory. The observations of the *Yale Alumni Weekly*
(November 25) may be of interest to historians of
culture: before the game "over in the improvised
paddocks across the road stood upwards of a thousand polished yellow and red and white and green
automobiles, 'busses and spanking toolers," adding the picturesque detail "Harvard's team was

first on the field, coming out in a big open barge
that clattered clumsily among the trim touring
cars of the out of town automobilists."

Still a part of the tranquil first decade of the
century, 1909 was nevertheless a year of portents.
Louis Blériot flew across the English Channel in
a heavier-than-air machine, and Henry Ford announced his intention of manufacturing only

Model T Fords, destined soon to serve the multitude. If you found such events disconcerting for their implications you could turn to *A Girl of the Limberlost*, just out this year. In other areas, Yale's William Howard Taft, ample and amiable, moved into the White House in March, the first—and so far the only—son of old Eli to attain to that high office. (Harvard already had two and would have two more ere we come to the end of our story). In Cambridge, the patrician Lowell succeeded Eliot; both were men of vigor and imagination, both Unitarians of the old stock, but Lowell would prove to be less uneasy about the iniquities of football than his predecessor; to be sure, the new game left less scope for unseemly conduct. (It is hard to think of Eliot allowing a Harvard team to go to the Rose Bowl, as ten years later, Lowell would.) In New Haven, having no president to inaugurate, the clan of Eli could rejoice in the founding of the Whiffenpoofs.

Haughton's '09 delegation, entering the lists against the Blue in the Stadium, had an even better record than his inaugural team; it was undefeated, untied, and had allowed a mere nine points to be scored against it. It was, in fact, one of the strongest teams ever fielded by the Crimson, at least up to that time, with many lustrous names in the lineup: Hamilton Fish, one of the great paladins in Harvard football, captained the team from his tackle position; Bob Fisher, destined to succeed Haughton as coach, stood beside him at right guard; Paul Withington flanked him at center; in the backfield were such stalwarts as Hamilton Corbett and Dong Minot, with the skill-ful Dan O'Flaherty at quarter. The line was a sturdy one, averaging 189 pounds. It was not a high-scoring team but the defense was all but impregnable, allowing the opponents only one touchdown in the entire season. It was, in fact, a team of similar nature and almost similar record to the Blue squad which it confronted. Ted Coy's Elis (with Howard Jones as field coach) also included memorable names on its register: the elusive Steve Philbin was Coy's running mate in the backfield, as was Fred Daly; the line included Kilpatrick trick at left end, Hobbs at left tackle, and the massive Cooney (232 lbs.) at center. Andrus and Goebel were as good a pair of guards as ever wore the Blue. Between them the opposing companies fielded the most glittering array of stars the game has ever known; Bealle's census is impressive.[6] Like Harvard, the Bulldog was notable mainly for his defensive strength; he came to Cambridge unscored on. For the first time in the century Blue and Crimson met with both contestants unbeaten and untied; this would not happen again for fifty-nine years. The game attracted almost nationwide attention, the Stadium was filled, and James Sherman, vice-president of the United States, was in the stands.

Both squads were keyed up for the meeting. Ted Coy on the eve of the battle affirmed that the game would be "the greatest that two elevens from the universities have ever played"; Harvard's Ham Fish, who was reported as "ailing," gave an interview in which he vowed that he would "start the game against Yale and play it through, unless he was killed." On which a Yale player com-

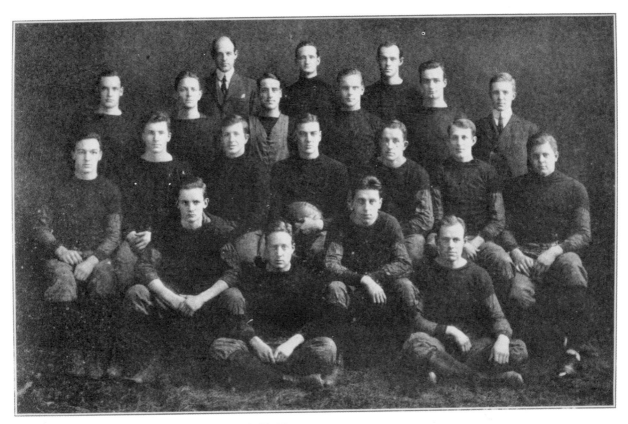

The 1909 Harvard team, one of the strongest ever fielded by
the Crimson, was captained by Hamilton Fish (holding ball).

mented: "He won't be killed unless he commits
suicide when he hears the final score."[7] Yale was
a slight favorite, although there was plenty of Harvard money abroad. Harvard had two new football
songs, the stirring "Harvardiana" and "Score";
the latter was a *riposte* to the Blue "undertaker
song," and its climactic "poor old Yale" was every

bit as lugubrious as "no hope for Harvard." But
as a dirge, it was, in 1909, a little premature.

The weather, sunny but cold and windy,
seemed to be in harmony with the Homeric nature
of the combat. Thirty-eight thousand spectators
turned up at the Stadium, "special wires" carried
a play-by-play account not only to the Harvard

Ted Coy led Yale's 1909 team to an undefeated, untied, and unscored on season.

Club in New York but also to the Heidelberger Restaurant in Berlin, where the sons of John and Eli gathered for a special fête. As might have been expected, the battle was hard and grim. It was a war of attrition, a dour confrontation of unyielding lines. Tim Cohane quotes the remark of a sideline observer and sometime Army coach: "At one point of the play the two lines were right opposite me and I could look right down between them. It was the most magnificent sight I ever saw. Every lineman's face was dripping with blood."[8] The *New York Times* correspondent, less enchanted by the sight of gore, found the Crimson incompetence on offense "made the match inordinately slow and stupid."[9] Ideally the game should have ended in a tie (as the next meeting between a flawless Blue and Crimson would do in 1968), but in fact, although the performances were of equal virtue and tenacity, with Harvard gaining a little more yardage than Yale, the Elis won by a score of 8–0. Neither goal line was crossed, but Coy kicked two field goals (this year the field goal had been devalued from four points to three) out of five attempts, one late in the first half and one toward the end of the game, and a kick blocked by Cooney led to a Harvard safety. Harvard might have made a better showing had it not been for the number of penalties incurred at crucial moments (infractions lost the Crimson ninety-two yards against Yale's five; the *Times* noted the officiating was "sloppy" and led to "bickering"); as it was, the Cantabs never got beyond the Yale 28-yard line; the Bulldogs for that matter could come no closer than the Crimson sixteen. Baker

Ted Coy kicking the first of the two field goals he scored in the 1909 game. Yale won 8–0.

faults the play of O'Flaherty, Harvard's quarterback, who, he avers, was "nervous" after fumbling a punt in the first quarter.[10] The decisive factor in the game was Coy's kicking, his long and lofty punts being frequently fumbled or mishandled by the Harvard receiver. It was a battle of giants and it marked, for Yale, a kind of watershed in her gridiron history. Never since has a Blue team gone through a season unscored on (to be sure, very few teams anywhere have in the last seventy years) nor has the Bulldog since stood on quite the same lofty pinnacle of pigskin prestige. The worst of the Haughton years were ahead and by the time they were over Crimson and Blue alike would be overshadowed by the exploits of teams beyond the cozy circle of the Northeast. For a few brief years, however, Harvard would uphold the honor of the ancient cradle of the game.

Before the next meeting of the old friends took place the authorities took another step toward the abolition of collective brawling that the invention of the neutral zone had failed to effect. "This time," writes Parke H. Davis, "the rule makers decided to remove the mass play wholly from the game. This was accomplished by prescribing that when the ball was put in play seven men should be on the line of scrimmage and, most revolutionary of all, that no player of the side in possession of the ball should use his hands or arms to assist the player carrying the ball, but that the latter should run unassisted and alone and that the players of the attacking side should not interlock arms or bodies."[11] Concurrently the old flying tackle was banned. So vanished the donnybrooks of yore, although a power play through the line can still attract quite a crowd and provide a reasonable amount of pushing and shoving.

In the revisional operations of the committee Haughton played a leading role. Lothrop Withington writes:

Haughton's greatest contribution to the modern game of football . . . came with his struggle with Walter Camp for control of the Rules Committee. In the winter of 1909—10, after cadet Byrne was killed in the Army game and Wilson, a Navy player, also died as the result of an injury received in a game, there was great clamor for reform or radical change in the mass play then prevailing.

The forward pass was little used. It had to be thrown five yards right or left and five yards back of the place the ball was put in play and, if incomplete, called for a fifteen yard penalty. With only three downs to make ten yards it is small wonder that it was little used. Camp, who incidentally had sponsored the forward pass when it was first permitted in 1906, urged its elimination and the introduction of steps to encourage end runs. Haughton, after experimenting in spring practice, became convinced that defensive steps would make end runs nothing but beautiful lateral sprints and championed the retention of the forward pass and the liberalization of the rules relating to its use.

A bitter fight ensued in which Haughton, E. K. Hall and Bill Roper finally prevailed over Camp and his supporters. . . . From this revolt came noteworthy developments—the elimination of restrictions in the pass, the addition of a down [in 1912] and the rigid protection of the receiver, who had hitherto been a fair target for any defensive man, both before the pass and while [the ball was] in flight.[12]

It seems likely that this defeat moved Camp to abdicate from his post of graduate advisor at Yale. His biographer states: "Camp's resignation from all official connection with Yale athletics came in 1910. He retired after long and anxious thought with the conviction that this action would be best for Yale. In this conclusion . . . he was seriously mistaken; . . . the old system disappeared with him, and the amazing series of Yale victories disappeared too."[13]

Another less controversial innovation of the rules committee was the shortening of playing time: four fifteen-minute quarters replaced the two thirty-five-minute halves which had been in vogue since 1893. (Through the eighties the halves had been of forty-five-minute duration. Clearly, American youth was growing more effete with each succeeding decade. What the rule makers of 1910 would have thought of the present style, with alternation of platoons and frequent intervention of specialists, it is perhaps best not to ask. Few warriors today are called upon to endure more than half an hour of actual combat.)

The performance of Coy's invincibles must have persuaded followers of the Blue that the Harvard victory in 1908 was merely a passing episode and that there was no particular reason to feel more uneasy about the new coaching staff in Cambridge than about any of their predecessors. And in fact for two years the Haughton tornado was held in abeyance; in 1910 and '11 the teams played scoreless ties. The two encounters were similar in nature, featuring defensive play, the kicking game, and recurrent frustrations. In the fall of 1910, the year of Victor Herbert's "Naughty Marietta" and Franz Lehár's "Gipsy Love," crowning a decade of innocence, Haughton's liberalizing plan became effective; from now on a pass could be thrown and a quarterback could run from any point behind the scrimmage line. But that year neither quarterback runs nor passes were features in the game at the Stadium. Harvard went in the favorite; she was undefeated and untied. Yale had had her troubles, losing to Army and—incredibly—to Brown (for the first time in history) and tied by Vanderbilt. At the end of the season, Walter Camp, previously ignored, had been called on to come to the rescue; he in turn had brought in Tom Shevlin with his newfangled Minnesota shift. The shift—and the good will of the pigskin gods—had enabled the Blue to beat a good Princeton team. The favor of the pigskin gods was with the Bulldog again in Cambridge. Harvard's clearly superior outfit, featuring a pair of outstanding guards in Captain Lothrop Withington and Bob Fisher, piled up massive yardage but somehow never got the ball over the goal line; a fumble spoiled her best chance. In fact, Captain Fred Daly's kick could have won it for Yale in the waning moments of the game had it not gone awry. In the following year on an icy field the pattern was the same. Neither side was quite as strong as it had been in 1910. Bob Fisher's platoon had lost not only to Princeton but to the Carlisle Indians. Art Howe's Elis had already suffered a licking at the hands of Army as well as, like Harvard, a mauling by the Tiger. It was an even money game, and the stalemate was a fair verdict on the performance of

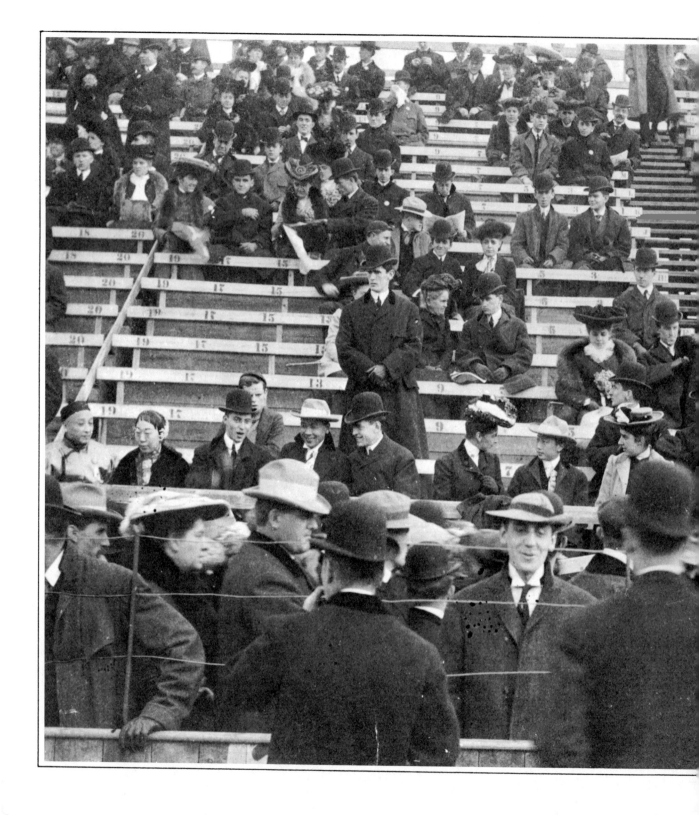

Football spectators, ca. 1910.

Art Howe, captain of the 1911 Yale team and coach of the 1912 team.

the two squads, enlivened (if that is the word) chiefly by a kicking duel between Harvard's Sam Felton and Yale's Walter Camp, Jr. It should be noted that for the first time since 1896 Princeton appeared on the Harvard schedule. Perhaps the Cantabs should have waited a year; the Tigers lost no time in making themselves Big Three champions again.

To the historian, political, social, or agonistical, 1912 is not a year to be passed over lightly. In the spring of that year the unsinkable *Titanic* sank, carrying with it John Jacob Astor and some illusions about the invulnerability of man-made creations. In the fall, while Crimson and Blue were running through their preliminary exercises, the Balkan allies were fighting a bitter war with the Turks; out of the strife would grow crises and confrontations that would in a short time bring about the downfall of the old European structure. At home it was a hard time generally speaking for Harvard and Yale men (most of whom were Republicans): the schism between Harvard's Teddy and Yale's Bill resulted in the election of Woodrow Wilson, not only a Democrat but a Princeton man to boot. (It was the first time the electorate was obliged to vote for one of the Big Three.) Needless to say, Wilson lost no time in bringing in the income tax. It was also the year of "Alexander's Ragtime Band," with its innovative syncopations prophetic of the jazz era in the offing. Nineteen-twelve left its mark also on the hometowns of the Bulldog and his sparring partner: in New Haven a fourteen-story "skyscraper" hotel, called appropriately The Taft, replaced the old New Haven House, and in Cambridge the subway came to unite Harvard Square with South Station. The Game of that year is a landmark, too, as being the last Harvard–Yale match played on old Yale Field, and the first in which Haughton really routed the Bulldog—in spite of Cole Porter's blithe "Bingo" and "Bulldog," and Douglas Moore's "Good-night, Poor Harvard," composed in this era.

For the 1912 season the rule makers had thought up a few more improvements. The field of play was shortened from 110 yards to 100, with "end zones" ten yards deep behind each goal line; forward passes could now be legally caught in these zones. Passes covering more than twenty yards were ruled illegal. The offensive team was now given four downs instead of three to make the necessary ten yards. (The older limitation goes far to explain the prevalence and the importance of the kicking game; of necessity a team had to kick more often with only three downs to cover the required yardage.) The additional down, too, made life a little easier for the offense; fewer games were to be decided by field goals than had been the case in the past; and, finally, the value of a touchdown was raised to six points—another detail that downgraded the field goal. The new freedom of motion permitted the quarterback in 1910 was beginning to bear fruit; gradually the direct pass to the runner came in to replace the old quarterback handoff—the single wing attack came into fashion.

At the end of the 1911 season the Haughton record against Yale was not especially impressive; one victory, one loss, and two ties. Had they had the benefit of hindsight, Yale men might well have felt pleased with the Bulldog's performance under the assaults of the artful canine-mangler. In fact, they were not. They were used to winning, and two successive scoreless ties brought them no satisfaction. Clearly Yale players could never be inferior to Harvard players; the fault must lie with the coaching. Yale was still faithful to the old tradition under which the captain appointed the field coach (usually the captain of the preceding year) and the field coach in turn invited the old Blues to help out on an informal basis; and of course (usually but not always) consulted Camp. Camp's influence; however, was fading; there was a growing consensus that the time had come to follow Harvard's example and hire a professional coach on a long-term basis. To be sure, Harvard men did not like scoreless ties either, but they did not lose their confidence in Haughton. If not this year, then probably next year and assuredly some day he would teach the Bulldog humility. And in 1912 his course of instruction began. Harvard won by a convincing 20–0, and the Crimson parade had started. Things would get much worse for the Blue before they got better.

The Eli contingent of that fateful year was, on the record, by no means a bad team. Captained by Jesse Spalding, coached by Art Howe, captain of the '11 delegation, it came to its doom undefeated, tied to be sure by Princeton, but owning a good defense (which had yielded no touchdowns) and a first-class dropkicker, Harold Pumpelly. Perhaps it could have beaten most Harvard teams, even some Haughton teams. But in 1912 Haughton's horses were blue ribbon. They had trampled down all opposition. Captain Percy Wendell, Tack Hardwick, and the talented sophomore Charley Brickley, who had already kicked eleven field goals in the course of the season, were in the backfield; the line included immortals such as Pennock and Trumbull and at left end was Sam Felton, renowned for the length, altitude, and vicious English of his left-footed kicking. The first Harvard touchdown followed the Yale receiver's fumble of

Percy Wendell, fullback and captain of Harvard's undefeated 1912 team.

one such kick (Hardwick's bruising tackle helped). This occurred early in the first quarter; shortly after, Brickley scored a thirty-three-yard dropkick. The second period was scoreless; the third repeated the pattern of the first: Brickley carried a Yale fumbled ball over the Blue goal line and kicked his second field goal from seventeen yards out. But for the Blue fumbles (seven of Felton's spiraling bombs were dropped) clearly the score would have been much lower; the Bulldog himself, however, though he actually outgained his tormentor by forty-two yards and made nine first downs to the Crimson's four, scarcely showed his teeth. The *New York Times* commented: "Harvard's play embraced every known maneuver in modern football. The punting was immense, the handling of kicks was without a flaw, the line-plunging was irresistible, and the end running was brilliant. The tackling was of the fiercest nature and the forwards broke through so rapidly that many of Yale's assaults were smothered for no gain."[14] The Haughton hurricane was gathering force.

Repercussions of the defeat among the High Command in New Haven were swift and decisive. A meeting of old Blues was called by Harry Ketcham, captain-elect for the '13 season; out of it came the formation of a graduate committee of which Camp was simply a member. The committee for the first time in the annals of the Bulldog engaged a salaried coach. He was Howard Jones, '08S, who had been field coach of Coy's team and had subsequently coached an undefeated team at Ohio State and had also, like all loyal Yalies,

come back to give informal and unpaid assistance to the squads of '11 and '12. His salary was $2,500, $500 less than the "expense money" he had received in '09.

It cannot be said that Jones "turned the fortunes of the Blue around" but it appears more than likely, in view of his subsequent very successful career, that he simply didn't have the material. It is taking nothing from Haughton's undisputed merits if the chronicler is obliged to point out that the Bulldogs of '13, '14, and '15 simply were not of the same caliber as the Blue delegations of the early century; one has merely to note their performance against opponents other than the Crimson. Ketcham's battalion assuredly demonstrates the truth of this statement; it came to the Stadium with a record of three ties (Princeton, *passons*— but Maine and the College of Washington and Jefferson!) and had taken a licking from Colgate. Harvard, on the other hand, fielded another unbeaten team, though the win over Princeton was a squeaker; Brickley was back, flanked by a new scourge of the Blue, the scintillant Eddie Mahan; Hardwick was back, this time at end, as were Pennock and Storer, among others. Yale men should have been grateful the result wasn't worse. For in fact the Bulldog defense did itself proud; the Yale goal line was not crossed. Containing Brickley was another matter; he booted five field goals; four dropkicks and one placement, from the 35-, 38-, 32-, 24-, and 40-yard lines. It was quite enough; an absentminded Harvard back gave Yale a safety in the first quarter, and Otis Guernsey, after missing two rather long attempts, finally booted one

HARVARD-YALE GAME TICKETS COUNTERFEITS

1913

The management of the Harvard-Yale football game wishes again to warn the public against the purchase of tickets from speculators or other unauthorized persons. Counterfeit tickets are said to be on sale.

SPECULATORS' TICKETS

A fairly complete record of tickets offered by speculators has been secured by our detectives and unless validated as provided below, these tickets will be dishonored and the seats for which they were issued resold. Such tickets as are now on the list as void, if presented to the management which they were purchased, will be indorsed officially as good. For this as herein provided, with a full explanation of the circumstances under purpose a representative of the Harvard Athletic Association will be in attendance at the Alumni office, 50 State St., Boston, between the hours of nine and twelve today, November 22nd. Tickets may also be validated at the office of the Harvard Athletic Association, Cambridge.

Two years ago a large number of speculators' tickets were dishonored at the game and only the face value of $2.00 each returned to the holders. The same course will be followed this year, absolutely, except for those cases in which tickets have been officially validated.

FRED W. MOORE, Graduate Treasurer.

Notice warning the public about counterfeit tickets that were being sold for the 1913 game.

Charley Brickley kicked five field goals in the 1913 game, leading Harvard to a 15−5 victory.

over from the 38-yard line in the last quarter; a total, far from adequate, of 5 points.

This was the year of the new Yale song "Goodnight Poor Harvard," tried out on the occasion of the Brown game—a stirring tune, too, but not much help to Ketcham's cause. Bealle notes an interesting statistic: only three penalties were called in the course of the combat; one against Harvard and two against Yale.[15] Perhaps the game has its place in literary history, too: replacing Knowles

Charley Brickley kicking the first of his two field goals in the
1912 game, won by Harvard 20−0.

at right half, a substitute named Archibald Mac-
Leish saw quite a bit of action. Jones left at the
end of the season to begin a distinguished career
far from New Haven, having learned from Haughton, as Cohane remarks, that the first law of coaching is to get the horses. His place was taken by
Frank Hinkey, the "disembodied spirit" of the
mid-nineties. Hinkey had frequently taken part
in the auxiliary coaching of Yale squads; he was
given a three-year contract. No better player ever
wore the Blue, no Yale coach ever endured such

frustration and humiliation; Haughton had by no
means said his last word.

Nineteen fourteen was a somber page in the
history of the Western world. It was for many, as
I once heard from an Italian scholar, "the year
God abdicated." On September 18 of that year, as
Yale and Harvard opened their football season,
the battle of Artois was launched by the Allies in
a vain attempt to drive the German invaders further back, and in the east von Hindenburg assumed command of the Imperial armies, pursuing

the battered Russians ever deeper into Poland. It is difficult to realize today how remote such events could seem to the America of the early years of the century. But in simple truth the suicide of Europe was followed from this side of the Atlantic with varying degrees of horror and amazement but with very little sense of involvement. For most of us in 1914 the great war was a spectacle; our leaders were in agreement that it was all no business of ours. As for the war between the Crimson and the Blue, well, the duello of 1914 attracted more spectators than ever before in history; the new Yale Bowl, dedicated on the day of the Harvard game, could and did accommodate some 78,000. Its seating capacity, a social historian notes, "would have more than sufficed for every member of the University and all living alumni."[16] It is a handsome and remarkable monument to the cult of the pigskin. It was built on a simple yet very original plan: the contractors simply dug a very large hole in the ground and used the excavated dirt to make an oval mound surrounding the hole. The construction had nothing of the imperial majesty of the Harvard Stadium (President Hadley was pleased by the designation "Bowl," eschewing pretentious classicism), but its design was eminently practical and it was probably the most comfortable amphitheater for the spectator ever built. The throngs enter through thirty spacious portals and, coming in at ground level, with half the rows of seats below and half above, are spared at least most of the climbing that was and is necessary in the ordinary stadium. Back rests are provided, too, an unusual comfort,

and carved to fit the contours of the seated spectator. The construction was financed by a cunning stratagem; contributors of $100 or more were guaranteed a number of choice seats (the number depending on the size of the contribution) for twenty years. The Bowl in fact soon paid for itself. Those privileged to watch the opening game were delighted and somewhat awed by the generous dimensions of the amphitheater, though we may suspect that some of them were a little distressed to find the builders had forgotten about rest rooms.[17] The day of the Bowl's christening was sunny and not at all cold for November; it was a great day for football. Greater, as it fell out, if you sat on the visitors' side, for the combat was a debacle for the Blue. Harvard ran up 36 points to 0 for the Bulldog; as the papers reported next day: "Yale had the Bowl but Harvard had the punch." This was the year of the Crimson war song: "Ten thousand men of Harvard want victory today." Couldn't have been more timely. It was also the year the rule makers thought up the penalties for intentional grounding of an aborted pass and decided the old "sleeper" tactic "unsportsmanlike." Neither ruling affected the outcome of the battle.

Retrospectively one may say that a Harvard victory was predictable but the score was a little surprising and perhaps not quite fair to the sons of Eli. Hinkey, in his first year, had shown himself resourceful and inventive. He had an All-American tackle in Captain Nelson Talbot[18] and a backfield of three competent veterans, Wilson, Knowles, and Ainsworth, reinforced by the talented sophomore Harry LeGore, and he made use

The Yale Bowl was dedicated on the day of The Game, November 21, 1914.

of the speed of his runners through the use of the lateral pass (he had brought the Hamilton Tigers down from Canada to illustrate the uses of this tactic); it had been particularly effective in Yale's victory over Notre Dame in midseason. He was the first coach to use "movies" as an educational adjunct, and the 1914 game was the first of the series to be filmed—an innovation authorized by the Yale authorities, who should have waited for Harvard's next visit. Hinkey's flaw—and it was a grave one—lay in his temperament. Essentially a loner, he found it difficult to communicate with his charges. Aside from his own assistants, he wanted no help from alumni, who, traditionally, had always come back to help out with the coaching. Even the great Walter was not seen on the sidelines during practice sessions in the Hinkey years. "The silent man," too, for all his inventiveness or perhaps because of it, tended to overlook fundamentals. No doubt he assumed that blocking and tackling "came naturally"—as it had to him in the glory days. In the Eli camp a sense of strain and uneasiness was felt, and of course the loss to Washington and Jefferson—a week after the Notre Dame encounter—was a shock. Yet Hinkey's forces regrouped and beat Brown (which Harvard could not do) and Princeton (for the first time since Daly's *bravi* of 1910).

Admittedly Harvard was strong too. Haughton brought a number of formidable veterans with him to the Bowl: Hardwick, Coolidge, Pennock, Francke, and, now in his second year, the elusive Eddie Mahan. Brickley captained the team but owing to injuries made only a token appearance on the field of the Bowl. The Crimson had lost no games but had suffered two ties, against Penn State and Brown (on the latter occasion the coaching staff and six varsity starters were in Princeton, scouting the Bulldog). All in all, one might have predicted a Harvard victory after a close game. To the great delight of Crimson followers the match turned out to be a "rabbit hunt"—and beginning almost with the opening whistle. A fifty-yard punt return by Mahan set up the first Crimson score; very shortly after, a long sixty-nine-yard march made it 12–0. In between the Harvard touchdowns there occurred an incident that seemed to indicate the gridiron gods had turned their backs on the Bulldog. Mahan, trying to handle a punt, kicked the ball over his own goal line and had to fall on it himself. The play should have been scored as a safety for Yale; instead the referee ruled it a touchback. But clearer evidence of Fate's animus followed the second Harvard score. Somehow Yale managed to get her machine into gear and carried the ball to the Harvard 4-yard line, making good use of the passing game. On the plunge for the touchdown, a Yale back fumbled, Jeff Coolidge of Harvard picked the ball up and went ninety-eight yards for a touchdown, Harvard's longest run in the Bowl. The score was 18–0 and the half was not yet over. Undeniably the Blue spirit was broken. Harvard got two more touchdowns and a field goal by Eddie Mahan. Final score 36–0: Harvard's highest total in history until then—but more was to come.

As for Yale's lateral passing, Haughton had scouted it well (all Haughton opponents were

Haughton's 1914 Harvard team, captained by Charley Brickley (holding ball), defeated Yale 36−0. The newspapers called the team "Harvard's greatest eleven."

thoroughly scouted) and destroyed its effectiveness by spreading his ends and tackles at some distance from the center trio, facilitating the disruption of the lateral game by hard charges on the wide-running ballcarriers.[19]

The papers next day unanimously called Haughton's '14 delegation "Harvard's greatest eleven."

This is debatable but no Yale man would have argued the point. In Flanders and in Poland operations slowed down as the winter closed in; in New Haven, the Bulldog licked his wounds and pondered, not too optimistically, his chances of revenge.

Tack Hardwick played a key role offensively and defensively in Harvard's three straight victories over Yale in 1912–14.

Harvard scoring in the 1914 game.

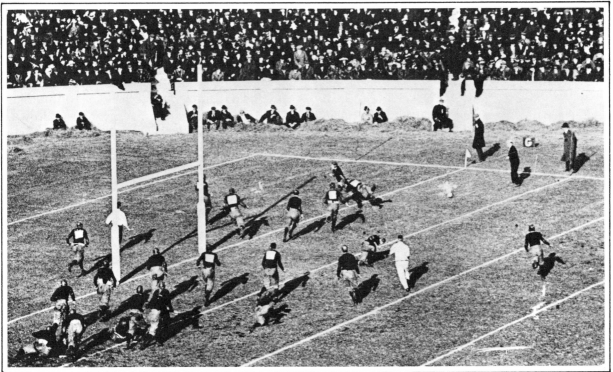

Captain Eddie Mahan led Harvard to a 41–0 drubbing of Yale in 1915. It was the Crimson's highest score ever against the Blue until 1982.

Nineteen fifteen marked the zenith of the Haughton star in the blue sky of the ancient rivalry. It is a year that will live forever in the memory of all Cantabrigian aficionados, and a year that the sons of Eli would be happy to forget. On the 20th of November of that fateful year under ideal weather conditions Captain Eddie Mahan and his mates rolled up the largest score ever made up to that point by the Crimson over the Blue, 41–0.

No Harvard team since has matched that intoxicating margin. It may have been the greatest mismatch in the history of The Game; yet most who witnessed the debacle were probably surprised by the final score because Yale had come to Cambridge with a guarded optimism based on a surprising victory over Princeton the week before the fatal encounter. But the snaring of the Tiger in truth served only to obscure the disparity between Crimson and Blue. Save for the happy hour with Old Nassau, Captain Wilson's Bulldogs had compiled the poorest record in all the annals of the Blue. The Bulldog's miseries began even before the opening game, when Harry LeGore, assuredly one of the most versatile of Yale backs ever to play in the Bowl, was declared ineligible for the season. (He and a few other athletes had injudiciously accepted compensation for playing on a semipro baseball team in the summer of 1915.) His loss was a great blow to Hinkey, already under fire as a result of the sad performance of his 1914 squad. In the games preceding the Big Three encounters the Bulldogs had managed to defeat only Maine, Springfield, and Lehigh (the latter by a scant 7–6); and had lost to Virginia, Washington and Jefferson, Colgate, and Brown. It was the first losing season in Yale history. In despair, shortly before the Brown game, Wilson summoned a meeting of Old Blues. It was decided to call on Tom Shevlin, who effectively displaced Hinkey as head coach for the climax games. Shevlin brought back his "Minnesota shift"—a variation of the momentum play—and, perhaps more significantly, he infected the squad with his own cheery and flamboyant optimism. Undoubtedly his inspiration was responsible for the surprising win over the favored Tigers. But Harvard was ready for the shift, as she had been for the lateral passes of 1914, and she quite simply rejoiced in a much more competent personnel.

Versatile Harry LeGore, a member of the Yale teams of 1914 and 1916, was a threat to run, pass, or kick.

The Harvard graph for 1915 had, in fact, been very different from that of the confused Bulldogs. Haughton had a number of experienced veterans (eight of the eleven starters against Yale were seniors), and all of them had not only unusual skills but also the habit of victory. Save for the Cornell game (nobody beat Cornell that year, not even Michigan), Harvard had gone through an undefeated season. They were ready for Yale. Strangely enough, for the first few minutes the Blue looked good, with Wilson running the ball on a fake kick thirty-three yards to the Crimson 25-yard line. At which point Harvard recovered a Yale fumble, quick-kicked to Guernsey, who dropped the ball, giving the Crimson's left end, Harte, a chance to score the first touchdown ever made against Yale in the Stadium. Three more—all by Mahan— followed before the end of the half. In the second half Mahan scored another, and, toward the end of the game, King cantered fifty-seven yards from scrimmage to seal the anguish of the Blue. After the first few minutes Yale was not in the game at all. The *Boston Globe* summed up the afternoon's operations with exultant accuracy: "Never before in a big game has the winning team played the better football in every department of the game or the loser been so helpless to stave off an overwhelming defeat. It was the worst beating the Blue ever has experienced at Harvard's hands and it was a beating that was administered with an exhibition of superior play that was simply overwhelming."[20] If the writer tends to make excessive use of *overwhelming* one can understand him. It is the right word.

Yale followers, whose hopes had been raised by the miracle victory over Princeton, were downcast. Shevlin was not shaken. Mac Baldridge, who played in the game, tells the following story:

Coming back on the train that night I was sitting next to Tom Shevlin with the rest of the team and you could cut the gloom with a knife. A bibulous Yale rooter came through the car, slapped Tom on the back, and said, "How could you coach a team that played so magnificently against Princeton last Saturday and was so lousy today against Harvard?"

Shevlin looked up at him, smiled and replied, "You just can't make two lemonades out of one lemon."[21]

The ebullient Tom would not have time left for many more witticisms; he died of pneumonia less than six weeks later. Within two years Captain Alex Wilson, whose qualities deserved better treatment by the pigskin gods, and two Harvard players—McKinlock and Doherty—would be killed in action.

For some weeks after the rout of the Bulldog the clan of Eli was in a state of shocked bewilderment; surely such a humiliation of the Blue was against the laws of nature.

Searching its soul, the *Yale Alumni Weekly* found the answer, affirming that "under conditions that prevailed in the older days the team would not have met such disaster at Cambridge last week. Under conditions that ought to prevail from now on, a repetition of that afternoon's football should never occur," and went on to suggest the remedy: "The Yale undergraduate spirit and football material are as good as they ever were; Yale graduate coaches are as ready as ever before to cooperate and help the undergraduate build anew; what is needed is to utilize that support under a coach and coaching system which will do for the present Yale student body what the old system did for its generations."[22] This sage counsel did not fall on deaf ears.

The spectacular resurgence of the Bulldog, humiliated in 1915 and triumphant in 1916, is amazing to contemplate. Alternation of victory and defeat is common enough in The Game, but a successful regrouping after the most disastrous defeat in the chronicles partakes of the miraculous. (Harvard would repeat the performance, leaping from a deeper pit to a higher summit in the years 1957–58, but in 1916 there was as yet no precedent.) For James L. Knox, writing in *The H Book of Harvard Athletics*, Yale's win simply illustrated the axiom that no good thing can go on forever.[23] Yale men might have quoted the proverb that the hour is darkest before the dawn. The practical minded might simply note that the Bulldog really had no direction to go but up after the mauling by Mahan and Co. in 1915. Whatever arcane forces may have been at work it was enough for the followers of the Blue that "Cupie" Black led his band to a hard-earned victory in the last game of Haughton's reign and in the last year of American immunity from European involvement.

The miracle, if such it was, is yet subject to naturalistic explanations. On the Crimson side, Haughton had, temporarily, run out of horses.

(RIGHT) The 1916 Yale team, captained by "Cupie" Black, was 8–1, including a 6–3 win over Harvard.

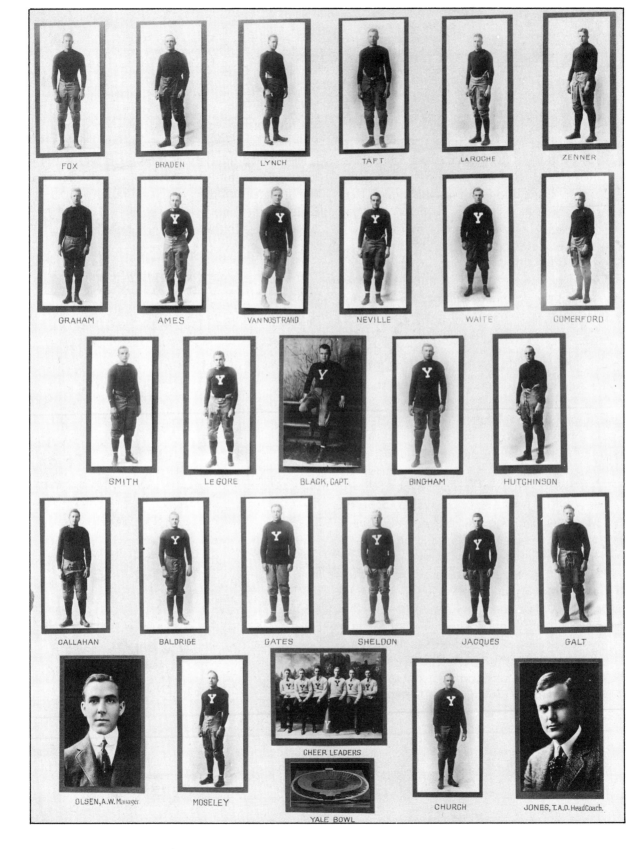

FOX   BRADEN   LYNCH   TAFT   LaROCHE   ZENNER

GRAHAM   AMES   VAN NOSTRAND   NEVILLE   WAITE   COMERFORD

SMITH   LE GORE   BLACK, CAPT.   BINGHAM   HUTCHINSON

CALLAHAN   BALDRIGE   GATES   SHELDON   JACQUES   GALT

OLSEN, A.W. Manager   MOSELEY   CHEER LEADERS   CHURCH   JONES, T.A.D. Head Coach.

YALE BOWL

The eight seniors of 1915 were gone, and their places were taken by raw troops. Captain Dadmun at guard was the only veteran of the '15 lineup to start in '16. The early season had indicated that the Crimson momentum was slowing down; Harvard lost not only to Brown (Yale did too, for that matter) but also, *horresco referens*, to Tufts and barely squeaked through her tussle with the Tiger. On the Yale side things were very different. LeGore was back and a crop of new and able players had replaced the doomed battalion of a year earlier: Callahan and Comerford in the line and LaRoche at quarterback, for example. Like his opposite number, Cupie Black was the only player on his side to repeat as starter. But for the Blue the new replacements were more talented than the men they succeeded. However, perhaps the change in personnel was less important than the appointment of a new coach, and a lion's share of the credit for Yale's rehabilitation must go to Tad Jones, quarterback of the 1907 and '08 teams, All-American in his time, and brought back to Yale after successful tours of duty at Syracuse University and Exeter. Tad was not an especially inventive coach but he was a good teacher of fundamentals, a stern yet kindly disciplinarian, winning the respect of his charges and simultaneously firing them with confidence and assurance.

Evidence of his competence is supplied by the record of the '16 Bulldogs. The defeats suffered the previous season at the hands of such parvenus as Virginia, Washington and Jefferson, and Colgate were avenged; Princeton was shut out and if Yale was stunned by Brown's wing-footed Pollard,

well, it was the common fate of all who encountered the Brunonians that year. As for Tad's inspirational gifts, Cohane quotes his words to the young Elis before the Harvard game (anticipating the approach of the more celebrated words of Knute Rockne a few years later): "If any of you boys believe in the hereafter," he said, "you will

Tad Jones, coach of the resurgent 1916 Bulldogs.

know that Tom Shevlin is pacing up and down across the river, smoking that big black cigar and asking you boys to go out there and do it once again for papa."[24] And so they did. (One may remark in passing that Haughton, peerless as he may have been, had a hard time with the Jones boys. Howard checked him in '09 and Tad brought him down in 1916; it was the only encounter between Tad and P.D.)

Played in New Haven on a fine autumn day— not too cold but with a sharp wind blowing—the Jones–Haughton duello aroused great interest and attracted a throng of massive proportions. The *New York Times* (November 26) estimated the attendance at 80,000; official records claim only 77,000; by either measurement it was a record breaker. "No spectacle of the kind, perhaps, has ever rivaled [the crowd] for enthusiasm and grandeur," the *Times* commented lyrically, noting that the number of fur coats in evidence was "so large as to suggest the jungles must have been scoured." The *New Haven Register* of the same date remarked with awe that the throng in the Bowl was equal to the population of Hartford or Kansas City or Nevada and estimated that some 7,000 cars had converged upon the city. Perhaps the large attendance was occasioned by a deep suspicion that one couldn't count on a game the following year. The first-page headlines of the *Times* of that Saturday blazoned, "U-Boat Alarms Sent to Incoming Ships," suggestive, to the percipient, of the prospect of speedy erosion of American neutrality. But war talk aside, Yale's captain, Cupie Black, so-called from his striking resemblance to the Kewpie dolls of contemporary vogue, had somehow won the affection of town and gown alike, and the showing of the Blue in the early games seemed to promise an exciting match.

The betting was on Harvard with odds of nine or ten to eight, not, as the chroniclers of the time noted, because of lack of confidence in Yale's personnel, considered overall superior to Harvard's, but because the Crimson had the better "system" (that is, Haughton would be hard to beat).

As indeed he was. The Elis not only had to work hard for their triumph but also be grateful to the alertness of an official at a crucial and perhaps decisive moment. It was a combat worthy of the large and distinguished public that it attracted. In the first quarter a fumbled punt gave Harvard's Robinson a chance to put his team ahead with a thirty-yard field goal. Shortly afterward, Eddie Casey, taking up the role of the great Mahan, dashed seventy-two yards to cross the Bulldog goal line. Happily for the Elis the run was called back on a penalty, and Harvard never came really close to scoring again. Encouraged by the providential reprieve, Yale started her own drive, of which the best ground-gaining play was a "forward fumble" from LeGore to Gates, and by grim determination succeeded in propelling Neville over the Crimson goal line for the only Yale touchdown ever made against a Haughton team—and the first touchdown against Harvard since 1907.[25] (It was a long wait—and it would be another seven years before the '16 touchdown would have a successor.) The kick was missed: 6–3, but quite enough. There was no scoring in the second half,

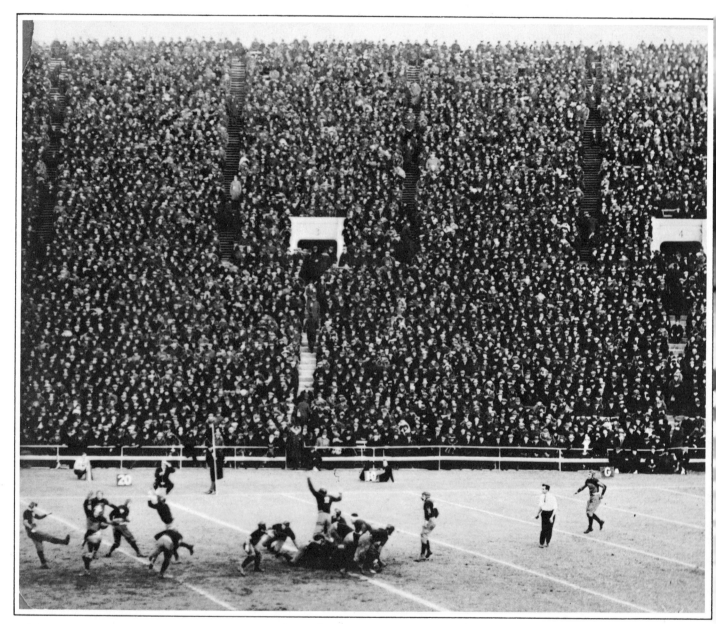

Harvard's W. F. Robinson kicks a field goal in first quarter of the 1916 game, giving the Crimson a short-lived 3–0 lead.

(OPPOSITE AND OVERLEAF) The sequence shows the Yale series of downs in the 1916 game that culminated in Neville's score. It was the only Blue touchdown ever made against a Haughton-coached team and the first Yale touchdown against Harvard since 1907.

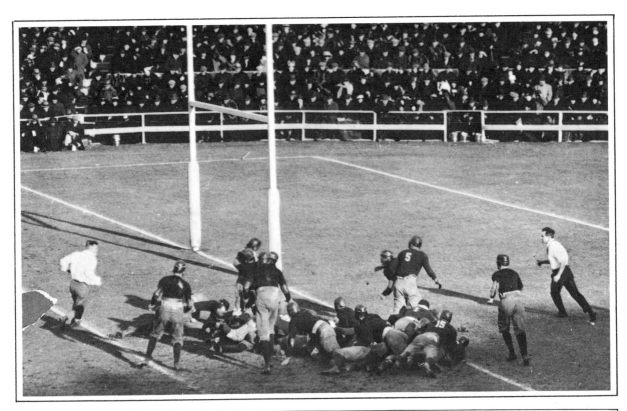

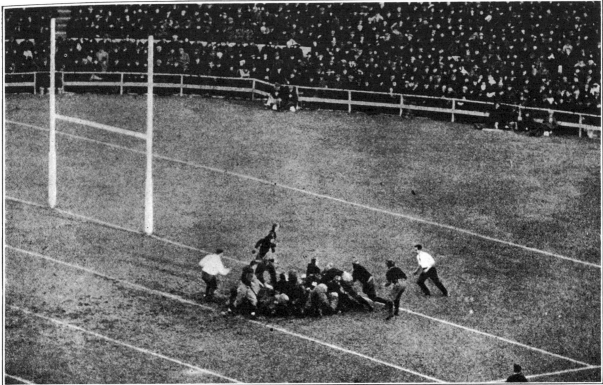

though Yale once moved the ball to the Crimson 7-yard line. In keeping with the Spartan ways of old, ten Bulldog starters played every minute of the game. At the end of the game, the *New York Times* reports, the victorious Elis were "mobbed" by their admirers, who "shot off Roman candles and fireworks, writhed in snake dances and 'caroused' far into the night."

In the spring of 1917 the sinking of the *Lusitania* had begun to move a large segment of American public opinion to the thought of intervention on the side of the Allies. During the course of the football season Woodrow Wilson had won a very close victory over Charles Evans Hughes, aided considerably by the slogan "He kept us out of war." How much longer he could keep us out began to be a matter of concern; it turned out to be less than half a year. On April 6 war was declared. Campuses were deserted as the youth of America flocked to the colors. Intercollegiate football was one of the war's early casualties; the young men had more important things to do than block kicks or run for touchdowns. Of the thirty-three warriors who participated in the 1916 game, thirty were in military uniform a year later. Haughton departed to enter the armed services; Tad Jones shifted his efforts to shipbuilding on the West Coast. Both institutions fielded only informal teams in '17 and '18; they did not meet in combat. Action was resumed in 1919, when things were safely settled "over there."

The renewal of the old rivalry took place in a new cultural setting. It was a different America,

more sophisticated and more affluent than the sober and somewhat isolated Republic of the prewar years. The war had bred, as wars always do, significant changes in manners and mores, abetted this time by the advent of Prohibition, which occurred less than a year after the Armistice. The twenties would go down in history as "the Jazz Age," "flamboyant," "roaring," characterized by its "flaming youth," often raccoon-coated, sometimes at the wheel of a Stutz Bearcat, always with an available hip flask. The tempo of the times was allegro, and frequently scherzoso. If the twenties could be accused of a kind of nonchalant materialism, they could be credited, too, with bringing in a new kind of exuberant *spensieratezza*, observable particularly, if not exclusively, on college campuses.

More intensely than in any previous generation, the public, the press, and writers of fiction focused their attention on the undergraduate scene. Perhaps it was simply because there were more campuses than ever, and all of them were densely populated. The college-going segment of the country greatly increased in numbers during the twenties; for the first time in their histories the older institutions, including Harvard, Yale, and Princeton, were obliged to set a limit to the number of admissions. Or perhaps it was their life style that fascinated observers—a style characterized by a kind of naive hedonism and a programmatic dismissal of the old proprieties. Emancipation was the watchword—from starched collars and three-piece suits for the male, from corsets for the female, from formal codes of behavior for both sexes. F. Scott Fitzgerald, prophet of the new student generation, and other novelists dramatized their foibles and their angst, on the whole sympathetically. It was a good time to be young, and the youngsters made the most of it. Seen in retrospect, the period has an undeniable charm: those melodious strains of the saxophone, the rendezvous under the Biltmore clock, the summer sallies to Paris to pass the hours at Zelli's or the Crillon bar, returning of course with a smuggled copy of *Ulysses*. And, after all, there was nothing to worry about; most people had plenty of money; and the destinies of the Republic were in the hands of a succession of laissez-faire presidents, eager to maintain "normalcy" and not to meddle with the status quo.

Undergraduates were content to live in their own Eden, not greatly concerned with the world beyond the campus gates; it is true that the Boston police strike and the Sacco–Vanzetti case were not without repercussions, particularly on the Square, but in the main isolationism flourished on the campus, as it did in the politics of the nation.

In the twenties (which, culturally speaking, began in July of 1919 when Prohibition, which had so much to do with shaping the mores of the period, came in) entertainment and sports flourished as never before; the country was blessed with figures of monumental dimensions such as Bill Tilden, Bobby Jones, Babe Ruth, and Jack Dempsey, to say nothing of John Barrymore, Douglas Fairbanks, and Mary Pickford. In the empire of football, the most noticeable change was the rise to

preeminence of hitherto unknown or, at least, hardly prominent institutions such as Notre Dame, Pittsburgh, the clan of the Big Ten, and the powers of the Pacific. The center of pigskin prominence continued its westward march with ever-increasing acceleration. To be sure, there were glories yet ahead for the old Eastern schools. Both Harvard and Columbia would have triumphs in the Rose Bowl—the latter as late as 1935; Yale in the late thirties had two successive Heisman Trophy winners, and in 1939 and 1940 Cornell took two games from Ohio State. But these were sparks thrown from a log rapidly burning out.

Unaware of or indifferent to such dislocations, the Crimson and the Blue regrouped for a renewal of their interrupted rivalry. Both clubs hired new coaches. Haughton's business interest obliged him to give up coaching,[26] and he was succeeded by his disciple Bob Fisher, captain of the 1911 team and a very able mentor, whose competence was masked by a retiring modesty of manner. If Yale had expected to have her own way again, with Haughton no longer guiding the Crimson destinies, it did not take her long to realize her mistake. Tad Jones, who had been appointed only for a year in 1916, was unavailable; like Haughton, he too had his business affairs to manage. Yale turned instead to Al Sharpe, a veteran of Gordon Brown's Team of the Century who had a record of outstanding accomplishment at Cornell (his team of 1915 was one of the few teams to beat Harvard's Haughton-coached delegation). Such was the enthusiasm of Yale followers that when Sharpe detrained at New Haven he was met by a cheering throng, complete with brass band.

On both sides the troops that these neophyte generals were to command were, for the most part, untried. Eddie Casey was the only starter for the Crimson who had played in the '16 game; for the Blue, Callahan and Neville were back, as was La Roche, although he did not start against Harvard, his place being taken by "Fido" Kempton of the blonde, free-flying locks. The season had not progressed very far before it became evident to connoisseurs that Harvard had fielded the

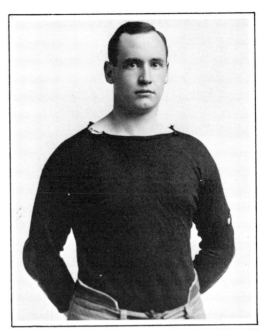

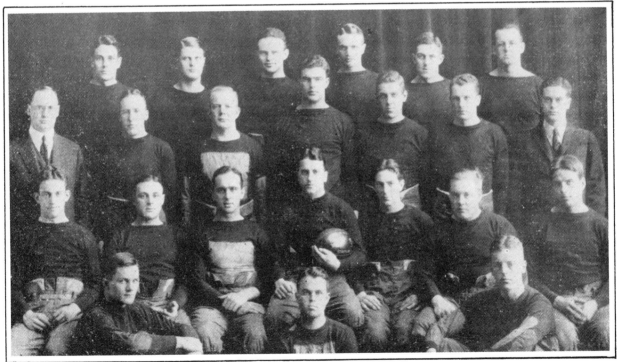

The 1919 Harvard team, winner in the Rose Bowl.

(TOP) Robert T. Fisher, who had been captain of the 1911 Harvard team, succeeded Haughton as coach in 1919.

stronger delegation. As it turned out, the Cantabs would not only go through the season unbeaten but would also defend victoriously the honor of the East against Oregon in the Rose Bowl game of 1920. A talented and versatile backfield included Casey, the newcomer Arnold Horween, with the deft Captain Murray at quarterback; a stalwart line: Desmond, Kane, and Sedgwick among them gave the ball handlers ample protection and were impregnable on defense: only one touchdown was scored against them that year. Only a tie with Princeton spoiled their record. Yale, on the other hand, lost not only to Princeton but surprisingly to ''little'' Boston College, whom Harvard had disposed of with relative ease.

So Harvard was favored. Even so it turned out to be a very close game, ''one of the hardest ever fought between the two old rivals,'' in the words of Bealle. Harvard got a field goal of forty-two yards from the toe of Arnold Horween in the first quarter and a touchdown on a brilliant pass from Winslow (yclept ''Babe'') Felton to Casey for thirty-five yards in the second. In the second half Yale scored three points on Jim Braden's fifty-three-yard dropkick (the longest in the series), and toward the end of the game carried the ball to the Crimson one-foot line, where a missed signal gave Harvard the ball. There was honor on both sides. Yale outgained Harvard and made seven first downs to her opponent's two. Grantland Rice faulted Yale for her stubborn allegiance to the running game; the Blue threw not one pass in the first half. Then in the last quarter Kempton turned to the air, ''emerging,'' as Rice puts it,

''from the stone age of football just exactly twelve minutes too late''[27] This assessment may be true, but what really cost the Elis the game was loose ball handling; there were simply too many Blue fumbles. And somehow there was always a Crimson jersey to cover the ball. Some of Yale's best running that day was done by the sophomore M. P. Aldrich, substituting for Neville at left half.

If Harvard's 1919 machine was one of the Crimson's best, the Yale squad, which came within a foot of tieing the game, could hardly be called a poor team. But Bulldog followers, unhappy with losses, however close, to both the Tigers and the Cantabs, were not willing to give Al Sharpe (who probably deserved a better fate) another chance. He resigned at the end of the season (although remaining as basketball coach for another two years), and Tad Jones, who had turned the trick in '16, was summoned back and given a three-year contract. It was a good thing for him that such great confidence was placed in him, for his first year was, in truth, less successful than that of his predecessor. Again Yale lost to Princeton and to Boston College and by wider margins than the previous year. And again in The Game, played under sunny skies in New Haven, the Crimson prevailed. The luckless Blue delegation of 1920 was the first since 1898 to be blanked by both of its Big Three rivals. (Nor has such a doleful record been matched since.) In contrast to the unrest at Yale all was serene for the Cambridge coaching staff. It had done superlatively well in 1919; there was no reason to assume 1920 would not be just as successful. As indeed it turned out to be. And even as with the Bulldog so for Harvard the season closely duplicated the profile of the previous year. Once more Harvard was undefeated, once more she fought to a tie with Princeton, and once more the defense was outstanding; only two teams scored on the Cantabs in 1920.

To be sure, Arnold Horween's *bravi* did not get to the Rose Bowl; one suspects that had they done so they would have racked up another win for the East. The personnel was one of the most talented ever to wear the Crimson; in the backfield aside from Horween, Charley Buell and George Owen,

The 1920 Harvard team, captained by Arnold Horween (holding ball), tied Princeton but defeated her other eight opponents, including Yale 9–0.

a pair of sophomores destined to give the Blue three years of anguish, performed brilliantly; the line, from end to end (that is, from Kane to Crocker, with such luminaries as Sedgwick, Havemeyer, and Hubbard in between), was smart and rugged. Yale had the tawny-haired Kempton and the fleet Aldrich in the backfield and Tim Callahan, re-elected captain, back again at center, but overall the Crimson had the stronger combination. The Cantab defense was stout enough to hold Yale scoreless—in fact, the Blue never seriously threatened. But to the credit of the Bulldog the Eli goal line was not crossed, and the visitors, for all their strength, had to settle for field goals. Buell scored the first one, from thirty-two yards out, following a Yale fumble. This was in the first quarter and was the only score in the half, giving Blue supporters some reason to hope. After all, only one breakaway run by either Aldrich or Kempton could have changed the face of things. Horween added another goal to the Harvard total at the end of the third quarter, and finally, after a Crimson march halted on the Yale six, Buell kicked his second goal of the day. The Bulldog could tell himself that he had fought hard and with honor; he hadn't, however, won, nor even, on the statistics of the game, really deserved to. An interesting feature of the combat was the Harvard passing game: sixteen attempts were made and nine were successful, a sizable number for those days. So in the Jones–Fisher competition, the latter drew first blood. (For those who see games as coaching duels we may note here that Fisher was destined to come out ahead; he faced Jones six times, winning three times and tieing once.)

In March of 1921 President Warren Harding was inaugurated. He looked more like a president than any man who has ever held the office; he would be succeeded two years later by Calvin Coolidge, who didn't look presidential at all but followed scrupulously the policy established by his predecessor: "normalcy" at home and "no foreign entanglements." Everyone seemed to like it. "Silent Cal" was given his own term by a substantial majority in 1924. There was new direction at Yale, too; in the fall of 1921 James Rowland Angell was installed as Yale's president, the first non-Yalie to be chosen for that office since the days of the founding fathers. The trustees and a considerable number of alumni felt that a fresh western breeze might blow away some of the mustiness that in their view was beginning to hover over the Old Campus. Angell, like Lowell of Harvard, was seriously concerned about the living conditions of undergraduate Yale, rapidly increasing in the postwar years and losing its old sense of intimacy. Within the decade both presidents would find the same solution to the problem. In 1921, beyond doubt the coming of Angell did somehow seem to portend refreshing changes in the old scene, and in the sector of football new hopes were in the air, too.

For such a sanguine attitude there was a sound foundation. The freshman team of 1924, playing in 1920, had revealed an unusual amount of new talent, particularly in Charlie O'Hearn at quarterback, Neidlinger and Mallory in the supporting

Mac Aldrich, captain of Yale's football and baseball teams in his senior year, was an exceptionally intense and dedicated figure on the playing fields.

cast, and Ted Blair at end. These along with their classmates Diller and Hulman immediately found places on a rejuvenated Bulldog task force, which had the further asset of being captained by one of the most versatile and inspiring heroes of the Blue pantheon. Mac Aldrich could not only kick, run, and pass (he played baseball, too, and captained both teams in his senior year), but on the field displayed a fire and dedication of exceptional intensity. Lean and handsome, Aldrich was an arresting and commanding figure; his style of running, too, with high knee action, made him difficult to tackle. His inspirational presence and the new recruits combined to give Yale its most exciting team in many a year. The pre-Harvard games were all won; admittedly there was not a lot of first-class opposition, but West Point and Princeton were disposed of, if not easily at least comfortably. The victory over Princeton was especially cheering, as the Tigers a week before their visit to the Bowl had finally, for the first time in ten years, defeated Harvard. In Cambridge circles it was recognized that Fisher's delegation this time was not quite as strong as its predecessors. On their record as they prepared to meet the invading Elis were losses not only to Princeton but to Centre College, a kind of midget comet in the football world of the early twenties, noted for the perhaps unfair practice of publicly invoking the assistance of the deity before running off their plays. Further, Penn State had played the Crimson to a tie and both Holy Cross and Brown had pressed the Cantabs hard. As Yale smothered Brown the week before the Princeton game, comparatists could see

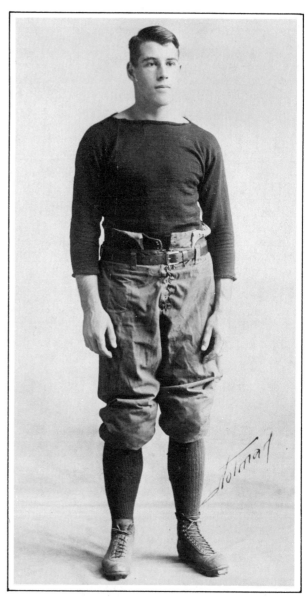

Charley Buell quarterbacked the underdog Harvard team to a stunning victory over Yale in 1921. Final: Harvard 10–Yale 3.

George Owen scored nine of Harvard's points in the Crimson's victory over Yale in 1921.

nothing but a rather one-sided Bulldog victory. "Only a miracle can save Harvard," wrote the Sage of the Pigskin, Grantland Rice. And the miracle came to pass, thanks to the aggressive genius of Charley Buell and George Owen and a grim Harvard defense led by the unyielding Captain Kane (destined to head the Office of War Information's bureau of intelligence). It was a fine battle, won essentially through the guile of Buell, surely one of the wiliest engineers ever to direct a Crimson machine.

Yale started off well and had the advantage most of the first quarter, in which Aldrich's drop-kick gave the Elis a three-point lead. In the second period Owen had three chances to score field goals but missed them all, and O'Hearn likewise failed to get a second one for Yale. The turning point came toward the end of the third period. Buell, who handled punts, had all afternoon signaled for a fair catch when receiving Yale kicks. For once he didn't; the Yale defenders were caught napping and Buell was off from midfield to the Yale 12-yard line. A clever inside fake got the Crimson to the Yale 3-yard line. In two bucks Owen was over for the touchdown. Time was now running out, but Yale fought back and carried the ball to the Crimson 15-yard line, where Harvard's Chapin intercepted a pass and ran it back into Yale territory. He would have gone all the way save for a magnificent chase by Mac Aldrich, who caught him from behind. Owen subsequently crossed the line again but was called back on a

George Owen advances to Yale's 5-yard line on a fake forward pass.

penalty. Shortly after, he kicked a field goal from twenty yards out, making the final score 10–3— and the Bulldog was frustrated once more. As a spectacle it was a great game to watch; Harvard's beating the odds was stirring to observe, and Buell and Owen were grand performers. Even so, the *Harvard Alumni Bulletin* bestowed its accolade elsewhere, chivalrously affirming that "Aldrich, the Yale captain, was the most brilliant player seen in the Stadium or anywhere else in a long time. He ran beautifully, made many long gains, punted, kicked drops, tackled and led his team with superb spirit."[28] Such tribute from an adversary is rare but on this occasion it was justified. Aldrich's performance in defeat went far to console the disappointed Yalies on the long ride back to New Haven.

The season of '22 (it was the year of Mussolini's march on Rome, hardly noticed by Americans, obsessed at that time by Mah-Jongg, which swept the country in the early twenties) was almost a replica of the preceding year. One might reasonably have expected the Elis, with the stalwarts of the class of 1924 returning to the fray with a year's experience in back of them and the sophomores of '25 (also undefeated in their freshman year—and what's more, unscored on), to give Tad the day he had been waiting for. And *in posse* the delegation of '22 was a powerful club, with a strong defensive line, now reinforced by two recruits of '25, Joss at tackle and Win Lovejoy at center; and Mallory, O'Hearn, and Neidlinger supporting Captain Jordan in the backfield. Yet somehow the team never quite lived up to its potential.

Perhaps the spark of Aldrich was missing. Certainly on the eve of the Harvard game the Bulldog could look back on a performance which was hardly more than mediocre. He had vanquished none of the opponents truly worthy of him: there had been a tie with Army, a loss to Iowa (an encounter that brought Tad and his younger brother Howard in confrontation; there was not a great deal to choose between the teams, but the westerners ground out a 6–0 win), and a defeat at the hands of the Tiger's "team of destiny." (A 3–0 squeaker; it was somehow characteristic of the Blue that year that Jordan should be stopped inches short of the Nassau goal line.) To be sure, Harvard had her troubles, too; Buell, now captain, was injured in the course of the season; his absence probably cost Harvard the Brown game, and, like Yale, Harvard found the Tigers of destiny a bit too much for them. On the record one might have said, waiting for the kickoff on that clear but cold afternoon in the Bowl, that Harvard had a more resourceful company, but Yale (slightly favored) was perhaps a little stronger. And, in fact, Yale showed her strength consistently during the combat, moving five times into Harvard territory and dominating in every statistical category. But all she got for it was a field goal by Charlie O'Hearn in the second quarter. By that time the Crimson had won the contest in a manner reminiscent of the action in the Stadium the previous year. In the first period a Yale punt was fumbled by a Harvard receiver; Owen, standing by, picked up the ball and ran over fifty yards to the Yale 4-yard line. Buell, who had not started, came limping in from the bench and in two plays sent Owen over for the only touchdown of the game. Pfaffman's field goal in the last quarter rounded out the 10–3 victory that seemed to be Harvard's specialty. Harvard men had a right to exult; alertness and fire had triumphed over strength. Yale men, going home in the twilight, could find comfort in the thought that while Mallory, O'Hearn et al. would be back next year, Buell and Owen would no more return to have their way with the Bulldog. The show, incidentally, had been witnessed by Georges Clemenceau, who found the game "sporting." It was a grand day for raccoon coats, too. Seventy-eight thousand aficionados packed the Bowl, thousands more throughout the country could follow the action, which was for the first time broadcast over the airways by that newfangled device called radio. (To be sure, strange as it may now seem, not everyone had a set in those days.)

Nineteen twenty-two marked the conclusion of the most glorious Crimson chapter in the chronicles of the rivalry. The Haughton–Fisher era, spanning fifteen seasons, matched Yale's great sequence in the primordial years of the game; over the period Harvard had outscored the Bulldog by 116 points to 28 and had allowed only one Blue touchdown—and none at all on the home field of the Stadium. Neither side has had such a run since.

Captain Charley Buell was injured for much of the 1922 season but managed to lead Harvard to its only touchdown in The Game that year. Here he is shown kicking a field goal against Holy Cross.

TOWARD PARITY THROUGH BOOM AND BUST

Football fan as seen by cartoonist R. C. Osborn in 1928.

The successive frustrations of 1921 and 1922 were hard for Bulldog fanciers to endure. One heard a lot in those days of the unfairness of the schedule. As it stood and still stands Yale is obliged to meet its two dearest rivals on successive Saturdays; the team has to be "up" two weeks in succession; any guru of the game will tell you this is asking a lot. However, Harvard never meets Princeton and Yale in succession. For many years the Crimson would be engaged with Brown, normally no grave challenge, and even when it was, yet not to be taken too seriously; meanwhile the Elis were wrestling with the Tiger. There is some foundation for the Blue querulousness in this matter, yet in fact most years it doesn't greatly signify since it is a rare season when both Princeton and Harvard are truly formidable. For four years ending in 1922, however, both Tigers and Redshirts had been very strong; hence the recurrence of the old complaint, of which one would hear very little for the rest of the twenties. For at last in 1923 Tad's tenacity was rewarded and finally he got the better of Bob Fisher, bringing back happier days for the Bulldog. The Elis of 1923 in fact turned out to be one of the really great Blue delegations, one of two teams to go through the season unbeaten and untied since the end of World War I. (The twentieth century so far records only four such stainless companies; Harvard has had three.) Fortune (or was it singularly foresighted recruiting?) was an invaluable aid to Tad; the starting lineup of the '23 immortals included no fewer than four extremely talented transfers whose times of eligibility were happily synchronized. Their contribution in addition to that of the classes of 1924 and '25, now experienced veterans, enabled Jones to field a company of rare quality. Was it better than Coy's team? On the offense, certainly, although it could not claim Coy's record of leaving the opposition scoreless. Was it superior to Mike Pyle's team, which would emerge in 1960 with another unstained escutcheon? This is debatable; probably it was stronger, if less versatile. The lineup, as the henchmen of Bill Mallory faced Harvard, is worthy of recording. At the ends were Bingham, '26S, and Luman, '25; the tackles—perhaps the most accomplished pair ever to wear the Blue—were Century Milstead, '26 (a transfer), and Blair, '24. Eckert, '25S, and Diller, '25, were

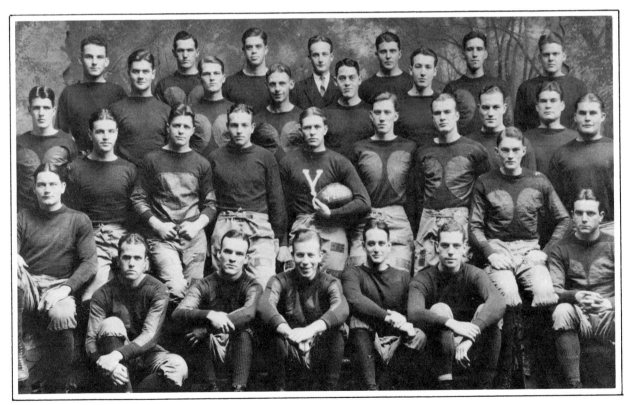

The 1923 Yale team is one of only four unbeaten and untied Yale delegations so far in the twentieth century.

"Memphis" Bill Mallory, captain of the 1923 Yale team.

Marvin Stevens, probably the most versatile back on the 1923 Yale squad, was head coach from 1928 to 1932.

the guards, and Lovejoy, '25, played center. Riche-son, '24S (a transfer), started at quarter, Neale, '25S (a transfer), and Pond, '25, were at the half-back posts, and blond and doughty "Memphis" Bill Mallory was the fullback. It should be noted that Neale and Pond, though starters, regularly alternated with Stevens ('25 and a transfer) and Neidlinger, '24. Probably Stevens was the most versatile of the backs, being not only a dangerous runner with a high-stepping style reminiscent of Mac Aldrich but a fine punter. But Pond, Neale, and Neidlinger were also excellent ballcarriers; Mallory on defense stands at the pinnacle of Yale linebackers. Had he not been injured, Charlie O'Hearn would have added even more power to a potent combination; both within the confines of the pigskin world and in the larger sphere of athletics O'Hearn was truly outstanding; he had already demonstrated his prowess on the gridiron in the seasons of 1921 and '22; he was also, in his senior year, captain of both the hockey and baseball teams. Unfortunately, he suffered a broken leg in the third game of the '23 season and made only a token appearance against Harvard.

Mallory's men achieved recognition by victories over Army and Princeton, both by comfortable margins. (The win over Maryland was unexpectedly a squeaker; the coaching staff had taken off to Princeton on a scouting expedition, and the team was undoubtedly looking ahead to the Big Three games; for whatever reason only Stevens's heroics in the second half gave the Bulldog a come-from-behind 16–14 win.)

At Cambridge the situation, as the season began, was quite different. Buell and Owen were gone; all members of the Crimson outfit had lost to their Yale opponents as freshmen—and Harvard had no talented transfers at hand. Captain Charley Hubbard and Greenough were sturdy linemen, McGlone a good quarterback, and Dolph Cheek an able runner, but none was quite of the caliber of their Eli counterparts. Fisher did well to eke out a 5–0 victory over Princeton (but it was a mediocre year for the Tiger, too); his troops had been beaten by Dartmouth and Brown and even tied by little Middlebury. Bulldog aficionados, as the annual tryst neared, began to have rosy dreams of not only winning but putting the Crimson to rout, an unbecoming attitude, no doubt, but a natural result of four successive lickings, the last two by underdogs in the betting. For these humiliations Harvard would now pay—and heavily.

In fact, Harvard got off relatively easily, thanks to a potent and unexpected ally—the weather. When the coin was tossed on that November 24 in the Stadium the rain was pouring copiously down. It had been doing so for twenty-four hours, nor did it cease throughout the whole time of combat. The field was already a swamp and by the time of the final whistle it more closely resembled a lake. Grantland Rice called it "a gridiron of seventeen lakes, five quagmires and a water hazard."[1] All dreams of blue-clad backs cantering over the goal line in joyous sequence went by the board. From an artistic standpoint, the *New York Times* remarked, the game was "a farce." For both squads the only play was the punt. Harvard punted twenty-five times and Yale twenty-nine. The

MANY THOUSAND FREE R. R. PASSES ISSUED ANNUALLY

Boston & Maine Reports 30,000 and the New Haven Company About 42,000

PUBLIC UTILITIES INFORMED

Employees and Their Families, American Express and Western Union Favored

More than 30,000 free passes are issued annually by the Boston & Maine Railroad, besides about 96,000 single-trip passes.

The New York, New Haven & Hartford Railroad issues about 42,000 free passes annually.

These passes are given to officials and employees of the companies and to their wives, and to employees of the American Railway Express and of the Western Union Telegraph Company. Statements relative to the passes have been filed with the Massachusetts Public Utilities Department in connection with the pending consideration of the proposed increase in rate for 12-ride and other commutation tickets.

In the case of both railroads it is claimed that all the passes are issued wholly under the provisions of the laws of Massachusetts, and the rules and regulations of the Interstate Commerce Commission, and that the passes are regarded as part compensation to the employees, so that their cancellation would occasion an increase in wages.

Following is the report made by the New York, New Haven & Hartford Railroad:

Passes on the New Haven

"The great bulk of passes issued by the New York, New Haven & Hartford at any time, and especially during 1922, were issued to our employes. Nearly all of these were governed by schedules in force constituting the agreements between the company and the different labor organizations.

"These passes were issued in part compensation for their services, and if abrogated would doubtless result in necessity of increased wages." These passes have been recognized, and in fact to some extent

Continued on Page Thirteen

ARMY PLANE WRECKED

Machine Flying from Boston to Mitchel Field Has Forced Landing in Connecticut—Occupants Unhurt

Stamford, Conn., Nov. 24—An Army plane flying from Boston to Mitchel Field was wrecked when a landing was made on the fairway of the Wood Way Country Club late yesterday. Sergeant Turner and his

---

door leading to the consul's offices. The blasts shattered window panes and shook houses in a wide radius.

At the Spanish consulate many persons were thrown from their beds, some being cut and bruised by flying glass. The bomb, concealed in a wooden box, was found on the doorstep by Emilio De Motta, the consul, when he returned from the theatre. He placed it inside the hallway, but, after retiring, he told the police, he had concluded that a passerby had left the box on the doorstep temporarily and might return for it. Without a thought of the deadly bomb concealed within, he got out of bed and replaced the box on the doorstep. A few minutes after returning to his room, the explosion occurred, tearing out the entire front of the building and wrecking the consul's room on the second floor.

The Sons of Italy Bank building was badly wrecked by the second explosion and a number of houses in the neighborhood damaged.

Today's Lineups

AT THE STADIUM

HARVARD			YALE
Combs, le		re,	Loman
Eastman, lt		rt,	Blair
Capt. Hubbard, lg		rg,	Diller
Greenough, c		c,	Lovejoy
Dunker, rg		lg,	Eckart
Evans, rt		lt,	Milstead
Mill, re		le,	Bingham
McGlone, qb		qb,	Richeson
Cheek, lhb		rhb,	Capt. Mallory
Coburn, rhb		lhb,	Neale
Hammond, fb		fb,	Pond

Referee—Ernest V. Quigley, Moot Institute. Umpire—Thomas J. Thorpe, Columbia. Field Judge—Edward J. O'Brien, Tufts. Linesman—Fred W. Murphy, Brown.

AT BRAVES FIELD

BOSTON COLLEGE			VERMONT
Duffy, le		re,	Eastburn
Donahue, lt		rt,	Johnson
Beaver, lg		rg,	Hill
Doyle, c		c,	Kendricks
Elbery, rg		lg,	Hawley
O'Brien, rt		lt,	Harms
O'Connell, re		le, Capt.	Semansky
McKenney, qb		qb,	Gooch
W. Cronin, lhb		rhb,	Yarnell
Wilson, rhb		lhb,	Tarpey
Capt. Darling, fb		fb,	Douglass

Referee—John J. Hallahan, Boston. Umpire—T. J. McCabe, Holy Cross. Field Judge—F. W. Lowe, Dartmouth. Linesman—James C. Donnelly, Dartmouth.

AT THE POLO GROUNDS, NEW YORK

ARMY			NAVY
Baxter, le		r.e.,	Brown
Penney, l.t		r.t.,	Shewell
Ellinger, l.g		r.g.,	Levensky
Garbisch, c		c.,	Zuber
Farwick, r.g		l.g.,	Carney
Goodman, r.t		l.t.,	Clyde
Doyle, r.e		l.e.,	Bernet
Smythe, qb		qb.,	McKee
Gillmore, l.h.b		r.h.b.,	Cullen
Hewitt, r.h.b		l.h.b.,	

---

probable time of the earthquake be predicted, pointing out the difficulty of such an estimate and declaring that the range of years it would have it would be practically valueless. Japanese catastrophe, he declared, was forecast in 1921 by the Imperial Seismological Bureau, which fixed the time within six years, and at the same time predicted a second serious disturbance between 1927 and 1933.

Clearing Tonight; Sunday Fair

(For This Evening's News, Entertainments, What Is Going On Tonight, Full U. S. Weather Report See Page 2, Part 1.)

Death Notices on Page 9, Part One

Rain for Harvard-Yale Game

FOR the first time in years, a Harvard-Yale game will be played in the rain. The storm which has been headed this way for the past two days, and which it was hoped would pass before the time of the Stadium encounter, sprung a surprise shift last night, when instead of taking the normal course out through the St. Lawrence Valley, it made an overhead pass for the coast. This means that clearing weather cannot be expected before tonight. The best that Weather Forecaster John W. Smith can promise is that the rain will come in showers instead of in a heavy downpour. Fair weather is probable tomorrow.

CAPPER FAVORS CURTIS AS AGAINST CUMMINS

HEAD OF FARM BLOC ASSERTS A VIGOROUS MAN IS NEEDED AS PRESIDING OFFICER IN SENATE

Washington, Nov. 24— Senator Capper, Republican, Kansas, chairman of the farm bloc, announced on his return to Washington today that he favored Senator Curtis of Kansas, the Republican whip for president of the Senate in opposition to Senator Cummins, Republican, Iowa. He said that "at this session more than ever the Senate needs a vigorous man as its presiding officer."

Selection of Senator Cummins as presiding officer of the Senate has been regarded generally as almost a foregone conclusion. He served last season as president protem, and neither Senator Curtis nor any other Senator on the Republican side has announced himself as a candidate for the place. With the elevation of Vice-President Coolidge to the Presidency, the president of the Senate will draw $4500 additional salary and be provided with an automobile and other perquisites of office.

Outlining his attitude toward legislation,

WORST FIELD EVER FOR HARVARD-YALE FOOTBALL CONTEST

Approximately Two Inches of Slimy Mud Covers Gridiron at the Stadium

REMOVE EIGHT TONS OF HAY

And Workmen Find a Field That Is Hopeless—Long Cleats for Players

TICKET HOLDERS HOPEFUL

Dash to H. A. A. by Ticket Seekers and Not Those Returning Pasteboards

By George C. Carens

With storm warnings up along the rugged Bay State coastline and with the most slimy, slippery and hopeless conditions underfoot that ever have existed for a Harvard-Yale game, there was a bleak prospect for some 53,000 football enthusiasts as they prepared to wend their way to the Harvard Stadium. It can be stated with positiveness that the Harvard field is in the worst possible condition for a modern football struggle and if the threatened rainstorm of the mid-afternoon materializes there is every likelihood that the game will go down into athletic annals as the dirtiest ever—a real mud-slinging battle.

Safety First on Catching Punts

Such a little matter as a pouring rain won't interfere with plans to hold the game. It may have an adverse effect on either or both teams; it may make scoring a matter of sheer luck, or it may even result in injury to the contestants. But the game will be played just the same and the football fans know it.

After strolling across the heavy blanket of hay at mid-forenoon, the reporter walked on a portion of the gridiron which had been cleared of its covering. And immediately his rubbers sunk down an inch or more in the slimy ooze. Even where turf remained the field fairly reeked with water and if there aren't some grotesque figures cut by the Crimson and Blue "skaters" it will be most surprising. The rival coaches said this morning that the rain would not interfere with their plans for the only offensive weapon either side could count on was the opponent's fumble. Harvard fumbled more often and recovered less often. In the first quarter a Crimson fumble was picked up by "Ducky" Pond, who ran (or waddled) sixty-three yards for the game's only touchdown. In the second half another Harvard fumble and a blocked kick by Blair put Mallory in a position to practice his recently acquired skill as a placekicker. With Lovejoy centering and Richeson holding a mud-encrusted ball, heavy as lead, Memphis Bill put two shots over the goal posts, one from the 24- and one from the 29-yard line. Yale 13, Harvard 0—and there was no further scoring. The Crimson never seriously threatened, though she might find statistical consolation in the fact that she outrushed Yale by sixty-nine yards to fifty-two. Even though the victory was not quite the kind that Eli followers had hoped for, they were content. At least it was a victory and the lean years were at last over. As for Harvard—well, it might have been worse. (Indeed, the following year it would be.)

For the first time in history of the rivalry the loser's goalposts were torn down and pieces were whittled off by exultant Eli souvenir hunters. "Yale at last was having its emotional debauch," wrote Grantland Rice, adding, "There will probably never be another game just like it. If there is, we hope to be somewhere else."[2] The *Yale Daily News* (November 28) commented that "complete wreckage of Harvard's football furniture seemed somewhat drastic though the wonder was that after the lean years the sons of Eli did not attempt

to remove the Stadium itself." The Crimson had an illustrious rooter that day. Babe Ruth sat on the Harvard side making his debut as a news commentator; he proudly proclaimed himself a Harvard man and said allusions to Harvard "snobbery" made him "sore." As for Haughton, he called the Yale victory "richly deserved" because the Elis "steadfastly refused to make mistakes and took full advantage of Harvard's." For Tad Jones, of course, even though the weather made the game "the most disappointing football spectacle ever waged (*sic*) by two major teams," Mallory's team was "the greatest fighting eleven ever to trot on a gridiron."

In 1924 Silent Cal was returned to the White House with a substantial margin, symbolizing no doubt the country's satisfaction with the status quo. The Bulldog too was quite satisfied with the way things were going since the reassuring result of the '23 game. In a way the Elis of '24 were a Coolidge-like team, not particularly adventurous (the off-tackle play with an occasional pass was their principal weapon), but a more than competent company of pigskin chasers. The glamorous transfers of the previous year had gone—having run out of eligibility—and the class of '24 had likewise departed. But the class of '25 included such stalwarts as Ducky Pond, Eddie Bench (at quarterback), and Lovejoy, now captain, Dick Eckart, and Luman in the line. There were a few good newcomers from '26 as well. Like its predecessors of '23, the squad of the Coolidge year went through the season undefeated, although it suffered two ties in the Dartmouth and Army en-

Bad field conditions for the 1923 game were front-page news in Boston.

counters. Its scoring total was modest but on defense it had only four touchdowns scored against it all season. It awaited Harvard in late November with a hard-earned win over Princeton to its credit and no doubts whatsoever about its ability to take the measure of the Crimson.

Such confidence could be based as much on Harvard's performance as on the Bulldog's own record. Bealle entitles his chapter on the year "A Disastrous Season"; "The Haughton momentum was ebbing," he remarks, and adds, with reason, that "lack of material was a factor in the decline"[3]—a little hard on Captain Greenough, the sophomores Dean and Cody, and the reliable Cheek. In fact, '24 was Harvard's poorest season up to that time in its long history, with only four victories against as many losses. It could have been said this year as it had been said in 1921 that only a miracle could save the Cantabs as they deployed for their forty-third joust with the sons of Eli. This time there was no miracle, although at the end of the first half with the Crimson leading 6–0 it seemed to the anxious Yale stands that the gods might once more be at work in red jerseys. Even as in '23, the weather was appalling. As if New Haven were trying to prove it would not be surpassed by Cambridge, the rain came down all the morning of the game and all through the game—a chilly, persistent downpour ("a deluge that might have drowned a dolphin" was W. O. McGeehan's phrase)[4] that made any kind of running all but impossible and completely ruled out the passing game. Mud is a great equalizer. To

everyone's surprise Harvard had the better of the battle in the quagmire throughout the first half and pressed Yale hard. No touchdown was forthcoming, but Erwin Gehrke scored two field goals, a dropkick from the 19-yard line and a placekick from thirty-five yards out, a notable feature considering the weather. But in the second half Yale rallied. Alternating Pond and the sophomore Kline for short but repeated and unstoppable gains through a weary Crimson line, the Blue crashed over for two touchdowns in the third quarter and one in the fourth ("One of the greatest marches in football history, 80 yards through the seven seas," *selon* McGeehan.)[5] It was grim, old-fashioned football, not beautiful but effective. The marvel was not that Yale's two aggressive backs could gain yardage but that they could consistently hang on to the slippery ball. It was the fairest licking Harvard had suffered at the hands of the Blue in many a long year (twenty-four, to be precise). And yet the individual hero of the game may well have been Harvard's Gehrke. Not only did he score all the visitor's points; he also gained more yardage than all the other Crimson backs and was a lion on defense. This even though he had not played or practiced for two weeks and had come to the Bowl on crutches—a brave warrior in a lost cause. A somewhat unusual feature of the action was that the rival captains, Lovejoy for Yale and Greenough for Harvard, both played center and faced each other across the line.

In the spring of 1925 Walter Camp died. Cohane describes the circumstances:

On March 13, he said good-by to Allie at the door of their home. . . . He never looked or seemed happier. Yale was on top again, and he was heading to catch the train for New York and the rules meeting. He walked down the street, shoulders erect, straight, with all his old brisk zest, turned once and waved. At the rules meeting that day, he was as quietly sharp as he had ever been, enjoying fully work that was to his taste and the association of old friends.

The night of March 13–14, he died during his sleep in his hotel room. When they found him, he lay peacefully, with his hands, palms together, under one cheek, his typical repose.''

He was in his sixty-sixth year. Cohane adds, "His name will live as long as American college football, his game, is played. His is the most important single name, not only in Yale, but in all football history."[6]

Three years after his death the Walter Camp Memorial Gateway to the field, now known as the Walter Camp Field on which the Bowl stands, was dedicated to memorialize him. He could not have wished for a more appropriate monument.[7]

Perhaps, returning to our chronicle, it was just as well for Camp's peace of mind that he did not live to see The Game of 1925, a sad and frustrating experience for the Blue and, on the comparative records of the rivals, quite inexplicable. The disintegration among the Cambridge clan which had set in the previous year showed no signs of slowing down. Harvard, now captained by Cheek, was beaten by Holy Cross, Dartmouth, and

The Walter Camp Memorial Gateway.

Princeton; the Tigers ran up the largest score ever made (up to then) against the Crimson. Fisher, early in the season, abandoned the sober style of offense he had taken from Haughton and indulged in tactical experiments that in the words of Will Cloney "were sometimes more confusing to Harvard than to the opponent."[8] Wisely in the last weeks of the season he went back to a simpler style of attack and concentrated heavily on defense. In New Haven, things started inauspiciously before the season began when "Shep" Bingham, captain-elect, was made ineligible because of academic disabilities. His place was taken by Johnny Joss, originally of the class of '25 and a veteran of the '22 and '24 campaigns, now enrolled with 1926. The stalwarts of the classes of '24 and '25 who had given the Blue two successive years without a defeat were no longer on hand. Still, the Bulldog record might have been worse; he came to Cambridge having suffered a defeat by Penn (a close one, though) and a sound licking at the hand of the Tiger (Jake Slagle was too slippery for his clutch); yet he had shown signs of vigor, notably in an easy conquest of Army, victor that year over Notre Dame. Bettors quite rightly made Yale a three to one favorite for The Game. Yet something *unheimlich* happened on Soldiers Field that fateful day. Work on defense had paid off for the Cantabs; they had rallied to beat Brown the previous week (for the first time in four years). And they were ready for Yale. Six times the Elis carried the ball deep into Crimson territory (twice inside the 5-yard line), and six times misplays, mental errors, and Harvard stubbornness turned them back.

The story of the last two minutes is the story of the game. Yale's end Bradley took a pass covering nearly fifty yards to put the ball on the 5-yard line. Three smashes at the line brought the Bulldogs within a foot of the promised land. Whereupon the Blue backfield, neglecting to call time-out, fell into earnest discussion about the next move and the last second ticked off while the parley went on. On her part, Harvard, though all but faultless on defense, never approached the Yale goal. "The game," as Bealle well says, "was played almost entirely in front of Harvard's goal line," adding what is only too true, "that the Bulldog gave one of the greatest exhibitions of futility and wasted opportunity in the history of football."[9] In its dismal way it was certainly an unusual game. *Passons*—with a salute to Dolph Cheek's stalwarts, who refused to acknowledge their inferiority. The *Crimson* (November 26) was accurate in calling the game "a scoreless victory." The result enabled Bob Fisher to end his coaching career on a happy if not truly high note. Against Tad his score was 3-2-1, better than Haughton's.

Nineteen twenty-six can hardly be described as a vintage year either in Blue or Crimson annals. Harvard's uninspiring season total was three wins and five losses, her first losing season in history; the Bulldogs didn't do much better, emerging with four wins and four defeats (it was the first Yale team to lose four consecutive games). Both teams lost to Brown and Princeton. Both managed to edge out a subpar Dartmouth delegation. One could hardly claim the championship of the East was at stake when the Cantabs came to the Bowl on November 20. The plain fact was that talent

Arnold Horween (*right*), a star of Robert Fisher's first team in 1919, succeeded his mentor as Harvard's coach in 1926. Here he is shown with C. D. Coady, captain of the 1926 squad.

was lacking in both squads. Harvard labored under the additional disadvantage of adapting to a new coaching staff. Arnold Horween, who had been a star of Fisher's first team in 1919, was appointed to succeed his mentor. The appointment was made by the outspoken and self-confident Bill Bingham, Harvard's first director of athletics, an office created that year by President Lowell with the purpose of taking athletics out of the hands of the alumni; the director was ex officio a member of the faculty. (Yale would move in the same direction later. In 1939 football would be stripped of its long-standing budgetary autonomy, and athletics in general would become more closely integrated with the other branches of the

university. The title of director of athletics was first bestowed upon Ogden Miller, concurrently head of admissions, in 1941.) Horween was a native of Chicago and had come to admire the style of the game as played in the Middle West. Among other things he brought the huddle to Cambridge. He did away with the Haughton–Fisher system and the coaching personnel of his predecessor; his broom swept cleaner than any since Haughton's intervention in 1908. Horween would spend four years on Charlesside and would have his successes, but the first year was a rough one for him. Jones had no such problem—only how to get his willing but somewhat undistinguished Bulldogs to play above their heads.

However, the level of competence has very little to do with the zest and even the quality of the ancient duello, and the '26 game was a good one to watch (nearly 75,000 spectators turned up) and one from which both sides could take a certain amount of satisfaction. After a scoreless first quarter Yale's Gene Richards blocked a Harvard punt on the Crimson 10-yard line; the veteran All-American Sturhahn fell on the ball over the goal line, giving Yale a 6–0 lead. In the third quarter Harvard went ahead on the most spectacular play of the game, a pass from Henry Chauncey to Nat Saltonstall covering fifty yards. Chauncey's conversion was good; Yale retaliated with two long passes of her own, putting the ball on the Harvard twenty; when resistance was stubborn, Jerry Wadsworth (who thirty-four years later would be his country's chief representative to the United Nations) went in and kicked a field goal from twenty-three yards out. In the last quarter Captain Bunnell swelled the Eli total with a forty-yard placement kick. Harvard had only one other chance to score and couldn't manage it. It was a well-earned victory for the Blue, but Harvard certainly provided the most exciting play of the game.

The Harvard–Princeton encounter, which is not our concern here, must be mentioned for its effect on the Big Three round robin. It was an engagement waged with unusual intemperance, to such a degree indeed that Harvard deemed it wise to suspend relations for a while. The regrettable hiatus would last for eight years. Yale, desiring to treat both old friends alike, altered her schedule as soon as it was possible to give Princeton the climactic final date in alternate years. Hence in 1931 and 1933 Princeton closed the Bulldog season. In 1934 Tigers and Cantabs got together again.

Nineteen twenty-seven may be said to mark the high tide of the carefree twenties. There seemed to be lots of money around; the stock market attracted investors from all classes of society and rewarded them richly. There was a trick called buying on margin which was very useful indeed. Besides, wonderful things were happening. Lucky Lindy, a prince of the skies, flew nonstop to Paris—and met his princess; talking movies came out. *Show Boat* enlivened the air with its enduring melodies, and Thornton Wilder's *Bridge of San Luis Rey* charmed and inspired thousands of readers. Less exhilarating was the execution of Sacco and Vanzetti in Massachusetts, which caused President Lowell a lot of trouble and has left a legacy of uneasiness in the national memory. It also left its mark on American letters, inspiring a poem by Edna St. Vincent Millay, a novel by Upton Sinclair, and a play by Maxwell Anderson. To come closer to our own muttons, it was in 1927 that the goalposts were moved ten yards behind the goal line, making field goals a little rare for a while. It was also the year in which the president's committee decreed that fall practice should begin no earlier than September 15— thus assuring for Harvard and Yale and their Ivy sisters a permanent second-rate status in the gridiron world. And it marked the last year of Tad Jones's term of coaching, and the first appearance of the Harvard band's massive drum, which like a medieval *carroccio* became a kind of mascot in the years to come.

For both schools things were looking up a bit after the rather drab year of 1926. Harvard's record—4 and 4—does not sound impressive but it was a valiant outfit for all that, featuring the two gifted ball handlers Art French and Dave Guarnaccia, now juniors and clearly on their way to high achievement. The Crimson, however, was weak on defense and would not really be ready for Yale for another year. For in New Haven the Bulldog was himself again. Tad came very close to fielding an undefeated team, losing only, and just barely, to Georgia. The '27 line was one of the best in twentieth-century Blue annals. Fishwick and Scott at ends were experienced seniors; their classmates Captain Webster at guard and Quarrier at tackle were also well-seasoned and talented; their younger comrades Eddy, Charlesworth and Marting were a good deal better than average. Only thirty-two points were scored against the Bulldogs in the course of the campaign. On offense, Hoben was an able quarterback and Cox a placekicking fullback in the style of Bill Mallory, but the star of the team was Bruce Caldwell, who, having seen some action in 1925, had sat out most of the '26 season with a broken

leg: he came suddenly into his own and became one of Yale's outstanding backs of the twenties. He could kick, run (some say like Ted Coy), and pass; he did most of Yale's ballcarrying—until the climax games. For as it fell out, just before the Princeton game the news broke that Caldwell was

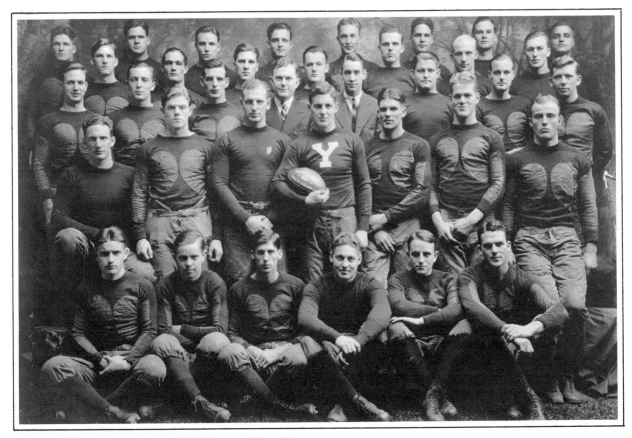

The 1927 Yale team, captained by Bill Webster, defeated Harvard 14–0 and overall allowed its eight opponents a total of only thirty-two points.

ineligible, having played a few games as a substitute on the Brown freshman team before entering Yale—strictly against the Big Three rules. It is an indication of the gentler mores of the new century that Harvard (in generous contrast to her censorious stance in the Glass case), as well as Princeton, petitioned that Caldwell, who had sinned in innocence (he didn't know that freshman football counted), be allowed to play. Yale, however, stuck by the rules, and Caldwell faced neither of the old Big Three rivals. The Yale camp was in despair. But both John Garvey and Bill Hammersley turned out to have the same shoe size as Caldwell, and the story—for the Blue—had a happy ending. Princeton, coming to the Bowl undefeated, as Dartmouth and Army had been before their visits to New Haven, was turned back in a thrilling game which is not part of our story here, and the Bulldogs, reassured, entrained for Cambridge with considerable confidence.

Even so, the climactic battle, fought under a chilly but sunny sky, was no walkover. Yale won it on two long runs, one by Garvey in the first period covering fifty-two yards, the other by Hammersley in the third period for forty-two yards. Otherwise the game was quite even; a third Yale score was averted by a determined Crimson defense in the last quarter. Harvard had her best chance, thanks to French and Guarnaccia, early in the game but could get no closer than the Yale ten. So Tad could retire in glory; counting his 1916 win, he had triumphed over the Crimson five times as against three losses and a tie, almost as good a record as Haughton's. And perhaps, having had the last word, he could move off the scene with a happier heart than P.D. did in 1916.

One could argue that the carefree and innocent twenties died a little before their time—in October 1929. That date was still more than a year off when Mal Stevens, '25, a disciple of Tad Jones and an assistant coach on his staff since 1924, was appointed to succeed his master—but '28 had its own portents of change too. It was the year that Henry made a lady out of Lizzie; without the old Model T something of America's spirit of adventure was missing. With Fords purring along, indistinguishable from Buicks and Oldsmobiles and almost as expensive, the age of the car came truly into its own. Soon there would be turnpikes and thruways and traffic lights—and suburbia in bloom. In 1928, too, Americans had for the first time a chance to vote a Roman Catholic into the presidency; probably no election in the twentieth century—which has had a good many exciting ones—occasioned more enthusiastic participation. A year adumbrating, if not actually witnessing, significant transitions. Incidentally, it was the first year one had to pay $5.00 for a ticket to The Game—up $2.00 over the previous year.

In New Haven things went not too well. Fortune was not kind to Tad's successor, as he took the Bulldog's leash in hand. The sturdy line of the 1927 delegation had graduated, replacements were inexperienced and in some cases prone to injury. (Captain Max Eddy injured himself falling off a chair while studying; legend has it that Eddy, in his senior year, had been seduced from total dedication to gridiron affairs by the charm of the classroom.) Nor did the '28 delegation field any runner of the Caldwell stamp. The season's record was four wins and four losses; looking back, one can't help thinking it might have been worse. At least there was a win over Dartmouth—but then Yale had always triumphed over the green.

In Cambridge, skies were brighter. Horween was in his second year; his pupils had mastered his style of play. Art French (now captain) and Dave Guarnaccia had come of age, each one formidable in his own right, but doubly so when teaming up, as they frequently did for their deft laterals. Horween's forwards also enlisted a new and redoubtable recruit in Ben Ticknor, a husky soph-

Art French, Crimson captain in 1928.

Ben Ticknor played center on the Harvard line from 1928 to 1930. In his senior year he was elected captain.

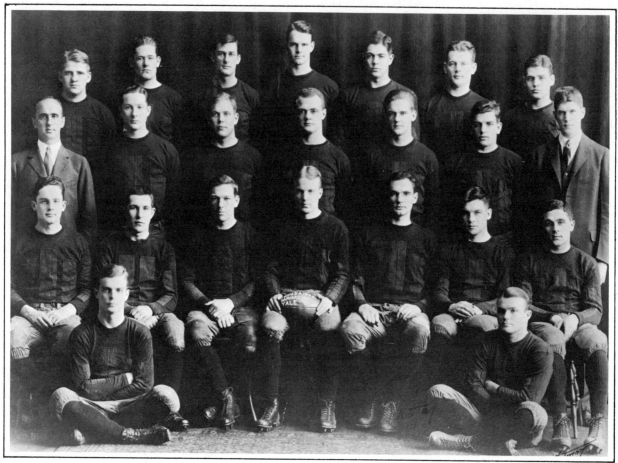

The 1928 Harvard team, captained by Art French, was a 17−0
victor over Yale.

omore. So for The Game of '28, Harvard came in a
favorite (the squad had a won−lost record only a
little better than Yale's but had performed with
greater finesse) and had no trouble justifying the
confidence of her backers. It was all French and
Guarnaccia; the Yale defense found no solution
to their smooth laterals: Guarnaccia as it happened scored both Crimson touchdowns, one in
the first quarter and one in the third. Eliot Putnam kicked a field goal from the 17-yard line to
complete the scoring. A very workmanlike job all
around for the Cantabs; what was sad from the
Blue point of view was the total inability of Yale
to counterattack. The Bulldogs made only five

first downs; driven to pass more often than they could have wished, they had but one completion in twenty attempts—and six interceptions. To Baker the French–Guarnaccia sleight of hand was less impressive than the Harvard defense; he notes that "not once was Yale able to get within the Harvard 38-yard line."[10] W. O. McGeehan found the capacity crowd, "befurred and feathered," brilliant to look upon, "but the game itself a drab sort of affair."[11] But McGeehan was not a Harvard alumnus.

For Americans who remember it, the year 1929 has an ominous ring which successive decades have not muffled. An era ended on that fateful Friday of October, and the country, for better or for worse, has never been the same since. Yet at the time no one had any notion of the lasting impact of the great crash. The market was drastically down—well, it would be up again, these things happen. Recovery was just around the corner. It took a year and more before the realization set in that it might be a very long and laborious walk to reach that corner. With no prevision of shrinking enrollments—and faculties—to say nothing of diminishing attendance at football games, the season of 1929 went along with easy normality. In Cambridge 20,000 seats were added in the course of renovating the venerable Stadium, enabling close to 60,000 to watch the game. Harvard and Yale came out with matching records (5–2–1) and matching neophyte paladins in the persons, respectively, of Barry Wood and Albie Booth. (Their competition had begun in freshman year, when Harvard won 7–6 and Booth amazed the

spectators with his all-around play, including a defensive ardor that staved off a few Crimson touchdowns.) In the course of his first year on the varsity Booth had already dazzled the football world with his single-handed defeat of Army (Cagle and all). He had a stout companion in "Hoot" Ellis and a pair of good forwards in Captain "Firpo" Greene and Fay Vincent, and the Bulldogs had pulled out a win over Dartmouth and taken care of a good Princeton team (without Booth in the lineup). The Blue came to Cambridge slight favorites and with some confidence. In fact, on the record it should have been Yale's day. Wood, like Booth, had come off the bench to star against Army and had performed valiantly in the Crimson's narrow defeat by Michigan. Like Albie, he had a good supporting cast, featuring a duo of aggressive Ticknors to clear the way. Just the same, Harvard had merely tied Army and had taken a real beating from Dartmouth. But things were different in the Stadium. Booth had two kicks blocked, both in the second quarter. The first was a would-be field goal from the Harvard twenty-five. The Crimson recovered and marched eighty-two yards to a touchdown, thirty-five of them made by a lateral pass, Devens to Eddy Mays. After the ensuing kickoff, Booth's attempted punt was blocked by Douglas. Harvard took over on the Blue 17-yard line, but this time had to settle for a field goal—by Wood, of course. Just before the end of the half it was Yale's turn to block a kick, the blocker being Yale's rugged captain. This put the ball inside the Crimson twenty; after two completions Booth's pass to Ellis was

(LEFT) In his first year on the Yale varsity in 1929, Albie Booth dazzled the football world with his single-handed defeat of Army. He later captained the 1931 squad.

(ABOVE) Barry Wood, captain of the 1931 Harvard team, quarterbacked the Crimson for three straight years. He later became a prominent member of the medical profession.

good for a Blue touchdown. The kick was missed, making the score 10–6—and so it ended. The second half began with Albie carrying the kickoff through the Crimson defenders and breaking into the clear, only to be hauled down by Ben Ticknor coming up from behind. Observing that Ticknor grabbed Booth by his "billowy blue sweater," Grantland Rice adds, "if he had been arrayed in the garb of a South Sea Island swimmer, he would have run 96 yards for a touchdown and would also have won the most dramatic game of football ever played."[12] Yale dominated the play in the second half but whenever it was necessary the Crimson defense was ready. It was not a great game for Booth. He may not have been at full strength, but in any case the Harvard defense "keyed" on him remorselessly and efficiently. In truth, Albie never had a spectacular day against the Crimson, although he would have a highly satisfactory one in '31. There were no fumbles on either side in the duello of '29—a phenomenon unique in the records.

The last year of the decade brings in "the thirties"—syllables which still awaken uneasy memories for Americans who can remember living through that era of anxiety. The early years of the fourth decade were particularly shattering as in the face of foreclosures, bankruptcies, and mounting unemployment confidence yielded to hopelessness and no remedy seemed in sight. Paradoxically, for Harvard and Yale undergraduates those years brought in a felicitous change in life style; they were the years in which the house plan at Harvard and the college plan at Yale came into

being. Their effect, as both Lowell and Angell had foreseen, was to greatly enrich the lives of the vast majority of the undergraduate body, restoring the sense of community that had characterized student life up to half a century earlier but which had been eroded by the steadily increasing enrollments over the years. Harvard's first two houses opened in 1930, Yale's first seven colleges three years later.[13] Both houses and colleges owed their existence to the generosity of Edward S. Harkness, Yale, '97. "Thus a Yale man became the greatest benefactor to Harvard in our entire history," says Morison handsomely.[14] The new residential units, though it was hardly their principal purpose, did a lot for Harvard–Yale football. Each house and college has its own football team; at the end of the season the champion teams of each group meet to battle for the Harkness Cup. Non-championship teams have their own special rivalries with their affiliates, whom they engage regularly on the Friday preceding The Game. On which occasion there are more pigskins flying through the air in the shadow of the Bowl or the Stadium than can be found anywhere else in the country. A great thing for the sport and a stirring prelude to the Great Event. But let us return to the saga of Little Albie and the red foxes.

The Bowl was once more filled to the brim, and it has been estimated that another 30,000 tickets could have been sold if there had been seats to accommodate their purchasers. The enthusiasm exemplified the irresistible attraction of The Game for its own sake, since that year neither side fielded an especially outstanding squad. Yale had the better record, with one loss to Georgia and two ties (with Army and Dartmouth); she could also boast of a powerful fullback in Joe Crowley and a trio of rugged forwards in Vincent (now captain), Linehan, and Freddy Loeser, built like a pocket battleship and no less dangerous. Horween, who had announced it would be his last year at the helm, had had a rougher time of it; as the Crimson entrained for the Bowl, the record stood at 3–4–1, with losses not only to Army and Dartmouth but also to Michigan and Holy Cross. But Barry Wood was coming into his own, and the second clash between him and Yale's mighty mite was anticipated eagerly on both sides of the field. Once more the Bulldog's Little Boy Blue was overshadowed; indeed, his statistics were decidedly mediocre, with a mere twenty-two yards rushing (Ben Ticknor, captain of the Crimson now, was back again to frustrate him) and no opportunity to exercise his dropkicking talents. Wood, on the other hand, had a superb day. He played sixty minutes of the game, passed twice to the elusive Huguly for touchdowns (once in the first and once in the third quarter), and seemed to be in command all the way. So it was 13–0 Harvard when the whistle blew. Yale, which on the basis of comparative scores—and in the eyes of the oddsmakers—should have won, never seriously threatened. "Three straight over Yale! What sweet music to Harvard ears!"[15] No wonder, as another journalist remarked, that "Harvard fans got a record for speed in toppling goal posts."[16] At the end of the season, players, coaches, and the athletic director pleaded with Horween to renew his contract. He had compiled a record of 21–17–3, not an especially impressive total. But he had beaten Yale three times running—which is all that Harvard hearts desire. Eddie Casey, star of Haughton's last team, was appointed to replace him.

For the '31 meeting Booth and Wood were captains (as they had been in freshman year) of the contending tribes. Little Albie had yet to win, and as *der Tag* drew near, his chances of victory this time seemed slighter than ever. In the melees of '29 and '30 he had been a member of Yale teams that had gone into The Game as favorites. This year it was another story. For the first time since 1913 the Crimson entered its climax match with a flawless record. (It would not do so again for thirty-seven years.) Under Wood's guidance, and with the collaboration of his running mates Crickard and Schereschewsky, an unusually strong line with Hageman and Nazro at the ends and Hallowell at center (yielding only four touchdowns in the entire season), the Crimson had defeated Army, Dartmouth, and Holy Cross in hard-fought battles and had disposed easily of Texas, reckoned to be a dangerous opponent. Wood had, as usual, shown rare talent both in performance and leadership; he had rallied his team to victory over Army with exploits, defensive and offensive, which somewhat resembled Booth's domination of the Cadets two years earlier. The Blue record was hardly comparable. For all Booth's efforts, the battles with Army and Dartmouth were draws and the game with Georgia was—again—lost. It could hardly be called a poor Yale team; the register of starters included Joe Crowley at fullback, Hans

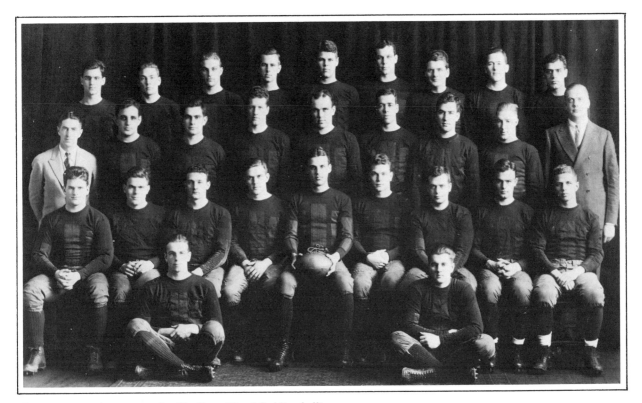

The 1931 Harvard team, captained by Barry Wood (holding ball).

Flygare and Hester Barres at the ends, and Johnny Wilbur at tackle. Still, it hardly seemed to be equal to Harvard, and the bettors gave the Crimson a ten-point edge.

The game, played in sunny but rather sultry weather, turned out to be one of the best in the series. (As if the gods realized it was the golden jubilee of the combative pair and wanted to make the anniversary memorable.) In style, the contest was a kind of throwback to the days of old; a grim battle of impregnable defenses, a test of endurance and dogged determination. Harvard almost won on the kickoff. The ball went to Barry, and all Elis converged on their most feared opponent. But Wood deftly and all but unobtrusively lateraled to Crickard, who was off like a flash down the west sideline. Booth tried desperately to seize him on Yale's 35-yard line; he failed, but the delay was sufficient to enable Barres, coming from across the field and far behind, to catch the ballcarrier on the Yale 7-yard line. At which the Bulldogs proved worthy of their name, and Harvard could get no further. Nor would the Redshirts ever get that close again. Cloney opines that the failure to exploit Crickard's run "broke Harvard's heart and spirit."[17] Yale kicked out of trouble and the game settled down to a tense struggle, with both sides battling for stingy gains. Yale had a slight edge in the tug-of-war and got close enough in the second period for Booth to try—and miss—a field goal from the Crimson 15-yard line. The half ended in a scoreless tie. Albie sat out the third quarter, being replaced by the sophomore Bob Lassiter. A Harvard fumble on her own 25-yard line gave the Blue another chance, but the Crimson line yielded nothing. It began to look as if a scoreless tie, again in the fashion of old, might be in the making. Booth came back for the last period. Halfway through the quarter he completed a thirty-yard pass to Barres which put the ball on the Crimson twelve. In three smashes, two by Booth, Yale reached the Harvard four. At which point, Cohane writes, "Pat Sullivan, who had alternated with Dud Parker, was in the game now. It was the first time he had ever played in the same backfield with Booth. He was calling the plays. He turned to Albie in the huddle and smiled grimly.

'Can you kick a field goal, you little b——?'

'Sure,' said Little Boy Blue.

And he did. And that was the game."[18]

George Carens, writing in the Boston *Transcript*, summed up the common sentiment when he wrote:

I hate to see Eddie Casey's boys lose their objective game after such a fine season, but no fair-minded person should begrudge Albie Booth the tribute which comes from a win over Harvard. Bostonians have previously had a tendency to belittle the Yale captain because he has never before seemed to hit his stride when playing against the Cantabs. However, his performance this afternoon leaves no doubt in their minds as to his ability. For three years he has been denied the taste of victory, and it was inevitable that he would at last come out the winner. Finally, as a Senior, Fate gave him his opportunity. It was merely delayed justice.[19]

It is possible, even from the Yale side, to feel some sympathy for Wood; it is hard to have a perfect season marred by a sad conclusion (it had happened to Yale's Mac Aldrich ten years before on the same field). But Barry could find comfort in his earlier triumphs. Journalists noted that at the end of the engagement the rival captains exchanged congratulations, which both had reason to offer and accept. Together they had written a great chapter in the history of The Game. They were to go on to very different destinies. Booth, on graduation, refused a number of invitations from sundry business firms; temperamentally almost without ambition, he married his high school sweetheart and lived out his years in his native town, employed on the management side of a New

(RIGHT, TOP) On the opening kickoff of the 1931 game, Wood (52) lateraled to Crickard, who skirted Yale's left end and ran to the Blue 7-yard line.

(RIGHT) Albie Booth drop-kicks field goal to beat Harvard, 1931.

Haven milk dispensing company and finding his pleasures in refereeing football games and counseling boys clubs. Wood, after getting his M.D., became a very prominent and highly respected member of the medical profession, to which his contributions achieved wide recognition.[20] And when death came, much too prematurely, to Albie in the spring of 1959, his old rival was present at the memorial service. One likes to think of them now gazing down from Valhalla as November comes around, cheering on their successors and exchanging reminiscences.

In 1932 Franklin D. Roosevelt was voted in; the country was desperately in need of a New Deal. Those who remember the Great Depression may recall 1932 as the grimmest year of all, with Hoovervilles springing up, apple sellers on street corners, and overall an uneasy suspicion that things were getting worse. Many worried citizens began to question even the viability of the American system; Coughlinites, Technocrats, and even Communists got a hearing. Yet, when the votes were in, it was refreshingly clear that the country didn't want revolution, only a new direction and the restoration of hope. (How comforting Walt Disney's "Three Little Pigs" and the hamburger-minded Wimpy were in those bleak years.) A not unhealthy side effect of the Depression was the change in undergraduate attitudes. In the twenties Joe College gave no thought to anything happening in the world outside the gates; the college-going youngsters of the thirties, on the other hand, many facing the dire possibility that tuition money would dry up and with odd jobs hard to find, became serious students of matters political and economical; departments of political science and government and even international relations flourished. The house/college system at Harvard and Yale made it possible to attract statesmen and pundits in great numbers. Youth had become committed. And the change was for keeps. Joe College has never come back; today, the old grads are more likely to fault "college kids" for their activism than for their indifference.

In the area in which we are dealing, a striking evidence of hard times is afforded by the attendance at the Bowl for the annual tilt. In 1930 it had been 74,000; in 1932 only 35,000 made their way to the rainy and muddy field of battle. (It would be fifteen years before the attendance would reach 70,000 again.) One cannot blame the low attendance on the weather; it had been much worse in '24 when 74,000 of the faithful had turned up—at least for the first quarter. In sharp contrast to the engagement of the previous year, neither Yale nor Harvard was a power to be reckoned with. The scintillant Booth and Wood were both gone, along with their talented classmates. With no intent to disparage the skills or valor of the young men of 1932, they were, on the record, less colorful and less gifted than their immediate predecessors. For Yale, Lassiter was a fine ball-carrier, and Sullivan at quarter and Crowley at fullback were able collaborators, and John Wilbur, now captain, and Curtin were prominent members of a sturdy line. Crickard was back for Harvard, which also fielded a pair of veteran ends in Nazro and Captain Hageman; Hallowell was an experienced and capable center. But for both squads the season had been mediocre. Yale came to the game with a record of three ties (unique in Yale annals), two losses, and one close victory over Dartmouth. (It was the shortest season in Yale's twentieth-century history.) Harvard's total (5−2−0) sounded better, but a 46−0 mauling by the Army did not boost the Cantabrigian stock. The Cadets had downed the Elis 20−0. Both teams had felt the heel of the Brunonians (Brown was strong that year), Harvard by a wider margin. Pretty much even money, one would have said, although Yale was a slight favorite. In fact, whether it was the nature of the field (Yale regularly does better in the mud than Harvard) or because Lassiter had his best day, the Bulldogs emerged with a rather easy victory (19−0). Lassiter completed only three passes but two went for touchdowns and, on the side, proved himself a better than average mudder. The Redshirts did not go down tamely; three times in the first half they brought the ball to the Yale 2-yard line, but three times, largely due to heroic work by Crowley and Levering backing up the line, their thrusts were frustrated. Summing up, one might say it was a match in which the Blue did a little better than had been expected and the Crimson considerably worse.

A few marginalia on that muddy weekend's activities may be cited. The night before the game, the *New Haven Register* (November 19) reported, "unknown malefactors" broke into the Bowl, uprooted and made off with the goalposts, and ran up Y banners upside down on the flagpoles. Costumes were of a distinctly picturesque style: the *New York Times* (November 20) observed some spectators wearing linoleum, and the *Register* (November 20) agreed that "ordinarily a coonskin convention, this year's game was an oilcloth contest." Babe Ruth, that loyal Crimson fan, was in attendance but (understandably) left early. During the game, a collection was taken up for unemployment relief, netting $2,315, according to the *Times*.

Starting with the season of 1933 the offense got a real "break." Hitherto the ball had to be put into play from where it was downed, even though that spot might be within an inch of the sidelines. Consequently the offensive team would have to waste a down to go offsides and gain the right to have the ball moved into a playable part of the field. Henceforth, however, if the ball was downed close to the sidelines it would be regularly moved back to ten yards (later fifteen) within the field. "Hashmarks" would now adorn the transverse stripes to facilitate measurement.

But there were other and more notable events in that same year. In 1933 James Conant succeeded Lowell as president of Harvard. Where his predecessor had vastly improved the social life of the undergraduates, Conant proposed to develop their intellectual potential, providing a more challenging curriculum and rewarding scholarly achievement, and thus no doubt adding to the hardships of coaching staffs. However, in the game that fall the Crimson scholars proved to be more than a match for the Bulldogs, giving Casey his one victory over the Blue.

This time he had a new adversary to face across the field, as Stevens, who had had enough of the job, yielded the reins to Reggie Root, a veteran of the '24 and '25 squads and so another disciple of Tad Jones. It may also be noted that in the summer of 1932 Malcolm Farmer had been appointed chairman of the board of athletic control at Yale; his title was the same as that of his predecessors, but he took a more active part in directing the destinies of Yale athletics; he was, in a way, the Yale Bingham. The new mentor faced a real problem. The material had fallen off in quality, and the Elis of '33 would end the season with a 4−4 record. It was the first Yale outfit since 1922 to lose both its big games. Entering the game in the Stadium the Bulldogs sported a 4−2 record, not bad under the circumstances but not truly impressive either. They could claim victories over Brown and Dartmouth—both by narrow margins—but they had been trounced by Army and nosed out by Georgia. The team did not lack gifted players. Lassiter was back this year as captain and Tommy Curtin was a good running mate. In the line, Clare Curtin and Jimmy De Angelis performed more than competently. But overall it was not a strong club. Nor were the Redshirts, who entered the fray with a 4−2−1 scorecard. Like Yale, the Crimson had lost to Army (and by a wider margin) and had had to settle for a tie with Dartmouth. Casey had very few veterans to work with; Wells at left half and Danny Dean (captain and son of the quarterback of Harvard's memorable delegation of 1890) at full were back and did yeoman service; in the line there was only the precocious Gundlach, still

a junior, at guard. Perhaps there wasn't much to choose between Crimson and Blue, but Yale went into the game a favorite. (Many of those new Stadium seats were unoccupied: attendance was down by 15,000 from the '31 total. The *Herald Tribune* (November 26) reported that of the 22,000 tickets reserved for the Yalies, 9,000 came back unsold.)

It wasn't long before Harvard proved how faulty odds-makers can be. Halfway through the first quarter Wells passed to Litman forty yards for a first down on the Blue six, and shortly after threw another pass to Haley in the end zone for the Cantabs' first touchdown. The second followed on an even more sensational toss from Wells covering over fifty yards to Teddy Crocker (destined to die in the service of his country a decade later). And lo, at halftime it was 13−0 Harvard, a score particularly galling to the Bulldogs, who, except for those thunderbolts, had done rather better than their adversaries in moving the ball. (The interval was enlivened by the release of a blue painted pig on the field.) Yale came out fighting in the second half and before the third period was over had pushed over her own touchdown, Lassiter making the score. Then came the crusher. On the ensuing kickoff, Fergie Locke, subbing for Wells, ran the ball back ninety yards down the sidelines, making the final score 19−6. (His run still stands as the Crimson record.) In effect, three electrical plays more than compensated for the superior statistics (eleven first downs to Harvard's four) of the plodding Elis, who seemed, through misplays and interceptions, determined to collaborate with doom.

Fergie Locke ran a kickoff back for a ninety-yard touchdown in Harvard's 19–6 victory in 1933, to date The Game's longest Crimson score on a kickoff return.

Raymond "Ducky" Pond, hero of the 1923 game, was named head coach at Yale in 1934, with "Greasy" Neale as chief assistant.

They were even more helpless the following week against the resurgent Tigers. Root, perhaps unfairly, was not given another chance. He went back to freshman coaching. Ducky Pond, the webfoot hero of the '23 game, was made head coach. And this time, rather exceptionally, his assistants were

Dick Harlow, the first Crimson head coach who was not a Harvard graduate, served from 1935 to 1947.

chosen for him by Farmer; of these, "Greasy" Neale was the chief of staff and, in effect, shared the head coaching with Pond. (For a few years Pond's staff included a young law student and former Michigan player named Gerald Ford.) An arrangement fraught with peril; but for a while it worked surprisingly well.

The years of the mid-thirties, '34–'36, were kind to Yale, even though, beginning with 1934, the schedule was made up almost entirely of adversaries of major stature (Cohane remarks that Malcolm Farmer, being a businessman, wanted to set up a program that would attract customers, whatever it might do to the win and loss column).[21] The cumulative record for those years was 18–7–0. Undoubtedly Pond and staff deserve a great deal of the credit for their successful handling of their novel and difficult assignment. But the coaches were happily blest with unusually good material; those years are the years of Kelley and Frank, both Heisman trophy winners. These paladins were flanked by a dozen or so stout comrades at various stages of the sequence, as we shall note in the course of our narrative. During the same span of years talent was scarcer on the banks of the Charles; although the Crimson did not play quite as challenging a schedule as the Elis, their cumulative record was a rather sad 9–14–1. Casey left at the end of the '34 season. Dick Harlow, an alumnus of Penn State, was appointed head coach—the first time the post had gone to a non-Harvard man. Harlow did not immediately improve on Casey's record. Surveying those central years of the decade, bright for the Blue and

The 1934 Elis upset heavily favored Princeton 7–0 and went
on to win The Game 14–0. *First row:* L. M. Kelley, H. J.
Wright, Jr., P. B. Grosscup, Jr., J. De Angelis, Captain F. C.
Curtin, M. L. Scott, Robert Train. *Second row:* S. L. Morton,
Jr., M. K. Whitehead, J. V. Roscoe, S. E. Fuller.

somber for her ancient rival, we may wonder that
Harvard did so well. There was never a Bulldog
runaway and all the games were hard fought.

In 1934, fresh from a spectacular win over highly favored Princeton (a match where the Elis had
called on no substitutes), Captain Curtin's "iron
men" ground out a 14–0 victory over the Crimson. A pass in the first quarter from Yale's cool
and competent quarterback Jerry Roscoe to Strat
Morton gave the Blue one touchdown, and in the
second period a Roscoe pass to the ubiquitous

Kelley (who was also magnificent on defense)
made the score 14–0. That was all the Bulldog
needed; the Cantabs, although they made a lot of
yardage and more first downs than Yale, could
not manage a score.[22]

It was in 1934, incidentally, that the circumfer-
ence of the official ball was reduced, making it a
smaller and lighter spheroid with pointed ends—
a better tool for the passing game and fatal to the
dropkick. (Albie Booth's game-winning effort
in 1931 was the last dropkick in the rivalry.) In

strictly Yale–Harvard terms the chronicler must note two other circumstances of Clare Curtin's happy weekend. First: a dastardly Cantabrigian act. On the eve of the encounter a party of marauders swept down from Charlesside, bore off Handsome Dan II, and, enticing the innocent canine by means of application of hamburger meat to the proper site, had him photographed licking the boots of the statue of John Harvard and then shamelessly published the picture on the front page of the *Crimson*. Handsome Dan was returned, to be sure, but sorely shaken and penitent. Segundo: taking part in the action on the field, though not a starter, was a young Eli end by the name of John R. Hersey, destined to hear not many years later the sweet chiming of a bell for Adano.

In 1935 the Blue margin was reduced. A number of the Iron Men had graduated, but Roscoe and Kelley were still on hand, as were Jack Wright at tackle and "Choo-choo" Train at end; Clint Frank made his first appearance and had immediate impact. Harlow, on the other hand, was off to a bad start. Captain-elect Haley was declared ineligible for unethically (though quite innocently) failing to disclose that he had received donations from admiring alumni; Shawn Kelley was elected to replace him. For this and other reasons Harlow's troops brought a mediocre scorecard to the annual rendezvous; three wins (over minor opponents) and four losses, while the Blue had a respectable 5–2 record.

Yet Captain Kim Whitehead's company did not have an easy time in the Stadium. The first half ended with no score and honors even. In the third

A modern-day descendant of Handsome Dan II.

period Kelley (who else?) took a touchdown pass from Roscoe, involuntarily relayed by a Harvard defender; the play covered fifty-four yards. In the first play of the final period, Fred Moseley, a Crimson substitute halfback, went over from the 2-yard line to even the score. It took a determined march by Yale, featuring a thirty-three-yard pass from Roscoe to Tommy Curtin, to set up a score by Al Hessberg and assure the Elis of a 14–7 victory. Curtin's catch was memorable; at that point in the action darkness had begun to close in and heavy snow was falling. It is hard to believe any receiver could see the ball, much less catch and hold it. And it is good to remember that Tommy had his moment of glory; he would die of leukemia a few months later.

In 1936 Franklin D. Roosevelt was reelected by a substantial margin. Taking office in March of 1933, after first shocking the country and the world by closing the banks and devaluating the dollar, he had gone on with a series of inventive and sometimes baffling servings of "alphabet soups" to provide employment and raise the spirits of the citizenry. True, economic recovery would—sadly—have to wait for the war but undeniably a corner had been turned; hope was abroad again. Perhaps the repeal of Prohibition in the fall of 1933 helped to create a new euphoria.

The year was a good one not only for New Dealers but for Blue football. With the irrepressible Kelley now captain the Bulldog fielded a strong and resourceful team, losing only to Dartmouth (for the first time in history) in a very close game.

Larry Kelley, captain of the Yale team in 1936, is the only player of the Big Three to have scored a touchdown against both rivals in each of three years of play.

Frank was coming into his own, and he had talented and robust associates. In Cambridge, on the other hand, the luckless Harlow had another attack of "Captain troubles"—he lost, in fact, not only Captain Dubiel but four other prospective starters through academic disability. (Perhaps Conant was to blame.) The Crimson came into the Bowl with a mediocre 3–3–1 scorecard, and Kelley and Company had every reason to look forward to a happy afternoon (a fine, sunny day it was, too).

The first half seemed to justify such an assumption. Yale scored twice: on a drive capped by a short run by Wilson and on a forty-two-yard pass, Frank to Kelley. But something happened between the halves. Perhaps Harlow was particularly inspirational. Or perhaps the Bulldogs forgot the old Confederate prescription: "When you have the other fellow down, stomp on him." For the second-half stomping was done by Harvard. Profiting by the skill and determination of Vernon Struck, using Harlow's hidden ball tactics to good advantage, the Crimson went seventy-nine yards for a score and came back to make a second touchdown on a pass. Unluckily for the Cantabs, Struck's kick for the extra point missed the post by a yard. It was Yale's win but by the closest of margins. The verdict was hardly fair to Harvard, which outgained the Elis by 317 to 265 yards. But as both parties had so often learned, the gridiron gods ignore statistics. Kelley could hang up his jersey with the knowledge that he was—and remains—the only wearer of the Blue (the only warrior of the Big Three, one might add) to score a

Vern Struck led the Crimson in their upset victory of 1937, when they defeated heavily favored Yale 13–6.

touchdown against both ancient rivals in each of three years of play. Harvard had the satisfaction of knowing she had outplayed a team *in posse* much stronger and more talented.

In 1937 James Rowland Angell laid down his burden of office and was succeeded in the presidency of Yale by Charles Seymour, '08. Angell had left a lasting mark on the architectonic face of Yale; he was the "buildingest" of all Yale presidents, and, perhaps more significantly, by the creation of the college plan also on the nature and color of undergraduate life. He left another precious legacy in the person of his wife, who would for another four decades play a prominent and gracious role in the social life of the Yale community. In choosing Seymour, the corporation followed the old practice, broken only by Angell's appointment, of nominating a president from the family circle. Given that premise, the choice of Seymour was inevitable. New Haven born, a graduate of Hillhouse High School, he was a historian of recognized stature and had for seven years served as provost. His role in the introduction of the college plan had been of major importance. He was himself master of Berkeley College at the time of his appointment. He was also, incidentally, a keen follower of Yale football—how could it be otherwise for one whose undergraduate years had been spent in the company of Hogan, Shevlin, Morse, and Biglow. Clint Frank's puissant company of the new president's inaugural year must have brought back happy memories.

To all Harvard and Yale alumni and even to a considerable segment of the followers of college football in general, all games between the venerable rivals are fascinating. Yet a great number are, when the book is closed and the record is not readily or frequently called to mind save by a few obsessed buffs, not especially memorable. In the long parade of victories, defeats, and ties, a score or so of engagements stand out—for the tension associated with their action, for the reversal of the odds by the underdog, or for sundry collateral circumstances. Of that stamp, certainly, was the battle of 1937, on which Harvard memories still fondly linger. The background and the outcome of that contest offer a kind of mirror image of the affair six years earlier. As the Crimson had in 1931, so this year the Blue could look back on a sequence of three victories and likewise was fielding an undefeated delegation, captained by an outstandingly gifted and valiant leader—yet doomed to defeat, even as the heroic Wood in 1931. In both cases, too, the battleground was the Stadium, which provided an appropriately classical setting for the enactment of the "hero's downfall" motif.

Assuredly Clint Frank's task force was a redoubtable one. In addition to the captain, "a team in himself," the Bulldog could call on such more than adequate backfield men as Chuck Ewart, the wing-footed Hessberg, and Colwell, a prodigious punter. In front of them there was a strong line, which included the experienced John Castle and Frank Gallagher (less than four years later he would die in battle) and the able junior Bill Platt. Perhaps not the stoutest line in Yale history but assuredly a tough one to crack. Coming into the Harvard game, only two touchdowns had been

Clint Frank, captain of Yale's 1937 team, was described as "the best football player since the war." He made fifty tackles in The Game that year in a losing effort.

scored on Frank's men, and they had no losses on their record (they had managed a tie with a strong Dartmouth outfit with less than a minute to play).

Harvard, too, presented a better team than she could have boasted of for some time. Struck was back, now captain and more deft than ever; Frank Foley, Torbie Macdonald, and "Chief" Boston filled out a very capable backfield, and up front a group of experienced juniors anchored by the veteran Kevorkian at tackle were gradually fashioned, as the season moved on, into a strong and aggressive company. Harvard's record was not as good as Yale's; she had lost a squeaker to Army and been manhandled by Dartmouth. But by this time the Yale coaching staff was well aware that Harlow-trained teams got better as the November games came along; even so the Blue went into the game a favorite—though the death of Handsome Dan II a few days before the combat could surely portend no good. The Stadium was crammed and even though the Depression lingered, scalpers got $50.00 for a pair of tickets.[23] Among the spectators was Herbert Hoover, who, according to the *New York Times* (November 21), rooted for Harvard, saying there is no neutral in football. (But the *Herald Tribune* of the same date reports that the ex-president didn't cheer—"at least not so you could hear him.")

It was a cold, dark day in the Stadium, and snow fell as the game moved into the second half. It was apparent very early in the combat that Harvard had come to win; the first quarter was even, but in the second period the Crimson's third thrust was crowned by a touchdown, scored on an eighteen-yard pass from Foley to Daughters.

Already the heroics of Frank on defense were attracting admiration; without his nose for the ball and hard tackling, Harvard would have gone in for the interval with a much larger lead. In the third quarter, though now injured and hobbling, he led a sixty-seven-yard Eli drive to tie the score. But Harvard was gaining in strength with every moment; Foley swept the Blue end for a nine-yard run and the tie-breaking touchdown. Yale made one more Herculean effort but could get no further than the enemy's 25-yard line. After which it was simply a matter of how many Red sorties Frank could contain; his teammates were now exhausted. Harvard nearly got another score when a receiver dropped a pass on the goal line—but thirteen points were all she needed. The game was over and the underdog Crimson had beaten what

Clint Frank, attempting to round Harvard's left end, is about to be tackled by Vern Struck in this shot from the 1937 game.

was one of Yale's best teams of the decade. But the image of the embattled and dauntless Frank, fighting to the end in a lost cause, would linger in the memory of many spectators long after the score was forgotten. Stanley Woodward in the *Herald Tribune* (November 21) wrote that "Clint Frank is the best football player we have seen since the war. He was the best defensive player on the field. He made fifty tackles. He kept the Yale team fighting to the finish. He drove and he fought and ultimately, for the first time this season, he lost."

Journalistic accounts of the last moments of the game have a Wagnerian flavor. Even before the final whistle blew, hordes of exultant young Cantabs poured into the field, like the overflowing Rhine waters in the final scene of the Ring cycle, tearing down the goalposts, firing pistols, and illuminating the dusk with red flares, while, according to Woodward, "the Yale adherents stood bareheaded in the stands, singing [appropriately] the New Haven version of Die Wacht am Rhein." Frank was "helped sobbing to the dressing room, exhausted and broken-hearted." Undeniably there was epic grandeur in Frank's performance that day. Yet, as another journalist observes, it would have been "an injustice if Yale had rallied to tie or win, for Harvard played the kind of football that deserved victory."[24] It was a happy day for Harlow and his charges, particularly for Captain Struck, so unkindly used by fortune the previous year.

After the downfall of Frank and his (almost) invincible company the *virtus* of the Blue withered.

In the four years from 1938 through 1941, the Bulldogs did not once have a winning season: the total for those dark years was 7–24–1, easily the unhappiest span in the Yale gridiron record. Perhaps the Blue was in arcane metaphysical harmony with the tone of those times, which were charged with alarms, mischance, and dire forebodings of things to come. Nineteen thirty-eight brought the ill-advised pilgrimage of Chamberlain to Godesberg as well as a hurricane which devastated New England; 1939 saw the beginnings of World War II; in 1940 France fell and late in 1941 Pearl Harbor brought America into the war. Years of anxiety and anguish, which aptly describes the state of mind of Yale aficionados—most of the time, anyway. Harvard, serene through change and through storm, as her sons loyally proclaim, did not seem affected by such matters. The Crimson teams of these years were not perhaps "great" teams but they were very good ones, and under the patient guidance of the ornithologist Harlow they consistently maintained their habit, disconcerting to the Elis, of getting better as the season wore on; invariably—well, not quite invariably—reaching their peak for their climax game. During these four years Harvard had no losing season; twice the Crimson broke even and twice her achievement was on the positive side. On the record the Cantabs should have won all four of the duelli; they took three and why they didn't make a clean sweep comes under the heading of Moleskin Mysteries.

In 1938—the year of Thornton Wilder's *Our Town* and those enchanting melodies "Jeepers

Creepers'' and ''Flat-Foot Floogie with a Floy Floy''—the fifty-seventh encounter took place on a drizzly afternoon in the Bowl (the rain got heavier as the game went on). It brought Captain Green's Harvard delegation (at that point 3−4−0) into a bruising affair with Captain Platt's Bulldogs (2−5−0 when the coin was tossed; the latter's finest hour had been a very close defeat by a strong Michigan team). For three quarters of the soggy day the Blue looked good, leading Harvard in all the statistical categories yet never getting close enough to the Red goal to be really dangerous. In the final quarter a short march ended in a frustrated field goal attempt. Whereupon Harvard, led by Torbie Macdonald, who was brilliant in both running and pass receiving, marched eighty yards for a score, Macdonald going over on a pass from Foley, who had engineered the downfall of Frank a year earlier. A grim struggle it was, but Harvard had more staying power and more tactical imagination.

The match in Cambridge in 1939 puzzles the historian. Harvard came on the field with a record a little better than that of 1938—4−3−0; it was a squad that was somewhat green perhaps, but Torbie Macdonald, now captain, was always a runner to be reckoned with, and the sophomore Endicott ''Chub'' Peabody (later to be governor of Massachusetts) had already distinguished himself. Yale at that point had won only two games while losing four and tieing one (with Brown). Not a very robust delegation; the outstanding back was Hovey Seymour (later a war casualty), who excelled more in kicking than in running. Captain

Endicott ''Chub'' Peabody, Harvard's standout left guard from 1939 to 1941, became governor of Massachusetts.

In the fourth quarter of the 1939 game, Harvard's Joe Gardella fumbled deep in Crimson territory, setting up Yale's third touchdown. Gardella redeemed himself grandly the following year, scoring twice in Harvard's win. (BELOW) On second down following Harvard's fumble, Yale's Hovey Seymour darted over right end into the end zone, making the final score Yale 20—Harvard 7.

Bill Stack at center was a more than competent forward; as it happened, however, he did not play in The Game because of injuries. Comparative scores with Army, Dartmouth, and Princeton gave Harvard a slight edge, and the Crimson was the favorite with the bettors. More often than not when Harvard goes in a favorite she wins: I cannot readily think of many exceptions to this rule. But in '39 the Bulldogs beat the odds and won— and rather easily, running up twenty points before Macdonald, in the fourth quarter, finally proved· his mettle and put Harvard at last on the scoreboard. As usual in such reversals, the vanquished collaborated with the victor. A Crimson fumble in her own territory put the Blue in position for the only score in the first half, on a pass Burr to Bartholemy. In the third quarter another Harvard misplay enabled the Elis to send Seymour over on a line buck, and in the last quarter Seymour again scored after the Cantabs had obligingly bobbled the ball on their own 6-yard line. Harvard's drive, when it came, was a good one but it yielded too little and came too late; the game went to Yale 20–7. It was a game that somehow exemplified "upness." I spoke years later with a Yale halfback who told me that after the first play he knew the Bulldogs would win. "But," I said, "on the first play Harvard went seven yards through the line." "Yes," he said, "I remember. But all the same, I had that feeling. I think we all did." Obviously the pigskin has a fourth dimension.

Any embarrassment the Cantabrigians may have felt for their indifferent performance in '39 was assuredly wiped away by the result of the 1940

contest. Harvard won 28–0, a blithe, easy victory that took the Crimson followers back to the glory days of the great P.D. It was a strong Harvard delegation, this time mostly veterans and including in its roster the doughty Joe Gardella at fullback (and captain), the fleet-footed Franny Lee, with Chub Peabody back and flanked by sturdy classmates in the line, such as Lauren MacKinney, Gardner, and Burgy Ayres. (The class of '42 had beaten the Elis in freshman year and waxed in strength with maturity.) Facing Yale, the Cantabs had behind them a unique (for Harvard) scorecard; they had lost only two games, one to Tom Harmon's powerful Wolverines and one (by the margin of 7–6) to Dartmouth. These losses were balanced by two wins, the opener against Amherst and a 14–0 defeat of Brown. Three other engagements had ended in ties. As usual, the Crimson performance improved as the season progressed. As for Yale, the win–loss record was the poorest in Blue annals— six losses as against one win (to be sure, a good one, at Dartmouth's expense). The Blue squad had been beaten by Brown, Cornell, and Virginia and positively humiliated by Penn (which played a tie with Harvard). And, characteristic of Yale's luckless years, for the second time running the Eli captain, Hal Whiteman (future dean of freshmen at Yale and president of Sweet Briar College), was unable to take the field. Things did not look good for the sons of Eli. A crowd of 47,000 was on hand (some complained that $3.85 was a lot to charge for a ticket; times had changed since 1928); it included such famous personages as Herbert Hoover (again!), Henry L. Stimson, the brother of Mme

Chiang Kai-shek, and the old Blue demigods, Pa Corbin and Pudge Heffelfinger.

The battle began with a surprising sixty-six-yard Bulldog drive, with good work by Fred Harrison and Chuck Willoughby, which carried the ball to the Harvard 14-yard line, as close as the Blue would ever get to a score. Striking back in the second quarter, MacKinney's forty-one-yard run brought the ball to the Yale twenty-eight, from where McNicol passed to Gardella for the first Crimson score. The half ended 7–0 Harvard, but in the second half the Cantabs really got to work. Gardella scored in the third period after another beautiful McNicol pass, this time to Kaufman. In the last period the most exciting play of the game took place when Franny Lee, back to receive a Yale punt, very skillfully faked a handoff to a colleague who came rushing by him and, with the Eli defenders (and most of the spectators) following the wrong man, cantered seventy-eight yards, untouched, for the third touchdown. Harvard's final score came when Charley Spreyer carried the ball twenty-six yards in six successive rushes over the Blue goal line. Spreyer, like Lee, was born and schooled in New Haven: "Too bad they didn't know that we have a seat of culture here too," said Pond.[25] But if the Harvard offense was brilliant perhaps their defense was even better. After Yale's first-quarter sortie the Blue was simply not in the game. In the remaining three quarters the Bulldogs could manage only two first downs—and both deep in their own territory. It was one of Harvard's finest victories, and although the score was lopsided it was a good game to

Franny Lee cantered seventy-eight yards for Harvard's third touchdown in the Crimson's lopsided 28–0 victory in 1940.

BARNES

McNICOL

GARDINER

PFISTER

AYRES

LEE

PEABODY

SEYMOUR (Y)

MILLER

MACKINNEY

T. HEIDEN

SUMMERS

A fortnight after the 1941 game came Pearl Harbor.

By the fall of '42 the war effort was in full swing. Unlike the case in World War I, the country was deliberate and disciplined in the lengthy process of girding for battle; young men were encouraged to finish their college careers if they had but a short time to go; commitments were deferred and undergraduate bodies did not simply melt away. The services brought a variety of training programs to the campuses, making it possible for undergraduates to prepare for their military duties and concurrently to work for their B.A.s. Abrogation of Christmas and summer vacations speeded up the process. Even so, both in Cambridge and New Haven turnouts for the varsity were lean when the squads began their spring practice. Harvard may have been a little worse off than Yale; even without the intervention of the war the Crimson would have suffered severely by the graduation of the class of '42, and the circumstances made it difficult to replace them. Yale had a few more veterans, but the Bulldog's new coach found less than two full teams ready to undergo the preliminary spring time calisthenics. Odell's appointment had come about in a novel fashion. After the debacle of '41, on the suggestion of Ted Blair, '24, President Seymour had created a graduate advisory committee with power to appoint a successor to the luckless Nelson; after considerable deliberation the appointment was given to Odell, sponsored zealously by Bob Hall, '30, a respected member of the committee. Odell, a graduate of the University of Pittsburgh, was only thirty-one when

he took on his responsibilities; he had served as assistant under Jock Sutherland and Dick Harlow, however, and his knowledge of the game and ability to impart it were already recognized. His record at Yale would turn out to be a very good one indeed. He made a good start in '42, bringing his pride of Bulldogs into the Bowl with four wins and three losses—the first time since Clint Frank's year that victories outnumbered defeats on the Blue register. Harvard had not done so well, having lost five and tied one of eight games played. Still, she had licked Princeton.

To those whose memories went back far enough, the '42 game seemed almost a replay of the 1916 encounter. As in 1916, so in 1942 the engagement came just before a break in the series occasioned by the interruption of the normal rhythm of a world at peace. So, too, the game came after a period of Crimson dominance and a time of sad frustration for the Blue. And, as in 1916, the Bulldogs at last broke the sequence of defeat and went off to war with the satisfaction of having finally triumphed over their ancient rivals. (There was one notable difference, of which one may be sure both athletic associations were well aware: in 1916, with war in the offing but not yet declared, 78,000 spectators found their way to the Bowl; in 1942, with the guns already blazing and gas rationing and travel limitations the order of the day, the crowd was a meager 26,000, the smallest to witness the traditional match in all of the twentieth century.)

The action on the field was curiously reminiscent, too, of the pattern of the earlier generation.

(LEFT, TOP) The 1941 Harvard team, captained by Franny Lee (holding ball).

(LEFT) Yale's Hovey Seymour attempting to penetrate the solid Harvard defense in the 1941 game. Harvard won 14–0.

Yale head coach Howie Odell (*right*) with Spence Moseley,
captain of the 1942 delegation.

Harvard scored first on a field goal by Bob Fisher, Jr., son of the erstwhile coach of the Cantabs, and the Crimson held grimly onto the lead until late in the game. As in 1916, a brilliant Harvard run (this time a punt return by Donald Richards for seventy yards and a touchdown) was nullified by a penalty. As in 1916, the Blue managed to come from behind (this time on a spectacular pass, Hugh Knowlton to Tim Hoopes, covering nearly seventy yards, which turned out to be the game-winning score). But this time, unlike 1916, Harvard, with less than five minutes left after Hoopes's touchdown, got down to work and went on a sustained drive some ninety yards to the Yale 7-yard line. She might have won on the last play of the game when a pass was dropped on the Yale goal line. The final minutes of the game were in fact more exciting than anything that took place on the same field in 1916, but the result was the same; Yale by 7–3—and Harvard with the justifiable feeling that the gods had not been entirely impartial. A spirited affair it was, and Yale's captain Spence Moseley—weighing 173 pounds, light for a center—was an inspirational leader and a Bulldog of the old stamp in his magnificent defensive performance.

In this year of the *risorgimento* of Bulldog power the Football Y Association was founded, with Clint Black, '17, Ted Blair, '24, and Bob Hall, '30, playing leading roles in its launching. The membership is made up primarily of Blue veterans; its purpose is to give moral and, where appropriate, financial support to the Blue pigskin cause. The association sponsors the *Football Y News*, edited by the director of sports information, which provides a weekly survey, with commentary, of the progress of the teams through the season. In membership and purpose the Harvard Stadium Club, dating from 1971, is similar to the Yale Association. But Harvard has also had for years—since 1886—the Varsity Club, covering all sports and hence with wider membership. The sports review *News and Views* has been sponsored by the club since 1958; its scope is not limited to football but in the gridiron season it fulfills the same function as the Yale *Football Y News*.

The ancient rivals did not meet in 1943 or 1944. With Harlow off to the wars, Harvard fielded only informal teams; Yale played regular schedules, giving Odell a chance to improve his techniques.

Under the captaincy of Macaulay Whiting the Blue even had an unbeaten (though once tied) record in 1944. But the conditions of the war years made it impossible to train and build up teams in the conventional way. The players were in large part in service, flitting from one airbase or training camp or military school to another at unpredictable intervals. It was rare that a coach could maintain the same lineup for more than two weeks. Some rather unusual situations came about: Harvard's Wayne Johnson, who had almost won the game for Harvard in 1942 (it was he who dropped O'Donnell's last-minute pass), found himself wearing a Blue uniform in 1944. He is the only football player in history to have won both his H and his Y.

We may take advantage of the interval to summarize the achievements of the Crimson and the Blue during the twenty years covered by this chapter. Yale, if she had by no means reasserted her ancient supremacy, yet had again taken the lead, with eleven victories, eight defeats, and two ties. In the point totals, thanks to the massacre of 1940, the Crimson has a slight edge, 164–161. Shutouts are even at six apiece. And some of the most spirited performers in the annals of the game—including Barry Wood and Franny Lee for Harvard and Albie Booth and Clint Frank for Yale—had played unforgettable parts in the drama. A sparkling twenty years' worth.

SAILING TO IVYLAND,
WITH OLLIE AT THE WHEEL

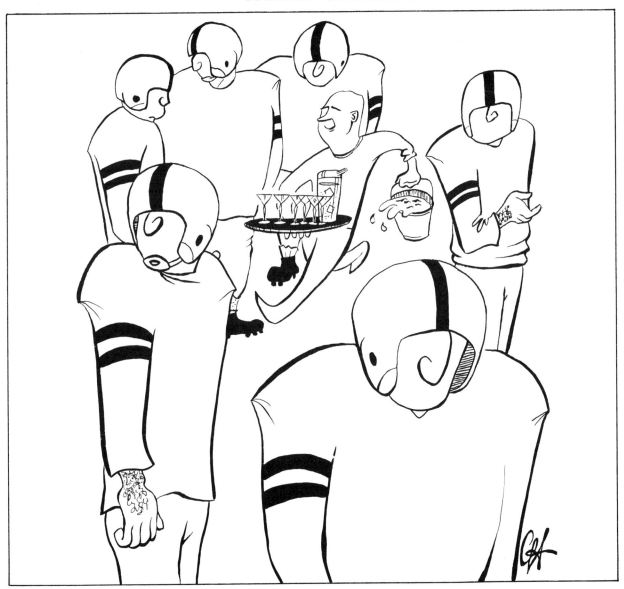

Cover of *The Yale Record*, October 1954. Cartoon by Christopher Harris.

So many innovations, so many changes in life style separate the world following World War II from the one of the thirties that it is difficult to take them all in, much less grasp their implications; indeed, sociologists are still grappling with the subject. Coming back from the four quarters of the embattled globe, the GIs found themselves suddenly in a world of television, thruways, air conditioning, miracle drugs, zippers, and the pizza, the latter destined to all but dislodge Wimpy's hamburger. All of a sudden everyone was rich, everyone had his own car, and if he didn't have his own house it was simply because housing could not keep up with the new affluence. Everyone could go to college, too, thanks to the GI bill, and lodging the hordes of students that poured in was a major problem for all institutions of higher learning— and still remains one, even though the Quonset hut era is no longer with us. For Yale and Harvard the influx signified the end of the gracious living in the colleges and houses; dormitories were forced to accommodate twice the numbers they were built for, and the elegant dining halls became cafeterias, with self-service and trays replacing the civilized table service of old. The delicate matter of admissions, no great problem in the thirties, became—and remains—an annual ordeal for applicants and administrators.

In the province of the pigskin it was likewise a new world. The pros, flexing their muscles in the thirties, took on with the next decade a dominant role in the sport. Had this dominance, as in the case of professional baseball years before, simply cut down attendance at college games, it probably would have been a healthy thing for the campus version of the sport. But it had other unhappy effects. For a great number of institutions it had—and has—a corruptive effect. Many schools have allowed their athletic departments to become training schools for the pros, with the seductions of athletic scholarships, tailored curricula, and sundry perquisites to lure muscular youth to their campuses. The competition for gridiron primacy at any cost began before the pros came of age, but the pros have done little to cool it off. They have to get their recruits somewhere and there are no minor leagues in professional football. From the point of view of many college administrators a stadium weekly crammed to the brim is a marvelous source of income—and publicity, of a sort. In the older, eastern institutions the dangers of glorifying muscle over mind had long been recognized; well before the pros were heard of, presidents like Eliot had been fearful that the dedication to the pigskin might be a distraction from the central purpose of an educational institution. And sporadically such administrators had taken appropriate measures, as we have had occasion to note.

As early as the mid-thirties the concept of an Ivy League, as it would later be called, had come into being.[1] At that time Harvard had been reluctant to surrender her autonomy, but by 1945 she too was ready. So it was that on the first of October of that year the presidents of the eight institutions "formed their first Ivy League agreement. The initial agreement pertained only to football. The presidents announced their purpose: to con-tinue intercollegiate football in such a way as to maintain the value of the game while keeping it in fitting proportion to the main purpose of academic life. Essential to this 1945 agreement was the intention that students engaged in intercollegiate athletics should not receive any financial aid except that provided by the GI Bill, by their families, from 'employment at normal wages' or from scholarships awarded through the regular official channels."[2] The first law of the Ivy League is, therefore, there shall be no athletic scholarships. Other regulations would follow and the Ivy code would be extended to cover other sports. Eleven years would ensue before the round robin schedule would make the league truly operational, but in essence its beginning may be dated from the presidents' compact of 1945.

There were novelties too on the field of battle. In 1941 unlimited substitution was legalized; this made it possible to train offensive platoons and defensive platoons, and in the course of time "special teams" for kickoffs, reception thereof, passing and rushing units, and the like. Players, in the words of an old Notre Dame veteran, learned to play not football but positions. Platooning was repealed in 1953 but came back a decade later and seems now destined to remain—for better or for worse.

Another new feature of the postwar game was a return to the old T formation; this, too, was in keeping with the example of the pros, who found it especially effective for the passing game—more crowd pleasing than the running game. The single wing gradually disappeared from college football;

Lloyd Jordan at Harvard used it, but only Princeton clung to it—and employed it with spectacular success—through the fifties. The T gives the quarterback a preeminence formerly enjoyed by a versatile tailback; he has become the sine qua non of the offense. A running back, to be sure, is still a valuable asset, though he rarely does anything but run; and all kickers are now full-blown specialists, coming in only when needed. Needless to say, a punter cannot be expected to placekick, and a placekicker seldom knows how to punt. But let us return to our chronicle.

After V-J Day in August of 1945 a steady and ever-growing trickle of veteran pigskin-chasers flowed back to their prewar campuses—or in some instances to campuses where they had undergone their military education. As the fortunes of war—or peace—would have it, the trickle turned out to be stronger and more revitalizing in New Haven than in Cambridge. The Bulldog got off to a slow start, losing to Holy Cross and Columbia, but by midseason he had picked up a number of unusually capable recruits: Fritz Barzilauskas, Bill Schuler, Marty Dwyer, and "Bolt" Elwell in the line and Art Fitzgerald, who had been a member of the Notre Dame squad before the war, in the backfield. Their talents, added to those of a few veterans of the 1944 season, notably Paul Walter, Dick Hollingshead, and John Prchlik, made the Blue a formidable machine by the time the first of December (latest date in the annals of The Game) rolled around, marking the resumption of the ancient rivalry. Harvard had not fared so well; most of the season they had depended on

the previous year's informals, calling on a mere seventeen-year-old freshman, Charley Roche, to lead them at quarterback. Yet, when the teams met, it was Harvard that had a slightly better record, with five wins against two losses; Yale's tally was five and three. The Harvard historian Will Cloney remarks that the Crimson had set up a light schedule—and paid the price. Still, Harvard had beaten Brown, a club that had been too much for the Bulldog.

In any event, the game turned out to be an easy win for Yale. It was a day of biting cold, and the field was damp as a result of snowfall on the preceding night. Such conditions did not trouble Art Fitzgerald, who passed brilliantly (as did his teammate Drakos) and ran authoritatively, scoring three of Yale's four touchdowns, thus tieing the record, set in 1884, for points scored against the Crimson. The first quarter was scoreless; Fitzgerald scored twice in the second and once more in the third period. Kirk made Yale's last touchdown, and a safety was added to the Blue count when the young Roche was trapped behind his goal line. In spite of the cold, 35,000 turned out for the spectacle. Happy days were here again—especially for the sons of Eli.

In 1946 Bob Kiphuth, Yale's genial and highly successful swimming coach, replaced Ogden Miller as director of athletics. He came in at a propitious time. The massive influx of discharged servicemen had bolstered the football forces of both Harvard and Yale. But for two years the latter made better use of her endowment than the Crimson did. It is possible that this was simply

Art Fitzgerald ran for three touchdowns in the 1945 game despite bad weather.

because the Bulldogs were a little more gifted than the Cantabs. But a sad and unhappy situation on the banks of the Charles had a lot to do with the results of the engagements of 1946. Will Cloney's narrative is revealing. "Dick [Harlow]," he writes,

had a new staff and new talent. But for the first time in his Harvard career he was faced with a squad of adults who already knew how to play football. Several men returned from the prewar days, including Captain Cleo O'Donnell [son of the famous Holy Cross coach] and a few came from the informal 1944 and 1945 teams, but the rest were G.I.s . . . transfers for the most part, and many of them had played excellent service football elsewhere. Without any question Harvard had more true talent than at any time in its long football history. . . . They were older, tougher and bigger than most players Dick had had in the past years.

This was a real problem, for Harlow could not adjust himself to the new breed, nor could they adjust themselves to his Harvard attitude. Most were combat veterans, many had been wounded and some had been prisoners of war. They wanted no part of the old "rah rah" spirit. The resulting estrangement between Harlow and his team was something which only a few of Dick's old boys could cope with, and even they found it difficult.[3]

To add to his troubles, Harlow's health was poor, which may well explain his sometimes querulous attitude toward his charges.

For some reason, principally because of the temperamental difference between the rival coaches (and possibly because Odell was younger than Harlow and closer to his pupils), no such tension existed in New Haven. And if Harvard could rejoice in her talent, so could Yale. There were plenty of veterans left from the sturdy 1945 team, and they were substantially reinforced by the addition of some really outstanding athletes, such as, for example, Levi Jackson (a freshman, returning from service, and originally a graduate of New Haven's Hillhouse High) and Ferdie Nadherny, whose style of running is indicated by his soubriquet, "the Bull," originally bestowed upon him for semiliterary reasons. He too was a freshman (that year the rule prohibiting freshmen from playing on varsity teams was suspended, as it had been in 1945; Gannon, Harvard's brilliant halfback, was also a freshman). Directed by "Tex" Furse, also back from the wars, and abetted by a veteran line, the Blue task force of '46 was a formidable company. A game was lost to Columbia, and the duel with Cornell ended in a tie; otherwise, the Bulldogs were all-victorious, and by mid-November were probably as redoubtable a lot as any Yale club in the twentieth century.

However, in spite of the tensions noted by Cloney, Harvard had a good season, too. In fact, on the eve of the final game, they had a record, deceptively perhaps, better than Yale, with only one loss (to Rutgers) and no ties—7–1 as compared to Yale's 6–1–1. Captain Cleo O'Donnell and Chief Gannon were first-class backs, and up front Fiorentino, Drvaric, and Wally Flynn were outstanding. For all that, percipient bettors made Yale a slight favorite.

The lineups for that afternoon's exercise suggest a digression on yet another feature of the rivalry in the years after World War II. In addition to Barzilauskas and Prchlik, whom we have had occasion to mention, the Bulldog roster includes such surnames as Cipolaro, DeNezzo, Jablonski, Montano, Nadherny, Pivcevich—and Jackson, the Elis' freshman sensation, was a black. In addition to Fiorentino and Drvaric, Harvard fielded Moravec at fullback. Such a variety of surnames is a token of the expansion of the ethnic range of Blue and Crimson warriors between the wars, destined to assume even greater proportions as the years pass. It must be said that although the Bulldog contingent of '46 provides an impressive illustration of this trend, it is Harvard who leads in this democratic expansion. Jackson was the first black to wear the blue; Harvard had already had two. So too for the Latin contribution; Jimmy DeAngelis in 1932 provided the first Ausonian cognomen on the Yale roster, but Harvard had fielded the deft Guarnaccia as early as 1926, and Gardella and Forte had captained Harvard teams in the forties. (Yale would not have a Latin leader until Fortunato in 1953.) Harvard could also show a pair of Armenians in the forties; Yale has yet to have one. However, for both squads names outside the Anglo-Saxon-Irish-Germanic orbit were relatively rare before the end of World War II; from that time on things would be different: blacks, Italians, Slavs, Greeks, and Lithuanians would all be joyously welcomed to the lineup.

The 1946 Yale team, captained by R. M. Hollingshead III.

Perhaps it should be added that this enrichment does not signify a new enlightenment on the part of the athletic administration in either Cambridge or New Haven, who would, from the beginning, have been happy to field any competent youth regardless of bloodlines; it is rather an indication of the assimilation of new ethnic groups into American society.

The combat that afternoon in '46 was noteworthy for two reasons. First of all, for the weather conditions. It was bitterly cold, and a wind of almost gale force blew from the south end of the

Stadium. And, segundo, because it provided an instance of a rare reversal of fortunes (unique up to that time). Harvard, in the first quarter, had the wind—as well as a bright, cold sun—at her back and lost no time in taking advantage of her situation. Very early in the quarter the Crimson launched a fifty-five-yard drive, culminating in Gannon's eight-yard run for a score. Shortly after, wind, sun, and Redshirts proving too much for the dazzled Elis, Gannon went to work again, passing to Wally Flynn for Harvard's second score. At this point the quarter ended and the teams changed sides—not a moment too soon for Odell, who had watched the first period's action with consternation.

In addition to facing wind and sun, the Blue had also during the first quarter been dealing with a hitherto unseen offensive formation; Harlow on this day unfolded for the first time a kind of "triple wing." To compound the Blue confusion, the Eli spotter, high in the stands, relaying his diagnosis of the new Crimson tactical pattern found the telephone line out of order, a casualty of the semityphoon. Most of the period had passed before a Bulldog courier could bring to the coaching staff on the bench the information necessary for readjustment.[4] Odell's plight, as he waited impatiently for the time for changing field and even more so for a lagging intelligence report, was dire indeed.

Practically everyone in the stands (57,000 had come out that day, the largest Stadium crowd since the Wood–Booth duel of '31—the Harvard AA had to return $100,000 to late applicants)[5]

knew that it was axiomatic in the rivalry that the first team to score a touchdown always wins. Since the beginning of things in 1875 there had never been an exception to this rule. It is possible, however, that this sacred law, known to all the spectators, may not have been known to Yale's freshmen. A long punt runback by Jackson, a few rushes by him and the Bull, and finally a pass, Jackson to Roderick, and the Blue was on the scoreboard. The next march, covering fifty yards, ended in a Jackson fifteen-yard sprint and a Nadherny carry for the score. Yale had missed the first conversion attempt, and the half ended 14–13 Harvard, with old-timers of the Blue stamp still uneasy about the record of history. Coming back to the third period, with the wind still at their backs, the Elis added two more touchdowns, one on a Furse to Roderick pass, one by Nadherny, who covered in two rushes the last twenty-eight yards of a Bulldog drive. In the fourth quarter the gale was again on Harvard's side, but it was not as strong as earlier in the afternoon. Nor was the Crimson; she simply lacked the resilience to come back after two quarters of severe pounding: 27–14 and the old saw was dead. As Cloney sums up: "Few Harvard teams have ever put together a better fifteen minutes of football. Unfortunately, however, there were forty-five minutes left."[6]

The following year most of Yale's great line was gone, though the veterans "Cottie" Davison (now captain, cousin of Harvard's Endicott Peabody, '42) and Prchlik survived; but the backfield remained intact. There was enough power left to punish the spoilers of '46, Columbia and Cornell,

Ferdie "the Bull" Nadherny (14) scoring Yale's second touchdown late in the second quarter of the 1946 game. Yale won 27–14.

but the puissance of '47 was not comparable to that of '46; the final record was 6–3, with losses to Wisconsin, Brown, and Princeton. It was clear to Odell at the end of the season that the glory days were running out. He decided to quit while he was ahead, and, although Yale did her best to keep him, he departed for the University of Washington. Coincidentally, the same year saw the end of Harlow's term at Harvard, but his departure was reluctant and a little sad. The underlying friction between mentor and charges that

had been a part (though unpublicized) of the '46 season worsened in '47, when, to quote Cloney again, "the total breakdown in communications finally took place."[7] After a humiliating loss to Virginia, disaffection grew and further defeats followed. The Crimson, although the material was still excellent (Drvaric and Wally Flynn were able forwards, and the class of '50 supplied a talented group, Moffie and Freedman in the backfield coming up to support Gannon), didn't do as well as it might have. The Cantabs came to New Haven with

Endicott Davison, captain of Yale's 1947 team.

yards to give the Elis the lead again, and early in the last period Furse plunged for his third touchdown; and Billy Booe kicked a twenty-yard field goal to round out the Bulldog total of 31 points. A last-minute march by Harvard put Moffie over the goal line for a consolation score, making the final count 31–21. Harvard historians note (and quite rightly) that the Blue got a few breaks from the officials, but no one argues that Yale did not have the stronger team. From a spectator's point of view it was certainly one of the better matches. A few weeks later Harlow was asked for his resignation. It was a sad moment. He had served Harvard thirteen years; he left with a record of 45–39–7; if he did not have a winning record against Yale he had nevertheless scored some notable triumphs over the Blue. As for Odell, his final score was 35–15–2, war years and all, and 4–0 against Harvard; he is unique among Yale coaches of this century in that his Bulldogs never lost to the Crimson. (He knew when to leave.)

To replace Harlow, Bingham called on Art Valpey, Crisler's assistant at Michigan. At Yale, under the aegis of Bob Kiphuth, Herman Hickman, graduate of Tennessee and assistant Army coach, took command of the Blue armed forces.

The two seasons in which Valpey and Hickman faced each other across the field were certainly not among the most glorious for either Blue or Crimson. During those years, although Yale held up better than Harvard, neither squad had the manpower to achieve greatness. Throughout those years, in fact, it was the Tiger who was consistently supreme in the ancient triumvirate; the sin-

a 4–3 record and underdogs (though not by much) in the betting. Seventy thousand came to see them, a crowd of pre-Depression dimensions. The game turned out to be a thriller. A Harvard fumble gave Yale her chance in the first quarter, and Furse plunged over for the Elis' first touchdown. A sensational pass Jim Kenary to Hal Moffie tied the score. Yale came back with a second touchdown by Furse in the second period, but the fleet-footed Lazzaro scampered sixteen yards to crown a Harvard match and again even the count. The third period was all Yale; Jackson went sixteen

Art Valpey assumed the head coaching duties at Harvard in 1948.

gle wing, employed with mastery by Caldwell, could and did mix power and deception to a degree that no T formation in those years could hope to match. Beginning in 1947 Princeton enjoyed a run of six successive victories over the Blue, the longest—up to that time—in the series. She had a seven-year sequence against Harvard. Probably for a few years at least the favorite enemy for the Bulldog was the apparently insatiable Tiger. And while all good Harvard men continued to look upon the Yale game as The Game, the Yale coaches, if not the players, would probably have

settled for one good drubbing of Old Nassau.

The neophyte coaches in 1948 were very different in temperament and personality. Valpey was a quiet, orderly theoretician of the game; he kept his squads well disciplined and brought in some new tactical maneuvers, sharply timed spinner plays of his own devising which might have worked well if he had better ball handlers and stronger linemen. He was not, however, really at home in the Harvard atmosphere and seems to have remained something of an alien throughout his tenure. Hickman, on the other hand, was possessed of an engaging "outsize" personality which matched his bulk. He was witty (it was he who defined his task as keeping the alumni sullen but not mutinous), and he soon became something of a personality in New Haven; before his coaching stint was finished he had set up a television program of his own, which probably distracted him somewhat from the business of building of the undernourished Bulldog in his charge. Indeed, by the end of his tenure his undeniable charm had ceased to appeal to some of his players, with whom he failed to establish rapport. One of his more prominent charges once told me that although he had been two years a starter Hickman could never remember his name. A more serious handicap perhaps was that Hickman had made his reputation as a defensive coach, and his tactical designs on offense often gave the impression of improvisation.

In any event the first round went to Valpey. In 1948 (it was the year Harry Truman was elected, suggesting that anything could happen and cheer-

On the first play from scrimmage in the 1948 game, Harvard's Hal Moffie (11) ran eighty yards untouched to score the Crimson's first touchdown. Here he crosses his own twenty at the start of his run.

ing all underdogs) the teams met in Cambridge with similar records, Yale's (4–4–0) slightly better than Harvard's (3–4–0). Both had lost to Dartmouth and, of course, to Princeton. Yale had had one moment of glory, a victory over Wisconsin (and in Madison, too, but in fact it was not a distinguished bevy of Badgers that year) and looked

perhaps a little more likely to win. After all, Jackson and Nadherny were still a pair to be reckoned with, and Furse was back at quarterback. Captain Bill Conway, Vic Frank, Bob Jablonski, and Setear were competent forwards. Not the '46 machine— but still quite ready for Harvard, one would have said. But the picture changed completely and immediately after the kickoff. On the first play from scrimmage, Hal Moffie took the ball on a reverse and ran eighty yards untouched into the Blue end zone. The kick was missed but the play fired up the Crimson, and even though a Yale counter-attack, led by the old reliable pair, Levi and the Bull, gave the Blue a second-period score and a 7–6 lead at the half, Bulldog confidence had been shaken. It was shaken further in the third period by a stout Crimson defense that turned back two long marches—one on the 2-yard line. From which spot, with Moffie and Roche making some fine runs and Gannon passing in the clutch, Harvard went out in front, Captain Ken O'Donnell going over for the score. And shortly after, start-ing from midfield, the Cantabs scored again; this time Roche carried the ball over on a beautiful twenty-nine-yard run off tackle. Valpey's strata-gems never looked better.

Things were quite different in 1949 (the year *South Pacific* premiered in New Haven's Shubert Theatre). Once more neither team was outstand-ing; Harvard particularly seemed to have run out of energy, coming to the Bowl with a 1–7 record, the worst in sixty-seven years. The team had suf-fered injuries in the course of the season and co-ordination was ragged, but even at full strength it was hardly a great Crimson team. Yale could not claim greatness either (3–4–0 on the eve of the game, with losses to practically all the major rivals, including, of course, Princeton), but its manpower was superior to Harvard's. Jackson was captain this year.[8] Hickman, with his usual wag-gery, had described his not too sturdy line as "the

Levi Jackson, the first black to wear the blue, captained Yale's 1949 team.

Lloyd Jordan became Harvard's head coach in 1950. He is shown here with Carroll Lowenstein, captain of the 1951 team.

seven dwarfs," to which Jackson had added, "I guess that makes me Snow White." The pounding of four years of combat had slowed Jackson up a little, but he was his old self on that sunny day in the Bowl, getting the Bulldog off to a good start with a thirty-four-yard touchdown run. He scored again on a pass from Tisdale, and while the game was still young Nadherny capped a fifty-seven-yard drive for a touchdown. It looked as if a rout might be in the making, but the feeble and outmanned Cantabs, led by Howard Houston, a formidable tackle, refused to be demoralized.

Crimson honor was saved by a fourth-quarter touchdown scored by Noonan after an impressive eighty-three-yard march; however, it came too late to make much difference: the final score was 29–6. It was a fine farewell for Jackson and Nadherny, but one could hardly call it one of the better games of the rivalry.

Hickman had evened the count with Valpey, and the latter, although he had a year left on his contract, did not stay for the rubber. The season had been dismal, and the prospects for the future were not encouraging. Valpey went off to try his hand at the young University of Connecticut; his place was taken by Lloyd Jordan, who had had a long and successful career at Amherst. He would serve Harvard for seven years and win some notable victories for the Crimson—but his first year, as it turned out, showed, on the record, no improvement over Valpey's performance. Once more the Redshirts managed only one victory, a squeaker with Brown, and absorbed some horrendous beatings, notably the one administered by Princeton, 63–26. Carroll Lowenstein, a very good back, labored hard in an unhappy campaign; Captain Isenberg and Wylie were valiant on defense but overall it was simply not a strong club. Yale, on the other hand, seemed somewhat improved; Senay, Spears, and Ryan came to fill the gaps left by the more renowned graduates of the '49 squad; in Captain Brad Quackenbush and the sophomore Ed Woodsum the Bulldogs had a fine pair of offensive ends. (Platooning had come in, not quite in full force because the manpower was lacking, but generally speaking offense and defense were autonomous groups. Hickman said he would have preferred a three-platoon system, one for defense, one for offense, and one to go to classes.) Chuck Masters and Pete Radulovic were outstanding up forward. The early games went well, but by the time the tryst in Cambridge was to be met, the Bulldogs had lost to Dartmouth, Cornell, and, inevitably, Princeton. (The Tigers were undefeated that year and ran up a combined total of 110 points against their ancient brothers of the Big Three.) A loss to the helpless Cantabs would have seemed impossible.

But somehow the encounter on Soldiers Field was no walkaway for the Blue. Indeed, it looked for a while as if Harvard might pull out with a tie. For this surprising state of affairs there were three reasons. First of all, the weather. As in 1946 the day was drizzly and cold, with a fifty-five-mile-per-hour wind roaring through the Stadium. It was a wind that was perhaps worse for Harvard than for Yale since the former depended chiefly on passing; even so it was a kind of leveling element. Second, for once the Harvard team presented a truly sturdy defense. And most of all because Lowenstein, at less than 150 pounds, put on a magnificent show in both punting and passing in the teeth of a quasi hurricane. Yale dominated the game for three quarters but somehow could never quite break the Crimson line; finally in the fourth period Senay, in three consecutive rushes, went fifty-seven yards for the touchdown. Lowenstein brought Harvard back, and his pass to Worden gave the Crimson her score. Unfortunately for the Cantab cause a caprice of the wind deprived Harvard of the point after touchdown. And fate dealt the final blow when, following the Yale kickoff, the ball was fumbled on the 17-yard line; Yale recovered and Captain Bob Spears went over to make the final score 14—6. It speaks well for the percipience of Harvard judgment in such matters that Lowenstein has his place among the elite of the Varsity Club's Hall of Fame, along with Barry Wood and his ilk. He well deserves it.

The early years of the sixth decade witnessed a changing of the guard in the high command of both Yale and Harvard. Seymour retired from the Yale presidency in 1950. His term of office had been characterized by "consolidation" rather than innovation, but under his aegis Yale's Dean W. C. DeVane had set up a number of pedagogical devices, similar to those of Conant in their intent to provide the more gifted students an opportunity to exercise their talents. Seymour had also been hospitable to the specialized training schools that were part of the war effort, and in the postwar years Yale had achieved a new eminence in such fields as linguistics and area studies. Seymour's successor, A. Whitney Griswold, 1929, was something of a dark horse; many of the Yale family had expected Dean DeVane to be chosen. Like Seymour, Griswold was a historian of prominence, but he had had little administrative experience, save as a director of one of the wartime programs. Witty, free-spirited, youthful, not to say boyish in appearance, he seemed to many to be not too "serious." But the Corporation's intuition was sound; Whit, never losing his charm, turned out to be a forceful leader, a dedicated champion

of the liberal arts, and an eloquent spokesman for his cause. He found a willing and able ally in Nathan Pusey, Harvard, 1928, who succeeded Conant in 1953. Unlike Griswold, Pusey came to his new office with a background of administrative experience; he was president of Lawrence College at the time his alma mater called him back. A scholar of English literature, he shared Griswold's views on the values of the humanities. The presidents were in accord, too, on their resolve to keep football a sport. They worked in successful collaboration toward the implementation of the Ivy League.

In New Haven, concurrently with the retirement of President Seymour a changing of the guard also took place in the province of the pigskin. Bob Kiphuth stepped down, handing the reins to Robert A. Hall, erstwhile quarterback of the 1929 team. He would remain in office only three years (but long enough to appoint Jordan Olivar as head coach), resigning in 1953. For a year Clare Mendell took over his old job (he had served as chairman of the board of control from 1919 to 1925) while the search for a permanent director was pursued. In 1954, DeLaney Kiphuth, son of Bob and a veteran of the grim campaign of 1940, was appointed to the post; he would serve for twenty-two years—a record term in office. But we are running ahead of our story.

Nineteen fifty-one was a year of some uneasiness in both Crimson and Blue camps. In spite of the valiant effort of Lowenstein's lost battalion, Harvard followers were not reassured. Spirits had been low in Cambridge since the disastrous

1–9 season of '49; some alumni felt that Harvard should imitate Chicago and give up football; others were thinking of "beefing up" the program in unspecified but probably dubious ways. In the spring of 1950 the provost gave a press conference in which he affirmed that Harvard had no intention of giving up the game. But a year later, "the ferment behind the scenes was still bubbling," Cloney writes,

and embattled Bill Bingham finally resigned on February 8, 1951. Three months later the post was virtually thrust upon Thomas D. Bolles, the Washington alumnus who had coached the varsity crew to eleven victories in twelve years over Yale. Quiet, unassuming, thoughtful and cooperative, he guided Harvard sports constructively toward new strength and achievement through twelve years. The path was still rocky, however, and when the hard economic facts dictated the dismantling of the steel stands in the summer of 1951, it was if the walls of Jericho had come tumbling down again.[9]

The demolition did in fact seem a kind of vote of no confidence; if so it was misplaced; there have probably been years since in which Harvard would have been happy to have room for a larger public. Concurrently with the appointment of Bolles, the Harvard athletic association became the department of athletics, budgeted, like other departments, by the faculty of arts and sciences.

Yet, in spite of such *Sturm und Drang* the Crimson fielded a tolerably good team in 1951— indeed, save for unusually cruel blows of fortune, it could have been a great team. But Lowenstein, now captain, was called up for service in Korea, Wylie, his replacement both as passer and captain, broke his arm in midseason, and Clasby, a sophomore of outstanding ability, was hounded by injuries. So the Red *condottieri* invaded New Haven with a 3–5 record, their proudest moment being a victory over Army. As it happened, things had not been going too well under the elms either, and Hickman, possibly distracted from his coaching by the demands of his television program, made the poorest showing of his tenure; the Bulldogs had lost five and tied one (with Navy) out of their eight games. For the fifth successive year they had bowed to the Tigers. There was talent on the squad, notably the Molloy–Woodsum passing combination, but it had not yet been brought out.

Odds-makers could pick no favorite for the engagement in the Bowl, and as it happened they were quite right. The final score was 21–21. If the quality of football, particularly as displayed by the defensive troops, was not particularly distinguished, the game was yet a stirring one to watch. Yale started bravely, running up fourteen points and bringing back memories of high-scoring times of old. (Let's see: 14 times 4, my, that would show those Cantabs!) But very near the end of the half, Clasby (quite healthy now, thank you) passed to Crowley to put the Crimson on the board. In the third period the red-shirted John Ederer ran eighty-three yards on a fake handoff, and the score was tied. Naturally a bit shaken by the turn of events the Bulldogs started perhaps too hastily to try to get back their lead; at which point Frederick

Ed Molloy (18) passed for 205 yards in Yale's 41−14 shellacking of Harvard in 1952.

Drill of Harvard intercepted a pass and carried it into the end zone. This was in the fourth quarter with time running out. The Blue did not panic this time and, largely on Molloy's good arm, went sixty-five yards to tie the score. Cloney reports that Hickman, in the closing minutes of the game, said to Ed Molloy, "You start pitching and I'll start walking" and then walked off toward the exit from the Bowl"[10]—and from Yale football, as it happened. The game was, I think, unusual among ties in that it left both sides reasonably content. Normally a so-called tie signifies a loss to one of the combatants; Harvard followers felt cheated by the tie of 1899, and Yale fanciers positively disgusted if not shamed by the result in 1925. (They would have an even more bitter pill to swallow in a certain year to come.) But in 1951 both sides had the satisfaction of having "come from behind," which always makes a tie feel like a victory. If there had to be disappointment it would surely have been felt in the Yale stands; the Blue outgained the Crimson by one hundred yards and was statistically top dog. But one can't be unhappy about a team that rallies in the last moment and pulls the game out of the fire.

The following year was one of change and new direction both for the nation and for the armed forces of the Blue. Dwight David Eisenhower, having served as president of Columbia just long enough to persuade Lou Little not to take the coaching job at Yale, was elected president of the United States, handily defeating Adlai Stevenson, the darling of intellectuals and academics. Ike could act vigorously when the need arose: he got us out of Korea, as he had promised he would, and he sent Marines to Lebanon and soldiers to Arkansas when the occasion seemed to require their presence. But his preference was to reign rather than to rule; he left the running of the country to his subordinates, coming in from the golf course only in emergencies. His style suited the voters, who were probably tired of activist presidents, and indeed, during his administration (which lasted eight years; he was easily re-elected) there was a comfortable feeling of security throughout the land, somewhat reminiscent of the Coolidge era. Campus life, too, took on something of the lighthearted insouciance of the twenties; it may have been even better, with no Prohibition to keep you from having a beer with your pizza, no obligation to wear neckties (though at Yale white shoes were de rigueur), and many happy hours tossing Frisbees around the courtyards.

As for Yale football, in the events that took place that summer the hand of a benevolent providence may readily be seen. In August Herman Hickman resigned. It was his own choice (though some alumni may have moved from the sullen to the mutinous in view of his record, 16–17–2, and four maulings by the Tiger). No hard feelings—but his timing was deplored; Yale had only a few weeks in which to find a replacement.

Time was too short to look far afield; the appointment would of necessity have to go to someone known to be immediately available (which for practical purposes meant someone on the staff) and with adequate skills and demonstrated experience. As chance would have it, Jordan Olivar had recently accepted an appointment as assistant coach; he had had long experience at Villanova and Loyola of California; the latter school had, however, given up football the preceding year. So Olivar was clearly indicated. But yet another circumstance worked for the fulfillment of the providential design. Olivar had made it a condition of his employment that he should serve only during the first term since he had an insurance business in California which took a lot of his time. For an assistant coach such an arrangement was acceptable; for a head coach it would have been, until 1952, a serious obstacle. But it happened that in that year the Ivy League presidents, reaffirming their compact, decreed in the interests of keeping the sport in its place that henceforth postseason games and spring practice periods would be banned. The latter restriction was unpalatable to the coaches, most of whom even today would like to see it rescinded. But it made it possible for Olivar to accept—and for Yale to acquire—an outstanding coach.

"Ollie" had many assets. He was very shrewd in choosing his assistants and within a short time had assembled an exceptionally able staff. He was an original and inventive tactician; he was, in fact, a man of unusual intellectual scope; it is not too much to say he was potentially a scholar. He had great inner self-assurance and his confidence infected his players. It must be said, too, that at least with regard to the 1952 season he was fortunate in his material, the best to wear the Blue in some years. Molloy and Woodsum were in full

strength, Jerry Jones, hitherto not especially noteworthy, turned out to be a fine running back, and up front, particularly on defense, there was considerable strength: Joe Mitinger, Pete Radulovic, and the linebacker Joe Fortunato, among others. From an almost catastrophic losing year in '51 the tide turned to give Yale a handsome 7–2 record, with tables at last turned on such tormentors as Cornell, Dartmouth, and Columbia. Princeton once more had a little too much power—actually it was speed—for the Bulldog to handle, but he made a brave effort even in that game. And he was ready for Harvard.

The Crimson, however, was also improving. The '52 team was the first since 1946 to finish with a winning record, and Clasby and John Culver gave the John Nichols outfit an offensive power that had to be respected. For the first time in six years Dartmouth was defeated. Subsequent losses to Princeton (but then almost everyone lost to Princeton) and Brown gave the Crimson backers second thoughts; even so, hopes were high when the team took the field against favored Yale. But the Bulldog had, if anything, been invigorated rather than depressed by his brush with the Tiger and proceeded to enjoy his best day of the season. Jones ran beautifully, scoring on a thirty-seven-yard scamper, the Molloy to Woodsum pattern was unbeatable (the latter made three touchdowns), and although the defense had some trouble with Crimson passing it cut off the Cantabs' running with ease. Yale ran up twenty points with a few minutes left in the first half. Harvard finally counterattacked and Clasby scored with two minutes to go. Whereupon the Bulldog almost effortlessly got another before the half ended. Two more Blue touchdowns were added in the second half, the final one followed by a bit of waggishness on the part of the Elis. Instead of kicking the extra point Molloy passed to an obscure and unknown "no. 99" from the Yale bench, who somehow managed to hold on to the ball, making the final score 41—14, and so forever carved his name (Charlie Yeager) in the annals. Yale followers

Yale head coach Jordan Olivar, appointed in 1952, flanked by the dangerous and productive passing combination of quarterback Ed Molloy *(right)* and end Ed Woodsum.

thought it was a fine gesture; some sensitive Harvard aficionados took it as an insult, or at best an example of New Haven boorishness, but most were simply amused. (There is no evidence that it worried Clasby much; he was probably content to "wait till next year.") It was a match that Yale, on the record, had every right to win, but the Crimson, one must admit, should have done a little better.

Beginning with the fall of 1953 the substitution rule was stiffened and platooning was no longer feasible. For a decade teams would be composed of players who "went both ways." In some cases the new—or revived—pattern caused drastic revisions in the lineup; not all "specialists" could acquire at once the versatility which had now become necessary. Yale's Joe Fortunato, captain this year, for example, had to learn how to be a blocking back as well as a linebacker. Coaches, too, as of old, had to make hard choices between the needs of offense and defense. Neither Jordan nor Olivar found the transition difficult; both had had experience with the traditional deployment of forces. In New Haven hopes were high for a good season. Woodsum would be missed, of course, as well as a few sturdy linemen of the class of '53, but Jones and Molloy were still on hand, each an already well-proved weapon in the Bulldog arsenal. But as it happened, Molloy suffered a wrist injury in a preseason scrimmage with Boston University and never was in condition to play more than a few minutes all season; Jones—perhaps because he could not adjust to the new one-platoon system—seemed to have lost some of his

virtus. The line remained strong (Thorne Shugart and Dick Polich were a first-class pair of guards); losses by graduation were offset by the arrival of sophomore stalwarts, of whom the most impressive was the monster-size Phil Tarasovic. Largely on the strength of its defense the Blue survived its first three games, then, after two ties with Cornell and Colgate, completely disintegrated in the confrontation with the Big Green. Yet, in one of the most stirring engagements in Big Three history, the underdog Elis, using three quarterbacks, supercharged tackling, and probably prayer, finally broke the six-year reign of the Tiger.

Meanwhile, Harvard, with Clasby at the helm, was enjoying her best season since 1946. Two one-touchdown losses to Princeton and Columbia marred her record; otherwise she had a string of five victories (including a fine triumph over Dartmouth) to boast of. Clasby, now captain, and John Culver had served the Crimson cause with distinction, abetted by a young center, Jeff Coolidge, Jr., a name to strike terror in all New Haven hearts (at least those old enough to remember 1914). Culver and Coolidge would have prominent careers: the former became a United States Senator, representing Iowa, the latter a distinguished director of a number of scientific societies. Both would serve on Harvard's Board of Overseers. Lowenstein was back, too, to break even more records with his passing. This year The Game looked like a toss-up; in the event it was a rather easy win for Harvard; not that the margin of victory (13–0) was especially wide, but because the Crimson had the Bulldog completely muzzled from whistle to

Harvard's 1953 varsity, captained by Dick Clasby (holding ball).

whistle. In fairness to the luckless canines it must be said that the engagement in Tigertown had drained them emotionally and also depleted their available strength. Of the three quarterbacks who had helped in the taming of the Tiger not one was in really good condition a week later, and four starters at Princeton did not appear at all in the Blue lineup. This game seemed to offer one example in support of the old Yale complaint that the Bulldog is at a unique disadvantage in facing his Big Three foes on successive Saturdays. And in 1953 both of his old rivals fairly fielded strong teams. This year the Elis simply couldn't manage two successive weeks of "upness." They made only one thrust, which ended in the neighborhood of the Crimson 10-yard line (this was in the third period); Harvard then marched back over eighty yards on a muddy field for her second touchdown, Culver carrying the last thirty-four on a very handsome run. Dexter Lewis had scored Harvard's first touchdown in the first period on a fine canter of twenty-two yards. In between, all Yale could do was to keep the score down, and in fact Harvard did not seriously threaten to get out of hand. Making all allowances for the Bulldog's handicaps, it was still a fine triumph for Harvard, "the most rugged and accomplished Harvard team of recent years,"[11] and for Clasby, highly esteemed by the Blue camp. Clasby was not only a record-breaking runner and skilled in every department of the game, he was also a leader and blessed with a warm personality and a happy temperament. Cloney tells the anecdote of

Clasby's running some eighty yards to score against Dartmouth, only to have the play called back because of a teammate's infraction of the rules. "How did you feel about it," he was asked. "Well," said Clasby, no whit crestfallen, "they can take away the yardage but not the thrill."[12] He played the game for the joy of it. The '53 game drew a crowd of 65,000; among the spectators were Dean Acheson, Robert Stevens, secretary of the army, and the new Handsome Dan IX, who took the result philosophically.

The Crimson task force of '54 is paradoxical to contemplate. With Clasby, Culver, and Co. gone, Jordan had to rebuild from scratch; he found some fine sophomores in Matt Botsford, Tony Gianelly,

Dick Clasby (40), shown here slicing through the Yale line in the 1953 game, was a record-breaking runner who was skilled in every department of the game.

(RIGHT) Harvard cheerleader, 1954.

and Ted Metropoulos, whose efforts gave the Crimson another winning season (4−3−1), though not quite such a good one as that of '53. Captain Tim Anderson's brigade lost to Dartmouth (always hard for both Bulldogs and Cantabs to take) and suffered a tie with Brown; good but not great. Yet, when it was all over, lo, they had brought Harvard the first Big Three championship since Franny Lee's prewar combination in 1941. The victory over Yale was well earned, too. In the Bowl the season started off well, as it had in '53; indeed, Thorne Shugart's team ran through six games without a defeat. The line was sturdy, featuring Shugart himself, Bill Lovejoy (son of Yale's captain in '24), the puissant Tarasovic, and a pair of exceptional ends in Paul Lopata and Vernon Loucks. In the backfield a flashy pair of sophomores, Al Ward and Denny McGill, were already making their mark. The Bulldog mistake in 1954 was not an operational error on the field but a grave gaffe on the part of the schedule makers, who had set up—"for old times' sake"—a match with Army. Over the years since World War II, Army had moved out of the Ivy class. Financially the game was a great success: the Bowl crowd ran to over 69,000, but the predictable slaughter left the Bulldog with shaken morale, to say nothing of physical bruises and contusions. He never recovered. He made a brave try against Princeton, coming from behind to tie the score but losing in the end; he should have been in shape for Harvard the following week but that one got away from him, too. This time it may not have been entirely his fault; Harvard won her victory by tenaciously hanging on till she saw her chance and employing a very clever tactical maneuver to profit by that chance. It was a game that gained in interest as it progressed. Yale seemed the better outfit in the first half, but the only Blue score came on a safety when Botsford was trapped behind the goal line after taking a deep Yale punt. In the third quarter the tempo became more *accelerato*. Yale scored again after a fifty-five-yard march, and with a nine-point lead, all that was needed to assure a Blue victory was a quarter and a half of the old Bulldog tenacity. Unhappily for Yale the Bulldog—perhaps still feeling the effects of the Army game and certainly not at full strength—did not have it. He was a little unlucky, too; Harvard made a fine march, was stopped at the five, whereupon a bad bounce on a kick gave them a fresh start inside the Yale thirty. On the first play of the last quarter Harvard was on the board. There was no serious counterattack from Yale, and halfway through the final period Harvard staged an eighty-yard march to win. The final play of that march proved that the Crimson was as smart in the clutch as Yale was unlucky. On that play Frank White, a substitute for Cowles, who was injured on the kickoff, took the ball on a reverse and passed to Bob Cochran; White had not thrown a pass all season and the Elis were totally surprised. It was not, in fact, a very good pass, but Cochran had time and room in which to juggle the ball half a dozen times, while spectators suffered agonies of suspense, before finally getting a firm clutch and scurrying untouched the last twenty yards for a score—12–9—a well-earned win. On

the statistics Yale had the better team but committed a few costly fumbles—and when the chips were down, the Blue was outsmarted. It was, incidentally, the first time that a Harvard team ever defied the Law of The Game, mentioned above, which decrees that the first side to score a touchdown wins. The *New York Times* noted that although the game was hard fought there were remarkably few penalties[13]—none against Harvard and a mere ten yards' worth against the Blue.

Although the last three encounters of Yale's '54 season had been somewhat disappointing to Blue followers, the personnel of that delegation was unusually competent and all the better after a year's seasoning, especially when reinforced by talented recruits from the sophomore class: Howie Phelan and Jack Embersits in the line and Dick Winterbauer, coming up to aid Loucks at quarterback. Ackerman, the formidable fullback of '54, was injured, but his place was taken by Gene Coker, another gift of the fruitful class of 1957. In the annals of the Blue, '55 has a special place; the aggressive band of Captain Tarasovic emerged victorious after a grim battle with Army in the Bowl, not only avenging the humiliation suffered in '54 but testifying to the quality of Ivy League football. As in '54 the price was paid, when the following week the Tiger unexpectedly came out on top in New Jersey, but it was generally admitted that Yale had bad luck that day, beginning with the loss of Winterbauer, victim not of the Army but of appendicitis. No soldier-caused disability was apparent in the contest with Harvard.

Harvard's Bob Cochran juggling the pass that he eventually
caught and carried into the end zone for the Crimson's clinch-
ing touchdown in 1954.

The Crimson had plenty of talent that year, too, with Botsford and Joslin reaching their peak, abetted by Gianelly and the blond sophomore Stahura. Yet the Harvard strength was not deep and the record for the season (3–4–1) hardly impressive: it must be noted, however, that the Cantabs did succeed (where the Bulldog had failed) in caging the Tiger. A good game was expected that November, and 56,000 came to the Bowl to see it, including Connecticut's governor Abe Ribicoff and New York's mayor Robert Wagner, who cheered for the Blue, and Senator John F. Kennedy, who must have been pleased by his young brother's performance.

The combat was fought out in a swirling snowstorm. Harvard had a stroke of bad luck at the start, when Gianelly was injured on the opening kickoff: his presence would assuredly have made a difference. Yale was also lucky in the breaks of the game, with a recovered fumble to set up a touchdown and a very timely pass interception that led to another score. Even so, and with all due allowances, the Bulldog deserved to win. Coker was an imposing figure that day, charging through the swirling snow like some Norse warrior of old; his yardage surpassed that of the entire Crimson backfield. And, when the occasion demanded it, the Bulldogs were smart, too. After a scoreless first quarter, a pass from one Loucks to another (not related save by the bond of comradeship) gave the Blue a touchdown; in the third quarter, Coker leading the charge, the Elis got their second touchdown and a comfortable 14–0 yield. But Harvard struck back, and on a spectacu-lar catch over the goal line made by Ted Kennedy cut down the Blue margin. In the last quarter came the aforementioned interception—by Denny McGill, whom no one ever caught once he got started. Considering the weather it was a fine game, well played and interesting to watch (if you weren't bothered by an occasional toe dropping off). Harvard's passing in the snow was remarkable, nine completions out of eighteen tries. Yale, with Winterbauer still unavailable, used four quarterbacks; they all looked good. Harvard inventiveness came to the fore again in the interval, when three slippery and squealing piglets were released on the field just as the Yale band began their ritualistic march. Harvard also had a journalistic triumph: the *Crimson* had its special edition out well under an hour after the game ended—and on sale outside the Bowl, thus "producing red faces among the editors of the *Yale Daily News*."[14]

In 1956 the Ivy League became truly operational. The "round robin" schedule was inaugurated, each team playing every one of its fellow members; as John McCallum puts it: "for the first time in history the Ivy League was no longer just a way of life—it was a football reality."[15] The schedule was not totally constrictive; since most of the members played a nine-game season two spots were left for local traditional rivals (UConn for Yale, New Hampshire for Dartmouth, and the like) or such long-established "cousins" as Colgate or Lehigh or for an occasional intersectional club or a service team. As we have noted, the creation of the league was a kind of affirmation on

The 1956 Yale delegation, first champions of the Ivy League,
scored 246 points (the highest since '03) in compiling a 9−1
record. *Front row, l. to r.*: Vern Loucks, Bob Mobley, Ted
Frembgen, Pete Fritzsche, Steve Ackerman, Captain Mike
Owseichik, Dennis McGill, Al Ward, Dean Loucks, Bide
Thomas, Paul Lopata. *Second row*: Charles Peet, Ted Loud,
Don Griffith, Bob Corry, Bill Ryland, Ralph Wisz, Henry Burt,
Bob Sigal, Jack Embersits, Oliver Henkel, Dick Winterbauer.
Third row: Howard Phelan, John Pendexter, Jim Kinney, Mike
Grean, Art Lubke, Dick Skewes, Pete Wight, Herbert Hallas,
Stuart Horwitz, Jim Hemphill, Gene Coker, Rolf Sandvoss
(manager). *Fourth row*: Bill MacLean, Mike Cavallon, Paul
Lynch, Tom Lorch, Alex Kroll, Bill West, Charles Griffith,
Lauren Williams, Ed Moore, Kent Bales, Nolan Baird.

the part of the member institutions that good football can coexist with the educational purpose for which colleges were founded. Many of the austere restrictions (banning of athletic scholarships and postseason games, limited practice periods, exclusion of freshmen from varsity competition, etc.) had already been imposed by the various members of the league; banding together, they could give each other strength, and, it was hoped— perhaps a little wistfully—encourage others to follow the example. If meanwhile the restrictions handicapped the members of the league when they took on non-league opponents, well, the principle justified the sacrifice. For the old Big Three, at least, the sacrifice has been real and a little painful; it is unlikely that ever again in our time will any of their names appear on journalistic roll calls of the "best ten" or even the "best thirty" teams of the nation. Sentimentally one may grieve for this state of affairs. But the alternative of laissez-faire and predictable competition with institutions of a different philosophy would have been intolerable and impossible for the members of the Ivy League. And in fact the attraction of the games played within the league has not waned; in contrast to the system fifty years ago, when only a few contests were fought out between peers, nowadays every Saturday pits one worthy foe against another, new rivalries develop, and every week brings an exciting challenge. And meanwhile, uniquely perhaps, on the campuses of the league, the players on weekdays actually go to classes, as a Navy coach recently remarked. One of the rules of league play prescribes

Denny McGill rushed for 116 yards in Yale's 42–14 victory in 1956.

that visiting teams must wear white; hosts play in their colors. This certainly makes it easier to follow the action, but some sentimental old-timers still regret the passing of the old days when honest blue and ardent crimson clashed in November afternoons.

The inauguration of the league schedule happily—for Blue aficionados—coincided with Olivar's most successful squad. One would almost suspect he had planned it. The Yalies of 1956, captained by the redoubtable Owseichik, were an awesome lot. The class of '57, which had been the mainstay of the two previous years, came fully into its own; no more talented and spirited backfield ever wore the Blue than the company of Dean Loucks, Al Ward, Denny McGill, and Ackerman, ably assisted by Winterbauer, the junior but well-tried signal caller. In the line the veterans Paul Lopata, Vern Loucks, Owseichik, Bide Thomas, and Fritzsche were formidable, and the juniors Cavallon and Baird (ends) and Jack Embersits and Howie Phelan (guards) no less so. Two rugged sophomores had come up to lend a hand: Charley Griffith (a New Haven high school recruit) and the massive Kroll, who started at center (and would conclude his career as captain of an undefeated Rutgers squad a few years later). Only a loss to Colgate marred '56's record. The point total of the team was 246, the highest since Rafferty's raiders of '03, who incidentally not only played three more games but took on teams that were far below their class. The '56 outfit still holds the record total of points (84) scored against the Blue's Big Three rivals—not outdone even by the high-scoring clubs of the Dowling era.

Harvard had good men too in the year of Ike's second election. Cloney comments: "This was an interesting team to watch with talented backs like Botsford, Simourian, Gianelly and Joslin sparking an attack that produced at least two touchdowns in every game. Unfortunately, Captain Metropoulos was the only line veteran on hand, and newcomers like Robert T. "Shag" Shaunessy, '59 were not quite ready."[16] And indeed, the Crimson had no difficulty in scoring but a regrettable lack of success in holding down the opposition. They had two wins against five losses as they prepared to meet the invading Elis.

The odds were simply too much for Harvard, although to their credit it must be noted that the Cantabs did get their ration of two touchdowns. Largely on Louck's passing, Yale got off to a 7–0 start in the first period. Midway in the second quarter there took place a truly spectacular sequence of *beaux gestes*. McGill broke out of the scrimmage and went seventy-seven yards to score. Four plays after the Yale kickoff Joslin ran a brilliant thirty-nine yards for Harvard's first touchdown. And then, when Harvard kicked off, Ward ran the ball back seventy-eight yards to swell the Bulldog total. But the Redshirts couldn't hold the pace; the half ended 28–7, Winterbauer picking up where Loucks left off, and, though the Crimson never gave up (she probably played her best game of the season), Yale, using many subs, went on to outscore her foe in the second half; the final score was 42–14. Perhaps it was poetically appropriate that the first champion of the new league should be Yale, who had played a major role in the development of the sport. It seemed so to Yale followers, anyway.

Though documentation is sparse and uncertain, it was probably during the period covered in this chapter that tailgating began to assume the prominence it now enjoys. Pregame refreshments, to be sure, are nothing new; there are occasional references to them in accounts of the early games, and one cannot imagine tally-hos trotting up Fifth Avenue to the Polo Grounds without some stock of bottles and baskets. But today the practice is more extensive than ever before. The term *tailgating* in this sense is relatively new. One cannot have tailgating without tailgates and while the horse-drawn wagons of old had them, one may reasonably surmise that the term derives from the tailgates of the station wagons which captured the fancy of suburbanites in the years after World War II. (To the best of my knowledge the locution was unknown in the twenties.) At a guess we may

date the modest beginnings of the present style from the mid-thirties, gaining increasingly large numbers of devotees in the succeeding decades. Certainly by the sixties the term and the practice had won recognition and acceptance. Today tailgating can be a Lucullan exercise; it is no longer a martini and a sandwich but a lavish production with substantial courses and not infrequently served on folding tables, complete with napery and glittering silver. Some zealous practitioners have been known to miss the first quarter of the game, reluctant to abandon the conviviality of the overture. "[The game] is a little anticlimactic after the tailgate," according to one of the cultists.[17]

Tailgating, an old practice, has now assumed Lucullan proportions.

Football spectators, 1958.

Nineteen fifty-seven was a notable year in Harvard gridiron annals, as it marked the appointment of John Yovicsin as head coach of the Crimson. Will Cloney comments on the circumstances of the appointment:

Lloyd Jordan had come to Harvard when football was in its weakest phase. A gentleman of character and strength he gave back to the teams he coached a great measure of their lost confidence. But by the autumn of 1956 there was a question whether some of those boys who had come to Harvard looking for an education first, plus an opportunity to play football, were getting the same level of fine instruction from their football coach that they were entitled to, and received, in a Harvard lecture hall. The Faculty Committee voted to pick up the remainder of Jordan's contract, and find a successor who might make the most, as a teacher, of the new material.[1]

Elsewhere Cloney recognizes, as does the Harvard committee, the value of Jordan's contribution—although his record was not impressive (24−31−3 overall and 2−4−1 against Yale) he had kept the fires burning through the Crimson's "most perilous period," when manpower was lacking and a cloud of apathy shrouded the Stadium.

The choice of Yovicsin, as Cloney notes, came as a surprise. He had compiled an excellent record at Gettysburg College, and he was warmly recommended by Dick Harlow. But he was not as yet a prominent figure in the field. His personality made a happy impression on the community, which was anxiously awaiting his coming. "Gracious, articulate and earnest," Cloney writes, "this handsome young man was readily accepted, though with a tinge of sympathy from those who knew what a formidable task he faced." Cloney specifies: "During the opening week all the centers on the squad gave up football, as did three starters from the previous year. Most of his end squad was injured in the first week."[2] Yovicsin did have, however, a few talented veterans to work with: Tom Hooper, now captain, Walt Stahura, "Shag" Shaunessy, for example, and a very promising, though "temperamentally explosive" sophomore, Chet Boulris. In spite of his preseason woes Yovicsin put together a respectable team. His squad came to the Bowl with a 3—4 record; the wins included one over Penn (which beat Yale that year), and the losses included a bruising battle with Princeton (which further decimated the Crimson starters; for the Yale game no experienced quarterback was available).

Things had gone much better in New Haven, although Olivar too might have had reason to complain of the casualties inflicted by graduation. The entire starting backfield was gone and most of the line as well, including the formidable Kroll, who had left Yale. Still, Jordan at least had experienced veterans to replace the departed: Winterbauer at quarterback, destined to have his finest season, Coker, back after a year's absense from action, and in the line, Jack Embersits, a truly dauntless captain, flanked by Howie Phelan and Lannie Baird, who had moved in from end to center for the good of the club. Cavallon was a sensational

John Yovicsin, Harvard's head coach from 1957 to 1970, had a record of 78—42—5; against Yale, 8—5—1. No Harvard coach has done better in the Stadium.

In 1957 Dick Winterbauer quarterbacked Yale to its most convincing win ever over Harvard, 54–0.

Jack Embersits captained Yale's 1957 team from his right guard position.

end, and the Winterbauer—Cavallon combination was as effective as the Woodsum—Molloy duo of five years earlier. Defensively the '57 team was probably as strong as its predecessor; of course the firepower of McGill and Ward was missed, even though Hallas turned out to be an excellent running back, ably supported, as the season wore on, by Winkler and Kangas. As he trotted out to meet his old rival on the uncertain footing of the Bowl—it was a drizzly day with rather soggy turf—the Bulldog carried a 5−2−1 record and had emerged in good shape from an arduous but triumphant tussle in Tigertown. He entered the game a favorite but no one could possibly have guessed at the awesome margin of victory.

Strangely enough, for a few minutes it seemed that the Crimson would, as had happened before, disappoint the odds-makers. Taking the opening kickoff, Harvard marched to the Blue 18-yard line. Yale took over; Winkler, a spirited combatant, ran thirty-four yards and the Elis never looked back. At the end of eight minutes Hallas went over for Yale's first score, five minutes later a twenty-six-yard pass, Winterbauer to Cavallon, was good for another. In the first minutes of the second quarter Hallas scored again; two more touchdowns followed in the first half, one on a forty-yard run by the second-string halfback Mike Curran, and at the interval the tally stood at 34−0, the fattest first half for either Crimson or Blue in their long history. By this time the Cantabs, who literally never had good field position since the opening moments of the game, could only resort to desperation moves—which invariably backfired. The final

score was 54−0, a record for the series. Olivar wrote some years later: "In the last quarter we told our quarterbacks, 'Don't throw the ball anymore'; it was getting a little embarrassing. Because I know that Harvard is a proud university with a proud team and we honestly didn't want to humble them."[3] And in fact, with few exceptions, coaches don't like to roll up large scores against traditional rivals; for one thing there is a natural compassion for the rival coach, who is after all a member of the guild—and besides, there will be another year in which you may need *his* compassion. But coaches cannot always apply the brakes. Every third- or fourth-stringer who gets into the fray wants to make the most of his moment of glory; restraint on his part is too much to expect. It was a sad moment for Yovicsin, but Harvard did not lose confidence in him; he was given a standing ovation at the Boston Harvard Club's Win-or-Lose Dinner shortly after the game. And he did not have long to wait for his revenge.

At New Haven, as September of 1958 (the portentous year of the Beatniks, the first moon rocket, and the optional two-point conversion, designed to give coaches nervous breakdowns)[4] rolled around, prospects for a good season were bleak indeed. The classes of 1957 and 1958 had been unusually rich in more-than-competent young athletes so that the decline (always to be expected in college football after a really good season, which invariably implies a predominantly senior team) from the pinnacle of 1956 had been postponed; in 1958, however, the material was scanty indeed. The class of '61, now sophomores, had some very promising candidates who would be heard from later, but as yet they were untried. Practically all the starters of '57 had departed (even Captain Paul Lynch had not been a regular starter); all had to be done *ex novo*. And, as Yovicsin had had to face the quarterback problem in '57, so Olivar in '58 found this a baffling concern to the very end of his long and frustrating road. Yale, which had been beaten by no Ivy club only two years earlier, was destined to lose to all of them this year; coming into the Harvard game, the Blue had won only two matches; neither against a league foe. For the camp on Charlesside, on the other hand, things were definitely looking up. Yovicsin had a core of sturdy veterans in Captain Shaunessy, Bob Foster, Jim Keating, and a few others in the line, all seniors, Chet Boulris and Sam Halaby in the backfield, and a glittering prospect in Charley Ravenel, a cocky and energetic quarterback. The won and lost record was not particularly impressive on the eve of the Yale game (3—5—0), but the Crimson had beaten Dartmouth and carried Princeton down to the wire (the Tigers had mangled the Bulldog 50—14). The Game of '58 was almost as much of a mismatch as that the previous season had provided, although it took the Crimson longer to get started and the final score was less spectacular. Yale, which could accomplish nothing on the offense all afternoon (less than fifty yards on total offense), managed to hold off destiny until the last play of the first half, when Ravenel, having a fine day, scooted over for the first Crimson score. In the second half the Blue appeared demoralized and yielded three

touchdowns, scored, respectively, by Boulris, Repsher, and Cullen. Blue followers had been looking forward to a duel between Ravenel and their own promising youngster, Tom Singleton, but as it fell out Singleton had been injured and did not play. He might have put a little spice in the Yale attack. Like the combat of '57, it was, after the first half, too one-sided to be called an exciting game, but it must have been enormously satisfying for Yovicsin; the performance of his troops that day set something of a record; they had shot up eighty-five points between the two years. (Tad Jones had brought Yale back to victory after the debacle in 1915, but that leap was, quantitatively, not so spectacular.) Even though Harvard had again come out with a losing season there was a feeling in Cambridge that somehow a corner had been turned. After all, Ravenel had two years to go. As for Yale, well, after the miseries of '58 surely there was no way to go but up, and the performance of the sophomore contingent, notably but not exclusively Mike Pyle and Tom Singleton (when they were healthy), seemed to point to a happier future. Backs of the junior class such as Nick Kangas and Rich Winkler had brightened a dark season, and Olivar, "Ollie's" son, and Puryear showed promise in the line. There was a good nucleus for 1959.

Beginning with the fall of 1959, the Powers That Be had widened by some five inches the space between the goalposts, possibly in belated compensation to the kicker for moving the posts back of the goal line years earlier. In New Haven Handsome Dan X began his reign, and Olivar

Under the quarterbacking of Charlie "Riverboat" Ravenel, Harvard rolled up 386 yards of total offense in the 1959 game and in the process trounced the Blue 35–6.

raised the spirits of the old grads by abandoning the gold trim which he had added to Blue jerseys when he took over; it seems to have taken him awhile to learn that Yale's colors were not those of Navy. And the wooden seats of the Bowl were repainted—not in gray as of old but in true blue. Such apparently irrelevant details may have had something to do with the rejuvenation of the battered Blue forces; the year would be a great improvement over '58. Olivar could not complain of lack of material, much of it now well seasoned. Rich Winkler at fullback was a captain who took his job seriously; his dedication gave the team an extra dimension, and he played with a commitment that alarmed his coaches. ("We thought he would kill himself," one of them confessed.) He had good company in the backfield: the speedy Kangas, now supported by extremely talented juniors, Singleton, Bob Blanchard, Kenny Wolfe, and Muller; the line was a good one, too, with Olivar, Mike Pyle, Hardy Will, and the sophomores Black and Brewster. The delegation got off to a good start and ran through the first five games not only victorious but unscored upon—hadn't happened since 1911. In the second part of the season the magic faded; the Bulldog was beaten by Dartmouth and Penn; he seemed to have aged before his time. But he rallied for a brilliant win over Princeton, and his followers looked for a good showing against the hereditary enemy. Harvard, of course, had no need to take the elevator; she had merely to hold her own. Which in fact she did. It was senior year for Boulris and Cullen and they were at their best. Ravenel had reached

In the Crimson's decisive victory over Yale in 1959, halfback Chet Boulris rushed for ninety-five yards and added an equal number passing. Here he cuts upfield against Cornell.

maturity. Keohane, now captain, Mossanbaugh, and Cappiello were also tried veterans, and a sturdy line was reinforced by sophomores like Bob Boyda, Wile, and Bill Swinford. This more-than-competent crew sailed into the Bowl with victories over Columbia, Penn, and Princeton—a rather unexpected licking by Brown gave their followers food for thought, but all in all it looked like an even-money contest.

It wasn't. In the first quarter a spectacular eighty-five-yard pass, Ravenel to Keohane, with a two-point conversion gave the Crimson an eight-point lead. Shortly after, Singleton passed to Wolfe for sixty yards and a crowd-pleasing score. Since Harvard had eight points, Yale felt obliged to try for a two-point conversion—and failed. Whether that failure was responsible for the deflation of the Blue or whether the latent power of the Cantabs had been simply lying dormant is hard to say; but from that point on the game became, in Olivar's terminology, "a fiasco." Harvard got in a second touchdown before the end of the half, and within fifteen minutes of the second half scored three times more, Ravenel, Boulris, and Cullen having their way with the baffled Bulldog. It was a muddy field and the Elis fumbled four times; they also suffered a disastrous interception, but the success of Harvard was not due to these little gifts of fortune but to the unflagging élan of a hard-charging line. The Crimson rolled up 386 yards of total offense—over a team which had yielded no more than 200 in any previous encounter. Why such things happen is part of the entrancing mystery of football. The Crimson was simply "up." The final score, 35−6, was the highest the Cantabs had made against the Blue since P.D.'s time. It was a grand day for Ravenel, who ran and passed with exciting assurance. Harvard seniors no doubt came away with quite a different impression of the Bowl from the one they had had two years earlier. Probably decided it was a nice place to visit after all. The stellar Bulldogs of the class of '61 licked their wounds and bided their time.

The sixties, destined to be a decade of confrontation, torment, and anguished soul-searching for Americans, came in on a deceptively optimistic note when John F. Kennedy, handsome, charismatic, and confident, won a hard-fought election; thus after a fifteen-year lapse, Harvard would return to the White House. The coming decade would bring assassinations, freedom rides, war, and antiwar demonstrations, to say nothing of the triumph of rock and roll, but in the first dawn of the sixties none of these calamities was predictable. It was a euphoric year. (Perhaps the country is always euphoric when a Harvard man moves into the White House.) On Soldiers Field, too, optimism prevailed. The experts, basing their opinion of Harvard's promise on 1959 and on the quality of the veterans returning for action, predicted the Cantabs would be Ivy League champions. Not only was "Riverboat" Ravenel, scourge of the tribe of Eli, available, he was flanked by Halaby, McIntyre, and the sophomore Hobie Armstrong in the backfield; the line was led by the puissant Terry Lenzner at guard and a supporting cast in-

cluding Eric Nelson, Bob Pillsbury, and Bill Swinford that gave the Crimson, as Cloney writes, "solid depth through two full units."[5] It was a strong, well-balanced outfit—save for one weakness; there was no one on the squad who could replace Ravenel, and, as the fates cruelly decreed, the effervescent Charley was injured in the second game of the season and never really recovered his full strength. Other injuries followed, notably that suffered by Lenzner, and the Crimson record suffered accordingly. The club came up to the Yale game with a 5−3−0 scorecard. Even so it was a redoubtable machine and would have held its own with most Yale teams. Unhappily for Harvard, the Bulldog combination of 1960 was among the very best to wear the Blue in the twentieth century.

It was a team, in fact, which had all the attributes a coach could wish for: talent, experience, and motivation. The starting backfield was made up of seasoned seniors: Singleton at quarterback, Wolfe and Muller at half, and Bob Blanchard at fullback. Pyle, now captain, had moved from his post at center (where he had been All-Ivy and All-East) to tackle, thus making room for his classmate and roommate, Hardy Will. King, also a senior, was at the other tackle spot. Ben Balme (good enough for a try at the pros) and Bursiek were the guards; at end were Jimmy Pappas and Hutcherson, also experienced. In fact, in the line there were only two juniors, Pappas and Bursiek. As for motivation—well, this would be the fourth encounter between the Blue and Crimson classes of '61; the former had three seasons of humiliation to think about. This year they were more nu-

Yale's undefeated Ivy League champions, 1960, a team with all the attributes: talent, experience, and motivation.

Tom Singleton quarterbacked an all-senior backfield at Yale in 1960: Ken Wolfe and Louis Muller at half and Bob Blanchard at fullback.

merous, on the whole more talented, and certainly healthier than their Crimson counterparts.

Able as they were, the Elis started slowly that year, barely taking the hard-fought opener from Connecticut and having not too easy a time with Brown. But by midseason they were awesome; Singleton excelled at the sprint-out (which Olivar had installed two years earlier). Blanchard was the kind of fullback that had to be watched and was therefore ideal for making Olivar's "belly series" work; Wolfe was an agile and fast runner and Lou Muller a skillful blocker. A high-scoring machine, it had run up over 100 points against Penn, Dartmouth, and Princeton on its way to the Stadium. It came into that venerable amphitheater the first unbeaten—untied Blue team since Mallory's day. It was, in fact, a more potent machine than Mallory's, scoring some thirty more points than the '23 delegation (and over stronger opposition), though yielding somewhat more on defense.

It was a mild, sunny day in Cambridge. Blue partisans were happy to be favorites, although a few with long memories remembered uneasily what had happened to Mac Aldrich and Clint Frank, who had also led unbeaten Elis to the banks of the Charles. Such disquieting memories were erased on the very first play of Yale's first possession, when Wolfe, profiting by Blanchard's fake thrust at the center, sped untouched for forty yards over left tackle for a score. Early in the second quarter Hutcherson intercepted a pitchout by Ravenel and went forty yards to make it 14—0. Kaake added a field goal and the Blue went off at the end of the half leading 17—0. By this time everyone knew it was just a question of how much. Yale added twenty-two points in the third period, one on a plunge by Blanchard, two following passes by Bill Leckonby, who had replaced Singelton; already in the third quarter, Olivar, true to his resolve not to humiliate a proud and cherished rival, had begun substituting; by the last period the Yale line up was made up entirely of second-stringers. Ravenel took advantage of this situation and, coming in from the bench after a short rest, hobbling through the action, yet managed to pilot the Crimson to its only touchdown, taking the ball over himself after a long march. No one in the Yale stands grudged him his score; while Yale has always respected its more gifted Crimson foemen, Ravenel seemed to inspire, to a unique degree, a kind of affection among Bulldogs. He was, in fact, later in the year invited to speak at the Yale senior dinner. It was good to watch Singleton, at the end of the game, run across the field to congratulate and console his three-year rival. Toward the end of the last quarter, as if in recognition of the historic hour of Yale football history, Olivar recalled his second-stringers and for one sequence of downs put in the varsity.[6] Harvard had the ball and in three downs lost ten yards. It was a magnificent display, and I shouldn't be surprised if even the Crimson stands appreciated Olivar's gesture; it was the last sight of a superb Yale team. Since 1960 the Blue has had no delegation to go through a season unbeaten and untied; three have gotten as far as the Harvard game only to encounter bitter disappointment. Since Mallory's year, Pyle's happy company stands alone.

As in the affairs of the world in general, so in football in particular—but even more so—triumph is a brief and transitory thing. Of the Yale starters against Harvard on the unforgettable day of the Invincibles of 1960 only one survived, Bursiek at guard, now captain, to enter the lists in 1961. The seniors had gone the way of seniors, and Pappas, the other junior in the lineup, had gone on to medical school. To be sure, during the campaign of the previous year, many second-stringers had looked good, sometimes almost as good as the starters. But it is one thing to come in fresh when your team has a lead against a weary and demoralized foe, and quite a different matter to start the game against an adversary as fresh as you and as full of confidence and fire. The personnel of '61 did its best; it could hardly, as the event proved, claim to be included in the "invincible" category. It was good enough to keep Olivar's victory string running for two more games—the openers against UConn and Brown; but when Columbia turned back the Bulldog in the third game the mystique of victory was shattered. Losses followed to Colgate, Dartmouth, and Princeton; it was a very bruised Bulldog whom the Cantabs found waiting for them in the Bowl.

Harvard, on the other hand, had, by the time of the meeting, done rather better than expected. A number of veterans carried over from the '60 squad: Pete Hart, now captain, Bob Boyda, Swinford, and Ted Halaby (Sam's younger brother); Dick Diehl; some promising sophomores, Bill Grana, Scotty Harshbarger, and a wily quarterback, Bill Humenuk, added their substantial con-

Harvard fullback Bill Grana passing off the fullback option in the 1961 game, won by the Crimson 27–0.

tributions. By the record it was not a great Harvard team; it was beaten, as Yale was, by Columbia and Colgate (this was the only year the Red Raiders beat all the members of the Big Three); but it was stronger than such mishaps would suggest; unlike Yale, the Crimson had subdued both Dartmouth and Princeton, a sure indication of mettle in any year. Another contrast between Crimson and Blue that became apparent before the game was five minutes old was that Harvard had saved its best game for its old rival, while Yale played what was assuredly its worst game of the season in the climactic match. A Yale fumble in the early minutes was covered by Pete Hart on the Eli 15-yard line; four plays later Taylor went over for the first Crimson score. Harvard then kicked off, and the Yale receivers, having apparently never been told that a kickoff means a free ball, calmly watched the spheroid roll about on the 26-yard line until Diehl picked it up. And again, four plays later Harvard had a touchdown, this time scored by the robust Grana. Harvard's third touchdown (in the second half) was more honestly come by, as Taylor capped a Crimson drive, taking a nine-yard pass from Bassett. And in the last quarter Yale obligingly allowed a pass from center to get away from Leckonby; Harvard's center, Nyhan, alertly fell on it. Final score 27–0. At no time was the Bulldog really in the game. Harvard ended the season in a tie for the Ivy League championship with Columbia; Yale fell from her proud supremacy of '60 to fifth place.

In 1962, as Dolph Samborski, '25, a stellar baseball player in his day and with long experience

Dick Diehl played tackle on the 1961 Harvard team that tied with Columbia for the Ivy League championship.

in guiding the intramural athletic program, replaced Bolles as director of athletics, Harvard football was in good shape. The redoubtable Diehl captained an outfit that in the course of the season developed a sturdy line out of somewhat inexperienced material and had ready at hand a veteran backfield in Bassett, Grana, Armstrong, and Taylor which (to quote Cloney) "on its good days was one of the finest Crimson units in years."[7] It took a while for the team to hit its stride, but in the three engagements immediately preceding the

Harvard band, 1961.

The 1962 Harvard team, captained by Dick Diehl (holding ball).

appointment with Yale, Harvard's warriors had run up a total of 81 points against Penn, Princeton, and Brown. As for Yale—well, if this were a history of Yale football the '62 delegation would call for special study as a kind of unusual case history. Admittedly less talented than the Cantabs, the Elis nevertheless could call on some good backs, Hank Higdon, now captain, Rich Egloff, and Jud Calkins at half, and Brian Rapp and McCarthy at quarter; and a line particularly strong on defense. (This year Olivar fielded three platoons, offense, defense, and general utility—a notion a number of coaches picked up from its successful use by a strong Louisiana State team in 1961.) Perhaps the "star" of '62 was Jack Cirie, a valiant laborer in the defensive backfield. George

Humphrey at center was another stalwart. The squad was reinforced by a number of promising sophomores: Cummings, Chuck Mercein, and McCarthy himself. Yet somehow the team never lived up to its potential. It was never badly beaten (no team scored more than two touchdowns against the Blue all season, not even mighty Dartmouth, held by the Bulldog to its lowest total in that undefeated year), but it consistently fell a little short of victory. Meeting Harvard, Yale stood at 3−4−2, with Cornell the only Ivy League conquest. Still, it was a convincing win, and the fact that the Ithacans had edged the Crimson gave the Bulldog some grounds for hope.

Harvard's News and Views report of the game has some interesting items.

Jack Cirie returned a punt sixty yards for Yale's only score in the 1962 game, won by Harvard 14—6.

A capacity crowd of close to 40,000 enjoyed itself on a cool but sometimes bright afternoon following a dismal morning that threatened to turn the game into a swimming meet. The early weather discouraged Harvard's distinguished alumnus, John F. Kennedy, from helicoptering up from

Hyannis Port as he had planned, but the announcement of the President's decision at least provoked noisy applause from the Yale stands; the Elis had little else to cheer about all afternoon. . . . Almost lost in the huge crowd were two prominent former H winners with political connections: All-American 'Chub' Peabody, the new governor of Massachusetts, and Bobby Kennedy, Attorney General of the United States.[8]

In the ensuing combat the Bulldogs ran true to their pattern. Like Yale's other opponents, Harvard could score no more than two touchdowns—but they were more than enough. The Elis looked promising in the first period and even had a shot at a field goal, but in the second quarter Harvard got rolling, carrying the ball from her own forty over the Blue goal line, Bill Taylor scoring over the Blue right flank. The third quarter produced the most exciting play of the game when Jack Cirie ran back a Harvard punt sixty yards for a touchdown. Olivar sent in a special play for a two-point conversion—it was no puzzle to Harvard's sophomore end, Mike Ulcickas, who smashed through to break it up. In the last quarter Harvard applied the clincher, when, following a brilliant return by Harshbarger of a short Yale punt, the Crimson got the ball on the Yale thirteen; four plays later Fred Bartl, subbing for the injured Dana, bolted over from the 2-yard line. The successful kick put the game out of the Bulldog's reach. In truth, Cirie's run was a kind of fluke; in spite of the closeness of the score, the Bulldog (outgained by some 150 yards) was never really in the game. But one must be grateful to Cirie for injecting a bit of excitement into what was otherwise a rather dull match. The victory gave Harvard second place in the Ivies that year; Olivar's last delegation finished seventh, saved from the cellar by the win over Cornell.

In 1963 the bright dawn of the seventh decade had given place to a cloudy and ominous morning. The assassination of President Kennedy put a tragic end to the blithe assurance of Camelot, already shaken by the confrontation with Russia and the sordid fiasco of the Bay of Pigs. A certain uneasiness about the goings-on in Southeast Asia was also beginning to trouble the American public. It was hardly a happy year for the world either; the death of the gentle and ecumenical-minded Pope John was mourned by all sects. Sixty-three also left its mark on the microcosm of the Yale family; A. Whitney Griswold, admired as much for his clear and courageous thinking as for his ready wit, died in the spring of the year, the first Yale president since the eighteenth century to die in office. Midway through the football season—in fact, on the morning of the Columbia game—the Yale Corporation named his successor: the provost, Kingman Brewster, Jr., '41, articulate, wise, and shrewd, who had served for a number of years on the faculty of the Harvard Law School. It would be his destiny to guide Yale through the trying times of activism and student unrest that the Vietnam War and the exacerbations of the civil rights issues would bring to most college campuses.

On the Yale football scene problems had arisen before the year began. After two rather unsatisfac-tory seasons Jordan Olivar's magic touch seemed to be missing and, as it happened, at a time when his contract came up for renewal. And would indeed have been renewed save that it had now become apparent that the arrangement under which he had been working (half the year in New Haven and half in California, where he maintained his business office) was no longer satisfactory. It was felt that a year-round coach was needed, primarily to carry on the task of recruiting, an aspect of his vocation that Olivar had never much cared for. Given the choice between full-time coaching and full-time pursuit of his business affairs, he opted for the latter. The Yale community, while regretting his departure, understood his position. Olivar resigned in January, and by March the selection committee, under the guidance of DeLaney Kiphuth, director of athletics, appointed John Pont, a graduate of Miami (Ohio) and at the time coach of his alma mater's team. In the '62 season he had achieved prominence when his squad defeated Purdue, a member of the Big Ten and normally out of the class of "little" Miami.

Pont came to Yale full of energy and confidence and was welcomed by the team, ready to hope that the change in coaches might signify a change in fortune. Pont's system was somewhat more dependent on power and less on deception than Olivar's style; his was essentially a version of Big Ten football. He discarded the notion of platooning that had crept in in 1962; his '63 squad featured a number of players equally at home on defense or offense. He gave Yale her best record since Olivar's champions of 1960. Perhaps Olivar would have done so, too, for this year Yale had veterans available at every position, including a talented quarterback in Brian Rapp, as well as the experienced Cummings, Mercein, and Egloff in the backfield. The line included Lawrence, Toby Hubbard, a doughty end who also did the punting for the team; and George Humphrey at center, whose inspirational play and leadership put him in the category of truly great Yale captains; Howard and Groninger added a sophomore punch to the backfield. One might even hazard the guess that Olivar could have done even better, for his pupils would not have had to learn, as Pont's did, a new system of play. For that reason the team was slow to gather momentum, losing to Brown and Cornell and beating Connecticut only by a field goal. But a smart and valiant win over Dartmouth at midseason indicated that this year's Blue company was a team of character.

Was it, however, quite up to the challenge offered by a strong Crimson squad which came to the Bowl with victories over Dartmouth, Princeton, Brown, and Cornell and counted on its roster two good quarterbacks in Humenuk and Bassett and a dozen well-tried veterans besides: Harshbarger, Grana, Walt Grant, and Dockery on offense and defensive stalwarts such as Boyda, Ulcickas, and Stephenson? (Following the reversal of 1960, Yovicsin had shifted his machine back into high gear; he had already given the Bulldog two successive lickings—and more were to come before his reign ended.) Coming down to the wire, Yale was rather easily beaten by Princeton's Tigers, a defeat that appeared to indicate that the Blue,

The inspirational play and leadership of center George Humphrey in 1963 put him in the category of truly great Yale captains.

though much improved, was probably in for another trying afternoon. So, at least, it seemed on the evening of Friday, November 22. Then—as the games between the Yale colleges and Harvard houses were in progress—came the news of the tragedy in Dallas. After hasty conference the presidents of Harvard and Yale decreed for the first time in history postponement of The Game.

When the old rivals came together a week after the scheduled date (on November 30), a subdued and somber air hung over the Bowl, though meteorologically it was a fine day, not too cold and surprisingly calm for that time of year. Attendance was (as one might have expected) relatively low, 51,000 as against the almost 62,000 that had come out to see the mismatch of two years before. The first quarter seemed to indicate that the Crimson would justify the betting odds; the Yale backfield was unsteady, and misplays gave Harvard an early chance at a field goal. It was missed but the Redshirts, unperturbed, launched a drive of their own capped by a brilliant screen pass which covered forty yards and gave them first blood. The kick went wide, which at that point hardly seemed to matter. But within seconds a surprising reversal of fortune took place. Harvard kicked off; the ball landed deep, inside the 5-yard line, and bounced over the goal: Bill Henderson, standing well back in the end zone, chose, rather brashly, to run with it—and carried it to the Harvard 20-yard line, where he was downed as much as by exhaustion as by the redshirted pursuit. In two plays, one for fifteen yards and one for five, Rapp sent Groninger over the Harvard goal line. The kick was good and as the second quarter began Yale was ahead 7−6. And ahead to stay. For some reason the Crimson counterattack never materialized. In the third quarter Rapp engineered a beautiful march, displaying Pont's slants and crossovers as if in a showcase, which ended in a second touchdown; an intercepted pass in the last period (by Merrill, Humphrey's replacement) sealed the 20−6 triumph of the Blue. Harvard passing in the second half was brillant but never really effective. The Crimson finished second to Princeton and Dartmouth, cochampions of the Ivies, Yale one place behind—and with the satisfaction of having beaten one cochampion and a runner-up. A good start for Pont. One wonders a little if the postponement of the game might not have worked to the advantage of the Blue. A week earlier Harvard would have been presumably "up" and ready: Yale would still have been in the process of recovering from the mental and physical damage wrought by the Tiger. The respite served her well; Harvard didn't need it and may have lost something of her keenness in the time of waiting. No doubt Henderson's run and the immediately following Yale lead shook the Crimson troops. From the Blue point of view one could simply say that it was *au fond* a good Yale team which that afternoon played its best game of the year, notably on defense.

In 1964, the year Lyndon Johnson swept all but unanimously into office prepared to launch the Great Society and to see to it that no American boy was sent to fight in an Asian war, both Yale and Harvard had unusually strong squads. In Cambridge, battle-scarred veterans such as Walt Grant, Dave Poe, John Dockery, and Tom Bilodeau were reinforced by the speedy sophomores Ray Kubacki and Tom Choquette; up forward, Skowronski and Hoffman were back at guard, flanked by a pair of good tackles and abetted by an unusually able duo of ends in Ulcickas and Ken Boyda. McCluskey, though not a letterman, was a good quarterback if

Chuck Mercein, in 1964 one of Yale's most gifted fullbacks in many years, was also a skilled placekicker.

not a great passer. Perhaps in New Haven things looked even more promising: Ab Lawrence, now captain, Shaftel, and Vandersloot ready for service in the line, McCaskey and Steve Lawrence at the ends, and a fine stable of backs, including three fullbacks of rare puissance and poundage— Mercein was the most gifted of Eli fullbacks in many a year, skilled also as a placekicker. McCar-

thy and Tone Grant were quarterbacks. John Mc-Callum rated the Blue squad as the strongest since 1960.[9] The team went undefeated (though tying with Columbia) up to the Princeton game, where the publicized "duel of fullbacks" between Mercein and the Tiger Iacavazzi was easily won by the latter, partly, to be sure, because Mercein was able to play only half the game. Save for an inexplicable humiliation at the hands of Dartmouth, the Crimson, too, had done well, although they too succumbed to an unbeaten Orange and Black.

The combat was a stirring one. Yale, though sadly missing Mercein, by this time the indispensable element in the Bulldog offense, went off at the half with a 14–12 lead and seemed likely to hang onto it. But in the last quarter Harvard's wing-footed Bobby Leo went forty-six yards on a wide sweep and the Blue was undone. It was a well-earned triumph for the Crimson, which had come onto the field as the underdog. The anticlimactic history of the 1964 Bulldogs is at first sight rather puzzling. Undefeated until the climax games—and then the loser in both of them; a strange performance for the "best team since 1960." Yet it was, in fact, not so much a matter of a Bulldog collapse as evidence that the other pair of the old Big Three were stronger than usual. (It is no derogation of the *virtus* of Mallory's undefeated 1923 *bravi*, for example, to point out that in their year neither Harvard nor Princeton was very powerful.) One doesn't have to make excuses for Harvard's '64 delegation; save for the embarrassing afternoon with Dartmouth, the Crimson made the best use of its potential and finished

Bobby Leo (15) breaks loose on his forty-six-yard run for the
winning touchdown in 1964. Final: Harvard 18—Yale 14.

runner-up to Princeton in the Ivies. Old-timers
were pleased to note that this year the old Big
Three were 1, 2 and 3 in the league—the only time
that has happened so far in the thirty-two years
of formal league play.

In 1965 the rules committee of the NCAA, in
McCallum's phrase, "lowered virtually all the remaining barriers against free substitution."[10]

Henceforth a coach could send in any number of
replacements more or less at will, most significantly after a change in ball possession. Platooning, which had been temporarily banished in 1953
and had been making persistent attempts to sneak
back again since the early sixties, was now lodged,
permanently it would appear, within the tent. The
coaches who had campaigned for it were greatly

pleased. One can see why; it is certainly easier to teach a football player, or anyone else for that matter, one thing rather than two. It was also argued that platooning gave more youngsters a chance to play, which is at least a half-truth. And it is beyond argument that specialization makes for greater individual competence. Squads with the personnel for it soon followed the pro style, fielding special units not only for offense and defense, but for kicking, receiving kickoffs, and the like. (Morris Bishop, in a sprightly exercise of prophesy, predicted the end of the game among smaller colleges when the entire undergraduate body, all specialists of the squad, would take up all the seating spaces in smaller grandstands, leaving no room for spectators.)[11] No doubt platooning may possess all the virtues claimed for it, but it is sad to think that versatility and endurance are no longer part of a player's equipment and that we shall see no more sixty-minute heroes. By 1966 game programs were listing separately offensive and defensive lineups; henceforth any player who "went both ways" even for a few plays was a rare phenomenon.

The new dispensation has brought about changes in coaching assignments; staffs must now include offensive and defensive coordinators to assure that the young specialists become acquainted. Concurrently a more sophisticated deployment of troops, particularly though not exclusively on defense, has come about, calling for novel and somewhat esoteric nomenclature. The Harvard–Yale program for 1983, for example, lists split ends and tight ends, erstwhile simply left and right ends. Split ends are sometimes called wide receivers. On defense one finds nose guards and monster backs for the first line of defenders, with safeties and cornerbacks trained to deal with the enemy's long-range artillery. In the basic sense that the quarterback regularly hands off to the runner, the standard formation may be still called the T (except of course when despair calls for the shotgun); the new style encourages such variations on the innocent T as wishbones, I formations, pro sets, and the like. Happily there are still (legally) only twenty-two men on the field at one time, and the purpose of the action is still to break through the line, circle the ends, or toss the ball over the other chap's head.

The year of 1965 was also marked by preseason concern in both the Cambridge and New Haven camps. In April Yovicsin underwent open-heart surgery; the Harvard community, in which he had won a place of regard and affection for both his success as a mentor and his personal qualities, was shaken. Fortunately he was restored to full health in time to take over the guidance of his pupils as they entered the fall campaign. As for Yale, in January of 1965 John Pont resigned his post to accept an offer from Indiana. His action was a blow to Yale followers; a few were a little resentful, since on his arrival in 1963 Pont had professed himself pleased with the New Haven atmosphere and prepared for a long stay. But most understood that a coach from the Middle West might well find an offer from the Big Ten hard to resist. Looking back from a distance of two decades, the Blue has every reason to be grateful to

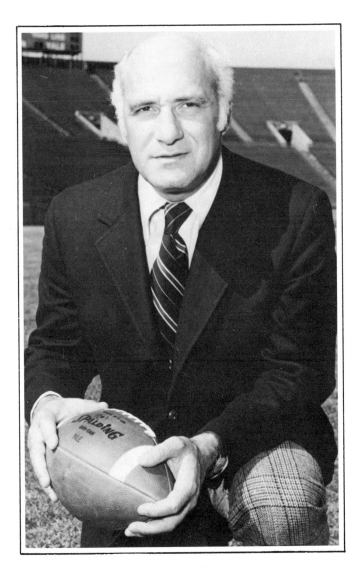

Carmen Cozza, Yale's head coach since 1965, has an intuitional talent for assigning his players to their best position and for assuring faultless execution of his plays.

Pont. His record was 12−5−1, not bad at all, and if his Big Three count (1−3−0) was less impressive, it must still be admitted that he had brought the Bulldog back from a very low estate and made him a real contender again. But perhaps the best thing Pont did for Yale was to leave behind him as his successor his Miami classmate and roommate, Carmen Cozza, destined, after a rough start, to become an outstanding coach and a respected and valued member of the Eli establishment. Pont took most of his assistants with him. An early indication of Carm's competence was the quality of his own appointments to fill the gaps in the coaching staff: Jim Root, Bill Narduzzi, Neil Putnam, and Seb LaSpina, an invaluable tactician. All were from Miami; later such able mentors as Buddy Amendola (Connecticut) and Paul Amodio (Kent) would join the brotherhood. A good deal of Cozza's success is a function of his talent for choosing his assistants and, for that matter, of his shrewdness in assigning his players to the best position for exercise of their skills. Just the same, Carm had a trying novitiate. His first year was disappointing. He had inherited a score of veterans from Pont's '64 delegation, but they were mostly replacements; the major performers of '64 (McCarthy, Mercein, Cummings, Henderson, Niglio, Vandersloot, et al.) had departed. Only Bob Kenney, at end, would repeat as a starter against the Crimson; even Captain Laidley had been a replacement in the '64 delegation. The season began inauspiciously, with the Blue losing for the first time to the University of Connecticut and picking up five more defeats (including the by-now-routine mauling at the hands of the single-wing Tiger) as against only three wins. But in midseason, against Cornell and against Dartmouth, the Elis had shown exciting potential (although the Green won, they had the narrowest escape of their undefeated season and needed a few crucial breaks to come out ahead). In the course of the campaign the defense had begun to jell, and Watts Humphrey had emerged as a very able signal caller.

Harvard had done much better. McCluskey was a veteran quarterback; Leo was still available, along with Walt Grant, John Dockery, and Tom Choquette. The veteran Tom Boyda and the sophomore Carter Lord gave the Crimson a fine pair of ends; the line was somewhat inexperienced but sturdy. At the beginning of the year the experts picked Harvard to vie with Dartmouth for the league championship. The Crimson task force didn't do quite that well, losing to Dartmouth and Princeton and tieing Cornell and Penn; but up to the Yale game its record (4–2–2) compared favorably with that of its host. So Harvard was the bettor's choice. And this time the bettors were right. The Crimson came out on top 13–0. The first half was a standoff; Yale's sophomore back, Fisher, ran the kickoff sixty yards deep into Harvard territory, and although the Bulldog couldn't score, it took the Cantabs a while to rally; Yale had a few yards' edge in statistics at the interval. The second half was a different story. Twice Humphrey's passes were intercepted (once in the third and once in the fourth quarter), and on both occasions Harvard used her field position to advantage; Leo scored the first touchdown from four yards out,

and Choquette carried over on a one-yard plunge for the second. The defense on both sides was good (the Bulldog was undone by the mistakes of his offense), but Harvard's was the better of the two. It was a well-played game, though with little real sparkle.

Nineteen sixty-six was not a happy year in the annals of the Republic. Race riots took place in a number of major cities; the most spectacular was the uprising in Watts, but even New Haven had a week of tension, with store fronts boarded up and commotion in the streets. Concurrently the protest against the adventure in Vietnam was mounting, as more and more American soldiers were sent to participate in a remote war, draining the nation's resources and polarizing its people. Campuses, responding to these national stresses, became restive and in some cases even rebellious. Drug addiction among undergraduates became a sorry fact of life. But The Game went on.

In a preseason interview Yovicsin bewailed the loss of seventeen seasoned veterans from his 1965 squad. All coaches are given to such mournful assessments of their prospects; it is a necessary part, it would seem, of the mentorial mentality. Few probably have had less reason for complaint than Yovicsin in 1966. For if many had gone, yet many a stalwart remained. By the time the team had jelled for the climax game, the Crimson lineup included five seniors on the offensive platoon and six on the defensive side. There was but one sophomore on each platoon. The Cantabs were not short on experience—nor on talent either. It is possible that the offensive backfield was the strongest to wear the Crimson since the days of Haughton. Ric Zimmerman, a junior, was a knowledgeable field general and a first-rate passer. Bobby Leo at left half was, in McCallum's opinion, "perhaps the finest runner ever enrolled at Harvard, certainly in modern times."[12] Tom Choquette at fullback, like Leo a senior of experience, was a good deal better than average back, and the one sophomore, Vic Gatto, 5'6" and 185 pounds, was an aggressive dynamo. Steve Diamond at right tackle anchored a robust line, which included two seniors, Bob Flanagan and Joe O'Donnell; Carter Lord, now a junior, was back at end. On defense, Dave Davis and Skip Sviokla, both seniors and weighing in at 230 pounds each, were truly formidable; another senior at the strategic left end position, Captain Justin Hughes, was a valiant element. On the eve of the Yale game the team had compiled the best record of any Crimson outfit since Barry Wood's time; seven wins against one loss (a close one to Princeton).

Cozza might have had better cause than Yovicsin for complaint, but at least it can be said that '66 promised to be an improvement over the delegation of the previous year. On defense he had two fine senior tackles in Glenn Greenberg, son of the baseball star, and Captain Bob Greenlee (inevitably they were known as the Jolly Green Giants, and, standing respectively at 6'2" and 6'4", weighing about 240 each, the designation was not inappropriate). Tom Schmidt, another senior, at middle guard was an outstanding performer, as was Watson at end. Elsewhere the Elis did not have the experience to match their Cantabri-

gian friends; facing Harvard, five of the Blue's twenty-two starters were sophomores. And it would have been a stronger team and a closer battle had there been seven yearlings on the field. For the cheering thing for Cozza as the season opened was the ample and spectacular contribution of the class of 1969, undefeated in freshman year and including not only two athletes destined for greatness, Brian Dowling and Calvin Hill, but a wealth of additional talent: Bruce Weinstein at end, Kyle Gee at tackle, and, on defense, Fran Gallagher, Bob Levin, and Ed Franklin, all of whom started in the Harvard game. If Carm was not quite as rich as Yovicsin in his flock he nevertheless had the makings of a fine team. But, as in 1962 only more so, the Bulldogs of 1966 were victimized by a cruel fate. Dowling started at quarterback, and his performance in the opening game justified his choice. Unhappily he was injured in the second game of the season and was out for the rest of the year. Hill, too, after surviving most of the season, sat out the Harvard game because of injuries sustained in the Princeton skirmish. Facing the ancient foe, the Elis had won only four of their eight games. Bad luck dogged them to the end. The duel with the Tiger was lost by a blocked kick in the last minute, undoing a truly heroic effort by the Blue (even the Princeton coach admitted that Yale should have won); and facing the Crimson, the weather was a factor in the undoing of old Eli. For, as the season wore on, it became increasingly clear that the Bulldog's fortunes depended on the arm of Pete Doherty, who had taken Dowling's place at quarterback. Doherty was no great runner but a superb passer; he was, as the rivals lined up in the Stadium, Yale's only weapon. And as the gods would have it, it was one of those days, not uncommon in Cambridge, when a strong wind whipped mercilessly through the amphitheater. Yale followers knew they had nothing to match the Crimson running game; when they took their seats in the Stadium and pulled their overcoats around them, they realized it was not to be a day for the Bulldog.

Nor was it. Doherty's first pass, on the first play of the game, wobbled in the thirty-mile-per-hour gale and was snapped up by a Harvard defender; in the whole game, peerless passer though he was, Doherty could complete only five of nineteen attempts, with two interceptions. And on the ground the Bulldog was powerless; the Blue offense never crossed midfield. Nor was the hard-pressed defense able to parry the Crimson thrusts. The real question was how much they would lose by. In the first quarter Babcock scored a field goal from twenty-nine yards out to start the Crimson scoring, and later in the same period Leo bucked over after Baker recovered one of Yale's two fumbles inside the Blue 30-yard line. Leo then ended the scoring in the last quarter in a fashion becoming his prestige, making a beautiful fifty-two-yard run from scrimmage through left tackle and nimbly reversing his field to outrun the Blue defense. Yale followers applauded vociferously—perhaps because they knew that would be the last they would see of a foeman who had thwarted them for three successive years. (Harvard's class of '67 had the all-but-unique experience of never losing

Pete Doherty, a superb passer, had no chance to exhibit his talents in the wind at Harvard Stadium in 1966, completing only five of nineteen passes in a losing effort. Final: Harvard 17−Yale 0.

a football game to Yale; hadn't happened since '31 graduated.) 17−0—it might have been worse but it was bad enough for the Bulldog; perhaps it would have been a different story if Dowling and Hill had been on hand, perhaps the Bulldogs had not recovered from the heartbreaking loss to Princeton; at any rate they played a rather slug-

gish game (making only five first downs). No penalties were called on the Blue; such sinless performance is not necessarily a good thing; a team
properly keyed up is likely to draw a few offside
penalties; a blameless record is often an indication of a certain lack of zest. (The Bulldogs did
not fumble either; the Eli delegation of '66 remains
the only team of either side ever to come through
the fray with no fumbles and no penalties.) On a
windless day Doherty would almost certainly have
put the Blue on the scoreboard, but overall Harvard had much the better team. One can't help,
in that connection, deploring the Harvard loss to
Princeton. Victory would have given the Crimson
its one untied, undefeated delegation since Campbell's clan of 1901. The great teams of 1919 and
1920 were tied by the Tigers, and Barry Wood
was undone by Booth's field goal; two years ahead,
another immaculate Crimson outfit, though covering itself with glory, would have its perfection
marred by a tie with Yale. This time, too, the loss
to Princeton cost the Cantabs the unchallenged
league championship; they had to share the cup
with Dartmouth and the Tigers (who were also
Big Three champions). Even so, it was a great Harvard squad, achieving the massive total of 3,192
yards against opponents' 1,949, a more impressive
tally than would be reached by the undefeated
company of 1968, for which the relative figures
are 2,833 to 2,313. Most of the yardage in '66
was made on the ground; a club with runners
like Gatto, Leo, and Choquette (there has never
been a more potent threesome in a Crimson backfield) had little need for the pass, though Ric

Zimmerman's percentage of completions was approximately 50 percent, quite good enough to
supplement a running game. On defense, Crimson
opponents were held to 60 points, the lowest total
since the low-scoring Harlow years—and 30 points
less than the '68 invincibles would yield. Yovicsin
admitted it was his best team to date; he would
never have a better one.

The games played in 1967 and 1968 were a pair
of back-to-back thrillers unique in the chronicles.
Both were filled with action, great individual efforts, and costly misplays, terminating in breath-
taking climaxes. Each would merit a special chapter, each had the outline of high melodrama, each
illustrated the unpredictable caprice of Fortune's
wheel.

Background study may properly begin in New
Haven, where in the early season of 1967 there
was a good deal of tension in the air. The seasons
of 1965 and '66 had not been particularly distinguished for the Blue, who had twice come out
lowest on the Big Three totem pole and who was
understandably getting a little restive. It was felt
that the class of '69, invincible as freshman but
not potent enough to save the Bulldog from disaster in their first varsity year, should by now be
sufficiently mature to make a difference. Particularly, of course, if Dowling was in good shape.
He did not, in fact, start the opener against Holy
Cross (which Yale lost, the first time in history
the Blue had been beaten in a season's curtain
raiser). He made no appearance in the Connecticut game either and went in for only one play
against Brown. In the fourth game, however,—

against Columbia—he started at quarterback and the Dowling era began. Yale would lose no games with the alert Brian at the helm. That he and his classmates were all that could have been hoped for was well proven by the rout of Dartmouth; the Blue scored 56 points against a better-than-average Green delegation. By the eve of the Harvard game the Dowling task force had rolled up 226 points against Ivy opponents, including a convincing victory over the Tigers, who had twisted the Bulldog's tail with impunity for six long years. On offense, with Dowling and Calvin Hill ably abetted by Fisher and Don Barrows in the backfield, ends of the caliber of Marting and Weinstein, and Morris to lead the charge at center, the Elis of '67 would by season's end roll up 278 points, the highest total since "Rif" Rafferty's band of 1903—and against more robust opposition. If defensively '67 was not quite as strong as the delegation of '56 or '60, it was certainly more than adequate, with Captain Watson in the line along with Paul Tully, Glenn Greenberg, and Tom Schmidt, and a very alert secondary featuring Don Begel (a first-class placekicker as well as a flutist), Paul Jones, and Ed Franklin.

In Cambridge, in early season, tension was absent. Harvard had taken the measure of the Blue three years running; there was no need for undue concern. Besides, it was a sturdy lot of Cantabrigians that Yovicsin fielded that year; Ric Zimmerman, the left-handed quarterback, broke all Crimson records for passing, and in Carter Lord he had an outstanding receiver, "the best end I have had in eleven years at Harvard," he said. Gatto and

Under quarterback Brian Dowling, who started the fourth game of the 1967 season—against Columbia—Yale's record was 14 wins, 1 tie, 0 losses.

The 1967 Elis, Ivy League champions, scored 278 points
against their opponents, the highest total since 1903. In 1968
Yale would do even better, with a total of 317 points.

Ric Zimmerman (26) fades to pass in the 1967 game. Despite
his heroic efforts—289 yards passing, including two touchdowns—Yale defeated Harvard 24–20.

Hornblower added a lot of power to the Crimson attack, and the defense, headed by Chiofaro and owning a very good secondary with Tom Williamson and Tom Wynne prominent among them, was consistently strong throughout the season, at least as strong as Yale's perhaps if one can overlook a singularly unhappy afternoon against the Tigers. It was a good club and, like Yale, well-equipped with offensive versatility. Still, the record was not as impressive as that of the Bulldogs; the Crimson had lost a squeaker to Dartmouth, barely edged out Cornell, and had been soundly thrashed by Old Nassau. But facing Yale, the Redshirts felt no lack of confidence. The habit of victory was strong.

The sun was shining brightly upon the 68,315 spectators in the Bowl ("the Ivy League's largest crowd ever," according to Will Cloney) [13] when the captains met for the toss of the coin. Yale immediately took command in the manner Blue followers had come to expect, for the '67 squad, after the loss in the season's opener, had never been at the short end of the score at any time in a game. Yet, though the Bulldog was dominant, an alert Harvard defense frustrated two scoring threats by interceptions, and a third blue attempt came to nought when Begel, for once, missed a field goal. The first quarter was scoreless. In the second period, however, the Blue power moved into high gear. A Crimson fumble gave Yale the ball on the Harvard forty; Dowling's pass to Weinstein moved it to the Crimson seventeen. Bob Levin, Barrows's replacement, made first down on the two, and Fisher carried the ball to the goal line, where his fumble was recovered by Marting for a touchdown. A few plays later Dowling made a spectacular contribution—taking the ball on his own forty, he embarked on a series of evasive scrambles that took him back to the ten before he could shake himself free and spot Hill waiting upfield. He found him on the Harvard forty, and Hill went the rest of the way for the second Blue touchdown. A few plays later Begel intercepted a Harvard pass and so earned his second try at a field goal. This time it was good and the Blue had a 17–0 lead. Finally Harvard struck back: Zimmerman got to work and, completing two passes to Lord and another to Hornblower, who crossed the Blue goal line, he brought Harvard back into the fray. At that point the Yale stands were not greatly troubled.

But in the second half the Crimson counterattack was irresistible. Zimmerman's incredibly accurate passing carried his team eighty yards, Gatto finally lugging the ball into pay dirt. Harvard's try for a two-point conversion failed. The rest of the third quarter saw both sides battling hard and vainly for another score. Early in the fourth quarter the Crimson, now clearly controlling the action, launched another drive which was stopped on the Yale six. But Yale was now penned in her own territory and compelled to punt from close to her goal line. Harvard got the ball on the Yale forty and in four plays, the last a fourth down pass, Zimmerman to Lord, that covered thirty-one yards, put the Crimson ahead 20–17. There were about three minutes of playing time left. Harvard kicked off and Yale took the ball on her 22-yard

In the last three minutes of the 1967 game, Del Marting caught two key passes, one of them for the winning touchdown.

line. Cool and poised, as if the game were safely in hand, Dowling sent Levin for five yards through the line, tossed a sideline pass to Marting, getting first down on his thirty-five. On the next play, for once without having to scramble, he found Marting alone beyond the Harvard secondary, and his graceful pass was caught and carried thirty yards to put the Bulldog back on top. Sixty-five yards in a few electric seconds! There were two minutes left—and the game was not over. Following the kickoff, three successive Zimmerman passes took the ball to the Yale 20-yard line; Harvard's O'Connell carried the pigskin another ten yards, where he was tackled by two Yale defenders and the ball fell from his hands, to be recovered by Madden of the Elis. And that was it. For the first time since 1960 the Bulldogs were league champions and Big Three champions as well.

The Harvard locker room was charged with mixed emotions after the game. Yovicsin, it is reported, had tears in his eyes. O'Connell was downcast by his fumble (he had been playing with a broken rib, a fact he had not disclosed to his coaches). Bill Cobb was seething with a sense of injustice; for him, Dowling was not to be compared with Zimmerman. It turned out that the defender meant to cover Marting had slipped on the turf. The general feeling was one of resentment against an unjust fate. [14] And it may be true that, as Dowling said years later, the Blue had won a game it shouldn't have won. Undeniably Zimmerman won the passing duel (if it could be called that, for Dowling passed infrequently); in fact, his performance remained a Crimson record in

The Game until Larry Brown came along eleven years later. (It is interesting that both Zimmerman's and Brown's records were made in a lost cause; the same could be said for Yale's Doyle, whose unmatched passing yardage would be amassed a few years later in an Eli defeat.) Statistically, too, Harvard did better than Yale both in total yardage and first downs, though the Bulldog had a fifty-yard edge in rushing. Yet it would be unfair to Watson's resilient band to see the game as merely an example of Fortune's mischief. The Bulldogs did not give up when the tide flowed against them, and the crucial fumble of the unhappy O'Connell resulted from hard, aggressive defensive play. It would have been a great game no matter which side had won.

The spectacle staged by the ancient rivals in 1967 was of such glitter that its splendor might linger undimmed for a decade or more, a radiant example of The Game at its best. Yet its glory was surpassed, if not obscured, by the drama of 1968, which may assuredly be regarded as a candidate for the designation of The Game of the Century. It had a special claim to distinction regardless of what might have taken place on the field of battle, for it was one of the very rare occasions on which the Blue and Crimson both came to the *momento de la verdad* unvanquished and untied. Such virginal confrontations had occurred only ten times in the course of history and only once in the twentieth century, when Ted Coy and Ham Fish had led their forces on to the field two generations earlier, the year the Model T was born.[15] That memorable encounter had taken place in the rela-

tively new Stadium on Soldiers Field; it was fitting that the warriors of 1968 should have the same trysting place. Admittedly, both athletic associations could have wished it had been in New Haven this time; by the day of the game even the Bowl would have been inadequate to contain the throngs who wanted to witness the spectacle. (One may suspect that in Cambridge there was sincere repentance for having dismantled those extra seats seventeen years earlier.)

In September, of course, such a grand climax to the season could not have been foreseen. It was clear enough to the pigskin world, in spite of Cozza's ritualistic laments over the loss of some of his '67 starters, that the Bulldogs would be mighty, if not invincible. As today one reads the lineup of the starters against Harvard the suspicion grows that Brian Dowling's band may well have been the most powerful delegation fielded by the Blue in the course of our century. On offense, the pair of senior ends, Bruce Weinstein and Del Marting were outstanding; their classmates at the tackle post, Kyle Gee and George Bass, were big and strong (the former stood 6'4" and weighed in at 235); Jack Perkowski and Bart Whiteman at guards were juniors but veterans; Fred Morris, another senior, was serving his second year at center. With Dowling and Hill in the backfield, firepower was assured, but their classmates Levin and Davidson were by no means unworthy of their company. Nine of the eleven had played together for three years. On defense, too, experience was not wanting; Pat Madden, Dick William, and Fran Gallagher—a truly outstanding

The undefeated 1968 Yale team, captained by Brian Dowling, was a scoring machine: the season's totals show 2,101 yards rushing and 2,006 passing, a twentieth-century record.

performer—were also of the class of '69; Tom Neville, a junior, and Jim Gallagher, a sophomore and brother of Fran, were on a level with their seniors (Neville would be captain two years later). The senior Mick Bouscaren and the veteran junior Andy Coe made up a redoubtable pair of linebackers; in the secondary Ed Franklin and J. P. Goldsmith, another pair of seasoned seniors, were assisted by Don Martin and the young "monster" Ron Kell, a sophomore but redoubtable. Yale had a strong bench, too; Dowling's backup man, Bob Bayless, versatile and resourceful, would have been a starter on most Yale teams, and he in turn was backed up by the sophomore Joe Massey, al-

ready showing signs of competence. In Bob Sokolowski the Blue could boast of a uniquely endowed returner of punts adept at picking up yardage—and such was his confidence that he never signaled for a fair catch. Never since the glory days of the nineteenth century had the Blue put together such a supercharged scoring machine; the season's totals would show 2,101 yards rushing and 2,006 passing, a twentieth-century record. It must be admitted that defensively the performance was a little less impressive; the opponents ran 2,278 yards and scored 147 points; to be sure, since the first team always got an early lead and substitutions were frequent many of the adver-

The undefeated 1968 Harvard team, captained by halfback Vic Gatto (holding ball), was deep in veteran defensemen.

sary's yards and points were scored against the reserves.

Yovicsin would have had much greater reason than Cozza to lament the attrition of graduation. From his good '67 combination he had lost the two most valuable players, Ric Zimmerman and Carter Lord. The offensive backfield that faced Yale, however, was a strong one, led by Captain Vic Gatto (at 5'6" the shortest man ever to be chosen to captain a Crimson squad; he was an inch shorter than Albie Booth, but no one ever called Gatto a mighty mite: the adjective would fit but he carried 185 pounds of fighting muscle). Ray Hornblower and Gus Crim, a pair of juniors, shared the ball-carrying chores with their captain; George Lalich, a senior, was a steady if not spectacular quarterback. To the offensive line, Tom Jones, Ted Skowronski, and Bob Giannino contributed the necessary experience; all were seniors and lettermen. Bob Dowd, a junior, was at right tackle, and his classmate John Kiernan played beside him at end. The sophomore Pete Varney, destined for greatness, stood large and menacing (6'2" and 245 pounds) at the other end.

As their performance during the season would attest, the Crimson offense was not to be scorned.

It must be said, however, that, on the record, they were not quite as awesome as Yale's attacking platoon. The Crimson point total was 236 and the total yardage compiled was 2,833. On the eve of The Game the totals against Ivy League rivals were: for Harvard, 121 to opponents' 41, for Yale, 208 to 90.

The figures suggest that if the Harvard offensive platoon may have been less puissant than that of the Bulldogs, the defense might be a little better. And in fact the defense was Harvard's chief asset in the campaign leading up to to the climactic battle. Here, the Crimson was not lacking in experience. Up front, Pete Hall, Steve Zebal, Alex Maclean, and Lonny Kaplan were all seniors, as were the linebacker John Emery and three of the four secondary defenders, John Ignacio, Tom Wynne, and Tom Conway. John Cramer at right end, though a junior, was well seasoned; only Gary Farneti and Rich Frisbie in back of the line were sophomores. Both sides fielded young men of sturdy build; Harvard's line averaged 216 both on offense and defense; Yale 219 and 200, respectively.

When two undefeated teams meet at the end of a season it is hard for odds-makers to make up their minds. On the record Yale looked a little better but not much.

November 23 brought a bright, shining sun, a pleasant if unseasonable warmth, and a blue and all but windless sky. Forty-one thousand packed the Stadium. And the game was on. It began in faithful conformity to the pattern of the '67 meeting. It took the Blue a little while to get into gear, but late in the first quarter, after Bouscaren recovered a Harvard fumble on the Bulldog twenty, Dowling engineered an eighty-yard march for a score, featuring a brilliant thirty-three-yard run by Davidson. The Eli captain took the ball over himself and, a few minutes later, early in the second period, passed to Hill for the second touchdown. Following Franklin's block of a Harvard punt on the Crimson's 8-yard line, Dowling passed to Marting for a third score, and the pair of Cleveland boys worked the same play again for a two-point conversion. 22–0 Yale; just like last year only a little better. And even as last year, just before the end of the half came the Crimson counterattack, and a pass from Champi (who had replaced Lalich) at quarterback was good for fifteen yards and a touchdown. The kick was missed. Yale 22–6 at the half. In the third quarter a Yale fumble was recovered by Freeman on the Blue twenty-five. Champi came off the bench again. He passed to Varney for a first down on the one and Crim bucked over. 22–13. Yale dominated play the rest of the period but twice fumbled the ball away. In the early moments of the fourth period, the Blue machine rolled again, and Dowling went around right end for the fourth Yale score, Bayless converting. It wasn't long before the Bulldogs were on the march once more, and Levin brought the ball to the Harvard fourteen, where a Crimson defender pried him loose from the leather. It didn't seem very significant; after all, only three and a half minutes were left to play and Yale had a sixteen-point lead. If I may insert a bit of personal recollection: I recall very clearly at that point

Calvin Hill, one of the all-time Yale great halfbacks, rushed for ninety-two yards in the 1968 game. He went on to a highly successful career in the pros.

thinking to myself: "There is time for Harvard to score another touchdown and it wouldn't surprise me if they did. But even to tie the game would take a combination of Harvard perfection, Yale ineptitude, and a few breaks. It is mathematically impossible." But the impossible happened. Of all the accounts of those last 200 seconds that I have read I think Will Cloney in the *News and Views of Harvard Sports* best chronicles the incredible exploits of the Crimson and the mishaps and mischances of the Blue. I quote it here:

John Ballantyne (Port Washington, NY) who had been brilliant on kickoffs and adequate as Hornblower's replacement, came up with a 17-yard gain. Then a moment later, Harvard got a big break. Champi was ganged for a 12-yard loss back at the 17-yard line as he tried to pass; Yale was caught holding downfield, however, and the penalty took the ball to the Eli 47.

A pass to Freeman carried to the Yale 30, but Champi was hit for a loss on the next play back to the 37. Now Harvard got another good break. Trapped again, Champi succeeded in shoveling a lateral toward tackle Fritz Reed (Lancaster, OH), an end last year. Fritz scooped up the ball and took off on a 26-yard gallop to the Yale 15. That was enough to unnerve the Elis, and on the next play, Champi threw to Freeman, who caught the ball at the five, and fought his way over the goal line. That was 14:18, and Harvard went for two points. Champi tried a pass to Varney which was knocked loose, but interference was called. On a second try from the one, Crim crashed over. It was 29–21.

Bruce Weinstein (89) lunges to make a difficult reception (1968).

Vic Gatto (40) drives through the line for a gain (1968).

That would have been a respectable final score, too, but Harvard still had hopes. All season long it had practiced onside kickoffs, and the practice paid off. Wynne approached the ball as usual, but Ken Thomas (Manchester, NH) moved in from the right, nudged it over toward the Yale bench, and the swift Kelley pounced on it at the Yale 49.

Champi went back to pass, couldn't find a receiver, and went 14 yards around left end. He was stopped by a facemask tackle that cost Yale 15 more yards, so it was first down on the Yale 20 with 32 seconds left. Two incomplete passes used up six seconds each, and it was third and 10, still on the 20, with 20 seconds left.

In came the gutsy Gatto, who hadn't played since early in the third period. He went out to the right as a flanker and Yale gave him respectful attention—so much so that Crim was able to get running room on a draw play and go 14 yards for a first down at the 6—and now there were 14 seconds left. (Harvard, of course, was using its time-outs to stop the clock after each play.)

Champi went back for what probably would be the final pass, ran right and was blocked, then ran left and was smothered for a two-yard loss. Three seconds to play—but enough to permit one final attempt.

Again Champi went back to pass, again he was ganged. For a split second he was on the verge of lateralling—but he was without friends back there. Then, a la Dowling, he squirmed free and threw to the far left corner of the end zone—to the unprotected spot occupied by the heroic Gatto. The catch was routine—but Harvard was still two points behind, 29–27, and the clock had run out.

The crowd exploded onto the field, and Champi took advantage of the confusion to run to the bench for instructions. When the field was cleared and play resumed, he got the ball from center, took a couple of steps backward, and threw a strike to big Pete Varney, who got his body between the ball and the Yale defender just over the goal line for one of the biggest catches in Harvard history. Nobody noticed—and nobody would have cared anyway—but officials later revealed that Yale was holding on the play and Harvard would have had another chance—but it didn't need one.

At that point, the *Harvard Alumni Bulletin* reports, "The Stadium exploded. Strangers embraced, full professors danced and the Yale people put their handkerchiefs to the use they were intended for."[16] Of that last minute Cozza said simply: "You felt that it had to be," and in fact, many Yale adherents confessed later that, watching the surrealistic series of mischances and misplays, they felt as if they were watching the working out of a preordained script. Journalists called on untapped wells of eloquence in their dispatches. One affirmed that "Harvard turned The Game into The Miracle."[17] Bob Barton opined that "In 83 years of Yale–Harvard football there has never been a game like this. If they go on playing for a thousand years, there will never be another one the same."[18] It is strange to think that there should be so much elation on one side and so much gloom on the other—after all, it was a tie. But then both sides knew who had "won" it.

Before we leave the Stadium it is right that we should take a last look at Brian Dowling, who had now joined Mac Aldrich and Clint Frank in the gallery of Yale's brave and doomed Rolands. The Harvard *News and Views* paid him generous tribute:

If there was irony at the end, it was on the Yale side of the field where Brian Dowling stood on the sidelines in total helplessness as the clock ticked off the final seconds of his career.[19] *In other circumstances, it is safe to assume that the day would have had a thrilling climax of another nature. Dowling would have been removed from the game to a long, thunderous, and well-deserved ovation, in which many Harvardians would have participated. He is a great athlete, and it took the greatest rally in Harvard football history to upstage him.*[20]

Crimson and Blue, alike in their Alpine eminence in 1968, were decreed—by the eternal laws of the game and the toll taken by graduation—to face massive reconstruction problems in '69. Of the starters in The Tie, thirteen out of Harvard's twenty-two were missing (platooning was in full swing at this point, and "starters" must no longer be counted as eleven but as twice that number). On first glance the state of the Bulldog was even more unhappy; sixteen of his twenty-two had gone the way of all good collegiate players, taken their diplomas and passed beyond the coach's wistful reach. In actual fact, however, Yale was much better off. The undefeated Blue of the previous year had been not only strong but deep in promising reserves—to a greater extent than Harvard, who had lost, along with so many starters, the real hero of the Great Battle; Champi, now a senior, had decided to give up football. (Probably the tension of the final moments in the Stadium had aged him before his time.) Yale had, if fewer starters, more experienced veterans, including Joe Massey at quarterback, all but unknown in '68, and Don Martin, whom the coaches shrewdly moved from defense to offense, giving the Blue a first-class running back. The pocket-size Klebanoff turned out to be an accurate and reliable field goal kicker, Billy Primps a sturdy fullback, and a defense which included the veterans Captain Andy Coe and Jack Perkowski was substantially bolstered by the massive Lolotai and Earl Matory, both sophomores. Harvard had veterans to count on in Varney and Fritz Reed but nothing like the depth of talent the Bulldog could field. The Blue was not downcast at the start of the season; Coe said the defense would be good and, as for the offense, "the coaches would think of something"; Cozza said he was counting on "the habit of victory." As it turned out, he was right. The Bulldogs lost their opener to Connecticut and a spirited match with Dartmouth; otherwise they were triumphant, even, surprisingly, taking the measure of the Tiger, who had at last—and perhaps mistakenly—forsaken the single wing. Things went not nearly so well for Harvard; unlike Yale they won their opener (over Holy Cross), and dispatched Columbia and Penn with ease, but sound drubbings at the hands of Cornell and Princeton showed a disquieting weakness on defense.

Joe Massey, quarterback of the 1969 Eli contingent, directed an eighty-yard march in the third quarter of the 1969 game that led to the game's only score. Final: Yale 7–Harvard 0.

If football were a computerized science, The Game of '69 should have been an easy triumph for the Blue. But no son or daughter (Yale "went coed" in '69, to the delight of the undergraduates and the dismay of the old Bourbons) of Eli who had sat in the Stadium the previous year was taking anything for granted. And, as it happened, the game was a close one, with the Blue clearly the stronger outfit but unable for a long time to demonstrate her superiority on the scoreboard. Three times in the first half the Bulldogs marched to no purpose into Crimsonland, once on a spectacular forty-two-yard pass, Martin to Milligan, who slipped on the wet grass thirty yards short of the goal. Harvard never threatened; still, at the half the score was 0–0, and Eli followers were beginning to worry. Finally, halfway through the third quarter Massey directed an eighty-yard march, with Martin running thirty-six yards in the course of it. Even so, with first down on the five, it took Primps three thrusts to carry the ball over the line. The real drama of an otherwise rather dull game came in the last few minutes. A roughing-the-kicker penalty gave Harvard the ball on the Yale forty; a pass to Varney brought it to the ten, and one could feel the tremor running through the Yale stands. Would it be '68 again—or worse?— for a touchdown and a two-point conversion would bring down the Blue. But the next sequence of downs justified Coe's faith in his defense; after three plays Harvard had the ball not on the ten but on the thirty-two; even the attempt at a consolation field goal went astray. One could hear the sigh of relief running through the Bowl. It may

Football fan, 1969.

have been Harvard's best game of the season—it was clearly so on the defensive side. Yale, shorn of yesteryear's paladins, managed to tie for the league championship.

In the spring of 1970 for both Harvard and Yale the tide of activism reached its peak. S. B. Sutton reports that on the night of April 15, "after a day of peaceful demonstration on Cambridge Common and Boston Common against American intervention in Cambodia, an estimated 2,000 people rioted in Harvard Square. . . . They smashed windows in banks and shops. Bystanders, some of whom had marched with them earlier in the day, and a few demonstrators and Cambridge policemen got injured before the crowd was dispersed. . . . The trashing of Harvard Square was the most violent interlude in Cambridge since 1778."[21]

A few weeks later, in New Haven, things could have been even uglier. The trial of Bobby Seale, a Black Panther accused of murder, was held in the courthouse on the New Haven Green. Hundreds of Seale sympathizers converged on the city. President Brewster, supported if not prompted by all the college councils, "defused" the potentially dangerous situation by opening the gates of the university to the visitors and inviting them to come as "guests"—and indeed hospitality was provided by the undergraduates. Yale escaped with only a minor fire in the hockey rink—and the lingering resentment of New Haven shopkeepers, who had thought it prudent to suspend activities and board up their windows for the duration of the "guests'" visit.[22]

Both administrations were thankful that the

school year ended shortly after these events, and both looked forward to the fall with some trepidation. But to everyone's surprise, all of a sudden the worst was over; the tide gradually receded. Brewster remarked that "an eerie silence seemed to pervade the Yale Campus" and a like tranquility descended on the Square. In fact, throughout the country by Christmas of 1970 it was apparent that undergraduates, sensing the end of the Viet Nam War and having, in most cases, won their battles for a greater share in the governance of their sundry almae matres, were willing to come down from the barricades and get back to their books. The seventies would witness a progressive détente; marches and demonstrations came to an end; even beards gradually disappeared or became, like beaded necklaces, optional rather than required accessories for the male.

It was to be Yovicsin's last year in Cambridge, and as he surveyed his prospects he was not too sanguine. Nineteen sixty-nine had not been a very bright year for the Crimson, and Yovicsin was putting what hopes he had in his small group of seniors, primarily defensemen led by Captain Gary Farneti. In fact, however, he was blessed with a pair of excellent sophomore backfield candidates, Eric Crone at quarterback and Ted DeMars, a fleet ballcarrier. The experienced Varney and Gatto were back at the end posts, and Richie Szaro was a gifted kicker. Facing Yale, the Crimson had behind her a 6–2 record, including four league victories. It was a very good team.

On paper at least Yale's should have been better. Captain Tom Neville, aside from being a Phi Beta Kappa student, anchored a good defense, with Gallagher and Lolotai giving aid and support. Massey was back as signal caller and Donny Martin returned to his halfback post. Yale's sophomore delegation was strong, too, with Dick Jauron already showing signs of greatness and Jim Nottingham displaying a rare skill in getting off high and long punts. The toe of the minuscule but unerring Klebanoff was again available for field goals. Yale lost only one game before entraining for Cambridge, a hard-fought battle with Dartmouth, who was destined to go undefeated.

The afternoon of November 21 was clear, cold, and windy, with a fairly steady twenty-five-mile-per-hour blast fighting its way out of the open end of the Stadium. In the first quarter the Elis had the wind at their backs and what's more had a bit of luck when a Harvard fumble on the second play of the game gave them excellent field position. Here, as if to prove the validity of Yovicsin's judgment, the Harvard defense showed its mettle; neither Massey's passes nor Bulldog running could get so much as a first down, and Klebanoff for once missed a field goal attempt. Harvard, encouraged by her show of defensive strength, lost no time in getting to work when in the second period it was her turn to profit by the gale. A Yale punt in the teeth of the wind covered only eight yards; the Cantabs got the ball on the Blue thirty-one-yard line, and, mixing brilliant passing with some running of his own, Crone had a touchdown (on a pass to DeMars) in no time. And even though Nottingham redeemed himself with a fifty-yard punt against the wind, the Crimson roared back

Captain Tom Neville, aside from being a Phi Beta Kappa student, anchored Yale's 1970 defensive line at tackle.

again, covering fifty-five yards in a march crowned by Crone's smart bootleg run around left end. At the half it was 14—0 Harvard.

That was the end of the Harvard scoring; the second half Yale came out fighting and held the Redshirts at bay; Szaro had a chance at three field goals (all unsuccessful) but otherwise the Bulldog contained the Crimson thrusts. But if the Blue had learned to protect her goal line she remained— thanks to the Redshirts' defense—all but incapable of moving the ball herself. The Elis mounted no consistent marches. In the third quarter Bulldog hopes were roused when, on a handoff from Sizemore (who had replaced the limping Massey), Donny Martin rocketed sixty-two yards untouched for a score. There was still plenty of time left but the Crimson defense held up. At the end of the quarter Yale recovered a fumble on the Harvard 13-yard line but again could not prevail and had to settle for a field goal. The last quarter ended in a flurry of excitement when Yale's third quarterback, the sophomore Rollie Purrington, led his desperate company on a sixty-yard march ending on the Harvard 20-yard line. The last play of the game carried drama to the very end. Crone, his back to the goal line, called two time-consuming plays and then, as Cloney tells it, "on the third, thinking time had run out, he traipsed joyfully back into the end zone. Yale's Ron Kell, plus about 2,000 spectators, tackled Eric for the safety that almost nobody saw. It didn't matter much, although think what a fumble would have done."[23]

The engagement of 1970—"a combined cliff hanger, farce and furious spectacle" in the words

of the *Yale Daily News*[24]—was a hard one for
Yale to lose. The Blue outrushed her adversary
by fifty-seven yards and was in the battle to the
end. But Harvard deserved to win. For the crucial
second quarter Crone was just too smart for the
Elis, and for the entire game the Cantab defensive
unit, Spencer Dreischarf at nose guard supported
by Captain Farneti, Jack Neal, Dave Ignacio, and
Rich Frisbie among others, was impregnable when
the occasion required it. Blue and Crimson tied
for second place among the Ivies that year.

It was a truly grand finale for Yovicsin. He left
behind him a record to be proud of; in fourteen
years at Harvard his statistics were 78–42–5;
against Yale it stands 8–5–1. No Harvard coach
has done better in the Stadium. At a press conference he revealed that the last years of his assignment had taken a heavy toll. Since undergoing
surgery five years earlier he had been "hustled
from the field" after each game. "Coaching," he
added, "is not an easy life even when you win."
No Harvard partisan would deny that he had
earned his rest.

THE BALLAD OF CARM AND JOE

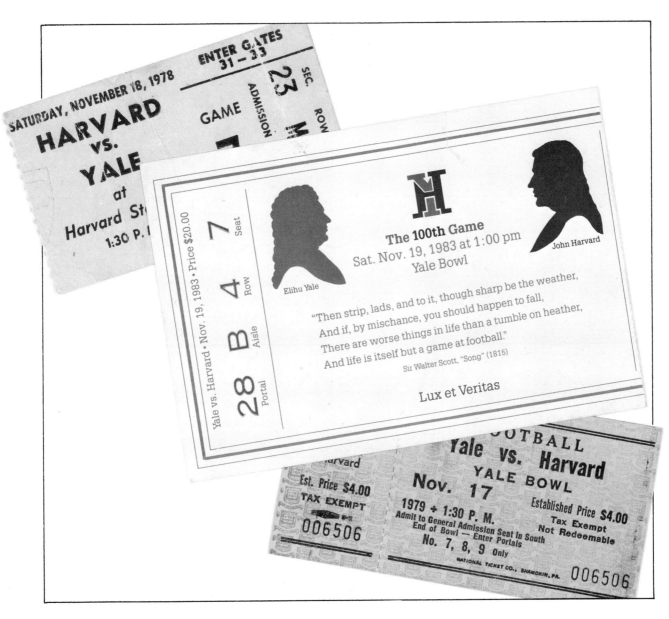

Yovicsin's last year coincided with the first year of the tenure of office of Robert D. Watson, appointed director of athletics in 1970 to succeed Adolph Samborski, who had reached retirement age. Watson had been dean of Harvard College and was a veteran of the gridiron wars of the mid-thirties. He was immediately faced with the necessity of finding a successor to Yovicsin. His choice fell on Joe Restic, at that time head coach of the Hamilton Tiger Cats of the Canadian Professional Football League. Restic was by no means unfamiliar with the American football scene, having served on the staffs of Colgate and Brown, earning the respect and even admiration of his colleagues; Alva Kelley of Brown said of him: "Joe has the best football mind in North America." His advent as commander of the Crimson armed forces marks a new chapter in the history of the rivalry. For thirteen years, at this time of writing, he and Carm Cozza have engaged in exciting competition. Off the field they are good friends, and many observers have remarked that a spirit of amicable sportsmanship has flourished over their years of rivalry. At the same time the two coaches have collaborated to give their followers some of the most crowd-pleasing and spirited performances in the long annals of The Game. Differences in style and tactics lend further interest to their sparring. Restic brought with him to Harvard what he calls a "multiflex offense." He will put not one but two and sometimes three backs in motion, he likes to use a "floating quarterback," he abandons the handoff or pitchout when it suits him in favor of

Joe Restic, Harvard's head coach since 1971, favors a "multi-flex offense" that allows for inventiveness and unpredictability.

the direct pass. He encourages the belief that the disconcerting antics of his backfield before the snap (which often cost them offside or delay of game penalties) are not planned at all but spontaneously invented by his deft and quick-witted ballcarriers. Cozza, on the other hand, is conservative; his strength is mainly in an intuitional talent for putting his players in the right spot; his formations are normally conventional and he depends much less on surprise than on faultless execution. Fanciful philosophers might see in these mentors a kind of incarnation of the spirit of the institutions they serve: Yale, steady, traditional, perfectionist; Harvard, adventurous and inventive. Of course, just to make things confusing, on any given occasion Harvard can look very staid (as she did in the deliberate, unhurried mauling of Yale in 1979) or once in a while Carm can pull his own surprises, as in occasionally making his quarterback a pass receiver or, every other year, calling for a smooth reverse. In any event, since the two rivals began their jousting, the games have more often than not been thrillers.

One cannot say as much, unfortunately, for the first meeting. Admittedly it did not lack sparkling plays, but from the first quarter on the issue was never in doubt. But let us look first at the personnel and the record of the rival battalions. A change of coaches, perhaps particularly from the traditional approach of Yovicsin to the exuberant style of Restic, is difficult for a squad to handle. However, on Charlesside a fairly good nucleus of veterans was on hand: Crone, the Bulldog tormentor, and DeMars and the fiery Rich Gatto (brother to the victorious Vic) in the offensive backfield, and, best of all perhaps, on defense Ignacio (now captain), Dreischarf, Steve Golden, Tom Bilodeau, and a few other robust comrades; the sophomore class supplied no fewer than five starters on the offensive line and the massive Floridian Mitch Berger at defensive end; Bruce Tetirick, class of '74, was a reliable kicker. All Harvard's games were close and hard fought; the record coming into the Yale game was an even four and four.

In New Haven, Cozza had his problems. The last survivors of the Dowling era had departed. The senior delegation had made, as freshmen, the poorest record in many a long year—and this somewhat underprivileged class made up the majority of the starting lineup. Jauron was back, a notable asset, but circumstances compelled him to play at fullback, not the best position for exercise of his talents. Cozza's major problem was at quarterback. Sizemore was not at his best; the choice seemed to lie between Purrington, a junior with little field experience, and his classmate Pfeil, with less. For the Harvard game it would be Purrington, Pfeil having suffered a concussion in the battle with Dartmouth. Still, one could not say that the Bulldogs, captained by Rich Maher, a competent end, lacked experience, and hopes were moderately high as the season began. Perhaps the record was not too bad; it was, like the Crimson's, an even four and four as the rivals squared off in the Bowl. Overall Harvard looked a little stronger, but the Elis had come fresh from their day of glory, having beaten a very good Princeton team the week previously. It was felt in

the Blue camp that if they could solve Restic's innovations, the game might be won.

They couldn't. Crone led his comrades on a dazzling forty-six-yard march halfway through the first quarter; his pass to Gatto gave the Crimson first blood. A few minutes later, moving from the Blue 29-yard line, where the Bulldogs had obligingly fumbled, Crone, using the floating quarterback play to advantage, passed twenty-nine yards to Denis Sullivan for the second Crimson tally. In the second quarter Yale cooperated with her adversary, giving up two touchdowns on a blocked kick and an interception by Mark Ferguson. In the interim Yale's one good drive had been frustrated by a fumble on the Harvard 2-yard line; the ensuing safety, when the Crimson kicker was rushed, was small comfort to the Blue. 28–2 at the half; the most opulent first half enjoyed by the Crimson in all the years of battle. Clearly the game was over. To the credit of the Bulldog he made the second half a fair contest; Jauron scored at the end of the third period, following a pass interference penalty against the Cantabs, and one more on a pretty fourteen-yard run capping a seventy-one-yard drive in the fourth quarter. Harvard's final score came after the interception of a Bulldog desperation pass deep in his own territory, Steve Harrison going over in the last seconds to make the count 35–16. Statistically the Elis didn't do badly, gaining 275 yards to Harvard's 321. But a good deal of Blue yardage was made after the game was out of sight; Harvard could afford to relax. Yale observers sadly observed that there might be something to be said for Restic's flying circus.

Harvard captain Dave Ignacio (42) blocks a punt to set up the winning touchdown against Yale (1971).

As in 1966, Yale drew no penalties; Harvard's count of 116 yards was rather high, a token not of Crimson wickedness but of the delicacy of timing necessary for Restic's tactical operations.

Restic was, incidentally, not the only newcomer to the Harvard high command in 1971. That same year Nathan Pusey stepped down and was succeeded by Derek Bok, Stanford '51, and at the time dean of the Harvard Law School. So he was at once that rare appointment, an alien—from the point of view of his undergraduate training—and also a member of the Harvard family. Kingman Brewster, too, had been a member of the Harvard law faculty before coming to Yale as provost in 1961. For a few years, unique in their annals, the sister universities would have their destinies directed by a pair of Harvard law professors. (Some alumni thought they looked alike, too.) And even as Brewster had, so Bok opened his administration with a football victory over the cherished enemy.

In the fall of 1972, as Richard Nixon was moving on to his rout of McGovern, generously leaving to his opponent the votes of Massachusetts and the District of Columbia, the Bulldog, who had suffered much ill-treatment at the hands of the ancient rival over the past two seasons, was striving mightily to put together a combination to end Cantabrigian domination. This year there was an added incentive—not that it was needed—for 1972 marked the hundredth anniversary of Yale football, which had begun, as noted, in 1872 with the meeting of the "picked twenties" of Columbia and Yale in old Hamilton Park. Such a centennial could not pass unobserved: in the summer plans were made for a memorial banquet, and the team trotting on the field for the opener had a blue and white oval bearing the number 100 discreetly engraved on their helmets. One thing the centennial committee could not plan for, although it was the most desirable of all desiderata, was a winning team worthy of celebrating such an illustrious tra-

dition. The record of 1971 was hardly cheering, viewed as a point of departure; but in fact, the survivors of that unhappy year included many competent youths, the better for their experience under fire—most of all Jauron, now in good shape and playing at tailback where he belonged. Donohue, Bob Perschel the captain, Wilhelm, Fehling, and others had also proven themselves in the baptism of fire of '71—and the sophomores were rich in talent, having gone undefeated in freshman year and carrying on their roster names like Tommy Doyle, Rudy Green, John Smoot—all destined for eventual Bulldog glory. Put together with Cozza's customary craftsmanship, the New Haven machine of '72 had some glorious moments on its way to the Stadium, demolishing Brown with the highest point total in history over the Bruins, sweeping Dartmouth off the field with a brilliant display by Doyle, who earned his starting job on that day; looking, at its best, unbeatable. But it was also a kind of Jekyll and Hyde team, undone by Cornell and almost blown off the field by Penn; it seemed somehow a mighty giant—yet susceptible to moments of panic and ineptitude. Journalists called it the yo-yo team. (Looking ahead for the moment, one might say that both personalities would be visible on Soldiers Field.)

Meanwhile in Cambridge there were similar uncertainties. Crone was back and Captain Ted DeMars likewise; there were good backfield men for all positions. The offensive line was strong, too, featuring the senior John Hagerty and the junior Jeff Bone at ends; but on defense, although Mike McHugh was fearsome at defensive end and

The 1972 Yale team, which compiled a 7−2 record, lost only to Cornell and Penn. Unbeatable when playing at its best, the squad won the Big Three championship.

Dave St. Pierre valiant in the secondary, the Crimson was not as sturdy as she had been; the season totals show a greater number of opponents' points than at any time since 1956. The skirmishes with Penn and Princeton had been setbacks. Yet De-Mars's battalion could be dangerous; it had taken the measure of Cornell (where Yale had failed) and won a tie with Dartmouth (league champions in spite of their mauling by the Elis). On a good day Harvard could be hard to beat. Besides, the *cognoscenti* pointed out, the Stadium had not been, in recent years, a healthy place for the Bulldog; he had not won on Soldiers Field since 1960.

The game showed both teams at their best and their worst and in the process provided one of the most thrilling spectacles in many a year— well, anyway, since The Tie. Weather was good, clear and not too much wind. For Yale followers the first quarter looked like a hideous reprise of the action on the Blue's last visit to Cambridge. On Harvard's second sequence of plays DeMars turned the Blue right flank for a run of eighty-six yards (longest Crimson run from scrimmage against Yale in history), and, as if to prove it was no fluke, Harvard quickly picked up another three points on a field goal following a Blue fumble;

Ted DeMars, escorted by Jeff Bone (89), races past Yale coach Carmen Cozza on record eighty-six-yard touchdown run (1972).

The turning point in the 1972 game came in the third quarter when, with Yale trailing 17–6, Dick Jauron broke through the Harvard line and cantered seventy-four yards for the touchdown. He is shown here about to cross the goal line. Final: Yale 28–Harvard 17. Photo S. Frinzi.

and in the second quarter Eric Crone, tamer of Bulldogs, engineered a sixty-eight-yard march through the Blue defenders, sneaking over himself to make the score 17–0. A bleak silence descended on the Yale stands. Never in the history of the rivalry had either team overcome a lead of such dimensions. Only the intervention of the gods could save the Bulldog. And intervene they did. Crowded back to its goal line after receiving a kick, the Crimson fumbled the ball on the one. Yale recovered and Tyrell Hennings pounded over to put the Blue on the scoreboard. Seconds later the Elis blocked a kick and recovered on the ten. On the last play of the half Jauron was stopped at the 1-yard line, and Harvard went off with a comfortable lead; but the last minutes before the interval seemed to presage better things for the Bulldogs. The change in momentum, aside from the divine intervention mentioned above, was in some part due to the substitution of Purrington for Tom Doyle. Restic had set up special defenses for Doyle's style of play and Cozza shrewdly reacted. Purrington played the rest of the game.

The early moments of the third quarter were marked by an interception of one of Purrington's passes that seemed to suggest the tide had turned again in Harvard's favor. But this time the Blue defense held, and Yale took the ball on her own twenty-eight. On second down came the turning point of the game, when Jauron broke through the Harvard forward line and cantered seventy-four yards for the touchdown. The score was now 17–13. Harvard was feeling the pressure. On the first play after the Yale kickoff Mike Noetzel re-

covered a Crimson fumble on the 39-yard line. Rudy Green and Purrington got the ball to the Harvard seven in two successive plays, and on a broken play from that point Purrington rolled into the end zone. A two-point conversion made it 21–17, and now the Cantabs had their backs to the wall. The pass was their only recourse, but at this point—very much unlike the first quarter—the Bulldogs were outcharging the Redshirts, and a Crone pass, hastily thrown, was snared by Yale's Willie Robinson at midfield. Yale beat her way down to the final score, giving the ball the Jauron to take over from the one. Out came the white handkerchiefs, and the Centennials had defied the demons of the Stadium. Neither Restic nor DeMars could find an explanation for the very marked reversal. "We were as fired up as any team I've ever coached," said Restic. "You have to give credit to that Yale ball club. We lost momentum and couldn't regain it."[1] The victory gave Yale second place in the Ivies (to Dartmouth, who had been easy Bulldog meat in the Bowl) and the Big Three championship for the first time since 1969.

Given the nature of the rivalry and the homogeneity of the pool from which both sides draw their recruits it is not surprising that a substantial proportion of the combats are upsets—on a given occasion when spirits are roused, one team or the other has shown itself quite capable of rising above the limits of its talents as indicated in past performances or as estimated by the odds-makers. Granted as much, there are a few cases in the files where the historian must remain baffled as he contemplates the final score. Nineteen seventy-three is an example of this sort of inexplicable phenomenon. Both competitors had strong squads that year; Yale had a well-rounded backfield in three seasoned juniors, Rudy Green, "Hurricane" Hennings, so he liked to style himself, at the running positions, and Doyle, now in his second year of service at quarterback. Sophomores of promise were Don Gesicki and Rod Gordon. Up front the Blue was strong, too, with Don Gallagher (third of the brothers to serve the Blue) and Bob Fernandez at the ends and sturdy warriors such as Ken Burkus and Ray Riddick; and on defense Captain Gary Wilhelm, Kelly Peddicord, Rich Feryok, and Rich Fehling in the line and a trio of agile sophomores in the secondary, with Ed Lewis and Willie Robinson adding their experience. But by the time the teams met in the Bowl, Harvard had the better record; on offense, Jim Stoeckel was a shrewd and experienced signal caller, Neal Miller a first-class fullback; nor should one overlook—indeed how could one, for he stood a lean and towering 6'6"—Pat McInally, destined for a brilliant career in the pros, a superb receiver, and a first-class punter as well. Dan Jiggetts, weighing in at 265, anchored a strong offensive line. On defense, six of the starting eleven were seniors, including Mike O'Hare at tackle, Mitch Berger and Joe Mackey at the ends, Bob Kristoff at linebacker, and St. Pierre, captain, at safety. The Crimson invaders came to the Bowl with only one loss on their record—to a very strong Dartmouth team, the league champions of the year. One might have expected the Cantabs to be favorites with the bet-

tors, but for some reason ("they must know something we don't," said Cozza on the eve of the combat) Yale was given a three-point edge. Blue followers were not reassured and were further downcast when it was learned that Tommy Doyle, still shaken by injuries received in the Princeton game, would be replaced at quarterback by Kevin Rogan, who had never started for the Blue and, now a senior, had been for two seasons a somewhat overlooked backup man, with little playing experience. One had a right to expect a close, hard-fought battle. Instead it was a Blue walk-away.

In the first quarter, following an interception in Harvard territory, Rogan, mixing passing and rushing, sent Donohue over for seven points. In the second quarter the Blue line chivvied Stoeckel unmercifully, and the Crimson could mount no attack; Yale, again guided by a confident Rogan, marched eighty yards for a second touchdown, and less than thirty seconds later, when another Harvard pass was intercepted, Rogan passed to Fencik for thirty-six yards and a touchdown. Spectators on both sides of the field, remembering the Harvard counterattacks of '67 and '68, expected a similar rebuttal from the Crimson in the second half. It never came. On the other hand, Yale added two more touchdowns (one each by Green and Hennings, both of whom carried for consistent gains) for the largest total, 35–0, over the Crimson since the golden year of 1960. It was a triumph for Rogan and equally so for the Yale defense, which seemed to penetrate the Harvard line at will, cutting off, with equal ease, the Crimson

Kevin Rogan quarterbacked the 1973 Elis to a 35–0 victory over Harvard, passing for 128 yards. Yale's total yardage in The Game that year was an awesome 523.

aerial thrusts; Stoeckel, compelled to pass more often than he would have liked to, had eleven completions out of twenty-seven attempts and suffered two interceptions; his stellar receiver McInally caught only three passes for a total of twenty-nine yards. Yale's total yardage was an awesome 523, with twenty-eight first downs, a record in the series. Harvard's tally of sixteen first downs was not contemptible, but they never came in significant clusters. Cozza described his pupils' performance as "probably as total a team effort as I've seen in many a year. . . . To cite standouts in the game I would have to name over fifty football players"[2] [fifty-six Elis saw action that day of glory].

The encounter of 1974 was one of special importance to Cambridge devotees of the pigskin. As 1972 had been for Yale, so for Harvard 1974 was a centennial year since the Crimson gridiron chronicle had begun in Montreal October 23, 1874, with a victory over McGill. Harvard claims in fact that her first game is also properly to be thought of as the first intercollegiate game of football since undeniably all preceding games, beginning with what the vulgar commonly regard as the first game (Rutgers vs. Princeton, 1869), were actually soccer and not football. While infidels might see in the Cantabrigian insistence on calling 1974 "the real centennial" just another example of Harvard haughtiness, their argument cannot be easily dismissed. In fact, as has been noted, American football did derive from rugby, not soccer. If there is a flaw in the Harvard case it lies in the simple fact that if American football is not soccer it is not rugby either. *Echt* American football came about when the scrum became a controlled scrimmage and when possession was tied to downs. Perhaps the accurate anniversary centennial would be 1982. But for Harvard it was 1974, and, as Yale followers had done two years earlier, the Crimson aficionados in 1974 took a special interest in the progress of their centennial team. It had better be a good one.

And in fact it was. Meeting the visiting Elis in the Stadium on a fine, fair day, the Crimson had a 6–2 record, their only league loss a rather surprising defeat at the hands of Brown (but they had probably been looking ahead, as Crimson squads do, to the climax match). The team had more than its share of competent athletes: "Pineapple" Milt Holt, the left-handed quarterback hailing from Honolulu, was an outstanding passer, Tom Winn, Al Tsitsos, and Neal Miller were first-class running backs—Winn in particular—and the offensive line had two fine ends in McInally and Curtin, with the mammoth Jiggetts heading a doughty company of "toads." On defense, Eric Kurzweil and Bob Shaw were a rugged pair of tacklers, and the secondary was well taken care of by Fran Cronin, Joe Sciolla, and the sophomore Bill Emper, among others. It added up to a resourceful and high-spirited combination.

Just the same, the Crimson went into battle a slight underdog. For 1974 was no less significant for Yale than for Harvard—for the simple reason that Cozza had fielded his best outfit since the Dowling years. The starting backfield, Tom Doyle at quarter, Hennings and Rudy Green, now cap-

Rudy Green, captain of Yale's 1974 team, ran for 142 yards in the 1973 game.

tain, and Gesicki as ballcarriers, was probably in all-around competence second to none in twentieth-century Blue annals. Cozza went back to the I formation this year, designed for a versatile and powerful attack. He had a star receiver in Gary Fencik, and Fernandez was not far behind in competence. He had an abundance of good "toads," Al Moras, Burkus, the massive veteran Greg Dubinetz (6'5", 235 lbs), and the sophomore Vic Staffieri, and a like abundance of stout defensemen: Brian Ameche and Sheldon Smith at ends and Feryok at tackle, with John Smoot and Brent Kirk backing up the line, and seasoned safeties such as Elvin Charity and Mark McAndrews. The Blue task force came to Cambridge undefeated in eight games and with more yardage to its credit than had been amassed even by the invincibles of 1960.

Everyone in the Stadium knew that the "real" centennial would be a genuine thriller. And such foreknowledge was amply justified. Yale, with Gordon in the place of the injured Gesicki,[3] started off as if about to duplicate the performance of the Blue in '73. In spite of a soggy field and a shrewd six-man line deployment that Restic had prepared to slow the Eli rushing attack, Yale scored one touchdown in the first quarter and another in the second, both by Rudy Green. It is true that both were set up by Crimson fumbles. At that point Harvard awoke and, in a fifty-six-yard drive culminating with a Holt–McInally pass, had her first score. With less than a minute left in the half, the Crimson had another, the main contribution being a fifty-six-yard "flea-flicker" from McInally,

on a lateral from Holt, to Jim Curry on the Yale two, a play verging on the melodramatic. Curtin scored on another pass and Harvard went off with a halftime lead of 14–13, since Yale had failed to make the second point after touchdown. Through the third quarter—which showed no advantage to either side, although there were some brilliant Doyle to Fencik passes—it began to seem as if 14–13 would be the final score. But another Harvard fumble gave Yale the ball on the Cantabs' 15-yard line. Such was the toughness of the Crimson resistance that the Blue ended up with only a field goal scored by Randy Carter from the 28-yard line. If the defense could hold, the Bulldog would have another undefeated year. But it was not to be. With five minutes to go, Harvard, taking a kick on her 10-yard line and immediately penalized five yards for delay of game, launched the most stirring come-from-behind march ever seen in the Stadium. With Holt passing to Steve Dart and McInally and alternatively faking, and Winn and Miller running, the Crimson was simply unstoppable, and with fifteen seconds left in the game Holt carried the ball over the Blue goal line himself. Ninety-five yards through a defense that had been called the best in the league! For Harvard it was a moment of delirious ecstasy. "Stop the clock, stop the calendar, stop the world right now," cried Joe Restic as the final whistle blew. "This is it. Now."[4]

For Yale the result was a bitter pill. Especially so for Tom Doyle, who played the best game of his career; he passed for 237 yards and his running gave him a total of 268 yards, both records

Milt Holt, Harvard's 1974 quarterback, receives blocks from
Steve Dart and Tom Winn before diving across the goal line
to score the winning touchdown in a 21–16 upset victory
over Yale.

that still stand. Fencik's eleven receptions made
another record. Looking at it from the Blue side
of the field, one could say it is probable that the
absence of Gesicki was a factor in the loss. Yet
Gordon, his replacement, was a good runner, and
three Harvard fumbles compensated for Gesicki's
absence. And in truth the Yale attack cannot be
faulted; sixteen points is a good total against a

strong opponent. That day, to be sure, they needed
more, and a good deal of credit for the Cantab victory must go to Restic's wily manipulation of the
Crimson defense, which held Yale's talented runners to their smallest total of the season. But even
more important than such tactics was the magnificent surge of last-minute determination, engineered by Holt but carried through by a band of

Harvards that would not give up. Blue hats were doffed to Holt that day. As Dave Matthews remarked: there would never be another "centennial" like it.[5]

Harvard and Yale tied for the league championship that year. But Harvard won the Big Three championship, which is of course the one that counts.

Following the year-by-year progression of The Game, one occasionally has the impression that the whole performance is in the hands of some masterful if invisible director. The rules of the sport change little and infrequently, the patterns of the conflicts' ebb and flow are often similar, yet there is, from year to year, likely to be a pleasing variety of moods—one might almost say, to carry out the figure of the orchestra, a constant change in movements. The combat of 1973 can be readily seen as a *scherzo*, 1974 was clearly an *andante mosso*—not to say *allegro*, particularly for the Harvards; the movement in 1975 was a rather dour *andante* if not quite a *maestoso*. That in spite of the fact that the graph of the game was very similar to that of the encounter of 1974, with Yale grinding out an early lead, then being tied and finally vanquished by a Crimson surge in the last minutes.

As in '74, so too this time both teams were playing for the championship. Each had lost but one league game, Harvard to a resurgent Tiger, Yale to a surprisingly powerful Brown outfit, also in competition for the Ivy championship. Both Crimson and Blue were strong, largely veteran delegations. Jim Kubacki was a brilliant passer and

actually surpassed Holt in total yardage gained during a season; Tom Winn piled up 630 yards rushing and Neal Miller, a fine blocker, added a fair total on his own. Again, Jiggetts, captain this year, led a rugged band of forwards, and the Crimson defense, featuring Kurzweil, Jon Judge, and Emper, was experienced and alert.

Dan Jiggetts, captain of Harvard's 1975 team.

Yale had suffered a few graduation losses that resulted in a somewhat less potent machine than the all-but-undefeated of the previous year: Doyle, Green, and Hennings were gone. Yet the Blue squad was a good one: Fencik was back and Gesicki was more redoubtable than ever. Both on offense and defense sturdy forwards were not lacking, notably Carfora and Staffieri as offensive guards and Smoot (now captain), McAndrews, Sheldon Smith, and Keller on defense. Stone Phillips at quarterback, if not quite as competent as Tom Doyle, was an able signal caller and on occasion a good runner.

The game, played on a pleasant if slightly overcast day, was in effect a battle of defenses. In the first half the Elis were notably superior, grinding out more than 100 yards to Harvard's 39. It was enough to give them one hard-earned touchdown; what was troublesome to Blue observers was a singularly ineffectual passing attack; so shrewd was the Harvard coverage that the Blue would complete only two out of thirteen tosses all afternoon—and suffer one interception, which turned out to be crucial. In the third quarter Restic readjusted his plan of attack and enabled Winn to find running room and to tie the score with a touchdown. For the rest of the game the burden was on the Yale defense. A surprise pass from Kubacki, who had injured his throwing arm in the second quarter, caught the Elis off guard and gave the Crimson the ball on the Blue fourteen. Yale held but could not block Mike Lynch's kick, which put the Crimson ahead with little time left to play. The Harvard march had begun after Yale had

brought the ball deep into Cantab territory only to have Phillips's would-be scoring pass intercepted by Judge. Yale fought back and, on Fencik's only catch of the day, brought the ball almost within the field goal range, but not quite close enough and time ran out with Phillips desperately trying to get a little closer to the Harvard goal. Yale outrushed Harvard by some thirty yards but was sadly behind in passing yardage; indeed, the coverage by the Crimson secondary was all but incredible. For all the intensity of the play it was a game fought with admirable sportsmanship; Yale drew no penalties and after the game Jiggetts said: "We really respect Yale. They came at us all day and never quit."[6] The victory gave Harvard the undisputed league championship—and gave Restic a 3−2 lead over his good friend Carm. The Bulldog could only lick his wounds and look hopefully to the future. The performance of the sophomore Pagliaro and the victory of the Bullpups over the Yardlings gave substance to their hopes.

From 1976 through 1978 the pigskin gods smiled on the wearers of the Blue. One may see in the Bulldog triumphs of those years an illustration of the Law of Impartial Alternation which seems to characterize the rivalry; in the years since World War II, while back-to-back victories are common enough, neither side had been able to put together a very long string of triumphs. Even Yale's run of four successive years (1949−52) without a defeat was marred by a tie in '51. So with the disasters of the past two years behind him the Bulldog felt that '76 should see that law

The 1976 Yale team, victors over Harvard by 21–7, compiled
a record of 8–1. Photo S. Frinzi.

come into operation. As indeed it did; but the Elis
that year and for several years to come had more
on their side than actuarial metaphysics; they had
a succession of outstanding ballcarriers and more
than their share of rugged forwards. In the three-
year span beginning with '76 the Bulldog would
put together twenty wins against five losses (only
three to brother Ivies) and two ties. The Crimson
over the same period managed fourteen victories
against twelve losses (eight within the league) and
one tie.

One could not, of course, have foreseen this in
the early fall of 1976. Indeed, most experts expected Harvard to repeat and sit again on top of
the Ivy throne. (After all, such luminaries as
Kubacki at quarter, "Framingham" Tommy Winn,

and the talented Bob McDermott gave the Crimson
a good nucleus, and Captain Bill Emper had
proved himself as a sturdy defender.) But both
coaches knew better. Cozza, who seldom speaks
to no purpose, had promised his troops at the end
of the '75 season that '76 would bring a Blue victory; Restic, without specifying where the losses
would come, predicted a 6–3 season. He knew
that in losing Danny Jiggets (who became Gary
Fencik's teammate with the Bears), an All-East
choice, and three All-Ivy forwards, the going
would not be easy. Linemen, either of the offensive or defensive brand, though less visible to the
naked eye than resourceful quarterbacks and
speedy runners, are no whit less valuable—and
often harder to replace.

Even so it was a good season for Harvard. The Crimson came into the Yale game with only two losses (unfortunately both in league play). Yale, like Harvard, had lost to Brown but otherwise had suffered no defeats. On the betting the Blue looked a little better, but one never knows (certainly after 1968) what may happen in the venerable bullring. Still, Yale had a notable asset in "Pags," known to the world as John Pagliaro, now a junior, whom Cozza had shrewdly recruited from Derby, in easy reach of the Bowl. Pags was fast, tough, and hard to bring down; if he ran with little style he made up for that deficiency with an explosive determination. Once on his way he was all but unstoppable. With Pags on hand the Bulldog didn't need much of a passing attack, especially as his running mates John Hatem and Bill Southworth were also more than competent ballcarriers. The Bulldog had as well, in Stone Phillips, a cool if not sparkling quarterback and an offensive line, anchored by Vic Staffieri ("the best captain I've had," said Cozza), that kept getting better as the season moved along. On defense Yale had two outstanding linebackers in the senior Jeff Waller and the sophomore Bill Crowley, with Keith Bassi, a junior, formidable at middle guard. But Harvard had sturdy defenders, too, notably Bob Baggott and Russ Savage at the ends and Tom Joyce at middle guard. The totals for offensive and defensive performance on the eve of the game seemed to indicate a Blue superiority; Yale had piled up 3,044 yards to opponents' 1,881; for Harvard the count was 2,455 to 1,941. It was a significant game for Cozza; he had consented in the summer to take

Captain of the 1976 squad, Vic Staffieri was, according to Coach Cozza, "the best captain I've had." Photo S. Frinzi.

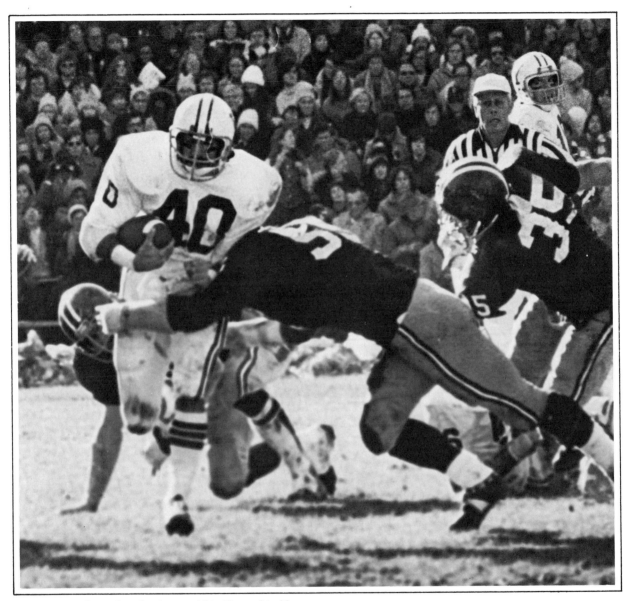

John Pagliaro, shown here leaving would-be Harvard tacklers in his trail in the 1976 game, was a fast, tough runner who was blessed with an explosive determination. He rushed for 128 yards in the 1976 game and for 172 in 1977. Photo S. Frinzi.

on the post of athletic director; this would entail his giving up the job of football coach.

November 13, although the earliest date for The Game since 1881, was bleak and cold, with a steady wind blowing toward the open end of the packed Stadium; 42,000 had come to watch. The first quarter was paradoxical in that the Elis not only controlled the game but even got a few breaks, and yet found themselves a touchdown behind as the period ended. Two successive penalties gave the Blue a first down on the Crimson eighteen, whereupon, on a second down, Stone Phillips tossed a rollout pass straight into the clutch of Russ Savage, who rambled unmolested seventy-four yards for a score. (It is the longest scoring run on an interception in the series.) Toward the end of the quarter the Crimson had another chance, with a first down on the Yale ten. A sack of Kubacki by Paul Denza pushed the Crimson back, and on fourth down a field goal attempt went wide. After some fruitless sparring in the second period Bob Rizzo came in at quarterback to replace the groggy Phillips and whether because of his presence or because the Blue was solving the Cantabs' defense, the Bulldog suddenly perked up and carried the ball deep into Crimson territory; the drive was spoiled when Rizzo fumbled on the twenty-five, but there was a feeling abroad that the momentum of the game had passed to Yale. Halfway through the third quarter this feeling was justified. Starting on the Crimson forty-two, Pags carried four successive times to bring the ball to the Harvard seven, where the rugged Mike Southworth took over and scored

the first Yale touchdown. Carter's kick was good and the game was tied. Shortly after the ensuing kickoff the alert Bassi recovered Kubacki's fumble on the Red thirty-one and four plays later Pagliaro bulled over from the five; one of Rizzo's two successful passes to Spagnola had covered most of the distance. The Bulldog's last score came on a well-planned march covering fifty-eight yards, with Pagliaro running for thirty-four yards and Hatem adding ten. Southworth was again called upon for the coup de grace. Carter, who seldom missed kicks, didn't this time. 21–7 and twelve minutes left. Harvard made them lively. In three minutes the ubiquitous Baggott intercepted a pass on the Yale nineteen, Winn carried to the seven. The Bulldog defense held, and on fourth down Kubacki's hurried pass was caught by Chris Doherty on the one, but a hard tackle by Yale's Steve Skrovan nailed him there. There were still seven minutes left, and the Yale stands, mindful of what the Crimson can do in much less time than that, were still anxious. Southworth, however, got off a fine kick from his end zone, and Yale got a big break when the ball grazed a Redshirt and Bob Krystyniak recovered it near midfield. The Blue got close enough for Carter to try a field goal; he missed, but at that point less than a minute remained and it was not enough—not even for Harvard.

The game was much more exciting than the score would lead one to believe. On statistics Yale certainly deserved to win, with twenty-two first downs to Harvard's nine and 316 yards to the Crimson's 143. But who knows what might have happened if Skrovan had missed that tackle? Pagliaro emerged from the game with a modern season record for the Blue of sixteen touchdowns and another for most points scored. (Only Bum McClung of the old days had done better.) The team made records for yardage by rushing (2,658) and most first downs by rushing (144). On the Harvard side, Kubacki, who deserved a better fate, playing valiantly and effectively throughout the game with an assortment of painful injuries, broke the Crimson individual record for career yardage, coming out with 3,042 yards, just a mite more than Dick Clasby's 3,028. The postgame comments gave happy evidence of the good feeling obtaining between the contending parties. "There is something special about the game" said Bill Emper; "there is so much mutual respect for one another. In four years I never saw Yale throw a cheap shot." On his part, Vic Staffieri remarked: "I went into the Harvard locker room and four guys came up and congratulated me. I can't say enough about the rivalry."[7]

Taking office in January of 1977, Jimmy Carter lost no time in appointing Kingman Brewster ambassador to the United Kingdom. Yale's president had assuredly given ample demonstration of his diplomatic talent during the trying years of his administration. On his departure Hanna Gray, then provost, moved into Woodbridge Hall as acting president. The following year A. Bartlett Giamatti, 1960, professor of English and comparative literature, was chosen president. He was the youngest Yale president in many a long year and the first to be chosen from the field of letters. He was also the first to bear an Italian surname. In these categories his appointment gave Yale a pair of "firsts" over Harvard. Even as Whit Griswold, Giamatti very soon emerged as a stout champion of the humanities and the liberal arts. He also (again in the tradition of Whit, who had been a staunch defender of the Ivy code) was determined to maintain amateur standards in collegiate sports. His remarks to the alumni in the fall of 1980 would stress the dangers of overzealous recruiting. In this objective he had the support of Harvard's Bok, though some old Blues have noted that in recent years Harvard has come up with squads outnumbering the Bulldog's armed forces. To be sure, Harvard has more males than Yale. In any event, the early Giamatti years witness no diminution of Blue power on the gridiron.

As in Woodbridge Hall, so too in Ray Tompkins House there was a change in the high command. In 1976 DeLaney Kiphuth, after twenty-two years of signal service to his alma mater, notably in the appointments of Pont and Cozza, stepped down from his post as director of athletics. Carm served as acting director through the season of 1976 and accepted appointment to the directorship—only to find, after much soul-searching that he could not comply with the requirement of the Corporation which would have obliged him to give up coaching. For him, coaching came first. Following Cozza's "gran rifiuto" in 1977, Frank Ryan, a graduate of Rice, a mathematician, and erstwhile stellar quarterback of the Cleveland Browns, was appointed director, leaving Cozza free to concentrate on the preparations for his thirteenth campaign, for which the prospects looked promising. Coincidentally Harvard that same year got a new director of athletics: John Riordan, '60 (from the office of admissions), replaced Robert Watson.

Harvard's 1977 season was a seesaw affair; certainly key losses by graduation were hard to make up for, notably Kubacki, who had performed so well in 1976. In fact, the quarterback spot was difficult to fill; the senior Tom Davenport was injured in early season and junior Larry Brown and the sophomore Buckley came into competition. Brown was the starter for the final games; occasionally, in the unorthodox scheme of Restic's multiflex, both would be on the field at once. Brown turned out to be very good at the job; he made a Harvard record both for passing yardage and total yardage in the Penn game. The senior Chris Doherty at fullback was a powerful and experienced runner, and Ralph Polillio, a junior, a reliable ballcarrier. Jim Curry, a first-class split end, also a senior, brought skill and experience to the offense. On defense, Restic could count on the able veterans Savage and Baggott at the ends and Captain Steve Kaseta at defensive tackle. It added up to a combination strong enough to win four Ivy League games, notably a fine victory over Dartmouth (which eked out a 3—0 win over Yale) —yet it was hardly a great team. The weakness was defense; for the first time since 1957 the Cantabs came up to the Yale game with more points scored against them than they had managed to score themselves. It was a team that had to win by outscoring the opposition and scoring

mostly by way of the pass: at the end of the season Kaseta's troops had amassed 1,113 yards rushing and 1,669 passing (in contrast to the Bulldog totals: 2,235 and 1,107, respectively).

In New Haven, the picture was quite different— even rosy. Pags was back again, flanked by the junior Angelone, a hard-charging fullback, and with a supporting cast that included the promising sophomore Mike Sullivan. (All were from New Haven suburbs; Carm was beginning to find treasures in his own backyard.) Bob Rizzo, who had changed the current of the game in '76, was now captain, an unusual vote of confidence in a player who had never started a game in his first two years. The offensive line was strong if not too experienced, and the defense was one of Yale's sturdiest in recent years, with Bassi, Denza, and Crowley all returning for service and Clint Streit, a junior, making a notable contribution. The Blue outgained opponents by more than 1,000 yards; the Crimson, on the other hand, was some 500 yards short of the opponents' total. Still, there was respect in the Eli camp for the Cantabrigian potential as they met on a sunny and pleasant afternoon in the Bowl.

When the smoke cleared, it was a clear-cut Yale victory. And the final score, 24—7, suggests it was an easy one. In fact, it was and it wasn't. The Bulldog triumph really came on one spectacular play, than which none more thrilling, I suspect, has been witnessed in the history of The Game. Late in the first quarter a sixty-yard drive, Pagliaro and Angelone alternating, led to the Elis first score, when, halted on the Crimson ten, Dave

Schwartz kicked a field goal. The Crimson counterattack came swiftly: good running by Doherty and Polillio and two passes Brown to Paul Sablock put the Crimson on top. The touchdown was made early in the second quarter; by the time the period ended Yale had retaliated, again on rushes by Pagliaro and Angelone, the latter crossing the Crimson goal line to give the Bulldogs a slim 10–7 lead at the half. The third quarter was scoreless, Yale backs piling up yardage but to no avail; Brown countered with Crimson passes that were rushed or dropped. Early in the final quarter came The Play. Following a display of unusual ineptness, the Bulldog found himself holding the ball on his own 35-yard line, fourth down and twenty to go. Mike Sullivan, a very good left-footed punter, came in to kick. The pass from center was wide; Mike had to step out of position to reach the ball and saw at once that he could not get the kick off. Instead, he ran, easily clearing the Harvard forwards, who overran him, and sidestepping the one safety man who stood in his way. It was a play that delighted old-timers, who saw in it at long last, even if purely by chance, the old "run from kick formation," which had been one of the attractions of the game of an earlier age.

In the 1977 game, Mike Sullivan (28), back to punt, fielded a wide pass from center and ran around Harvard's left end for a sixty-six-yard touchdown. Photo S. Frinzi.

The run was decisive for the outcome of the game. Now ten points behind and with little time left Harvard was forced to pass (which explains in part the low total of yards gained rushing) and the Eli defenders, well aware of the Crimson plight, hounded both Brown and Buckley; an interception by Sam Rapp set up the final Bulldog score, made, natch, on a buck by Pagliaro, who ended the season with no fewer than seven new Yale records, including a formidable rushing total of 1,159 yards. Once more the Bulldog sat at the top of the Big Three and held possession, this time unshared, of the Ivy cup. But the Crimson had nothing to be ashamed of. Until Sullivan's *beau geste* she was very much in the game; who knows what might have happened had Savage trapped him before he got away?

The abiding danger to the chronicler of the great rivalry is the seductive superlative, as irresistible as the appeals of the Siren. To the true aficionado, of course, be he or she of the Crimson or the Blue persuasion, every game is as a link on a glittering chain. Yet some sparkle more brightly than others, and when one of especial brilliance appears, the superlative lurks in wait. The exceptional sheen of the jousts of 1967 and 1968 has already been remarked, and it might be said that a scrupulous historian would hardly be justified in turning to his stock of superlatives to describe yet another contest a mere decade later. Yet in sober truth the battle of 1978 may well vie with its predecessors; it had a distinctive glamour of its own and, in one area, was a record breaker.

The Bulldogs and their old friends met in Cam-bridge that fall with profiles of performance very similar to those of the preceding year. For the latter it was again a year of the pass. Although Ralph Polillio was back and running well, the most potent weapon in the Red arsenal was the arm of Larry Brown, who set season and career records for Crimson passing. He had good receivers aplenty, of whom the most prominent were the split ends John MacLeod and Rich Horner, both veterans, the tight end Paul Sablock, an experienced senior, and Polillio himself, often used as a target. The offensive line, led by Mike Clark, another stalwart senior, gave the passer good protection. The Crimson scored a respectable 196 points in the course of the season. But, as in the previous year, in spite of the presence of individuals like the aggressive sophomore Chuck Durst and the senior middle guard Tom McDevitt up forward and alert ballhawks like Captain Steve Potysman and the junior Scott MacLeod in the secondary, the defense was not all that Restic could have hoped for. As in 1977, the total yardage gained by the Crimson was considerably less than that yielded to opponents. Coming into the final encounter, Harvard had a record of four wins (including a particularly impressive one over Dartmouth), three losses, and a tie with Princeton. For Yale, too, the style of the '78 squad resembled that of its predecessor. It was primarily a rushing team, as the '77 delegation had been; the speedy junior Ken Hill, heir to the peerless Pags, was the leading ballcarrier, and Angelone and Hatem were still on hand to make contributions, as was Mike Sullivan. Nor was the passing game overlooked. The sturdy offensive line gave the backs good running room and the defense was well above average, with Clint Streit and Bill Crowley (now captain), seasoned seniors, and the sophomores Kevin Czinger and Tim Tumpane perhaps the most

Larry Brown threw for 301 yards against Yale and set season records for passing (1978).

In the 1978 game, John Spagnola scored a key touchdown after wresting a pass intended for him out of the grasp of a Harvard defender who had intercepted the ball. "Spags" broke the Yale career record for pass receptions.

senior Pat O'Brien, having patiently awaited his turn, was a good quarterback; if he threw for less yardage and a lower percentage than Larry Brown, he was still a passer to be feared, and he had a spectacular receiver in the senior giant John Spagnola, standing 6'4'' and with a knack for hanging on to the ball; his classmate Bob Krystyniak was of like configuration and similar prowess. A prominent up forward. Nondorf, Pinkston, and Novosel were outstanding in the secondary. Retrospectively, one is inclined to wonder, in view of the exceptional talent, why the Blue record was not better than it turned out to be. As the Bulldog entrained for Cambridge, the tally was four wins, two losses (one to Dartmouth, which cost the Blue the league championship), and two rather surprising ties with Columbia and Penn. It was a powerful machine, but it had been known to stall.

In sum, Yale had the better runners and the better defense; Harvard had a uniquely effective passing game; against other rivals, in fact, the Crimson had run up a larger point total than the Blue. One could predict a high-scoring game; if the favored Bulldog was to win, he would have to outscore his opponent, sure to put a number of points on the board.

The action of the combat, fought out before a capacity crowd under ideal weather conditions, must have given the spectators a sense of *déjà vu*. As in '67 and '68 and '74, it began with a display of power by the Elis, followed by a strong Crimson counterattack, a vigorous Blue *riposte*, a second Red surge which almost undid the Bulldog. In the first quarter Yale land power proved its mettle: after a substantial march O'Brien scored on a nine-yard canter over his left flank. In the second quarter another long Blue drive was capped by Angelone's ten-yard burst through center. 14–0. Looked good for Cozza's lads. But then came the inevitable counterattack. In less than eight minutes Brown had passed his team to two touchdowns, one on a longish march with Matt Granger

catching the scoring toss, another on a thirty-yard pass to Rich Horner after the alert Potysman had recovered a Blue fumble. Then it was Yale's turn. On the first play after the kickoff Spagnola dropped back from the line of scrimmage, took a lateral from O'Brien and heaved the ball some fifty yards to Krystyniak, who covered the remaining distance untouched.

The play covered seventy-seven yards and, in pattern and execution, was a Bulldog version of the unforgettable McInally flea-flicker of four years earlier. (No doubt Cozza had seen many a rerun.) A minute later, following Nondorf's forty-three-yard punt return, O'Brien sent the wing-footed Hill around the Crimson flank for eighteen yards and another Blue score. The second quarter made history; with thirty-five points, it was the highest-scoring quarter in the ninety-five years of the venerable series.

So at the end of the half it was Yale 28, Harvard 14, but the Bulldog, mindful of old scars, was not content merely to sit on his lead. He went forth to get a third-period touchdown, scored in a singularly spectacular fashion as Spagnola wrested a pass intended for him out of the grasp of Fred Cordova, who had intercepted the throw.[8] And this exploit turned out to be decisive. Undaunted by the Bulldog's twenty-one-point lead, Harvard came storming back, and throughout the last fifteen minutes Brown was simply unstoppable. On the first play of the last quarter Horner scored on an eleven-yard pass from the peerless Larry to crown a ninety-yard march; and ten minutes later another ninety-yard parade, including a thrilling fifty-nine-yard Brown to Horner connection, gave the Crimson its fourth touchdown, John MacLeod making the score on an eight-yard pass from Brown. It was 35–28 with about six minutes to go. They were moments of quivering anxiety on both sides of the field. "I think we would have won the game if we had gotten the ball one more time," said Restic later. "There was magic in the air. We even had the two-point play all picked out for when we scored."[9] He wasn't telling the public anything it didn't know. Anyone who remembered 1968 was morally certain that if the Crimson got possession with even as little as a minute left, the game would end badly for the Bulldog. To his credit he held on to the ball, using a few guileful devices of his own, notably a pass from Mike Sullivan to quarterback O'Brien, and taking possession on his own twenty ticked off yardage to carry the ball into Crimson territory as the clock ran down. It was a magnificent game. Larry Brown broke all records for passing yardage and total offensive yardage (respectively, 301 and 306, surpassing Tommy Doyle's '74 figures). "Spags" broke the Yale career record for pass receptions, and the game itself broke a record for total points scored. It is certainly a candidate for The Game of the Century—or would be if one could forget '68 (as Yalies would like to).

The victory gave the Yale class of 1979 a sweep of four wins over their Harvard classmates, including the freshman game—a rare thing in the zigzag rivalry. It had happened, to be sure, a few times in the years of Bulldog dominance before World War I, and under the aegis of Haughton,

Fisher, and Harlow three Harvard classes (1916, 1923, and 1931) had managed it. Yale's class of 1958 had also turned the trick. The gallant Bill Crowley, however, instead of boasting of this distinction, expressed his sympathy for his Harvard adversaries: "I know how they must feel," he said.[10] And to think it all hung on Spagnola's opportunistic larceny!

The reader who has had the patience to follow this narrative through the preceding pages will be quite familiar with the high proportion of "upsets" that have characterized the century-old competition. Both sides have distressed the oddsmakers almost as often as they have followed their coldly calculated predictions. But there is a subcategory of upsets in which Harvard has a preeminence (delightful to her followers as it is disconcerting to Bulldog fanciers): the Crimson takes particular pleasure in frustrating otherwise unbeaten Yale teams. It happened in 1921, again in 1938, again in 1968 (to be sure, it was a kind of kamikaze victory since the Cantabrigian record was also blemished in the process, but it *felt* like a Harvard victory), and yet again in 1974. Since World War II only Mike Pyle's immortals of 1960 have come away from the combat unscarred. But of all the occasions cited, none was more impressive (or devastating, again, depending on where you sit) than the horrendous demolition of Cozza's delegation of 1979 by a Crimson outfit that, on the record, hardly belonged in the same league. Harvard came into the arena with only two victories—and those over the league's weaklings, Columbia and Penn. She had been outgained and outscored by the opposition, to whom she had yielded a juicy 150 points. Yale, on the other hand, had not suffered even so much as a tie to stain her perfection, had outscored the opponents by 186 points to 72, had demonstrated explosive if occasionally erratic power on offense, and was accounted to have the best defense in the league if not in the East. Yet Harvard won—and won with comparative ease. The game even got a bit dull. *Veniam peto, lector*, but I find yet another superlative bearing down on me and I fear I cannot elude it: 1979 witnessed the upset of upsets in all the years of our history.

November 17 was a beautiful day, all but windless and even a little warm. Seventy-two thousand made their way to the sunny Bowl, most of them prepared to see Tim Tumpane's battalion give Carm his first undefeated–untied season. Perhaps the spectacle would take their minds off the sad and humiliating plight of the hostages in Iran. Disillusionment came swiftly. Yale kicked off. Harvard took the ball on her 26-yard line and marched methodically and purposefully, with no hesitation on the way, seventy-four yards to a touchdown—Jon Hollingsworth going over for the score at the end of only five minutes of play. The Yale defense throughout the season had held the opponents to an average of sixty-five rushing yards per game, and lo, in five minutes, the Crimson had seventy-four. The sophomore Jim Callinan led the Harvard ballcarriers; it was to be his day of glory. But more was to come. Yale, which could not complain of lack of good breaks, recovered a Harvard fumbled punt—and promptly fumbled

back. Soon the Crimson was on the march again. Taking the ball on his own thirty, Burke St. John, the Crimson signal caller, drove his team to the Blue thirty-nine, at which point his pass to Callinan covered the rest of the distance. This score was made as the second quarter began; the rest of the period passed uneventfully as the Bulldog drew penalties, fumbled, and could not, even when he got started, move the Cantabs' defense. In the interval the benumbed spectators could only wonder and ask each other if Harvard could hold the pace.

Blue followers were greatly cheered when the Bulldogs took the second-half kickoff and marched sixty-three yards to cut the score to 13–7, Dennis Dunn carrying the last four yards for the tally. At this point the script should have called for a triumphant Blue resurgence. But Harvard did not panic. Early in the fourth quarter a Crimson penalty gave the Blue first down near midfield—and another fumble spoiled that chance. Harvard drove close enough for Dave Cody's field goal to make it 16–7. John Rogan, a sophomore and a good clutch passer, came in for Yale but was given no scope for his talents. The Blue's sixth fumble of the afternoon gave Harvard possession on the Yale forty-five, and in six plays, four of them substantial runs by Hollingsworth, the Crimson had the clincher, scored by the industrious and shrewd St. John. And there it was. Not a spectacular game by any means but to Harvard followers very satisfying.

Analysts, particularly of the New Haven breed, have long wondered about that unhappy after-

Mike Brown, captain of the 1979 Harvard team, which upset the previously unbeaten Bulldogs.

noon. A Harvard alumnus knowledgeable in these matters wrote me a week or so after the battle to say that he was not surprised by the outcome. He pointed out that the Harvard team had had a uniquely unfortunate early season, with injuries rampant among the starters; only in the last two games was the real first team healthy and ready. And it is certainly true that at the start of the year Restic had some very good veterans on hand; Hollingsworth and the diminutive but talented Rich Horner on offense with the puissant Callinan coming up from the freshman squad. He was even more richly endowed on defense, with a pair of good ends in Tom Kenna and the massive Tim Palmer, sturdy linemen like Chuck Durst, elected captain for 1980, and Steve Hollman at middle guard, with seniors of proven worth such as Terry Trusey and Scott MacLeod backing up the line. But, beginning with the Columbia game, injuries dogged the Crimson, particularly but by no means exclusively in the quarterback spot; St. John, though a senior, had not previously won his letter. (He looked good on November 17, though.)

But even granting that Harvard's ill luck was in great part responsible for a dismal record, it must be said that the Yale material was both richer and deeper. Ken Hill was a flashy runner, and the senior Dunn and the sophomore Rogan gave Cozza an unusual *richesse* of quarterbacks. It would have been a stronger offense if Mike Sullivan, now a senior, and the very promising sophomore Rich Diana had not been so persistently hampered by injuries; even so, in spite of sputtering occasionally, the Blue offense could be dangerous. And the defense included a veritable parade of stalwarts, of which Captain Tim Tumpane and the junior Kevin Czinger up front and Arnie Pinkston and Dave Novosel in the secondary were perhaps the most prominent. The Elis had marched from opening day on, straight toward the Ivy League championship; only in Ithaca did they really have to extend themselves. But something happened on the way to the Big Three crown. Three times now Cozza had fielded teams ambushed only by Redshirts. Back to the drawing board. A final note on the game: the Bulldog won the statistical battle, with seventeen first downs to Harvard's fifteen, and a total offensive yardage of 292 against the Crimson's 248. Unfortunately he also won the fumbling contest, committing six bobbles to Harvard's three. In part that statistic explains the game. But only in part. The determinant factor was that Harvard was "up"; one could sense an exuberant confidence among them as they took the field. They were ready. "[Harvard] . . . had nothing to lose going into the game. They were probably looser than we were, and they played an outstanding game," said Cozza philosophically.[11]

In the fall of 1980, hostages still in Iran, Jimmy Carter's time ran out, and the hero of *Death Valley Days* galloped toward the White House with his unerring six-shooter fixed on inflation, lavish spending, high interest rates, and Bad Guys in general. The Moral Majority cheered him on. By the time the votes were counted it was clear that the annual Crimson–Blue affair would be something worth seeing. Restic, euphoric one may suspect after pulverizing Yale's Ivy League champions of '79, had some reason to hope he might turn the trick again. Callinan was back, stronger than ever; he had a good running mate—and a fine pass receiver—in Tom Beatrice; Brian Buckley was shaping up well at quarterback; Lattanzi at guard led a hefty offensive line, and the defense was manned by experienced and able warriors—Captain Durst, Tim Palmer, and Bob Woolway up forward, with Pete Coppinger and Rocky Delgadillo starring in the secondary. The Crimson had a strong running game and air power good enough

The 1980 Yale team, captained by John Nitti (holding ball). Photo S. Frinzi.

(RIGHT) Split end Curt Grieve making his touchdown catch in the 1980 game. Grieve caught thirty-two passes for 580 yards and eight touchdowns in 1980.

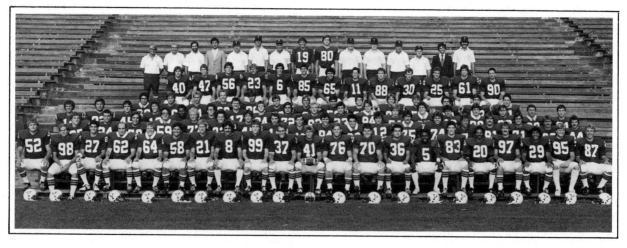

to assure versatility. As they prepared to meet their old New Haven friends, the Cantabs could contemplate with some satisfaction a record of seven wins against two losses. (In 1980 Ivy League members voted to allow themselves the luxury of playing ten games per season, a move intended to permit the teams to venture more frequently out of the family circle and, incidentally, to add to the income of the athletic associations. League attendance, under competition from the pros, had been dropping off.)

The Bulldogs brought to the Stadium a record similar to that of their hosts, seven wins and two defeats. Only one loss, however, had been suffered at the hands of an Ivy League foe; surprisingly, Cornell had rather easily taken the Bulldog's measure. Harvard had lost to both Princeton and Dartmouth, neither of whom had given the Bulldog much trouble. Records aside, most connoisseurs would have said the Elis were ahead of the Crimson in the matter of personnel. In Captain Nitti, the brilliant Diana, and Stratton (moved from end to wingback this year), Cozza had a very capable backfield guided by Rogan, a good quarterback and passer (if he was given enough time). It was a veteran group, too, as was Curt Grieve, a 6'4" end who could leap another six feet into the air. An offensive line, led by Regan at guard and Skarzynski at tackle, was more than adequate to open holes for Diana and give Rogan the time he needed. The defense—for the ninth successive year the most effective in the Ivies—included a number of stalwarts destined to interest the pros: Kelley and Leone at ends, Serge Mihaly and the incomparable

Czinger between them with Jeff Rohrer and Scott McKenzie in support; Dave Novosel and Pat Conran were brilliant in the secondary. In fact, it was the defense that turned the tide for Yale.

The afternoon was bright but a little too cold for comfort, and one of those pocket-sized gales that are the specialty of the majestic amphitheater blew lustily through the open end of the edifice. In the first quarter Harvard had the wind at her back and it took Yale some time to get good field position. Indeed, the Crimson high-water mark was reached halfway through the first period with a first down on the Yale twenty-four. It was there that the Blue defense showed its mettle. Three plays later the ball was back on the Bulldog forty-four, and on the following play Czinger scooped up a bad pass from the Crimson center and lo, it was first down for Yale on the Harvard forty-seven. Thus encouraged, the Blue offense revived and, after an exchange of punts, put on a march of eighty yards— eleven running plays and a spectacular fourth-down pass, Rogan to Grieve, for the score, with only sixteen seconds left in the quarter. Grieve was well covered by the alert Rocky Delgadillo, but the latter could not match the Blue receiver's prodigious *entrechat*. The touchdown was all the Bulldog would need; such was his defensive prowess that through the entire second half Harvard never carried the ball across the 50-yard line and ended the game with minus eleven yards rushing. The Cantab defense, however, had nothing to be ashamed of. Yale's second score came as a result of a mishandled kickoff which gave the Blue a first down on the Crimson twenty-five; it

took eight plays for Nitti to score (on fourth down with inches to go) and put Yale once more on the board. Later in the game the Blue had first down on the Harvard two—and was turned back. ("If it weren't for the color, you'd think they were Yale Bulldogs," an old friend of mine remarked in reluctant admiration.) The Cantab defense was playing without Captain Durst; undoubtedly he was missed, but it is hard to believe the defenders could have performed more valiantly than they did even if Ajax had come down from Olympus to join them. But a defense needs some help and the Harvard assault force was not able to give it. "They stuffed us," said Callinan, hero of the '79 upset and this afternoon held to thirty yards in nine attempts. "Their defensive line was the quickest I've seen."[12] Buckley performed gallantly, but he was always hurried and his successful passes yielded only short yardage; he was also twice intercepted. A fine day for the Blue; once more league and Big Three champions. But you couldn't blame the Harvard defense.

The first year of the century's ninth decade was an uneasy one for America and for the world in general. It has a grim distinction in history as being the only year in which assassination attempts were made both on the president of the United States and on the pope. The Middle East continued to be a center of international concern. At home the projected massive arms buildup troubled many citizens, and as inflation gradually subsided—but only gradually—unemployment went up. Such matters did not keep the crowds away from the Bowl on the bright and chilly November 22; in fact, the attendance, 75,300, was the largest since 1916, when the robust pair of guards Dadmun and Black had met for the toss of the coin in the middle of the vast saucer under the shadow of a war less than five months away.

This year in the annual battle of the old rivals the Bulldog had to be favored. Save for a totally unexpected and rather embarrassing loss to Princeton's aroused Tigers he came into the game undefeated and untied. (To be sure, he had had an even more glittering record in 1979.) Harvard, on the other hand, had a so-so record: five wins, three losses, and a tie. Among the Elis, renowned paladins were numerous and fearsome; above all towered Rich Diana, who did practically all the Blue ballcarrying and broke almost all Bulldog records for rushing, including a season's total of 293 carries for 1,442 yards. John Rogan set new Bulldog marks for attempts, completions, and yards gained (2,844) in passing, and his receiver Grieve made a season's record for receptions and tied the rugged Spagnola for the career records. All three, along with Tony Jones, a versatile kicker, were All-Ivy selections. Although no Blue "toads" won such recognition, they were collectively quite good enough to open holes for Diana, running from Cozza's favorite I formation, and to give the sometimes hesitant Rogan time to make his completions. The defense was, as usual, the best in the Ivies, and, save for the distressing lapse in Tigertown, all but impregnable: Captain Fred Leone, Serge Mihaly, and Jeff Rohrer won All-Ivy nominations and incidentally offers from the pros, as did Conran, the most prominent laborer in a

very good secondary. In personnel Harvard could not match the Bulldogs, though Greg Brown and Mike Corbat of the offensive line were All-Ivy, along with Scott Murrer at middle guard and the Californian Delgadillo at cornerback—and of course the now-veteran ballcarrier Jim Callinan. Ron Cuccia, though diminutive, was a good passer. But overall, on the record, Yale looked better. The Crimson had, however, some reasonable foundation for hope. After all, for two years running, Harvard freshmen had beaten the young Yalies, and the seniors on the Crimson squad had happy and inspiring memories of 1979. Furthermore, at game time it was not clear how the Elis would react to the reverse suffered in Tigertown; it had been a gruelling battle and had destroyed their hopes of an unbeaten season. Could they bounce back?

Well they could, and did, and by a score that made the contest seem much more uneven than it in fact was. Harvard started off as she had in 1979, taking the kickoff and marching purposefully with successive first downs toward the Eli goal. Then there was a fumble. Another brief Cantab march was stalled by a penalty. Meanwhile, Yale couldn't do much until finally, late in the first quarter, Diana took a pass from Rogan and cantered across the line for a Bulldog touchdown. Less than two minutes later Campbell recovered Callinan's fumble on the Crimson twenty-five and on the first play Rogan passed to Grieve for the second tally. At the interval it was 14−0 Yale (Tony Jones never missed). The third quarter was scoreless, but in the fourth another Rogan-to-

Rich Diana (33) broke almost all Bulldog rushing records, including a season's total of 293 carries for 1,442 yards in 1981. Here he prepares to block for quarterback John Rogan, who also set new Yale marks for attempts, completions, and yards gained (2,844 yards).

Grieve pass covered thirty-seven yards, and Diana scored a few plays later. Finally, after two Harvard misplays had given the Blue possession on the Cantabs' eleven, Joe Dufek (subbing for Rogan) passed to Grieve for the fourth score. Grieve had been inserted to give him a chance to equal Spagnola's career record of eighty-eight receptions. In the final moments Harvard made a brave effort to get on the scoreboard, but a very clever scoring play was ruled illegal. 28–0 and it sounds like a walkover. But in fact the statistics show quite a different picture. Harvard made more first downs than Yale and outrushed the Elis by twenty yards. The defense was consistently strong—there were no long Yale marches; in fact, the stellar Diana was held to eighty-seven yards in twenty-eight carries, a modest achievement for him but at least better than the sixty that Callinan could manage. (Callinan, incidentally, brought his season total to 1,054 yards, a Cantabrigian record.) But the Crimson offense could never function when it should have; four fumbles and two interceptions did not help their cause. As Buckley a year earlier, so this year Allard and Cuccia were hurried and harried by persistent and ubiquitous Bulldogs; they completed only thirteen out of thirty passes. Yale shared the Ivy title with Dartmouth; the Big Three crown went—for the first time in sixteen years—to Old Nassau.

It was the second year in a row that the Bulldog had shut out the Crimson. Hadn't happened since '31–'32, though Harvard had done it to the Blue in '65–'66. Perhaps the Rogan brothers deserve a special footnote. Together they had engineered 77 Bulldog points to 0 for Harvard. A puissant pair.

Having no world figure of sufficient stature to meet its standards *Time Magazine* for 1982 featured not the Man of the Year but the Machine of the Year; it was, so *Time* said, the year of the computer. Meeting Yale in the Stadium that November the Cantabs showed they were in accord with the times; they turned out a flawless and efficient machine. For in 1982 Restic indeed had the horses—or the parts, if we must keep to our figure. It was largely a senior team, which meant its members had not only experience but two years of unhappy memories to erase. Save for Don Allard at quarterback and possibly Greg Brown, an outstanding offensive tackle, it was not a team of stars, simply a company of competent partners. The Crimson came to the tryst with a 6–3 record and a chance for the Ivy League championship. Things had not gone so well on the shores of the Quinnipiac. Rogan and Grieve and Diana had departed along with some stalwart forwards; their replacements were not quite of the same calibre. Dufek, who could throw a very good pass, was inconsistent; his backup, the promising sophomore Mike Luzzi, was injured early in the season. The Bulldogs' major asset was Paul Andrie, a good ballcarrier if not quite a Diana. Still, although they had a losing record (4–5) coming into the game (Cozza had had no such dismal experience since 1971), the Elis had enjoyed a few happy moments, notably a stirring come-from-behind victory over Dartmouth—and the Greenies had eked out a win over Harvard. Coming into the Stadium, which during the year had been structurally reinforced

In 1982 the Crimson offense showed no mercy in routing the
Blue 45−7; it was the highest score ever made by Harvard
against her old foe. Photo S. Frinzi.

and provided with new seats (no more comfortable than the old ones to Blue posteriors), friends
of the Bulldog could hope.

Not, as it turned out, for long. Harvard was a
little slow getting under way, contenting herself
with one touchdown in the first quarter on a
twenty-three-yard run by Allard. Yale evened the
count in the second quarter on a pass from Dufek
to Crews, set up by an interference penalty on a
Harvard defender. Whereupon the red giant awoke
and got two more touchdowns before halftime,
both in virtue of Allard's passing. And in the second half the Crimson showed no mercy, adding
another three touchdowns and a field goal (by Jim
Villanueva, Harvard's all-time record holder in
this department), while Yale was powerless to
mount any kind of countercharge. Andrie never
found anywhere to go; the Blue made twelve yards
in rushing, and, although the passing statistics
were slightly in her favor, they produced no scores
nor even any serious threats. Final: 45–7—it was
the highest score ever made by the Cantabs against
their ancient foe; Haughton's margin in 1915 was
greater but his total a mere 41 points. In truth, the
underprivileged Elis of Alex Wilson's day had put
up a better show than Pat Ruwe's delegation sixty-
seven years later. Was Harvard really that good?
Or Yale that bad? A little of both perhaps; Don
Allard, guiding "a team without a superstar," put
on "one of the finest quarterbacking performances
in Crimson history,"[13] and certainly the Bulldogs
were a listless lot, particularly in the second half
of the game. The afternoon was enlivened by the
unexpected mushrooming of an ominous looking

Yale coach Carm Cozza had cause for concern following losing seasons in 1982 and 1983. Photo Stephen West.

black balloon, swelling in alarming fashion out of the grass in front of the Harvard bench. Courtesy of MIT it appeared, and Yale partisans felt grateful for the change of spectacle, which was less menacing than the Crimson's multiflex. The win gave Harvard the Big Three championship and a share of the league championship. The much-enduring Cozza went back once more to the drawing board. "The only good thing about a game like this is that we have a lot of young players and they will remember it," he said.[14]

As the season of the hundredth The Game loomed up, there was a good deal more sunshine pouring down in Massachusetts than in Connecticut. It was true that most of Restic's Bulldog tamers of 1982 had graduated; still, there were a few sturdy lads left, and for three successive years the Cantab freshmen had beaten the yearling Bulldogs. Quarterback, with Allard and Cuccia both gone, was admittedly a problem, and in the first half of the season the Crimson had her troubles. But following the old tradition Harvard got better as November came along. The October loss to Dartmouth was compensated for by a smashing victory over Penn, again threatening to take over the championship, just a week before the hundredth meeting with the Elis. Who, to the consternation of their aficionados, were undergoing the worst season in the whole history of Yale football, coming to the rendezvous with a record of one win and eight losses. The forwards were light and inexperienced—even Captain Tom Giella had not been a regular starter; the quarterback situation was problematical, though the sophomore Curtin

looked promising, and the Bulldog's real ace, Paul Andrie, a fine runner, broke his arm before the season began and, though he performed gallantly, he was never really in full vigor. Overall, it was a squad thin in talent (recruiting obviously had not been very successful), and it suffered some horrendous drubbings, notably at the hands of Boston College and Cornell. Even normally docile Columbia had her way with the Bulldog. Still, the Blue almost pulled off an upset against Dartmouth and did manage to cage the Tiger.

When the smoke of battle cleared away (it was actually a day of sparkling sunshine), the predictable had happened and Harvard went off the field the victor. Greg Gizzi at quarterback directed the multiflex with poise and confidence. After sputtering a bit in the first quarter, the red machine sent McGugan over the line early in the second period; and the Crimson defense stopped Andrie and gave Mike Curtin no breathing room at all. To the general surprise, the Blue came alive in the third quarter and marched from the kickoff to a touchdown by Jeff Bassette. For a short while the score was tied. Then Harvard got going again and in the last period a touchdown by Ernst and a field goal by Rob Steinberg gave the Cantabs a nine-point margin, and the last Blue hopes died when Mike Curtin's long pass to Moriarty was intercepted on the Harvard 2-yard line with four minutes left on the clock. The final score was 16–7. So the saddest season of the Blue ended with nine losses; yet it could be said that the delegation of '83 had put up an honorable resistance to the ancient foeman. At least, in the last game,

The Yale and Harvard coaching staffs in 1983. Yale *(top, l. to r.)*: Richard Pont, Bill Samko, Don Martin, Seb LaSpina, Head Coach Carm Cozza, Dave Kelley, Joe Benanto, Larry Story.

Harvard: Head Coach Joe Restic, George Clemens, Dick Corbin, Larry Glueck, Warren White, Bob McCarthy, Mac Singleton, Leo Fanning.

it looked like a Yale team. (Perhaps eighty-seven yards of penalties against Harvard—that multi-flex exacts its toll—helped a bit.) Connoisseurs agreed that Yale had played up to her potential, granting as well that Harvard, even if not as sharp as she might have been, was clearly the better team.

(LEFT) Defensive tackle Tom Giella, captain of Yale's 1983 team.

(RIGHT) Captain Joseph Azelby led Harvard to a 16—7 victory in 1983.

So the century of The Games ended as it had begun, with a Crimson victory on New Haven soil. Yet if we imagine the series as a long row of books bound in crimson and blue it must be said that in between the red volumes at the beginning and the end there are quite a few blue bound titles. The collection displays fifty-four blue bindings, 38 in crimson, and eight particolor. It's been a great hundred years.

If the home side couldn't quite manage an upset win, at least its performance as host was outstanding. A record-breaking cocktail party was given by the athletic director on the Friday preceding the battle. The Football Y Association not only set forth its traditional joyous Friday lunch but invited all the living captains of both parties to assist in the tossing of the coin. And a fine sight it was, with thirty-two representatives of the Blue and a like number for the Crimson.[15] The Harvard patriarch was the redoubtable Ham Fish of 1910, captain of the invincible (until they met Coy) brigade of 1909. Yale's senior representative was Henry Ketcham, captain of the 1913 band of Bulldogs that had suffered sorely from the toe of Charley Brickley. Intriguing, one might think, that the patriarchs of both sides had captained losers in The Game. But perhaps that's as it should be. It's The Game that counts—not victory or defeat. The coin toss took place upon a field emblazoned with the centennial logo at midfield and the inscription "100 YEARS" in each of the end zones. The encounter was preceded by the descent from the skies of nine Navy parachutists, all of whom made perfect landings. Some journalists opined

that the theatrical trappings were inappropriate for the anniversary of such a venerable rite, but most observers were pleased, feeling that once in a century a little froufrou was permissable even for a grande dame. It was regrettable that the Bowl was not completely filled; the crowd of 70,600 was substantial, but one might reasonably have hoped for another 5,000. Whether it was the mediocre record of the Bulldogs or the record-breaking price of the reserved seat ticket ($20.00) that was responsible for the unoccupied zone is hard to say.

Assuredly, if, as in 1968, both sides had brought unvanquished squads to the field of battle the Bowl would have been running over the brim, had the entrance charge been twice what it was. On the other hand, $20.00 is undeniably a lot of money. In any event, financially The Game was a great success; $5 million was spent in New Haven that weekend, $1 million "in receipts at the Bowl" and the rest in greater New Haven. The programs, too, were record breakers, selling for $5.00 each, but in this case the purchasers got their money's worth. Aside from the usual information and comment, the programs included twenty contributions from Cantabrigians and Yalensians, all distinguished either as veterans of the old wars or for their eminence as journalists, statemen, or men of letters; figures such as Bill Scranton, Clint Frank, Bill Buckley, and John Hersey on the Yale side and Roger Angell, Ted White, Ham Fish, and Endicott Peabody for Harvard, an anthology not likely to be matched in our lifetime and certainly not within the covers of a game program. It is a unique collection; the items range from the waggish to the philosophical, from anecdote to speculation, from memories to prophecies. Who comes out winner in this contest of the pen (or the typewriter) would be hard to say. I suspect Yale followers would vote for Ham Fish, who asserts that the time has come for the nation to issue a commemorative stamp in honor of Walter Camp.

In the journalistic sector Town collaborated with Gown. A special sixty-four-page supplement to the *Journal Courier* and the *New Haven Register* edited by Bob Barton for the Friday preceding The Game provided summaries of the previous ninety-nine games and other statistical lore, a number of lively and informative articles by specialists in the field, and a gallery of evocative photographs. A concise and readable survey of the rivalry, it should be bound in hardcover.

Watching the sun go down (in crimson, natch) at the end of the Day of the Hundredth Game, the sensitive observer could not fail to feel moved. The Game has had a long and robust life, flourishing in all kinds of political and economic climates, surviving wars and depressions and the more insidious mildew of ever-changing tastes and fashions. Though it is, to be sure, on the face of it, a family affair, it is also a national heritage and its kingdom is vaster than it might seem at first sight. Without the example of the Crimson and the Blue, loyally supported by the Tiger of Old Nassau—institutions which a hundred years ago were uniquely privileged in manpower, prestige, and athletic *élan vital*—it is difficult to see how the sport would have flourished as it has

throughout the country. Without the example of the early pioneers there would be no Super Bowl. But, more important, The Game has been, for a century now, played invariably with dedication and good sportsmanship by youngsters who are student-athletes, with emphasis on the first element. And on its hundredth birthday it is still in the prime of life.

SUMMARIES OF THE HUNDRED GAMES, INCLUDING LINEUPS

Summaries of games 1 through 99 are reprinted from the *New Haven Register*, *Journal Courier*, New Haven, Connecticut (special supplement November 18, 1983, edited by Bob Barton), by permission of the Jackson Newspapers. The summary of the 100th game is from the *Football Y News* of December 8, 1983. The lineups for the games through 1958 are from ''The Yale–Harvard Series,'' compiled by Edward Byrne and published with the official Yale football program for the Harvard–Yale game of 1959. Lineups for the games 1959–1966 are from *News and Views: Harvard Sports Review*. For 1966 and 1967 they are taken from the Yale *Football Y News*. From 1969 through 1983 Harvard lineups are from *News and Views*; Yale lineups from the *Football Y News*. All by courteous permission.

1st game
Saturday, Nov. 13, 1875
Hamilton Park, New Haven
Harvard 4, Yale 0
Harvard (3–0)   2   1   1—4G 4T
Yale (1–1)   0   0   0—0G 0T
H—H.C. Leeds punt return (Leeds kick)
H—FG W.S. Seamans
H—H.W. Cushing run (kick failed)
H—FG B.S. Blanchard
H—Blanchard lateral from N. Curtis (kick failed)
H—FG A.C. Tower
H—Seamans run (kick failed)
A—2,000 (est.)
NOTE: Fifteen players on a side. Only goals counted in scoring.

Harvard		Yale
Leeds (A.C.)	R*	Arnold (C.)
Cushing		Johnston
Blanchard		Phelps
Faucon		Trumbull
Tower		Vaille
Thayer		Wakeman
Keys		Wright
Curtis	HT	Alden
Seamans		Peters
Hall		Baker
Bacon		Elliot
Herrick		Camp
Wetherbee	T	Smith
Cate		Thompson
Morse		Wurts

Subs: Yale—Bushnell, HT; Harvard—none (Harvard Captain, Whiting, injured, did not play.)
*NOTE: Abbreviations for games 1–10 are as follows: B back, F forward, HB half back, HT half tend, QB quarterback, R rushers, T tend

2nd game
Saturday, Nov. 18, 1876
Hamilton Park, New Haven
Yale 1, Harvard 0
Harvard (2–1)   0   0—0G 3T
Yale (1–1)   0   1—1G 0T
H—J.B. Keys run (kick failed)
H—H.W. Cushing run (kick failed)
H—L. Cushing run (kick failed)
Y—FG Oliver Thompson
NOTE: Eleven players on a side. Only goals counted in scoring.

Harvard		Yale
H.W. Cushing	R	Walker
L. Cushing		Downer
Houston		Taylor
Keys		Clark
Rollins		C.C. Camp
Curtis, Capt.		Wurts
Herrick	HB	W. Camp
Seamans		Hatch
Faucon	B	Baker, Capt.
Jordan		Bigelow
Wetherbee		Thompson

Subs: Yale—none; Harvard—Blanchard

3rd game
Saturday, Nov. 23, 1878
National League baseball ground, Boston
Weather: Rain
Yale 1, Harvard 0
Yale (4–0–1)   0   1—1G 0T 7S
Harvard (1–1)   0   0—0G 0T 13S
Y—FG Oliver Thompson
A—600 (est.)
NOTE: Fifteen players on a side. Only goals counted in scoring; touchdowns used as tie-breaker.

Yale		Harvard
Farwell	F	H.W. Cushing
Fuller		Swift
Hull		Perry
Harding		Cowdin

Lamb   Morse
King   Holmes
Eaton   Warren
                Thacher
Peters   HB Blanchard
Thompson   L. Cushing (C.)
Watson   Winsor
Badger   Sedgwick
Camp (C.)
Wakeman   B   Wetherbee
Nixon   Eldridge
Lyman   Houston

Subs: Yale—none; Harvard—none

4th game
Saturday, Nov. 8, 1879
Hamilton Park, New Haven
Weather: Fair, warm
Yale 0, Harvard 0
Harvard (2-0-2) 0   0—0G 0T 4S
Yale (1-0-1)   0   0—0G 0T 2S
NOTE: Fifteen players on a side. Only
goals counted in scoring; touchdowns
used as tie-breaker.

Harvard   **Yale**
Morse   R   Eaton
Manning   Beck
H.W. Cushing   Moorhead
Burke   Lamb
Warren   Hull
Tebbets   Harding
Nickerson   Remington
Thatcher   Vernon
R. Bacon (C.)
Winsor   HB Peters
Austin   Badger
L. Cushing   Camp (C.)
Holden   Clark
Letherbee   B   Nixon
Shattuck   Lyman
                    B.W. Bacon ¾ b.

Subs: Yale—none; Harvard—Cabot

5th game
Saturday, Nov. 20, 1880
National League baseball ground, Boston
Weather: Rain
Yale 1, Harvard 0
Yale (4-0)   0   1—1G 1T 2S
Harvard (2-2-2) 0   0—0G 0T 9S
Y—Penalty goal Walter Camp 35
Y—Robert Watson 100 kickoff return
(kick failed)
NOTE: Eleven players on a side. Only
goals counted in scoring; touchdowns
used as tie-breaker.

Yale   **Harvard**
Fuller   R   Atkinson
Beck   Clark
Vernon   Cabot
Harding   Houston
Lamb   Perin
Storrs   Kent
Adams   Thatcher
Badger   QB Manning (C.)
Watson (C.)   HB Edmands
Camp   Foster
Bacon   FB Cutts

Subs: Yale—none; Harvard—Boyd, Keith

6th game
Saturday, Nov. 12, 1881
Hamilton Park, New Haven
Weather: Rain
Yale (winner) 0, Harvard 0
Harvard (6-1)   0   0—0G 0T 4S
Yale (3-0-1)   0   0—0G 0T 0S
A—1,500 (est.)
NOTE: Safeties counted as tie-breaker,
the victory being awarded to a team that
made 4 fewer safety touchdowns than its
opponents.

Harvard   **Yale**
Manning (C.)   R   Knapp
Cabot   Farwell
Houston   Tompkins

Kendall   Hull
Appleton   Storrs
Perin   Beck
Thatcher   Lamb
Mason   QB Badger
Henry   HB Richards
Keith   Camp (C.)
Edmands   FB Bacon

Subs: Yale—none; Harvard—Fuller

7th game
Saturday, Nov. 25, 1882
Holmes Field, Cambridge
Weather: Cold, windy
Yale 1, Harvard 0
Yale (7-0)   0   1—1G 4T 0S
Harvard (7-1)   0   0—0G 0T 2S
H—safety
Y—Louis Hull run (kick failed)
Y—Charles Beck recovered fumble in end
zone (kick failed)
H—safety
Y—Beck recovered fumble (Eugene Richards kick)
Y—Arthur Farwell run (kick failed)
A—3,000 (est.)
NOTE: Three downs to make 5 yards
introduced. Only goals counted in scoring except for tie-breakers.

Yale   **Harvard**
Hull   R   Morrison
Knapp   Kendall
Tompkins (C.)   Cabot (C.)
Farwell   Hammond
Peters   Appleton
Hyndman   Ayers
Beck   Wesselhoeft
Twombley   QB Mason
Richards   HB Coolidge
Terry   Keith
Bacon   FB Edmands

Subs: Yale—none; Harvard—Adams

8th game
Thursday, Nov. 29, 1883
Polo Grounds, New York
Yale 23, Harvard 2
Harvard (8−2)   0   2— 2
Yale (8−0)   6   17—23
Y—safety J.V. Cowling downed blocked punt
Y—FG Wyllys Terry
Y—William Hyndman run (Terry kick)
H—J. Codman run (kick failed)
Y—FG Terry
Y—Arthur Farwell 1 run (Terry kick)
A—10,000 (est.)
NOTE: Point values were established this year as follows:
Field goal—5 points
Goal from touchdown—4 points
Touchdown—2 points
Safety—1 point

Harvard		Yale
Simpkins	R	Robinson
Hartley		Williams
Gilman		Peters
Appleton (C.)		McCrary
Bonsal		Tompkins (C.)
Kendall		Bertron
Codman		Farwell
Crane	. QB	Twombley
Henry	HB	Richards
Cowling		Terry
Peabody	FB	Dennen

9th game
Saturday, Nov. 22, 1884
Yale Field, Orange
Weather: Sunny, muddy field
Yale 52, Harvard 0
Harvard (7−4)   0   0— 0
Yale (8−0)   24   28—52
Y—Alex Coxe run (Eugene Richards kick)
Y—Henry Flanders 100 run (Richards kick)

Y—Nervy Bayne run (Richards kick)
Y—Richards run (Wyllys Terry kick)
Y—Frank Peters run (kick failed)
Y—Coxe run (kick failed)
Y—Coxe run (kick failed)
Y—Richards run (Terry kick)
Y—Bayne run (Terry kick)
Y—Bayne run (no conversion attempt)
A—2,400 (est.)
NOTE: Point values were changed this year as follows:
Field goal—5 points
Touchdown—4 points
Goal after touchdown—2 points
Safety—2 points

Harvard		Yale
Hurd	R	Goodwin
Thayer		Coxe
Gilman		Peters
Burgess		Flanders
Brooks		Bertron
Homans		Robinson
Finney		Ronalds
Willard	QB	Bayne
Bemis	HB	Richards (C.)
Kimball (C.)		Terry
Peabody	FB	Marlin

Subs: Yale—Storrs; Harvard—none

10th game
Saturday, Nov. 20, 1886
Jarvis Field, Cambridge
Yale 29, Harvard 4
Yale (9−0)   18   11—29
Harvard (11−2) 4   0— 4
Y—Henry Beecher run (George Watkinson kick)
Y—Samuel Morison run (Watkinson kick)
Y—Beecher run (Watkinson kick)
H—A.F. Holden run (kick failed)
Y—Charles Gill run (Watkinson kick)
Y—FG Watkinson

Yale		Harvard
Wallace	R	Adams
Gill		Remington
Burke		Wood
Corbin		Burgess
Woodruff		Brooks (C.)
Carter		Butler
Corwin (C.)		Harding
Beecher	QB	Dudley
Watkinson	HB	Porter
Morrison		Holden
Bull	FB	Peabody

Subs: Yale—Buchanan; Harvard—Fletcher, Sears, Boyden

11th game
Thursday, Nov. 24, 1887
Polo Grounds, New York
Weather: Cloudy, chilly
Yale 17, Harvard 8
Harvard (10−1)   0   8— 8
Yale (9−0)   11   6—17
Y—FG Billy Bull 25
Y—Pa Corbin run with recovered kick (Bull kick)
H—safety, blocked punt downed in end zone
H—C.A. Porter 5 run (J.H. Sears kick)
Y—Billy Wurtenberg 35 run (Bull kick)
A—15,000 (est.)

Harvard		Yale
Bancroft	LE	Wallace
Butler	LT	Gill
Trafford	LG	Carter
Markoe	C	Corbin
Wood (A.C.)	RG	Woodruff
Woodman	RT	Cross
Cumnock	RE	Pratt
Harding	QB	Beecher (C.)
Porter	LH	W. Graves
Boyden	RH	A. Graves
Sears	FB	Bull

Subs: Yale—Wurtenburg, Robinson; Harvard—Appleton, Saxe

12th game
Saturday, Nov. 23, 1889
Hampden Park, Springfield
Weather: Fair, windy
Yale 6, Harvard 0
Yale (13—0)   6   0—6
Harvard (9—2)   0   0—0
Y—Bum McClung 1 run (McClung kick)
A—12,000 (est.)

Yale		Harvard
Stagg	LE	Hutchinson
Gill, Capt.	LT	Stickney
Heffelfinger	LG	P.D. Trafford
Hanson	C	Tilton
Newell	RG	Cranston
Rhodes	RT	Upton
Hartwell	RE	Cumnock, Capt.
Wurtenburg	QB	Dean
McClung	LH	Saxe
Morison	RH	Lee
McBride	FB	B.W. Trafford

Subs: Yale—Ferris, Heyworth; Harvard—
Blanchard, Hallowell

13th game
Saturday, Nov. 22, 1890
Hampden Park, Springfield
Harvard 12, Yale 6
Harvard (11—0)   0   12—12
Yale (12—1)   0   6— 6
H—Jimmy Lee 40 sweep (Bernie Trafford kick)
H—D.S. Dean 70 run with recovered fumble (Trafford kick)
Y—Bum McClung 6 run (McClung kick)
A—15,000 (est.)

Harvard		Yale
Cumnock, Capt.	LE	Hartwell
Upton	LT	Wallis
Finlay	LG	Heffelfinger
Cranston	C	Lewis
P.D. Trafford	RG	S.N. Morison
Newell	RT	Rhodes, Capt.
Hallowell	RE	Crosby
Dean	QB	Barbour
Corbett	LH	McClung
Lake	RH	Williams
B.W. Trafford	FB	S.B. Morison

Subs: Yale—Bliss; Harvard—Lee, Alward

14th game
Saturday, Nov. 21, 1891
Hampden Park, Springfield
Weather: Fair, warm
Yale 10, Harvard 0
Yale (12—0)   4   6—10
Harvard (13—1)   0   0— 0
Y—Stan Morison 1 run (kick failed)
Y—Laurie Bliss 25 run with recovered
fumble (Bum McClung kick)
A—25,000 (est.)

Yale		Harvard
Hinkey	LE	Emmons
Winter	LT	Waters
Heffelfinger	LG	Dexter
Sanford	C	Bangs
S.N. Morison	RG	Mackie
Wallis	RT	Newell
Hartwell	RE	Hartwell
Barbour	QB	Gage
Bliss	LH	Corbett
McClung (C.)	RH	Lake
McCormick	FB	B.W. Trafford (C.)

Subs: Yale—none; Harvard—none

15th game
Saturday, Nov. 19, 1892
Hampden Park, Springfield
Yale 6, Harvard 0
Harvard (10—1)   0   0—0
Yale (12—0)   0   6—6
Y—Pop Bliss 1 run (Frank Butterworth kick)
A—18,000 (est.)

Harvard		Yale
Emmons	LE	Hinkey
Upton	LT	Winter
Waters	LG	McCrea
Lewis	C	Stillman
Mackie	RG	Hickok
Newell	RT	Wallis
Hallowell	RE	Greenway
B.W. Trafford (C.)	QB	McCormick (C.)
Gray	LH	L. Bliss
Lake	RH	C. Bliss
Brewer	FB	Butterworth

Subs: Yale—none; Harvard—Mason, Shea

16th game
Saturday, Nov. 25, 1893
Hampden Park, Springfield
Weather: Clear, cold
Yale 6, Harvard 0
Yale (10—0)   0   6—6
Harvard (11—1)   0   0—0
Y—Frank Butterworth 1 run (Bill Hickok kick)
A—25,000 (est.)

Yale		Harvard
Hinkey	LE	Emmons
Murphy	LT	Manahan
McCrea	LG	Acton
Stillman	C	Lewis
Hickok	RG	Mackie
Beard	RT	Newell
Greenway	RE	Stevenson
Adee	QB	Beale
Thorne	LH	Waters, Capt.
Armstrong	RH	Wrightington
Butterworth	FB	Brewer

Subs: Yale—none; Harvard—Dunlop

17th game
Saturday, Nov. 24, 1894
Hampden Park, Springfield
Weather: Fair, cool
Yale 12, Harvard 4
Harvard (11−1)   4   0— 4
Yale (15−0)   12   0—12 ˙
Y—Phil Stillman run with blocked punt
(Bill Hickok kick)
H—J.J. Hayes 5 run (no kick attempted)
Y—Brinck Thorne 5 run (Hickok kick)
A—25,000 (est.)

Harvard		Yale
Cabot	LE	F. Hinkey (C.)
Hallowell	LT	Beard
Mackie	LG	McCrea
F.G. Shaw	C	Stillman
J.E.N. Shaw	RG	Hickok
Waters	RT	Murphy
A.H. Brewer	RE	L. Hinkey
Wrenn (A.C.)	QB	Adee
C. Brewer	LH	Thorne
Wrightington	RH	Jerrems
Fairchild	FB	Butterworth

Subs: Yale—Chadwick, Letten, Bass,
Armstrong; Harvard—Wheeler, Whittemore, Hayes, Gonterman
(Emmons, Harvard Capt., injured—unable to play).

18th game
Saturday, Nov. 13, 1897
Soldiers Field, Boston
Weather: Cloudy, windy
Yale 0, Harvard 0
Yale (8−0−2)   0   0—0
Harvard (10−0−1) 0 0—0
A—24,000 (est.)

Yale		Harvard
Hazen	LE	Cabot, Capt.
Rodgers, Capt.	LT	Swain
Chadwick	LG	Bouvé
Cadwalader	C	Doucette
Brown	RG	Haskell
Chamberlin	RT	Donald
Hall	RE	Moulton
deSaulles	QB	Garrison
Corwin	LH	Dibblee
Benjamin	RH	Warren
McBride	FB	Haughton

Subs: Yale—none; Harvard—Wheeler,
Shaw, Mills, Parker

19th game
Saturday, Nov. 19, 1898
Yale Field, Orange
Weather: Heavy rain
Harvard 17, Yale 0
Harvard (11−0)   11   6—17
Yale (9−2)   0   0— 0
H—Bill Reid 5 run (kick failed)
H—Ben Dibblee 5 run (Percy Haughton
kick)
H—Reid 12 run (Haughton kick)
A—17,500 (est.)
NOTE: Point values were changed this
year as follows:
Field goal—5 points
Touchdown—5 points
Goal after touchdown—1 point
Safety—2 points

Harvard		Yale
Cochrane	LE	Hubbell
Donald	LT	Stillman
Boal	LG	Brown
Jaffray	C	Cutten
Burden	RG	Marshall
Haughton	RT	Chamberlin, Capt.
Hallowell	RE	Eddy
Daly	QB	Ely
Dibblee, Capt.	LH	Dudley
Warren	RH	Durston
Reid	FB	Townshend

Subs: Yale—Thomas, McBride,
Schwepp; Harvard—Farley, Eaton, Burnett

20th game
Saturday, Nov. 18, 1899
Soldiers Field, Boston
Weather: Mild
Yale 0, Harvard 0
Yale (7−1−1)   0   0—0
Harvard (10−0−1) 0 0—0
A—36,000 (est.)

Yale		Harvard
Hubbell	LE	Campbell
Francis	LT	Donald
Brown	LG	Sargent
Hale	C	Burnett
Olcott	RG	Burden, Capt.
Stillman	RT	Lawrence
Gibson	RE	Hallowell
Fincke	QB	Daly
Sharpe	LH	Sawin
Richards	RH	Kendall
McBride, Capt.	FB	Ellis

Subs: Yale—Snitjer, Chadwick, Keane;
Harvard—Ristine, Eaton, Parker, Reid

21st game
Saturday, Nov. 24, 1900
Yale Field, Orange
Weather: Windy, showers
Yale 28, Harvard 0
Harvard (10−1)   0   0— 0
Yale (12−0)   12 16—28
Y—Ralph Bloomer 1 run (Perry Hale
kick)
Y—Bill Fincke 55 punt return (Hale kick)
Y—George Chadwick 18 run (no kick at-
tempted)
Y—Sherman Coy 75 run with recovered
fumble (Hale kick)
Y—FG Al Sharpe
A—20,000 (est.)

Harvard		Yale
Campbell	LE	Gould
Eaton	LT	Bloomer
Lee	LG	Brown, Capt.

Sargent	C	Olcott
Barnard	RG	Sheldon
Lawrence	RT	Stillman, G.S.
Hallowell	RE	S. Coy
Daly, Capt.	QB	Fincke, W.M.
Sawin	LH	Sharpe
Kendall	RH	Chadwick
Ellis	FB	Hale

Subs: Yale—Holt; Harvard—Bowditch, Clark, Graydon, Burnett, Roberts, Ristine, R. Fincke, Gierasch, A. Stillman, Devens

22nd game
Saturday, Nov. 23, 1901
Soldiers Field, Boston
Harvard 22, Yale 0
Yale (11−1−1)   0   0— 0
Harvard (12−0)   17   5—22
H—Crawford Blagden 1 run (Oliver Cutts kick)
H—Albert Ristine 1 run (Cutts kick)
H—FG Andrew Marshall 40
H—Thomas Graydon 1 run (kick failed)
A—36,000 (est.)

Yale		Harvard
Gould, Capt.	LE	Campbell, Capt.
Goss	LT	Blagden
Olcott	LG	Lee
Holt	C	Green
Hamlin	RG	Barnard
Hogan	RT	Cutts
Swan	RE	Bowditch
deSaulles	QB	Marshall
Hart	LH	Kernan
Chadwick	RH	Ristine
Weymouth	FB	Graydon

Subs: Yale—Rafferty, Johnson, Metcalf, Owsley, Vanderpoel; Harvard—none

23rd game
Saturday, Nov. 22, 1902
Yale Field, Orange
Weather: Warm, moist

Yale 23, Harvard 0
Harvard (11−1)   0   0— 0
Yale (11−0−1)   12   11—23
Y—George Chadwick 1 run (Morgan Bowman kick)
Y—Harold Metcalf 75 run (Bowman kick)
Y—Ralph Kinney 20 run (Metcalf kick)
Y—Jim Hogan 10 run (kick failed)
A—30,000 (est.)

Harvard		Yale
Mills	LE	Rafferty
Shea	LT	Kinney
Barnard	LG	Glass
Sugden	C	Holt
A. Marshall	RG	Goss
Knowlton	RT	Hogan
Bowditch	RE	Shevlin
C.B. Marshall	QB	Rockwell
Kernan, Capt.	LH	Metcalf
Putnam	RH	Chadwick, Capt.
Graydon	FB	Bowman

Subs: Yale—Farmer, Hamlin, Vanderpoel, Wilhelmi; Harvard—Clothier, Hurley, Whitwell, A. Stillman

24th game
Saturday, Nov. 21, 1903
Harvard Stadium, Boston
Yale 16, Harvard 0
Yale (11−1)   5   11—16
Harvard (9−3)   0   0— 0
Y—Ralph Kinney 3 run (kick failed)
Y—Jim Hogan recovered blocked punt in end zone (kick failed)
Y—Hogan run (Ledyard Mitchell kick)
A—38,000 (est.)

Yale		Harvard
Rafferty (C.)	LE	Clothier
Kinney	LT	Derby
Batchelder	LG	LeMoyne
Roraback	C	Parkinson
Miller	RG	A. Marshall
Hogan	RT	Knowlton

Shevlin	RE	Bowditch
Rockwell	QB	C.B. Marshall (C.)
Mitchell	LH	Nichols
Metcalf	RH	Hurley
Farmer	FB	Schoelkopf

Subs: Yale—Owsley, Bowman, Bissell, Morton, Soper; Harvard—Squires, Goodhue, Mills, Montgomery

25th game
Saturday, Nov. 19, 1904
Yale Field, Orange
Weather: Warm
Yale 12, Harvard 0
Harvard (7−2−1) 0   0— 0
Yale (10−1)   6   6—12
Y—Sammy Morse 2 run (Lydig Hoyt kick)
Y—Rex Flinn 1 run (Hoyt kick)
A—35,000 (est.)
NOTE: Point values were changed this year, a field goal being reduced to 4 points.

Harvard		Yale
Randall	LE	Shevlin
Brill	LT	Bloomer
White	LG	Kinney
Parker	C	Roraback
Squires	RG	Tripp
Derby	RT	Hogan, Capt.
Montgomery	RE	Neal
Starr	QB	Rockwell
Sperry	LH	Hoyt
Hurley, Capt.	RH	Morse
Mills	FB	Flinn

Subs: Yale—Flanders; Harvard—Matthews. Pruyn, Parkinson, Noyes, Nichols

26th game
Saturday, Nov. 25, 1905
Harvard Stadium, Boston
Yale 6, Harvard 0
Yale (10–0)   0   6—6
Harvard (8–2–1) 0   0—0
Y—Bob Forbes 4 run (Lydig Hoyt kick)
A—43,000 (est.)

Yale		Harvard
Cates	LE	Leary
Forbes	LT	Brill
Erwin	LG	Burr
Flanders	C	Parker
Tripp	RG	Kersburg
Biglow	RT	Squires
Shevlin (C.)	RE	Knowlton (A.C.)
T.A.D. Jones	QB	Starr
Roome	LH	Foster
Morse	RH	Wendell
Quill	FB	Carr

Subs: Yale—H.H. Jones, Hockenberger, Smith, Hutchinson, Hoyt, Knox, Levine, Flinn; Harvard—Montgomery, Barney, Newhall, Nichols
(Hurley, Capt., injured and unable to play.)

27th game
Saturday, Nov. 24, 1906
Yale Field, Orange
Weather: Cloudy, flurries
Yale 6, Harvard 0
Harvard (10–1) 0   0—0
Yale (9–0–1)   6   0—6
Y—Howard Roome 3 run (Paul Veeder kick)
A—32,000 (est.)

	Harv	Yale
First downs	4	7
Total offense	90	186
Punting	8–50	10–40
Penalties–yards	4–20	6–70

Harvard		Yale
McDonald	LE	Forbes
Osborne	LT	Paige
Burr	LG	Brides
Parker	C	Hockenberger
Kersburg	RG	Erwin
Peirce	RT	Biglow
Starr	RE	H.H. Jones
Newhall	QB	T.A.D. Jones
Foster, Capt.	LH	Veeder
Lincoln	RH	Knox
Wendell	FB	Morse, Capt.

Subs: Yale—Roome, Linn, Stuart, Alcott, Dines, Bomar, Wernecken; Harvard—Kennard, Fraser, Orr

28th game
Saturday, Nov. 23, 1907
Harvard Stadium, Boston
Weather: Cloudy
Yale 12, Harvard 0
Yale (9–0–1)   6   6—12
Harvard (7–3)   0   0— 0
Y—Ted Coy 4 run (Lucius Biglow kick)
Y—Coy 1 run (Biglow kick)
A—39,000 (est.)

	Yale	Harv
First downs	17	6
Rushes–yards	66–195	50–156
Passing yards	80	55
Punting	13–39	11–24
Penalties–yards	3–25	5–65

Yale		Harvard
H. Jones	LE	Starr
Paige	LT	Burr
Cooney	LG	Parker, Capt.
Dunbar	C	Grant
Goebel	RG	Peirce
Biglow, Capt.	RT	Fish
Alcott	RE	McDonald
T. Jones	QB	Newhall
Brides	LH	Wendell

Bomar | RH | Rand
Coy | FB | Apollonio

Subs: Yale—Foster, Burch, Dines, Beebe, Brown, Philbin, Wheaton, Wylie, Berger; Harvard—Browne, Hoar, Lockwood, Inches

29th game
Saturday, Nov. 21, 1908
Yale Field, Orange
Weather: Fair
Harvard 4, Yale 0
Harvard (9–0–1) 4   0—4
Yale (7–1–1)   0   0—0
H—FG Vic Kennard 25
A—35,000 (est.)

	Harv	Yale
First downs	13	7
Rushing yards	250	140
Passing yards	0	0
Return yards	55	35
Passes	0–1–0	0–2–0
Punting	12–35	10–44
Fumbles–lost	4–0	2–0
Penalties–yards	12–130	7–55

Harvard		Yale
Browne	LE	Logan
McKay	LT	Hobbs
Dunlap	LG	Andrus
Nourse	C	Biddle
Hoar	RG	Goebel
Fish, Act. Capt.	RT	Brides
Crowley	RE	Burch, Capt.
Cutler	QB	Corey
Corbett	LH	Philbin
White	RH	Wheaton
VerWiebe	FB	E. Coy

Subs: Yale—Daly, Lilley, Cooney, Haines, Johnson; Harvard—Withington, West, Sprague, Leslie, Kennard, Smith (Burr, Capt., injured and unable to play).

30th game

Saturday, Nov. 20, 1909
Harvard Stadium, Boston
Weather: Sunny, chilly
Yale 8, Harvard 0

Yale (10−0)   5   3—8
Harvard (8−1)   0   0—0
Y—safety, Wayland Minot recovered punt
blocked by Carroll Cooney
Y—FG Ted Coy 25
Y—FG Coy 32
A—38,000 (est.)

	Yale	Harv
First downs	2	8
Rushes−yards	60	136
Passing yards	0	0
Return yards	90	50
Passes	0−2−0	0−2−0
Punting	13−43	14−34
Fumbles−lost	3−1	8−1
Penalties−yards	0−1	9−105

NOTE: Point values were changed this
year, a field goal being reduced to 3
points.

Yale		Harvard
Kilpatrick	LE	Browne
Hobbs	LT	McKay
Andrus	LG	L. Withington
Cooney	C	P. Withington
Goebel	RG	Fisher
Lilley	RT	Fish, Capt.
Savage	RE	Smith
Howe	QB	O'Flaherty
Philbin	LH	Corbett
Daly	RH	Leslie
Coy, Capt.	FB	Minot

Subs: Yale—Spencer, Field, Holt,
Vaughan, Logan, Paul, Murphy; Harvard—Houston, Rogers, Wigglesworth,
Frothingham, Smith

31st game

Saturday, Nov. 19, 1910
Yale Field, Orange
Weather: Sunny
Harvard 0, Yale 0

Harvard (8−0−1) 0   0   0   0—0
Yale (6−2−2)   0   0   0   0—0
A—43,000 (est.)

	Harv	Yale
First downs	13	5
Rushing yards	200	110
Passing yards	22	0
Passes	2−4−1	0−0−0
Punting	15−30	22−31
Fumbles−lost	14−4	6−1
Penalties−yards	9−65	3−35

Harvard		Yale
Lewis	LE	Kilpatrick
McKay	LT	Scully
Minot	LG	Fuller
Perkins	C	Morris
Fisher	RG	McDevitt
L. Withington,	RT	Paul
Capt.		
Smith	RE	Brooks
Wigglesworth	QB	Howe
Corbett	LH	Field
Felton	RH	Daly, Capt.
Leslie	FB	Kistler

Subs: Yale—Childs, Vaughan, Corey;
Harvard—Smith, Potter, Gardner, Wendell, Campbell, Morrison

32nd game

Saturday, Nov. 25, 1911
Harvard Stadium, Boston
Weather: Sunny, mud
Yale 0, Harvard 0

Yale (7−2−1)   0   0   0   0—0
Harvard (6−2−1) 0   0   0   0—0
A—42,000 (est.)

	Yale	Harv
First downs	5	5
Rushing yards	145	106
Passing yards	0	27
Passes	0−4	1−6
Punting	18−30	16−37
Fumbles−lost	5−0	3−2
Penalties−yards	5−50	5−45

Yale		Harvard
Avery	LE	Felton
Scully	LT	Hitchcock
Francis	LG	Leslie
Ketcham	C	Parmenter
McDevitt	RG	Fisher, Capt.
Gallauer	RT	Storer
Bomeisler	RE	Smith
Howe, Capt.	QB	Gardner
Camp	LH	Campbell
Spalding	RH	Wendell
Philbin	FB	Huntington

Subs: Sheldon, Reilly, Paul, Tomlinson,
Loree, Perry, Freeman, Merritt, Dunn;
Harvard—Potter, Reynolds, Frothingham,
Blackall

33rd game

Saturday, Nov. 23, 1912
Yale Field, Orange
Weather: Warm, dry
Harvard 20, Yale 0

Harvard (9−0) 10   0   10   0—20
Yale (7−1−1)   0   0   0   0— 0
H—Bob Storer 30 run with recovered
fumble (Tack Hardwick kick)
H—FG Charley Brickley 30
H—Brickley 20 run (Hardwick kick)
H—FG Brickley 13
A—35,000 (est.)

	Harv	Yale
First downs	5	9
Rushing yards	125	54
Passing yards	11	12
Return yards	135	27
Passes	1−1−0	1−7−3
Punting	17−33	13−35
Fumbles−lost	4−2	11−3
Penalties−yards	3−25	6−45

NOTE: Touchdown increased to 6 points. Field shortened from 110 to 100 yards. Four downs to gain 10 yards.

Harvard		Yale
Felton	LE	Avery
Storer	LT	Gallauer
Pennock	LG	Cooney
Parmenter	C	Ketcham
Trumbull	RG	J. Pendleton
Hitchcock	RT	Warren
O'Brien	RE	Bomeisler
Gardner	QB	Wheeler
Hardwick	LH	Spalding, Capt.
Brickley	RH	Philbin
Wendell, Capt.	FB	Flynn

Subs: Yale—Read, Sheldon, Cornell, Markle, Pumpelly, Baker, Talbott, Avery, Carter, Dyer, W. Howe; Harvard—Frothingham, Wigglesworth, Driscoll, Lawson, Hollister, Bradley, Graustein, Lingard, Bradlee.

34 th game
Saturday, Nov. 22, 1913
Harvard Stadium, Boston
Weather: Sunny, warm
Harvard 15, Yale 5
Yale (5−2−3)   2   3   0   0— 5
Harvard (9−0)   3   3   6   3—15
H—FG Charley Brickley 26
Y—safety, F.J. O'Brien downed kickoff in own end zone
H—FG Brickley 39
Y—FG Otis Guernsey 36
H—FG Brickley 36

H—FG Brickley 30
H—FG Brickley 21
A—44,000 (est.)

	Yale	Harv
First downs	7	11
Rushing yards	163	221
Passing yards	10	0
Return yards	59	124
Passes	1−5−3	0−2−0
Punting	10−36	14−39
Fumbles−lost	3−0	3−0
Penalties−yards	2−30	1−5

Yale		Harvard
Avery	LE	O'Brien
Talbott	LT	Hitchcock
Ketcham, Capt.	LG	Gilman
Marting	C	Trumbull
Pendleton	RG	Pennock
Warren	RT	Storer, Capt.
Carter	RE	Hardwick
Wilson	QB	Logan
Ainsworth	LH	Mahan
Knowles	RH	Bradlee
Guernsey	FB	Brickley

Subs: Yale—Brann, Arnold, Way, McLeish; Harvard—Dana, Cowen, Mills, Freedley, Soucy, Bettle, Willetts

35 th game
Saturday, Nov. 21, 1914
Yale Bowl, New Haven
Weather: Overcast
Harvard 36, Yale 0
Harvard (7−0−2)6   16   7   7—36
Yale (7−2)   0   0   0   0— 0
H—Tack Hardwick 5 pass from Packy Mahan (kick failed)
H—H. Francke recovered fumble in end zone (kick failed)
H—Jeff Coolidge 98 run with recovered fumble (Hardwick kick)
H—FG Mahan 19
H—Francke 1 run (Hardwick kick)

H—Mahan 5 pass from D.C. Watson (Charley Brickley kick)
A—68,117 (est.) [Yale AA gives 71,000; Bealle, 75,000]

	Harv	Yale
First downs	16	5
Rushing yards	312	106
Passing yards	4	83
Return yards	223	137
Passes	4−5−0	6−12−1
Punting	7−36	9−33
Fumbles−lost	2−0	3−2
Penalties−yards	3−45	3−15

Harvard		Yale
T. Coolidge	LE	Brann
Parson	LT	Talbott (C.)
Weston	LG	Conroy
Wallace	C	White
Pennock	RG	Walden
Trumbull (A.C.)	RT	Betts
Hardwick	RE	Stillman
Logan	QB	Wilson
Bradlee	LH	Ainsworth
Mahan	RH	Knowles
Francke	FB	LeGore

Subs: Yale—Sheldon, Carter, Scovil, Waite; Harvard—Brickley, Watson (captain), King, Bigelow, C. Coolidge, Curtis, Withington, McKinlock, Swigert, Weatherhead, Underwood, Smith, Atkinson, Soucy

36 th game
Saturday, Nov. 20, 1915
Harvard Stadium, Boston
Weather: Sunny, windy
Harvard 41, Yale 0
Yale (4−5)   0   0   0   0— 0
Harvard (8−1) 13   14   7   7—41
H—R. Harte 21 run with recovered fumble (kick failed)
H—Mahan 1 run (Mahan kick)
H—Mahan 12 run (Mahan kick)

H—Bob King 58 run (Mahan kick)
H—Mahan 1 run (Mahan kick)
H—Mahan 5 run (Mahan kick)
A—47,000 (est.)

	Yale	Harv
First downs	3	8
Rushing yards	143	208
Passing yards	22	23
Return yards	90	126
Passes	4-7-2	2-2-0
Punting	12-35	14-43
Fumbles—lost	8-2	3-0
Penalties—yards	5-42	4-50

Yale		Harvard
Higginbotham	LE	Soucy
C. Sheldon	LT	Gilman
Black	LG	Cowen
White	C	Wallace
J. Sheldon	RG	Dadmun
Way	RT	Parson
Allen	RE	Harte
Van Nostrand	QB	Watson
A. Wilson, Capt.	LH	Boles
Bingham	RH	Mahan, Capt.
Guernsey	FB	King

Subs: Yale—Gates, E. Miller, Walden, Baldridge, Ames, Neville, Chatfield-Taylor, Scovil, Church, Roberts, Savage, Waite, Jacques; Harvard—R. Horween, C. Coolidge, Harris, Weatherhead, Taylor, McKinlock, R. Curtis, Robinson, Rollins, L. Curtis, Whitney, Doherty

37th game
Saturday, Nov. 25, 1916
Yale Bowl, New Haven
Weather: Overcast
Yale 6, Harvard 3
Harvard (7-3)   3   0   0   0—3
Yale (8-1)   0   6   0   0—6
H—FG W.F. Robinson 28
Y—Joe Neville 1 run (kick failed)
A—77,000 (est.)

	Harv	Yale
First downs	2	7
Rushing yards	74	158
Passing yards	45	19
Passes	3-14-4	2-5-0
Punting	18-46	17-42
Fumbles—lost	2-0	6-1
Penalties—yards	4-40	5-35

Harvard		Yale
Coolidge	LE	Moseley
Wheeler	LT	Gates
Dadmun, Capt.	LG	Black, Capt.
Harris	C	J. Callahan
Snow	RG	Fox
Caner	RT	Baldridge
Harte	RE	Comerford
Robinson	QB	LaRoche
Thacher	LH	Neville
Casey	RH	LeGore
R. Horween	FB	Jacques

Subs: Yale—Church; Harvard—Phinney, Batchelder, Sweetser, Wiggin, Murray, W. Felton, Minot, Bond, Flower, Willcox

38th game
Saturday, Nov. 22, 1919
Harvard Stadium, Boston
Harvard 10, Yale 3
Yale (5-3)   0   0   0   3— 3
Harvard (9-0-1)   3   7   0   0—10
H—FG Ralph Horween 41
H—Eddie Casey 40 pass from R. Horween (R. Horween kick)
Y—FG Jim Braden 55
A—50,000 (est.)

	Yale	Harv
First downs	7	4
Rushing yards	155	82
Passing yards	28	53
Passes	4-9-2	2-4-0
Punting	14-35	18-33
Fumbles—lost	9-5	4-1
Penalty yards	0-0	65

Yale		Harvard
Reinhardt	LE	Desmond
Dickens	LT	Sedgwick
Acosta	LG	Woods
J. Callahan (C.)	C	Havemeyer
Galt	RG	Clark
Walker	RT	Kane
Allen	RE	Steele
Kempton	QB	Murray (C.)
Neville	LH	Casey
Lay	RH	Humphrey
Braden	FB	A. Horween

Subs: Yale—Campbell, Hubbard, La-Roche, Webb, Aldrich, Walters; Harvard—Ryan, Philbin, Hubbard, Phinney, W. Felton, Gratwick, Nellson, Burnham, R. Horween

39th game
Saturday, Nov. 20, 1920
Yale Bowl, New Haven
Harvard 9, Yale 0
Harvard (8-0-1) 3   0   3   3—9
Yale (5-3)   0   0   0   0—0
H—FG Charley Buell 35
H—FG Arnold Horween 38
H—FG Buell 15
A—76,000 (est.)

	Harv	Yale
First downs	16	5
Rushes—yards	61-195	27-68
Passing yards	124	43
Return yards	92	80
Passes	9-16-3	3-17-3
Punting	12-38	13-39
Fumbles—lost	3-2	3-2
Penalty yards	66	35

Harvard		Yale
Kane	LE	Cutler
Sedgwick	LT	Dickens
Woods	LG	Acosta
Havemeyer	C	Cross

Tolbert	RG	J. Callahan (C.)
Hubbard	RT	Walker
Crocker	RE	Bean
Buell	QB	Kempton
Owen	LH	Aldrich
Fitts	RH	Kelly
A. Horween (C.)	FB	Sturm

Subs: Yale—Galvin, Quaile, French, Dilworth, Sherlin, Into, Mackay, Herr, Murphy, Wakelee, Jordan, Lay; Harvard—Gaston, Macomber, Faxon, Brocker, Tierney, Brown, Finley, Fitzgerald, Johnson, Gratwick, Hamilton, Humphrey, Churchill

40th game
Saturday, Nov. 19, 1921
Harvard Stadium, Boston
Weather: Warm, misty
Harvard 10, Yale 3
Yale (8–1)   3 0 0   0— 3
Harvard (7–2–1)0 0 0 10—10
Y—FG Mac Aldrich 12
H—George Owen 1 run (Charley Buell kick)
H—FG Owen 30
A—55,000 (est.)

	Yale	Harv
First downs	11	7
Rushing yards	264	130
Passing yards	5	8
Passes	1–7–3	2–7–2
Punting*	11–49	11–49
Fumbles—lost	1–1	1–0
Penalties—yards	2–20	4–30

*from point where ball was kicked.

Yale		Harvard
Hulman	LE	Macomber
Into	LT	Kane, Capt.
Cruikshank	LG	Brown
Landis	C	Clark
Guernsey	RG	Hubbard
Diller	RT	Tierney

Sturm	RE	Crocker
O'Hearn	QB	Buell
Aldrich, Capt.	LH	Fitts
Jordan	RH	Owen
Mallory	FB	Coburn

Subs: Yale—Cross, Deaver, Quaille, Herr, Norris, Miller, Blair, Becket, Wight, Knapp, Speiden; Harvard—Ladd, Lockwood, Holder, Grew, Brocker, Hartley, Johnson, Conlon, Gratwick, Churchill, Chapin, Hovey, Angier

41st game
Saturday, Nov. 25, 1922
Yale Bowl, New Haven
Weather: Cold
Harvard 10, Yale 3
Harvard (7–2)   7 0 0 3—10
Yale (6–3–1)   0 3 0 0— 3
H—George Owen 1 run (Owen kick)
Y—FG Charlie O'Hearn 20
H—FG Karl Pfaffman 34
A—78,000 (est.)

	Harv	Yale
First downs	8	10
Rushing yards	91	163
Passing yards	18	98
Return yards	104	66
Passes	3–6–0	8–16–1
Punting*	17–46	12–46
Fumbles—lost	3–2	0–0
Penalties—yards	3–12	4–30

*from point where ball was kicked.

Harvard		Yale
Jenkins	LE	Hulman
Dunker	LT	Miller
Hubbard	LG	Cruikshank
Clark	C	Lovejoy
Kunhardt	RG	Cross
Eastman	RT	Joss
Gordon	RE	Deaver
Spaulding	QB	Neidlinger

Owen	LH	O'Hearn
Gehrke	RH	Jordan, Capt.
Hammond	FB	Mallory

Subs: Yale—Luman, Bench, Lincoln, Herr, Greene, Pillsbury, Neale; Harvard—Buell (Capt.), Hill, Holder, Lee, Pfaffman, Greenough, Fitts, Chapin

42nd game
Saturday, Nov. 24, 1923
Harvard Stadium, Boston
Weather: Heavy rain
Yale 13, Harvard 0
Yale (8–0)   0 7 6 0—13
Harvard (4–3–1)0 0 0 0— 0
Y—Ducky Pond 67 run with recovered fumble (Bill Mallory kick)
Y—FG Mallory 24
Y—FG Mallory 27
A—55,000 (est.)

	Yale	Harv
First downs	1	1
Rushes—yards	30–43	24–23
Passing yards	0	0
Return yards	89	0
Passes	0–2–0	0–3–0
Punting	29–37	26–38
Fumbles—lost	6–1	8–5
Penalties—yards	3–12	3–25

Individual Leaders
Rushing: Yale, Eddie Cottle 10–25; Harvard, John Hammond 7–24.
Passing: Yale, Widdy Neale 0–2–0–0; Harvard, Phil Spaulding 0–3–0–0.

Yale		Harvard
Bingham	LE	Hill
Milstead	LT	Evans
Diller	LG	C. Hubbard (C.)
Lovejoy	C	Greenough
Eckart	RG	Dunker
Blair	RT	Eastman
Luman	RE	Combs

Richeson	QB	Lee
Neale	LH	Hammond
Pond	RH	Cheek
Mallory (C.)	FB	Coburn

Subs: Yale—Stevens, J. Miller, Deaver, Neidlinger, Esselstyn, Bench, Cottle, Hart, Haas, O'Hearn; Harvard—Crosby, R. Hubbard, Kernan, Bradford, Donovan, Hobson, Gordon, McGlone, Spaulding, Lockwood, Pfaffman, Jenkins, Cordingley

43rd game
Saturday, Nov. 22, 1924
Yale Bowl, New Haven
Weather: Rain
Yale 19, Harvard 6

Harvard (4–4)	6	0	0	0—	6
Yale (6–0–2)	0	0	13	6—	19

H—FG Erwin Gehrke 16
H—FG Gehrke 31
Y—Ducky Pond 1 run (Harry Scott kick)
Y—Bill Kline 1 run (kick blocked)
Y—Kline 1 run (kick blocked)
A—75,000 (est.)

	Harv	Yale
First downs	2	16
Rushing—yards	46	240
Passing yards	0	15
Passes	0–0–0	1–5–1
Punting*	11–41	12–49
Fumbles—lost	4–3	3–2
Penalties—yards	2–10	2–10

*from point where ball was kicked.

Harvard		**Yale**
Beals	LE	Bingham
Linder	LT	Joss
Theopold	LG	Sturhahn
Greenough, Capt.	C	Lovejoy, Capt.
Dunker	RG	Root
Coady	RT	Butterworth
Dean	RE	Luman
Stafford	QB	Bench

Miller	LH	Cottle
Gehrke	RH	Pond
Maher	FB	Allen

Subs: Yale—Bunnell, Scott, Eckart, Kline, Richards, Failing, Osborne, Gill, Wortham, Burt, Wadsworth; Harvard—Adie, Hoague, Gamanche, Hammond, Cheek

44th game
Saturday, Nov. 21, 1925
Harvard Stadium, Boston
Yale 0, Harvard 0

Yale (5–2–1)	0	0	0	0—0
Harvard (4–3–1)	0	0	0	0—0

A—51,000 (est.)

	Yale	Harv
First downs	13	3
Rushing yards	138	57
Passing yards	45	27
Return yards	69	22
Passes	5–18–0	2–6–2
Punting*	9–44	11–45
Fumbles—lost	1–0	2–1
Penalties—yards	1–15	4–20

*from point where ball was kicked.

Yale		**Harvard**
Gill	LE	Sayles
Joss, Capt.	LT	Linder
Sturhahn	LG	Bradford
Burt	C	Turner
Webster	RG	Kilgour
Butterworth	RT	Coady
Potts	RE	Bradford
Fishwick	QB	Cheek, Capt.
Noble	LH	Miller
Kline	RH	Zarakov
Allen	FB	Crosby

Subs: Yale—Wallace, Wadsworth, Bradley, Cutler, Bunnell, Cottle, Stone, Sanger, Scott, Foote, Caldwell; Harvard—Pratt, Chauncey, Coady, Maher, Doherty, Taylor, Daley, Hoague

45th game
Saturday, Nov. 20, 1926
Yale Bowl, New Haven
Weather: Sunny
Yale 12, Harvard 7

Harvard (3–5)	0	0	7	0—	7
Yale (4–4)	0	6	3	3—12

Y—Cobbles Sturhahn recovered blocked punt in end zone (kick failed)
H—Bill Saltonstall 35 pass from Henry Chauncey (Chauncey kick)
Y—FG Jerry Wadsworth 23
Y—FG Tibby Bunnell 38
A—74,782

	Harv	Yale
First downs	8	7
Rushing yards	104	110
Passing yards	64	55
Return yards	21	79
Passes	8–16–3	3–7–0
Punting*	12–45	11–53
Fumbles—lost	3–1	1–1
Penalties—yards	0–0	4–30

*from point where ball was kicked.

Harvard		**Yale**
Rudman	LE	Scott
Coady, Capt.	LT	Richards
Simonds	LG	Sturhahn
Gamache	C	Look
Stewart	RG	Webster
Pratt	RT	Benton
Meadows	RE	Fishwick
Stafford	QB	Bunnell, Capt.
Guarnaccia	LH	Noble
Clark	RH	Hoben
Sayles	FB	Kline

Subs: Yale—Switz, Holabird, Flaherty, McGunigle, Wylie, Quarrier, Goodwine, Harvey, Wadsworth, Wortham; Harvard—Chauncey, Putnam, Miller, Strong, Bell, Saltonstall, Kilgour, Goodwin, Lindner, French, Hamlen, Robinson

46th game
Saturday, Nov. 19, 1927
Harvard Stadium, Boston
Weather: Clear, chilly
Yale 14, Harvard 0
Yale (7–1)   7 0 7 0—14
Harvard (4–4)   0 0 0 0— 0
Y—Johnny Garvey 52 run (Duncan Cox kick)
Y—Bill Hammersley 42 run (Cox kick)
A—54,000 (est.)

	Yale	Harv
First downs	19	12
Rushing yards	384	219
Passing yards	27	0
Return yards	40	18
Passes	2–11–0	0–10–1
Punting*	11–45	14–40
Fumbles–lost	2–1	0–0
Penalties–yards	4–20	0–0

*from point where ball was kicked.

Yale		Harvard
Scott	LE	Strong
Quarrier	LT	Pratt, Capt.
Greene	LG	Parkinson
Charlesworth	C	Bell
Webster, Capt.	RG	Simonds
Eddy	RT	Clark
Fishwick	RE	Douglas
Hoben	QB	Brown
Garvey	LH	Guarnaccia
Decker	RH	Crosby
Cox	FB	Potter

Subs: Yale—West, Sanger, Mallory, Oldt, Flaherty, Spiel, Miner, Harvey, Crile, Billhardt, Switz, Lampe, Wilson, Marting, N. Hall, Ryan, R. Hall, Hammersley, Goodwine, Foote, Stone, Hubbard; Harvard—Lord, S. Burns, Prior, Stewart, Tripp, Turner, Combs, Fordyce, H. Burns, Kelly, French, Harper, Mason

47th game
Saturday, Nov. 24, 1928
Yale Bowl, New Haven
Weather: Cloudy
Harvard 17, Yale 0
Harvard (5–2–1) 7 0 7 3—17
Yale (4–4)   0 0 0 0— 0
H—Dave Guarnaccia 11 run (Eliot Putnam kick)
H—Guarnaccia 1 run (Putnam kick)
H—FG Putnam 26
A—74,786

	Harv	Yale
First downs	16	5
Rushing yards	236	90
Passing yards	45	10
Return yards	76	115
Passes	5–9–2	3–18–6
Punting*	10–41	9–41
Fumbles–lost	3–2	2–2
Penalties–yards	4–30	3–15

*from point where ball was kicked.

Harvard		Yale
Pichard	LE	Walker
Barrett	LT	Marting
Trainer	LG	Greene
B. Ticknor	C	Loeser
W. Ticknor	RG	Palmer
Clark	RT	Eddy, Capt.
O'Connell	RE	McEwen
Putnam	QB	Ellis
French, Capt.	LH	Loud
Guarnaccia	RH	Hubbard
Harper	FB	Decker

Subs: Yale—Stewart, Palmer, Garvey, Vincent, Miller, Wilson, Ladd, N. Hall, Ferris, Charlesworth, Godman, Crile, Hoben, Dunn, Snead; Harvard—Crawford, Douglas, Robinson, Huguley, Parkinson, Prior, Shaw, Dorman

48th game
Saturday, Nov. 23, 1929
Harvard Stadium, Boston
Weather: Cloudy
Harvard 10, Yale 6
Yale (5–2–1)   0 6 0 0— 6
Harvard (5–2–1) 0 10 0 0—10
H—Wally Harper 1 run (Barry Wood kick)
H—FG Wood 25
Y—Hoot Ellis 17 pass from Albie Booth (kick failed)
A—59,000 (est.)

	Yale	Harv
First downs	10	8
Rushing yards	128	151
Passing yards	78	10
Return yards	62	72
Passes	6–14–1	2–5–1
Punting	11–35	12–32
Fumbles–lost	0–0	0–0
Penalty yards	20	25

Yale		Harvard
Hickok	LE	Douglas
Marting	LT	Barrett, Capt.
Hare	LG	Trainer
Phillips	C	B. Ticknor
Greene, Capt.	RG	Talbot
Vincent	RT	W. Ticknor
Barres	RE	O'Connell
McLennan	QB	Wood
Snead	LH	Putnam
Miller	RH	Devens
Dunn	FB	Harper

Subs: Yale—Palmer, Tyson, Booth, Wilson, Austen, Stewart, Ellis, Taylor, Beane, Ferris, Hawley, McEwen; Harvard—Ogden, Harding, Richards, Kales, Cunningham, Gildea, Myerson, Kuehn, Davis, S. Burns, Mays, Wetmore, Huguley, White

49th game
Saturday, Nov. 22, 1930
Yale Bowl, New Haven
Weather: Fair, mild
Harvard 13, Yale 0
Harvard (4−4−1) 7 0 6 0—13
Yale (5−2−2) 0 0 0 0—0
H—Art Huguley 31 pass from Barry Wood (Wood kick)
H—Huguley 26 pass from Wood (kick failed)
A—74,679

	Harv	Yale
First downs	5	12
Rushing yards	82	129
Passing yards	117	81
Return yards	110	72
Passes	6−10−3	9−27−2
Punting*	15−38	14−41
Fumbles−lost	0−0	3−2
Penalty yards	35	50

*from point where ball was kicked.

Harvard		Yale
Harding	LE	Flygare
Richards	LT	Wilbur
Myerson	LG	Stewart
B. Ticknor, Capt.	C	Loeser
Trainer	RG	Linehan
Trafford	RT	Vincent, Capt.
Ogden	RE	Barres
Wood	QB	Booth
Crickard	LH	Austen
Huguley	RH	Dunn
White	FB	Crowley

Subs: Yale—Hare, Weiner, McLennan, Beane, Church, Wright, Levering, Tyson, Austin, Rotan, Avery, Sargent, Walker, Hall, Sullivan, Taylor, Muhlfeld, Heim; Harvard—Hageman, Kales, Batchelder, Upton, Baldwin, Talbot, Mays, Schereschewsky, Moushegian, Bancroft, Record, Fullam

50th game
Saturday, Nov. 21, 1931
Harvard Stadium, Boston
Weather: Clear
Yale 3, Harvard 0
Yale (4−1−2) 0 0 0 3—3
Harvard (7−1) 0 0 0 0—0
Y—FG Albie Booth 26
A—58,000 (est.)

	Yale	Harv
First downs	7	7
Rushes−yards	52−124	44−86
Passing yards	26	20
Return yards	44	69
Passes	1−9−1	3−9−1
Punting	14−40	9−27
Fumbles−lost	1−0	3−3
Penalties−yards	9−68	2−20

Individual Leaders
Rushing: Yale, Joe Crowley 20−49; Harvard, Jack Crickard 23−56.
Passing: Yale, Booth 1−4−1−26; Harvard, Barry Wood 3−9−1−20.
Receiving: Yale, Herty Barres 1−26; Harvard, Bernie White 2−13.

Yale		Harvard
Flygare	LE	Nazro
Wilbur	LT	Hardy
Nichols	LG	Ginman
Betner	C	Hallowell
Rotan	RG	Myerson
Hall	RT	Kopans
Barres	RE	Hageman
Parker	QB	Wood, Capt.
Booth, Capt.	LH	Schereschewsky
Crowley	RH	Crickard
Levering	FB	White

Subs: Yale—Strange, Lassiter, Hall, Hawley, Ingram, Sullivan, M. Williamson, Bachman, Converse, Bouscaren, Taylor, Doonan; Harvard—Esterley, Record, Francisco, Mays, Talbot, Kales, Finlayson, Bancroft, Faxon, Cunningham, Moushegian, Nevin, Gleason, Wells, Rogers, Dean

51st game
Saturday, Nov. 19, 1932
Yale Bowl, New Haven
Weather: Rain, mud
Yale 19, Harvard 0
Harvard (5−3) 0 0 0 0— 0
Yale (2−2−3) 7 0 6 6—19
Y—Walt Levering 1 run (Pat Sullivan run)
Y—Levering 4 run (kick failed)
Y—Walter Marting 24 pass from Bob Lassiter (kick failed)
A—35,000 (est.)

	Harv	Yale
First downs	10	9
Rushing yards	99	140
Passing yards	4	74
Return yards	83	26
Passes	1−8−0	3−4−0
Punting*	12−48	14−44
Fumbles−lost	7−2	5−1
Penalties−yards	3−10	8−40

*from point where ball was kicked.

Harvard		Yale
Nazro	LE	O'Connell
Hardy	LT	Wilbur, Capt.
Esterly	LG	Nichols
Hallowell	C	Howland
Gundlach	RG	Converse
Bancroft	RT	Curtin
Hageman, Capt.	RE	Parker
Wells	QB	Sullivan
Crickard	LH	Lassiter
Barrett	RH	Crowley
Dean	FB	Levering

Subs: Yale—Garnsey, Sargent, McCrudden, DeAngelis, Johnson, Holcombe, Kimball, Browne, C. Williamson, Callan, M. Williamson, Malin, Kilcullen, Marting; Harvard—Wolcott, Francisco, Crane, Healey, Rogers, Bartol, Cassedy, Whitney, Peter, Nevin, Leonard, Waters, Sherman, Pescosolido

52nd game
Saturday, Nov. 25, 1933
Harvard Stadium, Boston
Weather: Fair
Harvard 19, Yale 6
Yale (4–3)   0 0 6 0— 6
Harvard (5–2–1) 6 7 6 0—19
H—Bob Haley 5 pass from Harry Wells
(kick blocked)
H—Fred Crocker 56 pass from Wells
(Johnny Dean kick)
Y—Bob Lassiter 1 run (kick blocked)
H—Fergie Locke 90 kickoff return (kick
failed)
A—45,000 (est.)

	Yale	Harv
First downs	11	4
Rushing yards	139	56
Passing yards	81	107
Return yards	104	42
Passes	6–19–3	3–5–0
Punting*	14–48	18–47
Fumbles–lost	5–1	0–0
Penalties–yards	6–41	9–65

*from point where ball was kicked.

Yale		Harvard
Combs	LE	Choate
Kilcullen	LT	Francisco
Nichols	LG	Schumann
Malin	C	Casey
DeAngelis	RG	Gundlach
F. Curtin	RT	Kopans
Rankin	RE	Kelly
T. Curtin	QB	Haley
Lassiter, Capt.	LH	Wells
Keesling	RH	Litman
Nikkel	FB	Dean, Capt.

Subs: Yale—Callan, Roscoe, Morton,
Tarlton, Whitehead, McCrudden, Herold,
Grosscup, Johnson, Davis, Overall, Towle,
Childs; Harvard—Nazro, Crane, Lock-
wood, Crocker, Locke, Healey, Nevin,
Rogers, Whitney, Sherman, Beale, Peter,
White, Lowe, Janien

53rd game
Saturday, Nov. 24, 1934
Yale Bowl, New Haven
Weather: Overcast
Yale 14, Harvard 0
Harvard (3–5) 0 0 0 0— 0
Yale (5–3)   7 7 0 0—14
Y—Strat Morton 20 run (Clare Curtin
kick)
Y—Larry Kelley 8 pass from Jerry Roscoe
(Curtin kick)
A—55,000 (est.)

	Harv	Yale
First downs	14	10
Rushing yards	148	160
Passing yards	43	54
Return yards	87	42
Passes	5–19–1	5–6–0
Punting*	7–38	9–45
Fumbles–lost	3–3	3–2
Penalties–yards	3–11	4–20

*from point where ball was kicked.

Harvard		Yale
Dubiel	LE	Train
Burton	LT	Scott
Brookings	LG	Curtin (C.)
Comfort	C	DeAngelis
Gundlach (C.)	RG	Grosscup
Adlis	RT	Wright
Kelley	RE	Kelley
Haley	QB	Roscoe
Moseley	LH	Whitehead
Watt	RH	Morton
Jackson	FB	Fuller

Subs: Yale—Crampton, Rankin, Towle,
T. Curtin, Strauss, Johnson, Edmonds,
Hersey, Schultz, Callan; Harvard—Spring,
Adzigian, Knapp, Ecker, Hedblom, Black-
wood, Bilodeau, Locke, Litman, Parquette,
Lane, Ford, Casale, Littlefield

54th game
Saturday, Nov. 23, 1935
Harvard Stadium, Boston
Weather: Snow
Yale 14, Harvard 7
Yale (6–2)   0 0 7 7—14
Harvard (3–5) 0 0 0 7— 7
Y—Larry Kelley 35 pass from Jerry Roscoe
(Heinie Gardner kick)
H—Fred Moseley 2 run (Tom Bilodeau
kick)
Y—Al Hessberg 2 run (Tommy Curtin
kick)
A—52,000 (N.Y. *Times* est.)

	Yale	Harv
First downs	9	11
Rushing yards	131	126
Passing yards	83	74
Return yards	41	85
Passes	6–9–1	5–16–2
Punting*	12–37	10–41
Fumbles–lost	2–0	3–1
Penalties–yards	5–25	4–30

*from point where ball was kicked.

Yale		Harvard
Train	LE	Dubiel
Barr	LT	Burton
Snavely	LG	Gaffney
Herold	C	Jones
Davis	RG	Nee
Wright	RT	Maser
Kelley	RE	Kelly (C.)
Roscoe	QB	Blackwood
Whitehead (C.)	LH	Adzigian
Loomis	RH	Ecker
Miles	FB	Struck

Subs: Yale—Dickens, Gardner, Colwell,
Frank, Ewart, T. Curtin, Hessberg, Gal-
lagher, Hersey; Harvard—Allen, Husband,
Greeley, Kessler, Watson, Prout, Bilodeau,
Knapp, Ford, Moseley, Jackson, Hedblom,
Watt

55th game
Saturday, Nov. 21, 1936
Yale Bowl, New Haven
Yale 14, Harvard 13
Harvard (3–4–1) 0   0   7   6—13
Yale (7–1)   7   7   0   0—14
Y—Al Wilson 6 run (Bud Humphrey kick)
Y—Larry Kelley 42 pass from Clint Frank (Humphrey kick)
H—Vernon Struck 1 run (Struck kick)
H—George Ford 20 pass from Arthur Oakes (kick failed)
A—58,000 (est.)

	Harv	Yale
First downs	14	9
Rushes—yards	249	166
Passing yards	66	71
Return yards	51	41
Passes	3–10–4	3–9–2
Punting	3–20	6–39
Fumbles—lost	2–2	1–1
Penalties—yards	1–5	6–50

Harvard		Yale
Green	LE	Carey
Kevorkian	LT	Scott
Gaffney (C.)	LG	Caracciolo
Jones	C	Beckwith
Kessler	RG	Wright
Adlis	RT	John
Daughters	RE	Kelley (C.)
Wilson	QB	Ewart
Oakes	LH	Frank
Stuart	RH	Humphrey
Struck	FB	Miles

Subs: Yale—Castle, Dickens, Peterson, Higgins, Morse, Murtha, Love, Hoxton, Wilson, Mott, C. Miller, Platt, Hessberg, Colwell; Harvard—Allen, Boston, Watt, Roberts, Ford, Hedblom, Nee, Harding, Booth, McTernan, Staples, Winter

56th game
Saturday, Nov. 20, 1937
Harvard Stadium, Boston
Weather: Flurries
Harvard 13, Yale 6
Yale (6–1–1)   0   0   6   0— 6
Harvard (5–2–1) 0   6   0   7—13
H—Don Daughters 19 pass from Frank Foley (kick failed)
Y—Clint Frank 1 run (kick blocked)
H—Foley 10 run (Chief Boston kick)
A—38,000 (est.)

	Yale	Harv
First downs	10	16
Rushes—yards	38–178	51–256
Passing yards	28	57
Return yards	26	16
Passes	3–14–0	3–9–0
Punting	9–42	7–29
Fumbles—lost	1–1	1–1
Penalties—yards	7–45	1–5

Individual Leaders
Rushing: Yale, Al Hessberg 15–98, Frank 19–74; Harvard, Torby Macdonald 10–102, Vernon Struck 24–94, Foley 14–50.
Passing: Yale, Gil Humphrey 1–5–0–21; Harvard, Foley 3–9–0–57.
Receiving: Yale, Hessberg 1–21; Harvard, Daughters 2–39.

Yale		Harvard
J. Miller	LE	Green
John	LT	Kevorkian
Castle	LG	Nee
Gallagher	C	Wilson
C. Miller	RG	Klein
Platt	RT	Booth
Hoxton	RE	Daughters
Ewart	QB	Boston
Frank, Capt.	LH	Foley
Hessberg	RH	MacDonald
Colwell	FB	Struck

Subs: Yale—Rafferty, Dyess, Moody, C. Taylor, Heminway, Dickens, Caracciola, Wood, Stack, Watson, Snavely, Collins, Humphrey; Harvard—Allen (Capt.), Jameson, Downes, Hedblom, Russell, Jerome, Harding, Pope

57th game
Saturday, Nov. 19, 1938
Yale Bowl, New Haven
Weather: Rain
Harvard 7, Yale 0
Harvard (4–4) 0   0   0   7—7
Yale (2–6)   0   0   0   0—0
H—Torby Macdonald 10 pass from Frank Foley (Chief Boston kick)
A—62,000 (est.)

	Harv	Yale
First downs	5	10
Rushes—yards	72	129
Passing yards	70	43
Return yards	45	49
Passes	3–7–1	5–14–0
Punting*	10–46	12–44
Fumbles—lost	4–1	1–1
Penalties—yards	2–10	0–0

*from point where ball was kicked.

Harvard		Yale
Green (C.)	LE	J. Miller
Healey	LT	Brooks
Mellen	LG	Burnham
Russell	C	Stack
Glueck	RG	C. Miller
Booth	RT	Platt, Capt.
Daughters	RE	Dyess
Wilson	QB	Anderson
Harding	LH	Collins
MacDonald	RH	Wilson
Gardella	FB	Snavely

Subs: Yale—Moody, John, Burr, Humphrey, Zilly, Heminway, Dern; Harvard—Jamison, Lowry, Coleman, Fearon, Boston, Foley, Smith, Cohen, Hallett, Burnett

58th game
Saturday, Nov. 25, 1939
Harvard Stadium, Boston
Weather: Cloudy, raw
Yale 20, Harvard 7
Yale (3−4−1)   0   7   7   6—20
Harvard (4−4) 0   0   0   7— 7
Y—Al Bartholemy 5 pass from Fred Burr (Howie Kaye kick)
Y—Hovey Seymour 2 run (Kaye kick)
Y—Seymour 4 run (kick blocked)
H—Torby Macdonald 1 run (Charlie Spreyer kick)
A—52,000 (est.)

	Yale	Harv
First downs	4	11
Rushes−yards	82	126
Passing yards	19	100
Passes	3−6−1	7−22−2
Punting	44	38
Fumbles−lost	0	2
Penalties−yards	15	10

Individual Leaders
Rushing: Yale, Seymour 23−69; Harvard, Macdonald 22−109.

Yale		Harvard
Bartholemy	LE	MacKinney
Brooks	LT	Miller
Burnam	LG	Peabody
Starbuck	C	Ayers
Dern	RG	Pfister
Seabury	RT	Healey
Brinkley (A.C.)	RE	Lovett
Burr	QB	Coleman
Whiteman	LH	MacDonald (C.)
Seymour	RH	Lee
Wood	FB	Spreyer

Captain Stack did not play.

Subs: Yale—Lussen, Zilly, Kaye, Mc-Celland, Huffard, Reid, Taylor, Kemp, Knapp, Magee, Merrick, Wooster, Macomber, D. Kiphuth, Johnson, Turner, Harrison; Harvard—Devine, Kelly, Lowry, Hallett, Downing, Gardella, Heiden, Brown, Curtis

59th game
Saturday, Nov. 23, 1940
Yale Bowl, New Haven
Weather: Cloudy, mild
Harvard 28, Yale 0
Harvard (3−2−3)0 7 7 14—28
Yale (1−7)   0 0 0   0— 0
H—Joe Gardella 25 pass from Don Mc-Nicol (Hank Vander Eb kick)
H—Gardella 1 run (Vander Eb kick)
H—Fran Lee 78 punt return (Vander Eb kick)
H—Charley Spreyer 2 run (Greeley Summers kick)
A—47,000 (est.)

	Harv	Yale
First downs	10	8
Rushing yards	174	117
Passing yards	54	13
Passes	2−6−1	1−11−3
Punting	35	40
Fumbles lost	1	1
Penalty yards	20	20

Harvard		Yale
MacKinney	LE	Bartholemy
Elser	LT	Brooks
Peabody	LG	Burnam
Ayres	C	Moseley
Pfister	RG	Dern
Gardiner	RT	Knapp
Koufman	RE	Thompson
Heiden	QB	Harrison
Spreyer	LH	Willoughby
Lee	RH	Seymour
Brown	FB	Rewick

Subs: Yale—Greene, Miller, Eddy, Goldcamp, O'Rourke, Westfeldt, Anderson, McClelland, Bell, Whiteman (Capt.), Zilly, Magee, Millard, Turner, D. Kiphuth, Wheeler, Rewick, Kaye, Talbott, Detchon; Harvard—Morgan, Barnes, Duane, Fortes, Vander Eb, Miller, Lowry, Ferris, Dietz, Grover, Gardella (Capt.), McNicol, Lyman, Lyle, Summers, Townsend, Gordon

60th game
Saturday, Nov. 22, 1941
Harvard Stadium, Boston
Weather: Sunny
Harvard 14, Yale 0
Yale (1−7)   0 0 0 0— 0
Harvard (5−2−1)0 7 0 7—14
H—Don McNicol 1 run (Hank Vander Eb kick)
H—Don Forte 4 pass from Fran Lee (Vander Eb kick)
A—54,000 (est.)

	Yale	Harv
First downs	12	12
Rushing yards	164	270
Passing yards	97	4
Passes	7−27−1	1−4−0
Punting	38	40
Fumbles lost	0	1
Penalty yards	10	25

Individual Leaders
Rushing: Yale, Jigger Harrison 23−88, Hovey Seymour 20−67. Harvard, Mc-Nicol 25−179.

Yale		Harvard
Bartholemy (C.)	LE	MacKinney
Kemp	LT	Miller
Ruebel	LG	Peabody
Moseley	C	Page
Stack	RG	Pfister
Kiendl	RT	Gardiner
Thompson	RE	Forte
Potts	QB	Heiden
Taylor	LH	Summers
Harrison	RH	Lee, Capt.
Seymour	FB	McNicol

Subs: Yale—Greene, Collins, Overlock, Miller, Thompson, Westfeldt, Reid, Wheeler, Dwyer, Turner, Hoopes, Wallace, Ferguson; Harvard—Morgan, Barnes, Parsons, Stannard, Hibbard, Grunig, Whitehall, Ayers, LaCroix, Anderson, Wilson, Vander Eb, Goldthwait, Johnson, O'Donnell, Lyman, Lyle

61st game
Saturday, Nov. 21, 1942
Yale Bowl, New Haven
Yale 7, Harvard 3
Harvard (2–6–1) 0 3 0 0—3
Yale (5–3)   0 0 0 7—7
H—FG Bob Fisher Jr. 27
Y—Tim Hoopes 61 pass from Hugh
Knowlton (Fred Dent kick)
A—23,500 (est.)

	Harv	Yale
First Downs	9	5
Rushing Yards	167	70
Passing Yards	62	109
Passes	4–11–0	8–18–3
Punts	39	37
Fumbles lost	3	0
Penalties–yards	5	20

Harvard		Yale
Barnes	LE	Cooley
Durwood	LT	Elwell
Gudaitis	LG	Martin
Fisher	C	Moseley (C.)
Smith	RG	Davison
Stannard	RT	Kiendl
Forte (C.)	RE	Jenkins
Anderson	QB	Scovil
Richards	LH	Taylor
O'Donnell	RH	Hoopes
Johnson	FB	Ferguson

Subs: Yale—Dwyer, Furse, Macomber,
Ruebel, Warfield, Overlook, Knowlton,
Kirst, Miles, Meyer, Miller, Dent, Greene,
Dietrich, Stack, Smith, Whiting, B. Walk-
er, Pickett, Potts, Weiner, Town; Har-
vard—Cummings, Boston, W. Fisher, R.
Fisher, Hibbard, Kamp, L. Flynn, Comer-
ford, Harvey, Cowen

62nd game
Saturday, Dec. 1, 1945
Yale Bowl, New Haven
Weather: Cold, snow
Yale 28, Harvard 0

Harvard (5–3) 0 0 0 0— 0
Yale (6–3)   0 12 9 7—28
Y—Art Fitzgerald 1 run (kick failed)
Y—Fitzgerald 15 run (kick failed)
Y—safety, Charley Roche tackled by Paul
Walker in end zone
Y—Fitzgerald 4 run (Frank DeNezzo kick)
Y—Vandy Kirk 3 run (DeNezzo kick)
A—35,000 (est.)

	Harv	Yale
First downs	4	19
Rushing yards	62	169
Passing yards	46	202
Passes	2–13–3	13–22–0
Punting avg.	41	37
Fumbles lost	1	2
Penalty yards	1–5	30

Harvard		Yale
DiLuzio	LE	D. Hoopes
Pierce	LT	Barzilauskas
Dewey	LG	Schuler
Faber	C	Overlock
LeBart	RG	Elwell
Coan	RT	Hollingshead
Champion	RE	P. Walker (C.)
Tennant	QB	Dakos
Roche	LH	Penn
O'Donnell	RH	Kirk
Cowen (C.)	FB	Fitzgerald

Subs: Yale—Conway, Draper, Ritch,
Fusilli, Whiting, Thompson, Gehr,
Roderick, Furse, Lilley, M. Putnam,
Pivcevich, Florentine, Montano, Dwyer,
Warner, DeNezzo; Harvard—Kennedy,
Swegan, Mackintosh, W. Fisher, Mc-
Daniel, Foster, Malcolm, Grady, O'Leary,
Jenkins, Harwood, Fritts, Mielke, Miller

63rd game
Saturday, Nov. 23, 1946
Harvard Stadium, Boston
Weather: Cloudy, cold
Yale 27, Harvard 14

Yale (7–1–1) 0 13 14 0—27
Harvard (7–2) 14 0 0 0—14
H—Chip Gannon 2 run (Emil Drvaric
kick)
H—Wally Flynn 10 pass from Gannon
(Drvaric kick)
Y—Art Fitzgerald 17 pass from Levi Jack-
son (kick failed)
Y—Ferd Nadherny 9 run (Billy Booe
kick)
Y—Jack Roderick 37 pass from Tex Furse
(Booe kick)
Y—Nadherny 5 run (Booe kick)
A—57,000 (est.)

	Yale	Harv
First downs	14	9
Rushing yards	53–176	38–69
Passing yards	121	64
Passes	7–13–0	5–14–1
Punting	9–34	10–35
Fumbles–lost	2–0	4–0
Penalties–yards	6–40	1–15

Individual Leaders
Rushing: Yale, Nadherny 17–77, Jackson
19–68; Harvard, Gannon 13–71.
Passing: Yale, Furse 6–11–0–104; Harvard, Gannon 5–13–1–64.
Receiving: Yale, Roderick 2–54, Nadherny 2–37; Harvard, Fiorentino 2–29.

Yale		Harvard
Roderick	LE	Fiorentino
Schuler	LT	Dewey
Barzilauskas	LG	Rodis
Elwell	C	Fisher
Prchlik	RG	Drvaric
Hollingshead (C.)	RT	Davis
Lynch	RE	W. Flynn
Furse	QB	Goethals
Fitzgerald	LH	O'Donnell (C.)
Nadherny	RH	Gannon
Jackson	FB	Cowen

Subs: Yale—Setear, Hammer, Jenkins, Conway, Pivcevich, Whitridge, Davison, Kirk, Ernst, Frank, Florentine, Cipolaro, Jablonski, Whiting, Hansen, Larson, Scovil, J. Robertson, DeNezzo, Wagster, Gillis, Booe, Ferguson, Barksdale, Carey, Connelly; Harvard—Coulson, Felt, Kennedy, Fitz, Cummings, Garland, McDaniel, Houston, Allen, Markham, Pierce, Garvey, Feinberg, Smith, Drennan, Gutaitis, Fisher, Glynn, Grady, Petrillo, L. Flynn, Farrell, Jackson, P. O'Donnell, Lazzaro, Tennant, Moravec

64th game
Saturday, Nov. 22, 1947
Yale Bowl, New Haven
Weather: Freezing
Yale 31, Harvard 21
Harvard (4-5)   7   7   0   7—21
Yale (6-3)   7   7   7   10—31
Y—Tex Furse 2 run (Billy Booe kick)
H—Hal Moffie 35 pass from Jim Kenary (Emil Drvaric kick)
Y—Furse 2 run (Booe kick)
H—Paul Lazzaro 16 run (Drvaric kick)
Y—Levi Jackson 16 run (Booe kick)
Y—Furse 5 run (Booe kick)
Y—FG Booe 39
H—Moffie 5 run (Drvaric kick)
A—70,388

	Harv	Yale
First downs	15	22
Rushes—yards	31-133	59-243
Passing yards	158	183
Passes	9-22-2	11-18-2
Punts	4-39	3-27
Fumbles—lost	3-1	1-0
Penalties—yards	5-45	7-45

Individual Leaders
Rushing: Harvard, Lazzaro 13-54; Yale, Jackson 15-76, Nadherny 17-72
Passing: Harvard, Kenary 9-20-2-158; Yale, Furse 7-10-103-2.

Receiving: Harvard, Chip Gannon 4-61; Yale, John Setear 6-89.

Harvard		Yale
W. Flynn	LE	Setear
Houston	LT	Hanson
Drvaric	LG	V. Frank
Glynn	C	Conway
Feinberg (A.C.)	RG	Prchlik
Gorczynski	RT	Davison (C.)
Hill	RE	Jenkins
P. O'Donnell	QB	R. Furse
Moffie	LH	Fitzgerald
Gannon	RH	Nadherny
Freedman	FB	Jackson

Subs: Yale—Naffziger, Anderson, Kemp, Cirillo, Blanning, Kirk, Raines, Liechty, Keller, Adler, Dluzniewski, Kilroy, McQuade, DeVitt, Pivcevich, Fasano, Florentine, McAfee, Jablonski, Larson, Barksdale, Barnett, Booe, Connelly, Davis, Fuchs, Loh, Wagster, Tataronowicz; Harvard—Coulson, Kennedy, Felt, Mazzone, Fitz, Pierce, Markham, A. Stone, Drennan, Rodis, Middendorf, Guiders, Fiorentino, D. Stone, Kenary, Noonan, Niklas, L. Flynn, Brady, Roche, O'Connell, Shafer, Warren, Harrison, Lazzaro, Goodrich

65th game
Saturday, Nov. 20, 1948
Harvard Stadium, Boston
Weather: Overcast
Harvard 20, Yale 7
Yale (4-5)   0   7   0   0—7
Harvard (4-4)   6   0   0 14—20
H—Hal Moffie 80 run (kick failed)
Y—Tex Furse 1 run (Billy Booe kick)
H—Ken O'Donnell 2 run (Emil Drvaric kick)
H—Charley Roche 29 run (Drvaric kick)
A—57,495

	Yale	Harv
First downs	16	15
Rushes—yards	45-166	54-360
Passing yards	95	53
Passes	12-21-2	3-6-0
Punting	4-37	5-31
Fumbles—lost	1-1	2-1
Penalties—yards	4-40	3-35

Individual Leaders
Rushing: Yale, Ferd Nadherny, 18-81; Harvard, Moffie 11-149, Roche 13-130.
Passing: Yale, Furse 9-15-1-65; Harvard, Noon 2-3-0-44.
Receiving: Yale, John Setear, 5-55; Harvard, Fiorentino 1-30.

Yale		Harvard
Setear	LE	Hyde
Pivcevich	LT	Davis
Frank	LG	Houston
Conway, Capt.	C	O'Brien
Jablonski	RG	Coan
Emerson	RT	Bender
Quackenbush	RE	Fiorentino
Furse	QB	Henry
Tisdale	LH	Noonan
Peters	RH	Moffie
Larson	FB	Shafer

Subs: Yale—E. Kilroy, Anderson, Phillips, McAfee, Carr, Lovejoy, Clemens, McQuade, Booe, Keller, Barksdale, Fuchs, Lohnes, Fasano, Potter, Phillip, Albright, W. Kilroy, Robertson, Jackson, Nadherny, Raines, Wagster; Harvard—O'Donnell (Capt.), Hill, DiBlasio, Emmons, Coulson, Drvaric, Guiders, Powell, Bradlee, Coyne, Butler, Rosenau, Glynn, Hickey, D. Stone, O'Leary, Kanter, Rodis, A. Stone, Stensrud, Garvey, Dunker, Sedgwick, Mazzone, Bahn, Isenberg, Goodrich, Edmonds, Freedman, Roche, Kenary, Bolster, Athans, Warden, Gannon, Adams

66th game
Saturday, Nov. 19, 1949
Yale Bowl, New Haven
Weather: Cold
Yale 29, Harvard 6
Harvard (1–8)   0   0   0 6— 6
Yale (4–4)   7 16 0 6—29
Y—Levi Jackson 34 run (Palmer kick)
Y—Jackson 7 pass from Stu Tisdale (Palmer kick)
Y—safety, Ed Emerson blocked punt by Carroll Lowenstein
Y—Ferd Nadherny run (Palmer kick)
H—Jim Noonan 11 run (kick failed)
Y—Jim Fuchs 1 run (kick failed)
A—61,000 (est.)

	Harv	Yale
First downs	17	14
Rushes–yards	53–226	53–312
Passing yards	38	27
Passes	3–8–0	5–12–3
Punting	7–30	5–43
Fumbles–lost	3–1	1–0
Penalties–yards	4–20	3–23

Individual Leaders
Rushing: Harvard, Noonan 9–80; Yale, Bob Raines 9–99, Nadherny 19–81, Jackson 9–64.
Passing: Harvard, Noonan 2–6–2–17; Yale, Tisdale 3–7–0–27.
Receiving: Harvard, Henry 2–18; Yale, Jackson 1–9, Larry McQuade 1–9, Brad Quackenbush 1–9.

Harvard		Yale
Hyde	LE	Setear
Davis	LT	Finnegan
Houston (C.)	LG	Frank
O'Brien	C	Potter
Coan	RG	Fasano
Bender	RT	Anderson
Mazzone	RE	Gant
Henry	QB	Tisdale
Roche	LH	Raines
Moffie	RH	Jackson (C.)
West	FB	Nadherny

Subs: Yale—McAfee, LaBonte, McQuade, Emerson, Vorys, Phillipp, Masters, Jablonski, Clemens, Quackenbush, Robertson, Davis, Bowers, Naffziger, Barnett, Palmer, McDermott, Fuchs, DeCamp, Downey, R. Phillips, Gorman, Bishop, Carr, Lovejoy, Wooten, Peters, Senay, Hill, Test, Liechty, L. Phillips, Keller, Prince; Harvard—DiBlasio, Ray, Leavitt, Raverby, Bradlee, Guidera, Wilson, Sedgwick, Butler, Kanter, Connelly, Rosenau, Glynn, O'Leary, Isenberg, Edmonds, Noonan, Lowenstein, Warden, Bolster, Kenary, Lealey, Athans, Shafer, Bottenfield

67th game
Saturday, Nov. 25, 1950
Harvard Stadium, Boston
Weather: Hurricane
Yale 14, Harvard 6
Yale (6–3)   0 0 0 14—14
Harvard (1–7) 0 0 0 6— 6
Y—Ed Senay 3 run (John Bush kick)
H—Dave Warden 63 pass from Carroll Lowenstein (kick failed)
Y—Bob Spears 5 run (Bush kick)
A—38,000 (est.)

	Yale	Harv
First downs	15	9
Rushes–yards	66–348	41–75
Passing yards	1	127
Return yards	14	37
Passes	1–5–0	6–12–0
Punting	3–47	8–38
Fumbles–lost	5–4	7–2
Penalties–yards	8–50	4–30

Individual Leaders
Rushing: Yale, Senay 19–152, Spears 30–147; Harvard, Ossman 16–39.
Passing: Yale, Stu Tisdale 1–5–0–1; Harvard, Lowenstein 6–120–127.
Receiving: Yale, Spears 1–1, Harvard, Warden 2–68.

Yale		Harvard
Woodsum	LE	Hyde
Finnegan	LT	Toepke
Rowe	LG	Kanter
Brittingham	C	O'Brien
Downey	RG	Rosenau
Clemens	RT	Connelly
Quackenbush (C.)	RE	Ravreby
Tisdale	QB	O'Neil
Senay	LH	Lowenstein
Conway	RH	Warden
Spears	FB	West

Subs: Yale—Church, Gerstle, Borie, Kafoglis, Monroe, Marshall, Bright, Deen, Vorys, Phillips, Balme, Radulovic, Mitinger, Masters, May, Scott, J. Ryan, Peters, Parcells, E. Ryan, Martin, Polk, Bush, Lohnes, Prince, Rusnak; Harvard—Crowley, Emmons, Rate, Britton, Drill, Stargel, Culolias, Nichols, Heidtmann, Fallon, Lewis, Lemay, Isenberg (C.), Duback, Cox, Healey, Wylie, Blitz, Ossman

68th game
Saturday, Nov. 24, 1951
Yale Bowl, New Haven
Weather: Overcast
Yale 21, Harvard 21
Harvard (3–5–1) 0 7 7 7—21
Yale (2–5–2)   7 7 0 7—21
Y—Jim Ryan 47 run (Bob Parcells kick)
Y—Ryan 2 run (Parcells kick)
H—Paul Crowley 48 pass from Dick Clasby (Bill Monteith kick)
H—John Ederer 84 run (Monteith kick)
H—Fred Drill 18 interception (Monteith kick)
Y—Ray Bright 14 pass from Ed Molloy (Parcells kick)
A—43,000 (est.)

	Harv	Yale
First downs	11	17
Rushes—yards	46—140	54—259
Passing yards	133	135
Return yards	49	35
Passes	9—19—2	7—12—2
Punting	9—29	7—40
Fumbles—lost	2—0	3—2
Penalties—yards	2—10	8—80

Individual Leaders
Rushing: Harvard, Ederer 9—88; Yale,
Brock Martin 17—86, Gerry Conway 12—
68.
Passing: Harvard, Clasby 5—12—1—57,
Ederer 3—5—0—72; Yale, Molloy 5—9—
1—85, Ryan 2—3—1—50.
Receiving: Harvard, Crowley 3—76; Yale,
Ed Woodsum 2—50.

Harvard		Yale
Crowley	LE	Woodsum
Nichols	LT	Balme
Pappas	LG	Rowe
Lemay	C	Brittingham
Manos	RG	Polich
Thompson	RT	Radulovic
Rate	RE	Smith
O'Neil	QB	J. Ryan
Clasby	LH	Conway
Healy	RH	Shears
Ossman	FB	Spears (C.)

Subs: Yale—Ashton, Stefanelli, E. Ryan,
Senay, Vorys, Baldwin, Coudert, Rien-
hoff, Thompson, Merriman, Mitinger,
Marshall, Benninghoff, Caracciolo, Mol-
loy, Martin, Jones, Parcells, Bright, Polk,
Lemire, Ralston, Haase, Fortunato; Har-
vard—Drill, Dolan, Ravreby, Popell,
Burke, Toepke, Stargel, Horween, Caimi,
Batchelder, Jennings, Shaw, Yazejian,
Coolidge, Frothingham, Lewis, Weber,
Montieth, Cox, Hardy, Burke, Reynolds,
French, Duback, Ederer.
Capt. Wylie did not play (injured).

69th game
Saturday, Nov. 22, 1952
Harvard Stadium, Boston
Weather: Drizzle
Yale 41, Harvard 14
Yale (7—2)   7   20   14   0—41
Harvard (5—4) 0   7   0   7—14
Y—Jerry Jones 38 run (Bob Parcells kick)
Y—Ed Woodsum 4 pass from Ed Molloy
(Parcells kick)
Y—Pete Shears 3 run (kick failed)
H—Dick Clasby 10 run (Bill Monteith
kick)
Y—Hub Pruett 13 pass from Molloy (Par-
cells kick)
Y—Woodsum 26 pass from Molloy (Par-
cells kick)
Y—Woodsum 58 pass from Molloy (Char-
ley Yeager pass from Molloy)
H—John Culver 1 run (Monteith kick)
A—38,114

	Yale	Harv
First downs	8	18
Rushes—yards	33—155	59—80
Passing yards	205	219
Return yards	14	34
Passes	8—16—0	18—29—1
Punting	4—41	5—19
Fumbles—lost	0—0	1—0
Penalties—yards	4—28	5—35

Individual Leaders
Rushing: Yale, Jones 10—77; Harvard,
Clasby 25—47.
Passing: Yale, Molloy 8—12—0—205;
Harvard, Clasby 9—16—1—72; Howard
Cox 8—10—0—142.
Receiving: Yale, Woodsum 3—88; Shears
3—44; Harvard, Crowley 6—121; Ederer
4—65.

Yale		Harvard
Woodsum	LE	Crowley
Balme	LT	Nichols (C.)
Polich	LG	Pappas
Brittingham	C	Lomay
Coudert	RG	Manos
Radulovic	RT	Stargel
F. Smith	RE	Rate
Molloy	QB	O'Neil
Shears	LH	Clasby
Pruett	RH	Ederer
Jones	FB	Culver

Subs: Yale—Caracciolo, Gallaway, Deen,
Prentiss, Golden, Shugart, Hopewell,
Baldwin, Mitinger (Capt.), Ashton, Ben-
ninghoff, Hansen, Mathias, Armstrong,
Parcells, Fortunato, Conway, Poole, Mar-
tin, Ralston, Stout, Downey, Koplow,
Stefanelli, Doughan, Corelli, Shea, Holt,
Coker, Gambill, Wengert, Busch, Phillips,
Mallory, Yeager, Brink, Beni, Lemire,
Buss, Hawkins; Harvard—B. Weber, Pop-
ell, Toepke, Batchelder, Templeton,
Caimi, Messer, Coolidge, Jennings,
O'Brien, Culollas, Horwee, Cochran, Du-
beck, Montieth, Marsh, Cowles, Cox,
Murphy, Blitz, Campbell, French, Zuege

70th game
Saturday, Nov. 21, 1953
Yale Bowl, New Haven
Weather: Fog clearing
Harvard 13, Yale 0
Harvard (6—2) 0   6   7   0—13
Yale (5—2—2)   0   0   0   0— 0
H—Dexter Lewis 22 run (kick failed)
H—John Culver 35 run (Ross kick)
A—65,000 (est.)

	Harv	Yale
First downs	15	10
Rushes—yards	43—146	38—69
Passing yards	110	80
Return yards	104	40
Passes	7—18—1	6—18—2
Punting	5—47	8—38
Fumbles—lost	3—1	3—1
Penalties—yards	8—70	3—15

Individual Leaders
Rushing: Harvard, Culver 17–91; Yale, Connie Corelli 18–59.
Passing: Harvard, Dick Clasby 4–9–1–64; Yale, Bob Brink 4–11–1–54.
Receiving: Harvard, Bob Cowles 3–57; Yale, Bob Poole 3–48.

Harvard		Yale
Weber	LE	Prentiss
O'Brien	LT	Stout
Meigs	LG	Polich
Coolidge	C	Doughan
Anderson	RG	Shugart
Culollas	RT	Ashton
Ross	RE	Benninghoff
Marsh	QB	Brink
Clasby (C.)	LH	Shears
Cowles	RH	Pruett
Culver	FB	Corelli

Subs: Yale—F. Smith, Campbell, M. Armstrong, Tarasovic, Hawkins, Coker, Phillips, Gallaway, Lemire, Reno, Lopez, Molloy, J. Armstrong, Poole, Fortunato (Capt.), Jones, Hansen, Shulman, Hopewell, Johnson, Morgan, Killam; Harvard—Morrison, Yoffe, Cochran, Tice, Anthony, Meyer, Culbert, Rosenthal, Koch, Maher, Popell, Clark, Lowenstein, Reynolds, White, Lewis, Messer, MacDonald

71st game
Saturday, Nov. 20, 1954
Harvard Stadium, Boston
Weather: Sunny
Harvard 13, Yale 9
Yale (5–3–1)   2   0   7   0— 9
Harvard (4–3–1)0   0   0 13—13
Y—safety, Matt Botsford stepped into end zone with interception
Y—Byron Campbell 7 pass from Bob Brink (Phil Matthias kick)
H—Tony Gianelly 1 run (Joe Ross kick)
H—Bob Cochran 39 pass from Frank White (kick failed)
A—40,000 (est.)

	Yale	Harv
First downs	18	16
Rushes—yards	52–168	45–200
Passing yards	169	85
Return yards	11	24
Passes	8–13–2	4–12–0
Punting	4–26	6–30
Fumbles—lost	5–3	2–2
Penalties—yards	2–10	0–0

Individual Leaders
Rushing: Yale, Denny McGill 14–99, Mathias 11–47; Harvard, Jim Joslin 12–79, White 5–56.
Passing: Yale, Dean Loucks 4–5–0–77; Harvard, White 1–1–0–39.
Receiving: Yale, Campbell 2–60, Al Ward 3–49; Harvard, Cochran 3–64.

Yale		Harvard
Campbell	LE	Cochran
Lovejoy	LT	Tice
Phillips	LG	Meigs
Doughan	C	Painter
Shugart (C.)	RG	Anderson (C.)
Gallaway	RT	Maher
Hansen	RE	Ross
Brink	QB	Marsh
Lopez	LH	Botsford
McGill	RH	Cowles
Mathias	FB	Gianelly

Subs: Yale—Tarasovic, Henderson, D. Loucks, Guzeman, Sterns, Coker, Fritzsche, Mobley, Jones, Schainman, Ward, Griffith; Harvard—Eastabrooks, Yoffe, Frate, Anthony, Weber, Bodiker, Metropolous, Koch, Clark, Morrison, Kennedy, Daley, Haughey, Joslin, White, Simourian, Oehmler, MacDonald

72nd game
Saturday, Nov. 19, 1955
Yale Bowl, New Haven
Weather: Snow
Yale 21, Harvard 7
Harvard (3–4–1)0   0   7   0— 7
Yale (7–2)   0   7   7   7—21

Y—Vern Loucks 7 pass from Dean Loucks (V. Loucks kick)
Y—Al Ward 1 run (V. Loucks kick)
H—Ted Kennedy 7 pass from Walt Stahura (Bing Crosby kick)
Y—Denny McGill 39 interception (V. Loucks kick)
A—56,000 (est.)

	Harv	Yale
First downs	10	14
Rushes—yards	33–78	50–225
Passing yards	98	7
Return yards	12	58
Passes	9–18–2	1–3–0
Punting	4–46	4–32
Fumbles—lost	2–1	3–1
Penalties—yards	2–15	5–35

Individual Leaders
Rushing: Harvard, Stahura 10–49; Yale, Gene Coker 21–105, Ward 16–72, McGill 8–54.
Passing: Harvard, Stahura 7–13–2–79; Yale, D. Loucks 1–3–0–7.
Receiving: Harvard, Joe Crehore 3–39; Yale, V. Loucks 1–7.

Harvard		Yale
Morrison	LE	Lopata
Tice	LT	Tarasovic (C.)
Meigs, Capt.	LG	Embersits
Meyer	C	Owseichik
Metropoulos	RG	Lunsford
Maher	RT	Lovejoy
Kennedy	RE	Cavallon
Daley	QB	D. Loucks
Botsford	LH	Ward
Lewis	RH	McGill
Gianelly	FB	Coker

Subs: Yale—Loud, Ryland, Frembgen, Smith, Meeth, Moneymaker, Williams, Henkel, Mark, Triplett, Baird, Thomas, Bales, Burt, Wight, Phelan, Mobley, Grimes, V. Loucks, Peet, Morgan, Griffith, Wisz, Lorch, Sigal; Harvard—Copeland,

Markos, Jones, Eaton, Holzschuch, Rosenthal, Quartarone, Schein, Gill, Hooper, Crehore, Joslin, Stahura, Simourian, Crosby, Oehlmer, Hallett

73rd game
Saturday, Nov. 24, 1956
Harvard Stadium, Boston
Weather: Sunny, cold
Yale 42, Harvard 14
Yale (8−1)　7　21　0　14—42
Harvard (2−6)　0　7　7　0—14
Y—Denny McGill 2 run (Vern Loucks kick)
Y—McGill 78 run (V. Loucks kick)
H—Jim Joslin 39 run (Joslin kick)
Y—Al Ward 77 kickoff return (V. Loucks kick)
Y—Steve Ackerman 13 pass from Dean Loucks (V. Loucks kick)
H—John Simourian 1 run (Joslin kick)
Y—Paul Lopata 8 pass from Dick Winterbauer (V. Loucks kick)
Y—Herb Hallas 2 run (Mike Cavallon pass from Pudge Henkel)
A—38,240

	Yale	Harv
First downs	17	15
Rushes−yards	39−243	45−150
Passing yards	140	81
Return yards	55	5
Passes	9−17−1	7−22−1
Punting	3−23	5−41
Fumbles−lost	5−3	4−3
Penalties−yards	7−65	3−25

Individual Leaders
Rushing: Yale, McGill 8−116, Ackerman 8−59; Harvard, Joslin 3−48.
Passing: Yale, Winterbauer 5−7−0−86, D. Loucks 4−10−1−54; Harvard, Simourian 6−16−0−74.
Receiving: Yale, Hallas 1−38; Harvard, Damis 4−30.

Yale		**Harvard**
Lopata	LE	Haughey
Thomas	LT	Shaunessy
Owseichik (C.)	LG	Metropoulos (C.)
Kroll	C	Lebovitz
Embersits	RG	Harris
C. Griffith	RT	Briggs
V. Loucks	RE	Hooper
D. Loucks	QB	Simourian
Ward	LH	Botsford
McGill	RH	Joslin
Ackerman	FB	Gianelly

Subs: Yale—West, Burt, Frembgen, Lynch, Pendexter, Henkel, MacLean, Cavallon, Baird, Moneymaker, Williams, Simon, Phelan, Wight, Ryland, Lubke, Jones, Mobley, Bales, Loud, Skewes, Conners, Winterbauer, Peet, D. Griffith, Hallas, Hemphill, Horwitz, Wisz, Kinney, Corry, Lorch; Harvard—Erjy, Soucek, Holzschuch, Foker, Nelson, Hill, Newell, Altamonte, Anderson, Keating, Schein, Avery, Hershon, Cathcart, McLaughlin, Stahura, Dodge, Damis, Levin, Eikenberry, Gerety, Bell, Dinatale

74th game
Saturday, Nov. 23, 1957
Yale Bowl, New Haven
Weather: Cloudy
Yale 54, Harvard 0
Harvard (3−5)　0　0　0　0— 0
Yale (6−2−1)　13　21　14　6—54
Y—Herb Hallas 4 run (Art LaVallie kick)
Y—Mike Cavallon 27 pass from Dick Winterbauer (kick failed)
Y—Hallas 3 run (LaVallie kick)
Y—Cavallon 9 pass from Winterbauer (Winterbauer kick)
Y—Mike Curran 41 run (Pudge Henkel kick)
Y—Hallas 58 pass from Winterbauer (Don Wall kick)
Y—Matt Freeman 6 pass from LaVallie (LaVallie kick)

Y—Henkel 3 run (kick failed)
A—55,817

	Harv	Yale
First downs	9	22
Rushes−yards	42−108	45−254
Passing yards	43	240
Return yards	0	26
Passes	6−15−1	14−21−0
Punting	3−27	1−27
Fumbles−lost	2−1	2−1
Penalties−yards	3−35	4−40

Individual Leaders
Rushing: Harvard, Chris Hauge 12−51; Yale, Hallas 7−48.
Passing: Harvard, Ted Marmor 4−9−0−27; Yale, Winterbauer 9−12−0−164.
Receiving: Harvard, Sam Halaby 1−13; Yale, Cavallon 6−88, Hallas 2−64.

Harvard		**Yale**
Copeland	LE	Cavallon
Shaunessy	LT	West
Walker	LG	Lynch
Foster	C	Baird
Anderson	RG	Embersits (C.)
Briggs	RT	Olivar
Hooper (C.)	RE	Pendexter
Johanson	QB	Winterbauer
Boulris	LH	Hallas
Gerety	RH	Winkler
Hauge	FB	Coker

Subs: Yale—Puryear, Connors, Walters, Whipple, Mallano, Kohr, Simon, Ghent, Nowak, Wakefield, Wellemeyer, Lubke, Lamy, Wall, Blair, Skewes, Ernst, Schoettle, Klemm, Sigal, Kinney, Wisz, Horwitz, Wyatt, Grean, Forstman, Phelan, Wight, Davenport, Williams, Riddle, Freeman, Henkel, LaVallie, Curran, Hemphill, Kangas, Lorch; Harvard—Keohane, Soucek, Foker, Weidler, Robbins, Hill, Franke, Francis, Eliades, Schein, Huff, Hershon, Marmor, McLaughlin, Cullen, Leamy, Cappiello, Stahura, Levin, Halaby

75th game
Saturday, Nov. 22, 1958
Harvard Stadium, Boston
Weather: Sunny, windy
Harvard 28, Yale 0
Yale (2−7)   0   0   0   0— 0
Harvard (4−5)   0   6   8   14—28
H—Charlie Ravenel 7 run (run failed)
H—Chet Boulris 20 run (Warren Huff pass from Boulris)
H—Larry Repsher 17 run (run failed)
H—Albie Cullen 2 run (Cullen pass from Dick McLaughlin)
A—40,209

	Yale	Harv
First downs	7	19
Rushes−yards	46−12	57−284
Passing yards	23	36
Return yards	34	46
Passes	2−7−2	4−12−0
Punting	7−20	3−26
Fumbles−lost	6−2₁	5−3
Penalties−yards	1−5	7−75

Individual Leaders
Rushing: Yale, Rick Winkler 15−36; Harvard, Ravenel 16−105, Boulris 12−72.
Passing: Yale, Mike Curran, 1−1−0−17; Harvard, Ravenel 3−10−0−29.
Receiving: Yale, Nick Kangas 1−17; Harvard, Repsher 1−18.
NOTE: Conversion by rush or pass increased to 2 points.

Yale		Harvard
Freeman	LE	Keohane
Puryear	LT	Shaunessy (C.)
Balme	LG	Keating
Pyle	C	Foster
Lynch, Capt.	RG	Anderson
Olivar	RT	Briggs
Ernst	RE	Hershon
Singleton	QB	Ravenel
Winkler	LH	Boulris
Hallas	RH	Repsher
Muller	FB	Halaby

Subs: Yale—Riddle, Rogers, King, Kickham, Mallano, Davenport, Ghent, Gaede, West, Wall, Porvaznik, Williams, Ross, Simon, Murach, Hutcherson, Lundstedt, Kugler, Mallory, Welch, Curran, Blanchard, Creamer, Kangas, Wolfe, Sigal, Hard, Kahn; Harvard—Cappiello, Messenbaugh, Pillsbury, Greelish, Lenzner, Eliades, Christensen, Papalia, Wilson, Weidler, Nelson, Foker, Huff, Sullivan, Kirk, Deane, Johanson, McLaughlin, Gerety, MacIntyre, Cullen, Lawson, Haughie, Hauge, Newell

76th game
Saturday, Nov. 22, 1959
Yale Bowl, New Haven
Weather: Overcast
Harvard 35, Yale 6
Harvard (6−3)   8   0   7   20—35
Yale (6−3)   0   6   0   0— 6
H—Hank Keohane, 85 pass from Chet Boulris (Dave Cappiello pass from Charlie Ravenel)
Y—Ken Wolfe 60 pass from Tom Singleton (run failed)
H—Ravenel 1 run (Sam Halaby kick)
H—Boulris 13 run (Ravenel run)
H—Ravenel 7 run (run failed)
H—Albie Cullen 31 run (run failed)
A—66,053

	Harv	Yale
First downs	22	16
Rushes−yards	50−251	43−102
Passing yards	135	161
Return yards	29	37
Passes	6−19−0	6−14−1
Punting	5−40	5−42
Fumbles−lost	0−0	6−4
Penalties−yards	7−60	5−73

Individual Leaders
Rushing: Harvard, Boulris 18−95, Cullen 6−60; Yale, Nick Kangas 7−36, Rick Winkler 8−36.

Passing: Harvard, Boulris 2−7−0−95, Ravenel 4−12−0−40; Yale, Singleton 3−9−1−111.
Receiving: Harvard, Keohane 1−85; Yale, Wolfe 1−60.

Harvard—LE, *Keohane,** Boyda, Kirk; LT, Wile, Greelish, Nichols; LG, Lenzner, Swinford, Jacobs; C, Christensen, Watters, Cohen; RG, Waterman, Weidler, Wilson; RT, E. Nelson, Sheridan, Aadalen, Wynne; RE, Cappiello, Messenbaugh, Hart; QB, Ravenel, Watts; LH, Boulris, MacIntyre, Shipman; RH, Cullen, Repsher, Williams, Leamy; FB, S. Halaby, Haughie, Reed, J. Nelson.

Yale—LE, Freeman, Riddle, Hutcherson; LT, Olivar, Kickham, McCormick; LG, Davenport, Chimenti, Wakefield; C, Pyle, Will, Black; RG, Bursiek, Cochran, Brewster; RT, King, Ross, Stenzel; RE, Ernst, Pappas, Stocking; QB, Singleton, Mallory, Leckonby, Feldhaus; LH, Muller, Curran, Creamer; RH, Kangas, Wolfe, Snimer; FB, *Winkler*, Blanchard, Kenney.
*From 1959 through 1983 names of captains are given in italics.

77th game
Saturday, Nov. 19, 1960
Harvard Stadium, Boston
Weather: Fair
Yale 39, Harvard 6
Yale (9−0)   6   11   14   8—39
Harvard (5−4)   0   0   0   6— 6
Y—Ken Wolfe 41 run (run failed)
Y—John Hutcherson 42 interception (Ted Hard run)
Y—FG Ed Kaake 33 Y—Bob Blanchard 1 run (run failed)
Y—Connie Shimer 15 pass from Bill Leckonby (Hank Higdon pass from Leckonby)
Y—Shimer 3 pass from Leckonby (Lee Mallory pass from Leckonby)
H—Charlie Ravenel 2 run (pass failed)
A—40,000 (est.)

	Yale	Harv
First downs	15	9
Rushes—yards	42−188	37−7
Passing yards	108	132
Return yards	111	17
Passes	9−15−1	9−20−4
Punting	3−38	6−33
Fumbles—lost	8−4	4−3
Penalties—yards	7−60	1−15

Individual Leaders
Rushing: Yale, Wolfe 8−71, Blanchard 15−45; Harvard, Larry Repsher 7−26.
Passing: Yale, Tom Singleton 6−10−1−80; Harvard, Ravenel 5−8−2−96.
Receiving: Yale, Wolfe 3−48; Harvard, Pete Hart 1−58.

Yale—LE, Hutcherson, Carpenter, D. Jacunski, Ryan, Robertson, Hallas; LT, *Pyle*, Kickham, McCormick, Iezzi; LG, Balme, Brewster, Riveles, Dietrich; C, Will, Black, Thompson, R. Clark; RG, Kay, Bursiek, Truebner, Kiernan; RT, King, Cochran, Jensen, Mawicke, Keller; RE, Pappas, Lundstedt, Stocking, B. Jacunski, Andreae, Jones; QB, Singleton, Kaake, Leckonby, O'Connell, Grant; LH, Muller, Higdon, Mallory, C. Clark, Landa, Marsh; RH, Wolfe, Shimer, Creamer, Calkins, Duncan; FB, Blanchard, Hard, Zimmerman, Kenney, Gengarelly.

Harvard—LE, Boyda, Jordan; LT, Pillsbury, Wile, Greelish; LG, Swinford, Jacobs, Diehl; C, Christensen, Watters, Nyhan, Cohen, McLaughlin; RG, Gaston, Semeraro, *Lenzner*; RT, E. Nelson, Aadalen, Sheridan; RE, Messenbaugh, Hart, Hudepohl; QB, Halaby, Bartolet, Ravenel; LH, Armstrong, MacIntyre, Hunter, Williams; RH, Repsher, Boone, Hatch, Taylor; FB, J. Nelson, Haughie, Reed, Ward.

78th game
Saturday, Nov. 25, 1961
Yale Bowl, New Haven
Weather: Sunny
Harvard 27, Yale 0
Harvard (6−3)   14   0   7   6—27
Yale (4−5)   0   0   0   0— 0
H—Scott Harshbarger 2 run (Dave Ward kick)
H—Bill Grana 16 run (Ward kick)
H—Bill Taylor 9 pass from Mike Bassett (Ward kick)
H—Dave Nyhan recovered bad snap in end zone (run failed)
A—61,789

	Harv	Yale
First downs	13	11
Rushes—yards	59−192	40−91
Passing yards	28	76
Return yards	43	36
Passes	4−9−1	5−19−3
Punting	5−37	3−37
Fumbles—lost	3−2	7−5
Penalties—yards	2−19	8−54

Individual Leaders
Rushing: Harvard, Grana 16−62, Bill Taylor 14−43; Yale, Ted Hard 6−36.
Passing: Harvard, Bassett 2−3−0−19; Yale, Bill Leckonby 2−8−0−31.
Receiving: Harvard, Taylor 2−19; Yale, Randy Egloff 1−19.

Harvard—LE, Boyda, Juvonen, Stephenson, Young; LT, Wile, Sheridan, Neuenschwander; LG, Swinford, Zissis, Hagebak; C, Watters, Nyhan, Lozeau, Stephens, Minotti; RG, Gaston, Southmayd, Jacobs; RT, Smith, Diehl, Pochop; RE, *Hart*, Hudepohl, Gray; Q, Bassett, Halaby, Beizer, Adams, Humenuk; LH, Boone, Harshbarger, Leath, Connor; RH, Taylor, Hatch, Fiscina; FB, Grana, Bartl, Stringer, Ward.

Yale—LE, R. Carpenter, Sherman, Grant; LT, Mawicke, McCormick, Cochran; LG, Bursiek, Dietrich, Iverson; C, Black, Thompson; RG, Riveles, Kay; RT, Wickstrom, Jensen; RE, Shimer, Jones, Hallas, Hubbard; Q, Leckonby, Rapp, O'Connell, Cirie, Lavely; LH, Higdon, Marsh, Calkins, Thomas; RH, Egloff, Berk, C. Clark; FB, Hard, Niglio, Caviness.

79th game
Saturday, Nov. 24, 1962
Harvard Stadium, Boston
Weather: Blustery
Harvard 14, Yale 6
Yale (2−5−2)   0   0   6   0— 6
Harvard (6−3)   0   7   0   7—14
H—Bill Taylor 4 run (John Hartranft kick)
Y—Jack Cirie 59 punt return (run failed)
H—Fred Bartl 2 run (Hartranft kick)
A—39,000 (est.)

	Yale	Harv
First downs	9	16
Rushes—yards	37−85	60−234
Passing yards	42	23
Return yards	77	30
Passes	4−10−0	2−6−0
Punting	6−29	7−34
Fumbles—lost	3−1	2−1
Penalties—yards	3−31	8−70

Individual Leaders
Rushing: Yale, Jud Calkins 7−23; Harvard, Taylor 15−98, Hobie Armstrong 16−55.
Passing: Yale, Brian Rapp 4−8−0−42; Harvard, Bassett 2−6−0−23.
Receiving: Yale, DeWitt Jones 2−20; Harvard, Taylor 1−16.

Yale—LE: Duncan, Robertson, Carter, Hallas; LT: Wickstrom, Lawrence, A.; LG: Dietrich, Benoit, Riveles, Truebner, Jensen; C: Humphrey, Merrill; RG: Kay, Vanderslott; RT: Mawicke, Shaftel; RE:

Jones, Donnelley, Kenney, Lawrence, S., Hubbard; QB: McCarthy, O'Connell, Henderson, Rapp; LHB: *Higdon*, Thomas, Calkins; RHB: Berk, Cirie, Mercein, Marsh, Gengarelly, Landa; FB: Caviness, Cummings.

Harvard—LE: Young, Ulcickas, Stephenson; LT: Smith, Curtin, Jurek; LG: Zissis, Dobrzelecki, Skowronski; C: Stephens, Minotti, Beery; RG: Southmayd, Vinton, Kessler; RT: *Diehl*, Pochop; RE: Hudepohl, Gray, Hartranft; QB: Bassett, Mechling, Beizer; LHB: Armstrong, Bilodeau, Stringer; RHB: Taylor, Harshbarger, Hatch; FB: Grana, Bartl, Hunter.

80th game
Saturday, Nov. 30, 1963
Yale Bowl, New Haven
Weather: Cloudy, windy
Yale 20, Harvard 6
Harvard (5–2–2) 6   0   0   0— 6
Yale (6–3)   0   7   6   7—20
H—Scott Harshbarger 38 pass from Mike Bassett (kick failed)
Y—Jim Groninger 5 run (Chuck Mercein kick)
Y—Randy Egloff 5 run (kick failed)
Y—Egloff 2 run (Mercein kick)
A—51,000 (est.)

	Harv	Yale
First downs	12	17
Rushes–yards	34–114	61–237
Passing yards	177	48
Return yards	6	47
Passes	14–24–2	3–9–0
Punting	6–34	5–23
Fumbles–lost	0–0	2–2
Penalties–yards	5–38	2–30

Individual Leaders
Rushing: Harvard, Bill Grana 7–55; Yale, Mercein 14–63, Jim Howard 13–58, Egloff 16–56.

Passing: Harvard, Bassett 11–19–1–160; Yale, Brian Rapp 2–7–0–26.
Receiving: Harvard, Harshbarger 8–122, Mercein 2–32.

Harvard—LE: Stephenson, Boyda, Gray, Van Oudenallen; LT: Jurek, Pochop, Neuenschwander; LG: Dobrzelecki, Barrett, Hoffman; C: Stephens, Minotti, O'Brien; RG: *Southmayd*, Kessler, Reischel; RT: Curtin, Foley; RE: Ulcickas, Barringer, Hudak, Hartranft; QB: Bassett, Humenuk, Mechling; LH: Harshbarger, Bilodeau, Grant, Beizer; RH: Poe, Dockery; FB: Grana, Yastrzemski.

Yale—LE: S. Lawrence, McCaskey, O'Grady, Burton, Wick; LT: Wickstrom, Lonergan; LG: Benoit, Sullivan, Pollack; C: *G. Humphrey*, Merrill; RG: Vandersloot, Weiss; RT: A. Lawrence, Strong, Shaftel; RE: Hubbard, Donnelley, Carter; QB: Rapp, Cirie; LH: Howard, Henderson, S. Thomas; RH: Egloff, Groninger, Knapp; FB: Mercein, Caviness, Cummings.

81st game
Saturday, Nov. 21, 1964
Harvard Stadium, Boston
Weather: Sunny, cold
Harvard 18, Yale 14
Yale (6–2–1)   0 14 0 0—14
Harvard (6–3) 0 12 0 6—18
H—Wally Grant 5 run (kick failed)
Y—Dick Niglio 2 run (Bill Vance kick)
H—John McCluskey 7 run (run failed)
Y—Ed McCarthy 7 run (Vance kick)
H—Bobby Leo 46 run (run failed)
A—39,909

	Yale	Harv
First downs	9	15
Rushes–yards	37–133	54–255
Passing yards	83	72
Return yards	5	22
Passes	6–19–1	4–6–1
Punting	6–37	3–23
Fumbles–lost	1–1	2–1
Penalties–yards	3–35	2–10

Individual Leaders
Rushing: Yale, Niglio 8–36; Harvard, Stan Yastrzemski 17–85, Leo 10–81, Grant 20–56.
Passing: Yale, McCarthy 6–19–1–83; Harvard, McCluskey 3–5–1–46.
Receiving: Yale, Bill Henderson 1–26; Harvard, Grant 1–26.

Yale—LE: Kenney, O'Grady; LT: Strong, Lonergan, Shaftel, Brundage; LG: Benoit, Munson; C: Merrill, Laidly, Dohrmann; RG: Fargo, Vendersloot; RT: *Ab Lawrence*, Greenlee, Vance; RE: Carter, Steve Lawrence, Wick; QB: McCarthy, Grant; LH: Howard, Carey, Weigel, Henderson; RH: Niglio, Groinger, Beutler, Knapp; FB: Cummings, Foster.

Harvard—LE: Ulcickas, Hall, Calderwood; LT: Diamond, Jurek, Davis; LG: Berdik, Barrett; C: *O'Brien*, Driscoll, Lozeau; RG: Reischel, Noback, Skowronski; RT: Hoffman, Patterson, Peterson; RE: Barringer, Hughes, Boyda; QB: McCluskey, Bilodeau, Guzzi, Mechling; LH: Grant, Van Oudenallen; RH: Leo, Poe; FB: Yastrzemski, Dullea, Conway.

82nd game
Saturday, Nov. 20, 1965
Yale Bowl, New Haven
Weather: Overcast
Harvard 13, Yale 0
Harvard (5–2–2) 0   0   7   6—13
Yale (3–6)   0   0   0   0— 0
H—Bobby Leo 4 run (Maury Dullea kick)
H—Tom Choquette 1 run (kick blocked)
A—50,817

	Harv	Yale
First downs	13	8
Rushes—yards	57—156	35—59
Passing yards	71	97
Return yards	31	29
Passes	6—13—2	9—24—2
Punting	8—35	7—36
Fumbles—lost	1—0	2—2
Penalties—yards	1—5	0—0

Individual Leaders
Rushing: Harvard, Leo 14—61, Wally Grant 16—46; Yale, Don Barrows 9—35.
Passing: Harvard, John McCluskey 4—9—1—26; Watts Humphrey 8—20—2—90.
Receiving: Harvard, Leo 3—27, Dullea 1—34; Yale, Bob Kenney 3—40, Jim Groninger 3—23.

Harvard—E: Lord, Calderwood, *Boyda*, Hughes, Dullea, Cook, Welz, Petzey, Hoffman, Holland; T: Peterson, Diamond, Davis, Sviokla, Brooks, Burns, Patterson, deBettencourt; G: Noback, O'Donnell, Berdik, Evans; C: Zukerman, Gunn, St. Onge, Bindas; QB: McCluskey, Shevlin, Zimmerman, Berg; Off. B: Leo, W. Grant, Choquette, Sadoski, Robinson, Macdonald, Manchester, Goldberg, Kilkuskie, Hicks; Def. B: Poe, Dockery, Cobb, Baker, Norton, Williamson, Donnelly, Weber, Beasley; KSP: Van Oudenallen, Babcock, Krinsky.

Yale—E: Kenney, G. Jones, Watson, Saxon, Skubas, Thompson, Young, Grew, Somerville, Burr, Burton; T: Lonergan, Prewitt, Greenlee, Greenberg, Koerlin, Raymond, McLaughlin, Houston, Karas; G: Munson, G. Weiss, *Laidley*, Kiernan, Fargo, McCarthy, France, Livingston, DeVries; C: Lease, Emmons, Day, Hardesty; LB: Hildendorf, Kolar, Foster, Schmidt; QB: Humphrey, Doherty, Galen; Def. B: Brundige, Howard, P. Jones, Beutler, Begel, Vorpe, T. Grant, Mallory,

Fates, O'Keefe, Soper; Off. B: Shevelson, Groninger, Barrows, Weigel, Kovacs, Fisher, Kule, Bartlett; KSP: Carey, Spires.

83rd game
Saturday, Nov. 19, 1966
Harvard Stadium, Boston
Weather: Hurricane
Harvard 17, Yale 0
Yale (4—5)   0   0   0   0— 0
Harvard (8—1) 0   10   0   7—17
H—FG Jim Babcock 29.
H—Bobby Leo 1 run (Babcock kick)
H—Leo 52 run (Babcock kick)
A—41,000 (est.)

	Yale	Harv
First downs	5	14
Rushes—yards	28—82	59—218
Passing yards	33	26
Return yards	0	37
Passes	5—19—2	3—11—0
Punting	8—34	8—34
Fumbles—lost	5—2	6—2
Penalties—yards	0—0	3—25

Individual Leaders
Rushing: Yale, Jim Fisher 11—40; Harvard, Leo 16—106, Tom Choquette 15—56.
Passing: Yale, Pete Doherty 5—19—2—33; Harvard, Ric Zimmerman 3—9—0—26.
Receiving: Yale Court Shevelson 2—19; Harvard, Joe Cook 2—17.

Yale—ENDS—Kenney, Weinstein, Saxon, Watson, Somerville, Madden, Gallagher; TACKLES—Gee, Stroube, *Greenlee*, Greenberg, Bass, Heckler; GUARDS—France, McCarthy, Schmidt, McLaughlin, Gallico, Kleber, Williams; CENTERS—Emmons, Morris, Pace; QB—Doherty; HB—Kule, Fisher, Weigel, MacQueen, Shevelson; FB—Barrows; LB—Hilgendorf, Foster, Levin, Woolery, Day, Bouscaren; SAFETIES—Fates, Begel, Franklin.

Harvard—OFFENSE: ENDS—Cook, Lord, Dullea, Goodwin, Mortenson; TACKLES—Brooks, Diamond, Burns, Wilson; GUARDS—Flanagan, Bersin, Peterson, Jones, Brown, Georges; CENTERS—O'Donnell, Weiss, Skowronski, Collins; QB—Zimmerman, Shevlin; HB—Leo, Gatto, Goldberg, Stargel, Robinson; FB—Choquette, Strandemo, McKinney; KSP—Gahan, Babcock, Krinsky. DEFENSE: ENDS—*Justin Hughes*, Hoffman, Timpson; TACKLES—Davis, deBettencourt, Sviokla, Gloyd; GUARDS—Greenidge; LB—Cobb, Chiofaro, Donelan, Baker, Norton, Machin, Emery, Ananis, Donnelly, Marino; SAFETIES—Williamson, Tyson, Sadoski, Wynne.

84th game
Saturday, Nov. 25, 1967
Yale Bowl, New Haven
Weather: Clearing
Yale 24, Harvard 20
Harvard (6—3) 0   7   6   7—20
Yale (8—1)   0   17   0   7—24
Y—Del Marting 1 run with recovered fumble (Dan Begel kick)
Y—Calvin Hill 53 pass from Brian Dowling (Begel kick)
Y—FG Begel 36
H—Ray Hornblower 14 pass from Ric Zimmerman (Tom Wynne kick)
H—Vic Gatto 3 run (pass failed)
H—Carter Lord 31 pass from Zimmerman (Wynne kick)
Y—Marting 66 pass from Dowling (Begel kick)
A—68,135

	Harv	Yale
First downs	20	13
Rushes—yards	47—102	43—152
Passing yards	300	153
Return yards	11	27

Passes	15−30−1	5−20−5
Punting	6−28	4−34
Fumbles−lost	2−2	2−0
Penalties−yards	3−11	3−15

Individual Leaders
Rushing: Gatto 21−81; Yale, Hill 10−60, Bob Levin 16−55.
Passing: Harvard, Zimmerman 14−29−1−289; Yale, Dowling 5−19−4−153.
Receiving: Harvard, Lord 9−188, Gatto 3−68; Yale, Marting 3−76, Hill 1−53.

Harvard—ENDS: Reed, Timpson, Lord, Cook, Hoffmann, Hall, Ranere, Gloyd. TACKLES: Zebal, Dowd, Brooks, Kaplan, DeBettencourt, Wilson. GUARDS: Bersin, Jones, Greenidge, MacLean. CENTERS: Weiss. LINEBACKERS: *Chiofaro*, Emery, Marino, Machin. QUARTERBACKS: Zimmerman, Berg. OFFENSIVE BACKS: Gatto, Hornblower, Strandemo, O'Connell, Saba, Ballantyne. DEFENSIVE BACKS: Cobb, Wynne, Williamson, Ananis, Thomas, Sadoski, Ignacio.

Yale—ENDS: Weinstein, Roney, Downing, Marting, *Watson*, Hixon, Lussen. TACKLES: Gee, Bass, Stroube, Whiteman, Greenberg, Mattas. GUARDS: France, McCarthy, Gallico, McLaughlin, Schmidt, Williams, Boyer. CENTERS: Morris, Pace. LINEBACKERS: Coe, Bouscaren, Day, Kolar, Southwick. QUARTERBACKS: Dowling, Henley. OFFENSIVE BACKS: Hill, Fisher, Davidson, Levin, Shevelson, Sokolowski, Harper. DEFENSIVE BACKS: Begel, Jones, Franklin, Goldsmith, Madden, McKenna, Waldman.

85th game
Saturday, Nov. 23, 1968
Harvard Stadium, Boston
Weather: Sunny
Harvard 29, Yale 29
Yale (8−0−1)　　7　15　0　　7—29
Harvard (8−0−1)0　　6　7　16—29

Y—Brian Dowling 3 run (Bob Bayless kick)
Y—Calvin Hill 3 pass from Dowling (Bayless kick)
Y—Del Marting 5 pass from Dowling (Marting pass from Dowling)
H—Bruce Freeman 15 pass from Frank Champi (kick failed)
H—Gus Grim 1 run (Richie Szaro kick)
Y—Dowling 5 run (Bayless kick)
H—Freeman 15 pass from Champi (Crim run)
H—Vic Gatto 8 pass from Champi (Pete Varney pass from Champi)
A—40,280

	Yale	Harv
First downs	19	17
Rushes−yards	53−251	53−118
Passing yards	116	104
Return yards	60	30
Passes	13−21−1	8−22−0
Punting	3−36	8−36
Fumbles−lost	6−6	3−1
Penalties−yards	7−66	4−30

Individual Leaders
Rushing: Yale, Hill 23−92, Nick Davidson 7−63, Dowling 10−55; Harvard, John Ballantyne 13−65.
Passing: Yale, Dowling 13−21−1−116; Harvard, Champi 6−15−0−82.
Receiving: Yale, Marting 4−35, Hill 4−28; Harvard, Freeman 4−51.

Harvard—ENDS—Varney, Kiernan, Gloyd, T. Smith, Hall, Cramer, Ranere, Freeman, McKinney. TACKLES—Reed, Dowd, Zebol, Berne, Kaplan, Sadler. GUARDS—Jones, Jannino, MacLean, Georges. CENTERS—Skowronski, Teske. QUARTERBACKS—Lalich, Champi. HALFBACKS—Hornblower, *Gatto*, Ballantyne, Reynolds. FULLBACKS—Crim, Miller. LINEBACKERS—Farneti, Emery, Ignacio, Frisbie, Neal, Ananis, Koski,

Kundrat, Marino. SAFETIES—Wynne, Conway, Kelly, Martucci, Fenton, Thomas, Manny. KICKING SPECIALISTS—Singleberry, Szaro.

Yale—ENDS—Martin, Weinstein, Madden, Jim Gallagher, Robinson, Lussen, Roney. TACKLES—Bass, Gee, Neville, Fran Gallagher, Peacock, Kleber, Livingston, Mattas, Mackey. GUARDS—Whiteman, Perkowski, Dick Williams, Puryear, Lee, Jackson. CENTERS—Morris, Pace. QUARTERBACK—*Dowling*. HALFBACKS—Hill, Davidson, Kropke. FULLBACKS—Levin. LINEBACKERS—Bouscaren, Coe, Kell, Schmoke, Franklin, Martin, Dowling, Waldman, Boyer. SAFETIES—Goldsmith. KICKING SPECIALISTS—Bayless.

86th game
Saturday, Nov. 22, 1969
Yale Bowl, New Haven
Weather: Clear, cold
Yale 7, Harvard 0
Harvard (3−6)　　0　0　0　0—0
Yale (7−2)　　　0　0　7　0—7
Y—Bill Primps 2 run (Harry Klebanoff kick)
A—62,562

	Harv	Yale
First downs	10	13
Rushes−yards	48−27	56−198
Passing yards	94	93
Return yards	83	54
Passes	8−24−2	5−15−2
Punting	7−35	7−32
Fumbles−lost	5−4	3−1
Penalties−yards	4−32	9−59

Individual Leaders
Rushing: Harvard, Miller 17−70; Yale, Primps 24−91, Don Martin 21−71.
Passing: Harvard, Blankenship 4−11−2−30, Yale, Joe Massey 5−15−2−93.

Receiving: Harvard, Pete Varney 2–41, Reynolds 3–29; Yale, Lew Roney 3–32, Bob Milligan 1–42.

Harvard—OFFENSE: ENDS: Varney, Freeman, Kiernan, Sullivan, Sontgerath; TACKLES: Dowd, Reed, Pearson; GUARDS: Cassis, Czulewicz, Ferullo; CENTERS: Teske, Waldstein, Hevern; QUARTERBACKS: Blankenship, Roda; HALFBACKS: Hornblower, Harrison; FULLBACKS: Miller, Lukaska, Reynolds; KICKING SPECIALISTS: Singleberry, Szaro.
DEFENSE: ENDS: Cramer, Doyle, Mc-Crann; TACKLES: Berne, Steiner; MIDDLEGUARDS: Dreischarf, Piotrowski; LINEBACKERS: D. Neal, Farneti; CORNERBACKS: Frisbie, Fenton, Ignacio, J. Neal; SAFETIES: Martucci, Hurley, Johnson, Mottau.

Yale—ENDS—Roney, Maher, Gallagher, Jones, Brooks, Oldenburg. TACKLES—Jordan, Kerecz, Matory, Kessler, Neville, Lolotai, Wolak, Story. GUARDS—Whiteman, Lee, Perkowski, Jackson, Shields, Biancamano, Puryear, Train. CENTERS—Adair, McKeown. LINEBACKERS—Coe, Kell, Ford, Lindsey. QUARTERBACKS—Massey, Sizemore. OFFENSIVE BACKS—Primps, Martin, Potts, Kropke. DEFENSIVE BACKS—Roberti, Hartman, Bliss, Holahan, Cole. KICKER—Klebanoff.

87th game
Saturday, Nov. 21, 1970
Harvard Stadium, Boston
Weather: Clear
Harvard 14, Yale 12
Yale (7–2)　　0　0　10　2—12
Harvard (7–2)　0　14　0　0—14
H—Ted DeMars 7 pass from Eric Crone (Richie Szaro kick)
H—Crone 8 run (Szaro kick)
Y—Don Martin 62 run (Harry Klebanoff kick)

Y—FG Klebanoff 31
Y—safety, Crone tackled by Ron Kell
A—40,000 (est.)

	Yale	Harv
First downs	10	13
Rushes–yards	51–227	57–170
Passing yards	27	53
Return yards	2	20
Passes	4–19–0	5–19–0
Punting	6–35	9–28
Fumbles–lost	7–4	3–2
Penalties–yards	4–29	4–50

Individual Leaders
Rushing: Yale, Martin 29–137, Dick Jauron 13–77; Harvard, DeMars 22–95.
Passing: Yale, Roly Purrington 3–9–0–21; Harvard, Crone 5–19–0–53.
Receiving: Yale, Rich Maher 1–9; Harvard, Bruce Freeman 2–21, DeMars 2–20.

Yale—OFFENSE: ENDS—Brooks, Maher, Hammerberg. TACKLES—Kessler, Jordan, Matricciani, Kerecz. GUARDS—McKeown, Leyen, Inithar. CENTERS—Wilkins, Tolley. QUARTERBACKS—Massey, Sizemore, Purrington. HALFBACKS—Martin, Woodruff, Fox, Murphy, Milligan, FULLBACKS—Jauron, Primps. KICKING SPECIALISTS—Nottingham, Reed, Klebanoff. DEFENSE: ENDS—Gallagher, Michel, Jones, Barzilauskas. TACKLES—*Neville*, Wolak, Story. GUARDS—Lolotai, Petrie. LINEBACKERS—Kell, Danforth, Lindsey. HALFBACKS—Roberti, Bliss, Dore. SAFETIES—Holahan, Cangelosi.

Harvard—OFFENSE: ENDS: Freeman, Varney, Gatto, Hagerty, Kelly. TACKLES: Honick, Ferulio, Masaracchio. GUARDS: Hevern, Veteran. CENTER: Starck. QUARTERBACK: Crone. HALFBACKS: DeMars, Craven, Murr, Harrison. FULLBACKS: Miller, Hall, Mayberg. KICKING SPECIALIST: Szaro.

DEFENSE: ENDS: Doyle, Lukawski, Mc-Hugh. TACKLES: Vena, Steiner. GUARD: Dreischarf. LINEBACKERS: *Farneti*, Neal. CORNER/HALFBACKS: Ignacio, Frisbie, Shofner, Bridich, Broyer. SAFETIES: Fenton, Golden, Harvey, Malinowski, Johnson.

88th game
Saturday, Nov. 20, 1971
Yale Bowl, New Haven
Weather: Sunny, warm
Harvard 35, Yale 16
Harvard (5–4)　14　14　0　7—35
Yale (4–5)　　0　2　8　6—16
H—Rich Gatto 4 pass from Eric Crone (Bruce Tetirick kick)
H—Denis Sullivan 29 pass from Crone (Tetirick kick)
H—Jack Neal recovered punt blocked by Dave Ignacio (Tetirick kick)
Y—safety Rod Foster downed in end zone
H—Mark Ferguson 52 interception (Tetirick kick)
Y—Dick Jauron 4 run (John Donohue pass from Roly Purrington)
Y—Jauron 14 run (run failed)
H—Steve Harrison 3 run (Tetirick kick)
A—51,238

	Harv	Yale
First downs	12	17
Rushes–yards	48–182	46–123
Passing yards	139	152
Passes	9–15–0	15–35–4
Punting	6–34	5–31
Fumbles–lost	1	1
Penalties–yards	116	0–0

Individual Leaders
Rushing: Harvard, Ted DeMars 14–139, Gatto 13–57; Yale, Jauron 16–85, Fred Danforth 13–51.
Passing: Harvard, Crone 9–14–0–139; Yale, Purrington 15–33–4–152.
Receiving: Harvard, Sullivan 2–41, Gatto 2–22; Yale, Kim Hammerberg 5–78, Bob Milligan 5–46.

Harvard—OFFENSE: ENDS: Sullivan, Craven, Armstrong, Bone, Hagerty. TACKLES: Bowens, Ferullo, Manna, Ferry. GUARDS: Kircher, Veteran, Bauer, Schappert. CENTERS: Starck, Snavely, Rifkin. QUARTERBACKS: Crone, Foster, Guerra. HALFBACKS: DeMars, Gatto, Leone, Harrison, Crawford. FULLBACKS: Krohn, Hall, Mayberg. KICKING SPECIALISTS: Tetirick, Faust.
DEFENSE: ENDS: Berger, McHugh, Smith, Mackey, Hughes. TACKLES: Vena, Steiner, O'Hare, Butterworth, Kettlewell. LINEBACKERS: Ferguson, Dreischarf, Neal, Kristoff, Tennant, Westra, Stroffe. CORNER/HALFBACKS: Murr, Malinowski, Harvey, St. Pierre, Shofner. SAFETIES: Golden, *Ignacio*, Bridich, Broyer, Bilodeau.

Yale—ENDS—*Maher*, Hammerberg, Peddicord, Louden, Pettit, Cutler, Michel, Robinson, Jones. TACKLES—Jordan, Kessler, Matricciani, Kerecz, Leyen, Wolak, Riddick. GUARDS—Matory, Burnworth, Intihar, Story, Fehling, Kiernan. CENTER—Wilkins. LINEBACKERS—Wilhelm, Perschel, Jackson. QUARTERBACKS—Purrington, Sizemore. OFFENSIVE BACKS—Jauron, Sortal, Danforth, Donohue, Woodruff, Fox, Murphy, Milligan. DEFENSIVE BACKS—Ford, Lindsey, Hartman, Bliss, Noetzel, Lewis, Cangelosi, Dore, Johnson. KICKERS—Nottingham, Clarke.

89th game
Saturday, Nov. 25, 1972
Harvard Stadium, Boston
Weather: Sunny
Yale 28, Harvard 17
Yale (7–2)   0   6   15   7—28
Harvard (4–4–1)10   7   0   0—17
H—Ted DeMars 86 run (Bruce Tetirick kick)

H—FG Tetirick 32
H—Eric Crone 1 run (Tetirick kick)
Y—Tyrell Hennings 1 run (pass failed)
Y—Dick Jauron 74 run (Brian Clarke kick)
Y—Roly Purrington 7 run (Rudy Green pass from Purrington)
Y—Jauron 1 run (Clarke kick)
A—39,000 (est.)

	Yale	Harv
First downs	16	11
Rushes–yards	58–284	51–214
Passing yards	68	50
Return yards	92	86
Passes	6–21–3	6–17–3
Punting	7–31	7–35
Fumbles–lost	7–2	7–4
Penalties–yards	4–39	1–5

Individual Leaders
Rushing: Yale, Jauron 28–183; Harvard, DeMars 16–153.
Passing: Yale, Purrington 5–16–3–72; Harvard, Crone 5–14–2–33.
Receiving: Yale, Paul Sortal 3–35; Harvard, Rod Foster 3–42.

Yale—ENDS—Sortal, Hammerberg, Michel, Fehling, Fernandez, Cutler, Archier. TACKLES—Moras, Matricciani, Leyen, Peddicord, Feryok, Dubinetz. GUARDS—Burnworth, Burkus, Alcorn. CENTERS—Riddick, Walker, Resch. LINEBACKERS—*Perschel*, Wilhelm, Danforth, Burke. QUARTERBACKS—Doyle, Purrington. OFFENSIVE BACKS—Jauron, Green, Donohue, Hennings, Mierzwinski. DEFENSIVE BACKS—Robinson, Lewis, Charity, Noetzel, Volo, Viglione, Douglas. KICKERS—Nottingham, Clarke.

Harvard—OFFENSE: ENDS: Bone, Hagerty, Craven, Dobbs, McInally, Curtin. TACKLES: Manna, Ferry. CENTERS: Snavely, Rifkin. GUARDS: Hehir, Friar, Kircher, Crim, Bauer. QUARTERBACKS: Crone, Holt. HALFBACKS: Wheeler,

Tsitsos, *DeMars*, Dart, Leone, Cronin. FULLBACKS: Foster, Hall, Flood. KICKING SPECIALISTS: Tetirick, Stoeckel. DEFENSE: ENDS: Smith, McHugh, Mackey, Wiedemann. TACKLES: O'Hare, Vena, Shaw, Butterworth, Kettlewell, GUARDS: Tennant, Burlage, Schappert. LINEBACKERS: Ferguson, Westra, Kristoff. BACKS: Dowling, Murr, Sciolla, St. Pierre, Clarke, Malinowski, Shofner, Page, Broyer, Bridich, Golden, D. Staggers, Costello.

90th game
Saturday, Nov. 24, 1973
Yale Bowl, New Haven
Weather: Cloudy, drizzle
Yale 35, Harvard 0
Harvard (7–2)   0   0   0   0— 0
Yale (6–3)   7   14   7   7—35
Y—John Donohue 1 run (Clarke kick)
Y—Rudy Green 6 run (Clarke kick)
Y—Gary Fencik 36 pass from Kevin Rogan (Clarke kick)
Y—Green 4 run (Clarke kick)
Y—Tyrell Hennings 1 run (Clarke kick)
A—41,427

	Harv	Yale
First downs	16	28
Rushes–yards	32–93	68–395
Passing yards	139	128
Return yards	127	30
Passes	15–38–2	8–17–1
Punting	9–34	3–36
Fumbles–lost	4–1	2–2
Penalties–yards	4–30	5–42

Individual Leaders
Rushing: Harvard, Phil Allen 8–51; Yale, Green 22–142, Hennings 11–74, Greg Daniels 6–67.
Passing: Harvard, Jim Stoeckel 11–27–2–106; Yale, Rogan 8–17–1–128.
Receiving: Harvard, Pete Curtin 3–44; Yale, Fencik 6–63.

Harvard—OFFENSE: ENDS: McInally, Curtin, F. Cronin, Bone, Dobbs, Herbert, Hagerty. TACKLES: Manna, Jiggetts, Lowry, Wagner, Burlage. GUARDS: Kircher, Ferry, Antonellis, McCafferty, Dombrowski, Friar, Pisanelli. CENTERS: Culig, Forman, Hehir, QUARTERBACKS: Stoeckel, Holt. HALFBACKS: Dart, E. Cronin, Tsitsos, Yates, H. Staggers, Richter, Sandow, Quimby, Foye, Duvauchelle. FULLBACKS: Miller, Allen, Balko, Bennett, Flood. KICKING SPECIALIST: Tetirick, Collins.
DEFENSE: ENDS: Berger, Mackey, Wiedemann, Hartnett, Mee, O'Neill. TACKLES: Shaw, O'Hare, Harrington, Restivo, Downer, Pickard, Scott. GUARD: Tennant, D. Staggers, Gardner. LINEBACKERS: Kristoff, Kurzweil, Keough, Collatos, Dowling, Rolader. BACKS: Page, Costello, Lauricella, St. Pierre, Clarke, Newhouse, McDonald, Jadick, Bender, Carfagna, Eyen, Judge, Peel, Sciolia, Stockman, Tosetti.

Yale—ENDS—Fernandez, Gallagher, Fencik, Fehling, Ameche, Resch, Calland, Nadherny, Barker. TACKLES—Moras, Palmer, Peddicord, Feryok, Paprota, Johnson, Hellauer, Schwegman, McGann. GUARDS—Burkus, Alcorn, Dubinetz, Beams, Chodosh, Webb. CENTERS—Riddick, Walker, Jenson. LINEBACKERS—*Wilhelm*, Sellati, Kirk, Knowles, Burke, Zupsic. QUARTERBACKS—Rogan, Doyle McAndrews. HALFBACKS—Green, Hennings, Daniels, Gesicki. FULLBACKS—Donohue, Gordon, Perkowski. DEFENSIVE BACKS—Charity, Lewis, Cahill, Robinson, Day, Viglione, Jennings, Volo, Hanway, Hinkley, Connors. PUNTER—Westfall. KICKER—Clarke.

91st game
Saturday, Nov. 23, 1974
Harvard Stadium, Boston
Weather: Clear, cold
Harvard 21, Yale 16
Yale (8–1)   7   6   0   3—16
Harvard (7–2)   0 14   0   7—21
Y—Rudy Green 1 run (Randy Carter kick)
Y—Green 5 run (Carter kick)
H—Pat McInally 2 pass from Milt Holt (Alky Tsitsos kick)
H—Pete Curtis 1 pass from Holt (Tsitsos kick)
Y—FG Carter 38
H—Holt 1 run (Tsitsos kick)
A—40,500 (est.)

	Yale	Harv
First downs	19	20
Rushes–yards	57–101	40–79
Passing yards	237	258
Return yards	13	1
Passes	16–25–0	20–33–0
Punting	6–34	7–38
Fumbles–lost	3–1	4–3
Penalties–yards	5–55	5–63

Individual Leaders
Rushing: Yale, Green 20–45; Harvard, Tom Winn 12–56.
Passing: Yale, Tom Doyle 16–25–0–237; Harvard, Holt 19–32–0–212, McInally 1–1–0–46. •
Receiving: Yale, Gary Fencik 11–187; Harvard, McInally 6–62, Pete Curtis 6–57, Winn 4–51.

Yale—OFFENSE: ENDS—Fernandez, Fencik, Barker, Hall, Calland, Tyson. TACKLES—Moras, Palmer, McGann, Six. GUARDS—Burkus, Dubinetz, Staffieri. CENTERS—Walker, Bosch. QUARTERBACK—Doyle. HALFBACKS—Green, Hennings, Daniels, Lewis. FULLBACKS—Gordon, Southworth. KICKERS—Westfall, Carter.
DEFENSE: ENDS—Ameche, Bonacum, S.

Smith, Rooth, Rose. TACKLES—Feryok, Lawrence, Schwegman, Hellauer. LINEBACKERS—Smoot, Kirk, Knowles, Burke, Resch. BACKS—Cahill, Viglione, Charity, McAndrews, Jennings, Hill.

Harvard—OFFENSE: ENDS: McInally, Curtin, McDermott, Curry, Hagerty. TACKLES: *Hehir*, Jiggetts, Burlage, GUARDS: McCafferty, Antonellis, Benninger, Johnston. CENTERS: Culig, Forman. QUARTERBACKS: Holt, Gordon. HALFBACKS: Dart, Winn, Balko, Taylor, E. Cronin. FULLBACKS: Miller, Flood, Lincoln. KICKING SPECIALISTS: Tsitsos. DEFENSE: ENDS: Hartnett, Wiedemann, Herbert, MacGillivray. TACKLES: Shaw, Kaye, Witten, Scott. GUARDS: Restivo, Mee, Staggers. LINEBACKERS: Kurzweil, Joyce, Jadick, Keough, Collatos. BACKS: Sciolla, Page, F. Cronin, Clarke, Costello, Emper, Rice, Newhouse, McDonald, Judge.

92nd game
Saturday, Nov. 22, 1975
Yale Bowl, New Haven
Weather: Windy, cold
Harvard 10, Yale 7
Harvard (7–2)   0   0   7   3—10
Yale (7–2)   0   7   0   0— 7
Y—Stone Phillips 5 run (Randy Carter kick)
H—Tom Winn 2 run (Mike Lynch kick)
H—FG Lynch 26
A—66,846

	Harv	Yale
First downs	16	12
Rushes–yards	45–146	54–175
Passing yards	118	20
Return yards	44	29
Passes	11–27–3	2–13–1
Punting	7–41	9–42
Fumbles–lost	4–0	1–1
Penalties–yards	5–73	0–0

Individual Leaders
Rushing: Harvard, Winn 12−65; Yale,
Don Gesicki 26−78.
Passing: Harvard, Jim Kubacki 11−27−
3−118; Yale, Phillips 2−10−0−20.
Receiving: Harvard, Curry 4−41; Yale,
Gary Fencik 1−12.

Harvard—OFFENSE: ENDS: Curry, Mc-
Dermott. TACKLES: *Jiggetts*, Wagner,
Peabody. GUARDS: Antonellis, McCaf-
ferty. CENTER: Culig. QUARTERBACKS:
Kubacki, Davenport. HALFBACKS:
Winn, Taylor, Kinchen. FULLBACKS:
Miller. KICKING SPECIALISTS: Lynch,
Curry.
DEFENSE: ENDS: Savage, Baggott.
TACKLES: Mee, Kaseta, Witten, Taubes.
GUARDS: Bernieri. LINEBACKERS:
Kurzweil, Joyce. BACKS: Emper, Judge,
Cronin, Newhouse.

Yale—OFFENSE: ENDS—Fencik, Cal-
land, Hall, Kelly, Barker. TACKLES—
Palmer, Six, McDonnell, Mihalcik.
GUARDS—Staffieri, Carfora, Browning.
CENTERS—Litchman, Bosch. QUARTER-
BACKS—Phillips, Nubani. HALF-
BACKS—Gesicki, Pagliaro, Lewis. FULL-
BACKS—Gordon, Southworth, Bassi.
PUNTER—Southworth. KICKER—Carter.
DEFENSE: ENDS—Keller, Bonacum,
Smith. TACKLES—Lawrence, Denza,
Stadler. LINEBACKERS—*Smoot*, Sellati,
Zupsic, Simons, Waller, Knowles, Knapp.
BACKS—Cahill, Jennings, Day, McAn-
drews, Judge, Rooth, Weatherspoon.

93rd game
Saturday, Nov. 13, 1976
Harvard Stadium, Boston
Weather: Sunny, crisp
Yale 21, Harvard 7
Yale (8−1)   0 0 14 7—21
Harvard (1−7)   7 0   0 0— 7
H—Russ Savage 74 interception (Mike
Lynch kick)

Y—Mike Southworth 7 run (Randy Carter
kick)
Y—John Pagliaro 5 run (Carter kick)
Y—Southworth 2 run (Carter kick)
A—42,000 (est.)

	Yale	Harv
First downs	22	9
Rushes−yards	67−286	37−116
Passing yards	30	37
Return yards	2	77
Passes	2−10−3	5−12−1
Punting	6−33	6−31
Fumbles−lost	3−1	3−2
Penalties−yards	5−57	9−103

Individual Leaders
Rushing: Yale, Pagliaro 25−128, Bob
Rizzo 11−53; Harvard, Tom Winn 21−95.
Passing: Yale, Rizzo 2−6−1−30; Har-
vard, Jim Kubacki 5−12−1−37.
Receiving :Yale, John Spagnola 2−30;
Harvard, Winn 2−11.

Yale—OFFENSE: ENDS—Kelly, Hall,
Spagnola, Krystyniak, Calvin. TACK-
LES—Mihalcik, McDonnell, McNamara,
Zorio, DeCusati. GUARDS—*Staffieri*, Car-
fora, Noetzel, Melina. CENTERS—Bosch,
Browning, Ventresca. QUARTER-
BACKS—Phillips, Rizzo. HALFBACKS—
Pagliaro, Lewis, Hatem, Nubani. FULL-
BACK—Southworth. KICKER—Carter.
PUNTER—Southworth.
DEFENSE: ENDS—Bonacum, Smith,
Tomana, Corcoran. TACKLES—Denza,
Skoronski, Streit, Stadler. MIDDLE
GUARDS—Bassi, Humphreville. LINE-
BACKERS—Crowley, Waller, Goodfriend,
Rapp. BACKS—Rooth, Judge, Nondorf,
Skrovan, Gardner.

Harvard—OFFENSE: ENDS: Hobdy,
McDermott, Graham, Sablock, Kinney,
Saxon, McLeod. TACKLES: McKinnon,
Kross, Radakovich, Peabody. GUARDS:
Clark, Benninger, Gantley, Rubinstein,

Cocalis. CENTERS: Spagnola, DiNorfio,
Shea. QUARTERBACKS: Kubacki, Dav-
enport. HALFBACKS: Winn, Taylor,
Sigillito, Polillio, Schember. FULL-
BACKS: Doherty, Lincoln, Granger,
Woods. SPECIALISTS: Coolidge, Lynch,
Bosnic.
DEFENSE: ENDS: Savage, Baggott, Wal-
ton, Binning. TACKLES: Kaye, Kaseta,
Bailey. GUARDS: Bernieri, McDevitt,
Fiori. LINEBACKERS: Joyce, Taubes,
Beling, Jason. CORNERBACKS: *Emper*,
Puopolo, McCarthy, Royal, Potysman,
Masterson. SAFETIES: Wendel, Rice,
Halas, Tuke.

94th game
Saturday, Nov. 12, 1977
Yale Bowl, New Haven
Weather: Sunny
Yale 24, Harvard 7
Harvard (4−5) 0 7 0   0— 7
Yale (7−2)   3 7 0 14—24
Y—FG Dave Schwartz 22
H—Paul Sablock 14 pass from Larry
Brown (Gary Bosnic kick)
Y—Rich Angelone 5 run (Bill Moore kick)
Y—Mike Sullivan 66 run (Moore kick)
Y—John Pagliaro 2 run (Moore kick)
A—64,685

	Harv	Yale
First downs	11	24
Rushes−yards	32−49	69−353
Passing yards	114	43
Return yards	−4	35
Passes	9−24−2	3−7−1
Punting	8−38	5−33
Fumbles−lost	5−2	2−2
Penalties−yards	3−22	4−39

Individual Leaders
Rushing: Harvard, Chris Doherty 8−25;
Yale, Pagliaro 30−172, Angelone 17−75,
Sullivan 1−66.

Passing: Harvard, Brown 7–16–1–85; Yale, Bob Rizzo 3–7–1–43.
Receiving: Harvard, Sablock 3–53; Yale, Kevin Kelly 1–17.

Harvard—OFFENSE: ENDS: Curry, Sablock, Hobdy, Brady, Graham, Horner. TACKLES: Kross, McKinnon. GUARDS: Clark, Cocalis, Mike Brown, DeCamp. CENTERS: Pelegrini, Lauricella, Simmons, DeNofrio. QUARTERBACKS: Larry Brown, Buckley. HALFBACKS: Polillo, Sigillito, Kinchen, Moore. FULLBACKS: Doherty, Coolidge, Granger. KICKING SP: Bosnic
DEFENSE: ENDS: Baggott, Savage, Binning, MacMurray. TACKLES: Kaye, *Kaseta*, Murray, Kane, Malone, Bennett. GUARDS: McDevitt, Gaudio, Schned, Dowd. LINEBACKERS: Jason, Goodreault, Walton. CORNERBACKS: Potysman, Masterson, Cordova, Kinney, Ippolito. ADJUSTORS: Tuke, Stack. SAFETY: MacLeod, Halas, Olatunji, Kozlowski.

Yale—OFFENSE: ENDS—K. Kelly, Cardwell, Spagnola. TACKLES—McNamara, McDonnell, DeCusati. GUARDS—Noetzel, Carfora, Melina, Maples, Orlando, Hartman. CENTERS—Ventresca, Browning, Ross. QUARTERBACKS—Rizzo, O'Brien. TAILBACKS—Pagliaro, Austin, Sullivan. WINGBACKS—Nubani, Hill, Wallace. FULLBACKS—Angelone, McIntyre, Nitti. KICKERS—Moore, Schwartz. PUNTERS—Sullivan.
DEFENSE: ENDS: Streit, Tomana, Goodfriend, White, Faschan. TACKLES—Denza, Skoronski, Paci, Conrad. MIDDLE GUARDS: Bassi, Humphreville, Barlow. LINEBACKERS—Crowley, Rapp, Tumpane, Porter, Knapp. BACKS—Gardner, Weatherspoon, Nondorf, Skrovan, Meyer, Calvin, Pinkston, C. Kelly, Pace, Blagdon.

95th game
Saturday, Nov. 18, 1978
Harvard Stadium, Boston
Weather: Clear
Yale 35, Harvard 28
Yale (5–2–2) 7 21 7 0—35
Harvard (4–4–1)0 14 0 14—28
Y—Pat O'Brien 9 run (Dave Schwartz kick)
Y—Rich Angelone 10 run (Schwartz kick)
H—Matt Granger 4 pass from Larry Brown (Gary Bosnic kick)
H—Rich Horner 35 pass from Brown (Bosnic kick)
Y—Bob Krystyniak 77 pass from John Spagnola (Schwartz kick)
Y—Ken Hill 18 run (Schwartz kick)
Y—Spagnola 59 pass from O'Brien (Schwartz kick)
H—Horner 11 pass from Brown (Bosnic kick)
H—John MacLeod 8 pass from Brown (Bosnic kick)
A—41,500 (est.)

	Yale	Harv
First downs	28	19
Rushes–yards	65–327	37–59
Passing yards	212	301
Return yards	50	0
Passes	7–11–1	19–27–0
Punting	1–39	4–38
Fumbles–lost	3–3	2–1
Penalties–yards	10–89	8–85

Individual Leaders
Rushing: Yale, Hill 25–154, Angelone 19–93, Mike Sullivan 8–51; Harvard, Ralph Pilillio 19–46.
Passing: Yale, O'Brien 5–9–1–124, Spagnola 1–1–0–77; Harvard, Brown 19–27–0–301.
Receiving: Yale, Spagnola 4–102, Krystyniak 2–99; Harvard, Horner 6–163.

Yale—OFFENSE: ENDS—Spagnola, Krystyniak, Rostomily. TACKLES—McNamara, DeCusati, Skarzynski, Zorio, Regan. GUARDS—Noetzel, Maples, Hartman. CENTERS—Orlando, Repetti. QUARTERBACK—O'Brien. WINGBACKS—Hatem, Spizer, Grieve. KICKERS—Schwartz, Owens.
DEFENSE: ENDS—Streit, White, Dwyer, Faschan. TACKLES—Conrad, Paci, Skoronski. MIDDLE GUARDS—Barlow, Czinger, Kelley. LINEBACKERS—Crowley, Porter, Tumpane, Rohrer. BACKS—Gardner, Nondorf, Skrovan, Pinkston, Kelly, Novosel.

Harvard—OFFENSE: ENDS: MacLeod, Sablock, Kinney, Horner, Marshall. TACKLES: Durgin, Kross, Silvey. GUARDS: DeCamp, M. Clark, Lattanzi, M. Brown, J. Clark. CENTERS: Scheper, DeNofrio, J. Knoebel, Locke. QUARTERBACK: L. Brown. HALFBACKS: Polillio, Connors, Hollingsworth, Beatrice, Sandor, Carreon. FULLBACKS: Granger, Quantock, Beacom, Altieri. SPECIALISTS: Bosnic, MacMurray.
DEFENSE: ENDS: Coric, Otto, DeBello, Binning, Kenna. TACKLES: Durst, Palmer, Cosgrove. GUARDS: McDevitt, Gaudio. LINEBACKERS: Beling, Woolway, Cimmarrusti, Sabetti. CORNERBACKS: *Potysman*, Cordova, Kasanjian, Trusty. ADJUSTERS: Masterson, Casto. SAFETIES: Jacobs, S. McLeod, Casey.

96th game
Saturday, Nov. 17, 1979
Yale Bowl, New Haven
Weather: Sunny
Harvard 22, Yale 7
Harvard (3–6) 7 6 0 9—22
Yale (8–1) 0 0 7 0— 7
H—John Hollingsworth 4 run (Dave Cody kick)

H—Jim Callinan 39 pass from Burke St. John (kick failed)
Y—Dennis Dunn 4 run (Dave Schwartz kick)
H—FG Cody 22
H—St. John 2 run (kick failed)
A—69,592

	Harv	Yale
First downs	15	17
Rushes—yards	54—152	44—92
Passing yards	96	200
Return yards	50	16
Passes	5—13—0	14—31—3
Punting	7—31	3—36
Fumbles—lost	3—1	6—3
Penalties—yards	9—84	8—91

Individual Leaders
Rushing: Harvard, Callinan 18—73; Yale, Ken Hill 18—43.
Passing: Harvard, St. John 5—13—0—96; John Rogan 8—21—2—127, Dunn 6—9—0—73.
Receiving: Harvard, Callinan 2—62; Yale, Dan Stratton 6—121.

Harvard—OFFENSE: ENDS: Horner, Marshall, McGlone, O'Donnell. TACKLES: Durgin, Spiegel, Anderson. GUARDS: *Brown*, Lattanzi, J. Clark, Mee. CENTERS: D. Scheper, Piurkowsky, DeFeo. QUARTERBACK: St. John. HALFBACKS: Hollingsworth, Beatrice, Sandor, Connors, P. Scheper. FULLBACKS: Callinan, Altieri. SPECIALISTS: Millard, Arnold, Cody. DEFENSE: ENDS: Otto, DeBello, Kenna, Whittington. TACKLES: Durst, Palmer, Sauve, Kelley. GUARDS: Finan, Lohmiller, Jackson, T. Clark. LINEBACKERS: Sabetti, Woolway, Cimmarrusti, Stinn, Mills, Layden, McCormack. CORNERBACKS: Coppinger, Wool, Kazanjian, Crowley, Trusty. SAFETIES: Jacobs, Delgadillo, Casey. ADJUSTERS: Casto, M. Foley.

Yale—OFFENSE: ENDS—Stratton, Rostomily, Burkitt, Kokoska, Dawson. TACKLES—Skarsynski, Regan, Lata, Britt. GUARDS—Spears, Glanz, Dola. CENTERS—Corelli, Repetti. QUARTERBACKS—Dunn, Rogan. RUNNING BACKS—Hill, Sullivan, Nitti, McIntyre. WINGBACKS—Gaughan, Diana. KICKER—Schwartz. PUNTERS—Sullivan, Conran. DEFENSE: ENDS—Dwyer, Kelley, Tulsiak. TACKLES—Conrad, Barlow, Crane, Ford, Mihaly. MIDDLE GUARDS—Czinger, Barlow. LINEBACKERS—*Tumpane*, Porter, McKenzie. BACKS—Novosel, Kelly, Pinkston, Conran.

97th game
Saturday, Nov. 22, 1980
Harvard Stadium, Boston
Weather: Sunny, cold
Yale 14, Harvard 0
Yale (8—2)   7   0   7   0—14
Harvard (7—3)   0   0   0   0— 0
Y—Curt Grieve 25 pass from John Rogan (Tony Jones kick)
Y—John Nitti 1 run (Jones kick)
A—41,000 (est.)

	Yale	Harv
First downs	15	9
Rushes—yards	66—219	21—11
Passing yards	81	141
Return yards	24	8
Passes	5—10—0	14—33—2
Punting	7—35	8—31
Fumbles—lost	4—2	4—4
Penalties—yards	5—43	7—43

Individual Leaders
Rushing: Yale, Rich Diana 27—79, Nitti 19—69; Harvard, Jim Callinan 9—30.
Passing: Yale, Rogan 5—8—0—81; Harvard, Brian Buckley 14—33—2—141.
Receiving: Yale, Grieve 3—49; Harvard, Chuck Marshall 5—67.

Yale—OFFENSE: ENDS—Grieve, Burkitt, Kokoska, Bernhard. TACKLES—Skarzynski, Regan, Primrose, Deeb. GUARDS—Ruwe, Whitehurst, Bellisimo, Pekar. CENTERS—Mumford, Jaben, Manning. QUARTERBACKS—Rogan, Manley. RUNNING BACKS—Diana, *Nitti*, Harrington, Cottrell, Dalzell, WINGBACKS—Stratton, Dawson. PUNTER-KICKER—Jones. DEFENSE: ENDS—Kelley, Leone, Burkus, Englert, Tavera. TACKLES—Mihaly, Ford, Tulsiak, Mattick. MIDDLE GUARDS—Czinger, Debasitis. LINEBACKERS—Snyder, McKenzie, Joiner. BACKS—Novosel, Duncan, Conran, McCullom, Muscatello, Daugherty.

Harvard—OFFENSE: ENDS: Cuccia, Marshall, O'Donnell, McGlone, Quartararo, Thompson. TACKLES: Anderson, Durgin, Hinton, Brown, Pendergast, Corbat. GUARDS: Lattanzi, Mee, J. Clark, Cash. CENTERS: Francis, Jacobs. QUARTERBACK: Buckley. HALFBACKS: Connors, Beatrice, McCabe, Acheson, Scheper. FULLBACKS: Callinan, Ernst. SPECIALISTS: Flach, Cody. DEFENSE: ENDS: Otto, Whittington, Connolly, McHugh, Zumbrum, Margolis. TACKLES: T. Clark, Palmer, Fleming, Sauve. GUARDS: Finan, Murrer, Kelley. LINEBACKERS: Woolway, Stinn, Layden, Mills. CORNERBACKS: Coppinger, Delgadillo, Mullen, Wool, Crowley. SAFETY: Jacobs. ADJUSTERS: Foley, Kazanjian, Varsames. *C. F. Durst* did not play.

98th game
Saturday, Nov. 21, 1981
Yale Bowl, New Haven
Weather: Fair
Yale 28, Harvard 0
Harvard (5—4—1) 0   0   0   0— 0
Yale (9—1)   7   7   0 14—28

Y—Rich Diana 39 pass from John Rogan (Tony Jones kick)
Y—Curt Grieve 25 pass from Rogan (Jones kick)
Y—Diana 4 run (Jones kick)
H—Grieve 7 pass from Joe Dufek (Gary Whitman kick)
A—72,440

	Harv	Yale
First downs	17	15
Rushes–yards	48–138	48–115
Passing yards	107	146
Return yards	48	21
Passes	13–30–2	7–23–1
Punting	10–32	9–37
Fumbles–lost	5–4	0–0
Penalties–yards	10–81	9–74

Individual Leaders
Rushing: Harvard, Jim Callinan 21–60, Don Allard 6–53; Yale, Diana 28–87.
Passing: Harvard, Allard 11–23–1–107; Yale, Rogan 5–16–1–126.
Receiving: Harvard, Ron Cuccia 5–57; Yale, Grieve 4–82.

Harvard—OFFENSE: ENDS: O'Donnell, McGlone, Scheper, Killen. TACKLES: Hinton, Brown, Pendergast. GUARDS: Corbat, Cash, Hurty, Morse. CENTERS: Francis, Swan, Orban. QUARTER-BACKS: Cuccia, Allard. HALFBACKS: Bianucci, Acheson, McCabe, Garvey, S. Ernst. FULLBACKS: Callinan, Granger, M. Ernst. SPECIALISTS: Villanueva, Flach.
DEFENSE: ENDS: McHugh, Whittington, Fleming, Margolis, Connolly, Zumbrum. TACKLES: Clark, Martin, Sauve, Schlichting. GUARDS: Murrer, Kelley. LINEBACKERS: Azelby, Nolan, Mills, Rutt. CORNERBACKS: Delgadillo, Myers, Rollins, Dailey. SAFETIES: *Coppinger*, Howkins. ADJUSTERS: Varsames, Mullen.

Yale—OFFENSE: ENDS—Grieve, Kokoska, Moyer, Crews, Jadin, Dolan. TACKLES—Basa, Gates, Phelan, Britt. GUARDS—Lata, Bellissimo, Mackie, Ruwe, Donahoe. CENTERS—Lang, Mumford. QUARTERBACKS—Rogan, Dufek. RUNNING BACKS—Diana, Cottrell, Andrie, Neville. WINGBACKS—Dalzell, Burkitt. KICKERS—Jones, Whitman. PUNTER—Jones
DEFENSE: ENDS—Burkus, *Leone*, Crook, Holowinko, Lombardi, Manolukas, Hammersmith. TACKLES—Mihaly, Tulsiak, Batesky. MIDDLE GUARDS—Debasitis, Blue, Kirk, Levy, Giella. LINEBACKERS—Rohrer, Snyder, Joiner, Piazza. BACKS—Bensinger, Daugherty, Campbell, Conran, Duncan, Gaughan, Vitelli, Gordee, Burns.

99th game
Saturday, Nov. 20, 1982
Harvard Stadium, Boston
Weather: Cloudy
Harvard 45, Yale 7

| Yale (4–6) | 0 | 7 | 0 | 0— | 7 |
| Harvard (7–3) | 7 | 14 | 17 | 7— | 45 |

H—Don Allard 23 run (Jim Villanueva kick)
Y—Rick Crews 7 pass from Joe Dufek (Bill Moore kick)
H—Peter Quartararo 12 pass from Allard (Villanueva kick)
H—Jim Garvey 1 run (Villanueva kick)
H—Steve Ernst 1 run (Villanueva kick)
H—Mike Granger 23 run (Joe Abate kick)
H—FG Villanueva 42
H—Mike Ernst 13 run (Abate kick)
A—40,000 (est.)

	Yale	Harv
First downs	12	23
Rushes–yards	48–12	50–286
Passing yards	128	171
Return yards	0	6
Passes	12–27–0	11–21–0
Punting	8–37	3–39
Fumbles–lost	1–1	3–2
Penalties–yards	7–50	11–108

Individual Leaders
Rushing: Yale, Paul Andrie 17–21; Harvard, Allard 8–74, Granger 11–56.
Passing: Yale, Dufek 10–20–0–109; Harvard, Allard 10–20–0–159.
Receiving: Yale, Rick Crews 5–51; Harvard, John O'Brien 3–52, Quartararo 3–51.

Yale—OFFENSE: END—Crews, Jadin, O'Shea, Sheldon, Crook, Powers, Quinlivan, Clark. TACKLES—Gates, Primrose, Basa. GUARDS—Mackie, *Ruwe*, Williams. CENTER—Lang. QUARTERBACKS—Dufek, Luzzi, Rosales. HALFBACKS—Andrie, Dalzell, Javens, Thivierge, Casey, Gaughan. FULLBACKS—Neville, Lassette, Marwede, Bassett. SPECIALISTS—Baer, Moore.
DEFENSE: ENDS—Burkus, Keenan, Holowinko, Walsh, Kalinich. TACKLES—Batesky, Giella, MacLaren, Kolstad. GUARD—Zanieski. LINEBACKERS—Joiner, Piazza, Ilacqua, White. CORNERBACKS—Duncan, Myre, Gordee, Casey. SAFETIES—Dooley, Campbell.

Harvard—OFFENSE: ENDS: Quartararo, O'Brien, Abbott, Ceko, Rutecki, Farrell, Crudo. TACKLES: Hurty, *Brown*, Crotty, Scibelli, Sullivan, Fernandes. GUARDS: Corbat, Cash, Ippolito, Morse, Thio, Edgell, Pascucci. CENTERS: Bouley, Locke, Jensen, Orban, Curiel. QUARTERBACKS: Allard, Cuccia, Reardon, Columbo, Gizzi. HALFBACKS: Garvey, S. Ernst, McCabe, Vignali, Dunn, Lowe, Fadule, Saleeby, Nicholas, McGugan. FULLBACKS: Granger, M. Ernst, Cooke, Sharon, Mazzocco. SPECIALISTS: Villanueva, Swan, Abate

DEFENSE: ENDS: Fleming, Margolis, Clapacs, Mead, Rector, Chase. TACKLES: Martin, Schlichting, Scott, Ford, Welsh, Marcus, Boulris. GUARDS: Murrer, Perdoni, Holley. LINEBACKERS: Azelby, Nolan, Garvin, Cammett, Uecker. CORNERBACKS: Myers, Dailey, Bergstrom. SAFETIES: Dixon, Rice. ADJUSTERS: Varsames, Howkins, Cronin.

100th game
Saturday, Nov. 19, 1983
Yale Bowl, New Haven
Weather: Fair
Harvard 16, Yale 7

Harvard (6−2−2) 0   7   0   9−16
Yale (1−9)   0   0   7   0− 7
H—McGugan 1 run (Steinberg kick)
Y—Bassette 1 run (Moore kick)
H—Ernst 2 run (kick failed)
H—FG Steinberg 35
A—70,600

	Yale	Harv
First downs	13	15
Rushes−yards	40−61	51−259
Passing yards	139	94
Return yards	12	18
Passes	11−22−1	8−18−1
Punts−Avg.	7−39	6−35
Fumbles−lost	2−1	2−1
Penalties−yards	5−48	12−87

Individual Leaders
Rushing: Harvard, Ernst 19−113−1, Gizzi 14−97, McGugan 9−38−1, Vignali 7−15; Yale, Andrie 14−72, Bassette 13−38−1.
Passing: Harvard, Gizzi 18−8−1−94−0; Yale, Curtin 21−11−1−117−0, Luzzi 1−1−0−22−0.
Receiving: Harvard, O'Brien 4−47, Ernst 2−7, Santiago 1−22, Seko 1−18; Yale, Moriarty 6−76, Marwede 2−22, Javens, 2−21, O'Shea 1−11, Clark 1−9.

Harvard—OFFENSE: ENDS: Ceko, O'Brien, Coyne, Abbott, Crudo. TACKLES: Fitzsimmons, Caron, Curiel. GUARDS: Ippolito, Pascucci, Thio, Moffatt. CENTER: Jensen. QUARTERBACK: Gizzi. HALFBACKS: Vignali, Fadule, McGugan, Santiago, Sharon, Saleeby. FULLBACKS: Ernst, Cooke, Ridout. SPECIALISTS: Steinberg, Colombo, Mielach. DEFENSE: ENDS: Mead, Rector, Anderson, Chase. TACKLES: Boulris, Fanikos, Ford. NOSEGUARD: Perdoni. LINEBACKERS—*Azelby*, Nolan, Uecker, Garvin, Bennett, Wilkinson. CORNERBACKS: Bergstrom, Tarczy, Dailey, Oldenburg. ADJUSTERS: Howkins, Leone, Ciota. SAFETY: Dixon.

Yale—OFFENSE: ENDS—Moriarty, Quinlivan, Clark, Parker, O'Shea, Marwede. TACKLES—Anderson, Gates, Sweeney, Skwara, Powers. GUARDS—Anderer, Phelan, Sams, Wesoloski, Maxwell. CENTERS—Martinson, Leckowicz, Millet. QUARTERBACKS—Curtin, Luzzi. RUNNING BACKS—Andrie, Bassette, Neville, Kline, Spivack, Bonny. WINGBACKS—Javens, Profit, Tjarksen. PUNTER—Eaton. DEFENSE: ENDS—Keenan, Kalinich, Kay, Crook, Manolukas. TACKLES—*Giella*, Kolstad, MacLaren, Walsh, Batesky. MIDDLE GUARDS—Zanieski, Yacobucci, Rohal. LINEBACKERS—McKenna, White, DeNicola, Presnick, Litner, Weber. BACKS—Dooley, Kotkiewicz, Penders, Campbell, Resch, Lenskold, Ruffin, Pont. KICKER—Moore.

CAPTAINS AND COMMENT

The following lists include all captains of record from the beginnings of football at the two institutions down to the present. Names are followed by residence at the time of matriculation, scholastic preparation, and careers after graduation. For the last column I have used abbreviations as follows: B: business (used in a wide sense covering everything from banking and finance to manufacturing and salesmanship); E: education (teaching or administration); J: journalism (in which I include publishing); L: law; Med: medicine; PS: public service. Other vocations are spelled out. C indicates some experience in professional coaching, M military service, and P a career in professional athletics. In a number of cases more than one abbreviation is necessary. NI signifies no definite information available. I have carried the career survey only through the early sixties.

The names of acting captains, captains of·informal teams, and captains-elect who did not serve are omitted from the lists.

HARVARD CAPTAINS

1874 H. R. Grant '74; Boston; Boston Latin; B
1874* A. B. Ellis '75; Boston; L, minister
1875 William A. Whiting '77; Charlestown MA; Chauncey Hall School; L
1876 Nathaniel Curtis '77; Boston; Hopkinson's School; B
1877 Livingston Cushing '79; Boston; Private tutoring; L
1879 Robert Bacon '80; Jamaica Plain MA; Hopkinson's School; B
1880 William Manning; Jamaica Plain MA; Roxbury Latin; B

1882 Edward T. Cabot '83; Brookline MA; Roxbury Latin; died young
1883 Randolph Appleton '84; Staten Island NY; Exeter; L
1884 Marcus M. Kimball '86; Boston; NI; L, B
1885 No team
1886 W. A. Brooks '87; Haverill MA; NI; Med
1887 Albert F. Holden '88; Cleveland; Exeter; B
1888 Joseph H. Sears '89; Dorchester MA; NI; NI
1889 Arthur J. Cumnock '91; Lowell MA; Lowell HS; B
1890 Arthur J. Cumnock '91

1891 Bernard Trafford '93; Westport MA; Exeter; B
1892 Bernard Trafford '93
1893 Bertram G. Waters '94; Boston; Boston Latin; B, L
1894 Robert W. Emmons '95; Boston; Groton; B
1895 Arthur H. Brewer '96; Boston; Hopkinson's School; PS, M
1896 Edgar Wrightington '97; Brookline MA; Brookline HS; B
1897 Norman W. Cabot '98; Brookline MA; Hale School; B, M
1898 Benjamin H. Dibblee '99; Ross CA; Groton; B, M
1899 William A. M. Burden '00; Troy NY; Groton; B
1900 Charles D. Daly '01; Boston; Boston Latin; C, M

1901 David C. Campbell '02; Waltham MA; Worcester Academy; B
1902 Robert P. Kernan '03; Utica NY; Brooklyn Polytechnic; L, B
1903 C. B. Marshall '04; Boston; Brookline HS; B
1904 Daniel J. Hurley '05; Boston; Boston Latin; Med
1905 Daniel J. Hurley '05
1906 Hatherly Foster '07; Boston; Hackley School; B
1907 Bartold Parker '08; Lancaster MA; Milton Academy; L, B
1908 Francis H. Burr '09; Chestnut Hill MA; Noble and Greenough; L

1909 H. Fish '10; Garrison NY; St. Mark's; PS, M
1910 Lothrop Withington '11; Escondido CA; Oahu College; L, M
1911 R. M. Fisher '12; Boston; Andover; B, M, C
1912 Percy L. Wendell '13; Roxbury MA; Roxbury Latin; B, M, C
1913 R. T. P. Storer '14; Boston; Noble and Greenough; B, M, C
1914 Charles E. Brickley '15; Boston; Exeter; P
1915 E. W. Mahan '16; Natick MA; B, M
1916 Harrie H. Dadmun '17; Cambridge; Arlington HS; B
1919 William J. Murray '18; Natick MA; Andover; C
1920 Arnold Horween '21; Chicago; Parker School; B

1921 Richmond Kane '22; San Francisco; St. George School; L, E, PS
1922 Charles C. Buell '21; Hartford; Pomfret; E, M
1923 Charles Hubbard, Jr. '24; Kansas City MO; Milton; engineer/science, M
1924 M. W. Greenough '25; Philadelphia; Groton; B, M
1925 Marion A. Cheek '26; Oakland; Exeter; E
1926 C. D. Coady '27; Newton MA; Exeter; B, M
1927 Charles Pratt, Jr. '28; New Bedford MA; Loomis; E
1928 Arthur E. French '29; E. Milton MA; Worcester; E
1929 James E. Barrett '30; Ayer MA; Worcester; B, M
1930 Benjamin Ticknor '31; Canton MA; Milton Academy; B

1931 W. Barry Wood '32; Milton MA; Milton Academy; Med
1932 Carl Hageman, Jr. '33; Lorain OH; Lorain HS; B
1933 John H. Dean '34; Cohasset MA; Exeter; B, M
1934 H. W. Gundlach; Houghton MI; Houghton HS; B, M
1935 Shawn Kelly, Jr.; Freiburg; Groton; E, C, M
1936 James Gaffney, Jr. '37; Danvers MA; Danvers HS; B, PS, M
1937 Charles R. Allen '38; Belfast ME; Exeter; E, B, C, M
1938 Robert L. Green, Jr. '39; Baltimore; Baltimore Polytechnic; minister
1939 Torbert Macdonald '40; Malden MA; Andover; L, PS, M
1940 Joseph Gardella '41; Weston MA; Worcester Academy; Med, E

1941 Francis M. Lee '42; Branford CT; Choate; B, L
1942 Donald Forte '43; Wayland MA; Exeter; B, M
1945 Robert Cowen II '47; Chestnut Hill MA; Exeter; B, M
1946 Cleo A. O'Donnell, Jr. '46; Natick MA; Worcester; B
1947 Vincent P. Moravec '48; Hamburg NY; Beaver HS; B

1948 Kenneth O'Donnell '49; Jamaica Plain MA; Worcester HS; B, PS
1949 Howard E. Houston '50; Portland; Haverill MA HS; B
1950 Philip L. Isenberg '51; Hartford; Loomis; Med

1951† Carroll Lowenstein '52; Arlington MA; NI; B, M
       Warren D. Wylie '52; Lowell MA; Tilton School; B
1952 John D. Nichols, Jr. '53; Westport CT; Loomis; B
1953 Richard J. Clasby '54; Boston; Trinity Pawling; B, M
1954 J. Timothy Anderson '55; Bemis Pt. NY; Andover; architect
1955 William W. Meigs '56; Syracuse; Scott HS; B, M
1956 Theo N. Metropoulos '57; Aliquippa PA; Aliquippa HS; B
1957 Thomas B. Hooper '58; Needham MA; Needham HS; B
1958 Robert T. Shaunessy '59; N. Attleboro MA; N. Attleboro HS; B
1959 Harold J. Keohane '60; Arlington MA; Worcester; PS
1960 Terry F. Lenzner '61; New York City; Exeter; L

1961 Alex "Pete" Hart '62; Lancaster OH; Lancaster HS; B
1962 Richard C. Diehl '63; Pittsburgh; Choate; NI
1963 William Southmayd '64; Newton MA; Newton HS; Med, P
1964 John F. O'Brien '65; Brockton MA; Brockton HS; B
1965 Kenneth L. Boyda '66; Carnegie PA; Carnegie HS
1966 Justin Hughes '67; Natick MA; Natick HS
1967 Donald J. Chiofaro '68; Belmont MA; Exeter
1968 Victor E. Gatto, Jr. '69; Needham MA; Needham HS
1969 John F. Cramer '70; Portland; Sunset HS
1970 Gary Farneti '71; Binghamton NY; Binghamton N HS

1971 David A. Ignacio '72; Natick MA; Natick HS
1972 Theodore DeMars '73; Smithfield RI; Classical HS
1973 David P. St. Pierre '74; Salem MA; St. John's Preparatory
1974 Brian P. Hehir '75; E. Northport NY; Holy Family HS
1975 Danny M. Jiggetts '76; Quoque NY; W. Hampton Beach HS
1976 William D. Emper '77; Wallingford PA; Nether Providence HS
1977 Steven J. Kaseta '78; Framingham MA; Andover
1978 Steven C. Potysman '79; Northbrook IL; Glenbrook N HS
1979 Michael G. Brown '80; Danvers MA; St. John's Preparatory
1980 Charles F. Durst '81; Adrian MI; Adrian HS

1981 Peter M. Coppinger; Billerica MA; Billerica HS
1982 Gregory Brown; Santa Ana CA; Santa Ana HS
1983 Joseph Azelby; Dumont NJ; Bergen Catholic HS

*In 1874 Harvard had two football seasons: a spring season (two games with McGill) and a fall season (one game with McGill in October and a game with Tufts the following June [1875]). Hence two teams and two captains.
†After the second game of the season Lowenstein was called up for service in Korea and Wylie was elected to replace him.

YALE CAPTAINS

1872 D. S. Schaff '73; New York City; Andover; minister, E
1873 W. S. Halstead; New York City; Andover; Med
1874 H. J. McBirney; Cincinnati; Hopkins; B
1875 William Arnold '76; Brooklyn; Brooklyn Polytechnic; L
1876 Eugene V. Baker '77; Wilbraham MA; Wilbraham Academy; B
1877 Eugene V. Baker '77
1878 Walter Camp '79; New Haven; Hopkins; B, C
1879 Walter Camp '79
1880 Robert W. Watson '81; Harrisburg PA; Brooks Mill; engineer

1881 Franklin M. Eaton '82; New Brunswick, Canada; Andover; Med
1882 Ray Tompkins '84; Elmira NY; Williston; B
1883 Ray Tompkins '84
1884 Eugene L. Richards '85; New Haven; Hopkins; L
1885 Frank G. Peters '86; Syracuse; Exeter; L
1886 Robert N. Corwin; Baiting Hollow L.I.; Norwich Free Academy; E
1887 Henry W. Beecher; Yonkers NY; Private tutoring; B
1888 William H. Corbin; Union CT; Hartford HS; E, B
1889 Charles O. Gill; Orange NJ; Orange HS; minister
1890 William C. Rhodes '91; Cleveland; Exeter; B

1891 Thomas L. McClung; Knoxville; Exeter; B, PS
1892 Vance C. McCormick '93; Harrisburg; Andover; J, PS
1893 Frank A. Hinkey '95; Tonawanda NY; Andover; B, C
1894 Frank A. Hinkey '95
1895 S. B. Thorne '96; New York City; Berkely School NYC; engineer, B
1896 Fred T. Murphy; Detroit; Andover; Med, M

1897 James O. Rodgers; Toledo; Andover; B, C
1898 Burr C. Chamberlin '97; Pittsfield MA; Andover; B, C
1899 Malcolm McBride '00; Cleveland; University School; B
1900 F. Gordon Brown, Jr. '01; New York City; Groton; B

1901 Charles Gould '02; Albany; Albany Academy; B
1902 G. B. Chadwick '03; Brooklyn; Brooklyn Latin; B, E
1903 Charles D. Rafferty '04; Pittsburgh; Andover; B
1904 James J. Hogan '05; Torrington CT; Exeter; L
1905 Thomas L. Shevlin '06; Minneapolis; Hill School; B
1906 Samuel F. B. Morse; Newtonville MA; Andover; B
1907 Lucius H. Biglow; Brooklyn; Mr. Leal's School for Boys; L, Med
1908 Robert B. Burch; Cincinnati; Exeter; L, M
1909 Edward H. Coy '10; Andover MA; Hotchkiss, B, M
1910 Frederick J. Daly '11; Cambridge; NI; E, C, M

1911 Arthur Howe '12; South Orange NJ; Hotchkiss; minister, E (college president)
1912 Jesse Spalding '13; Chicago; Hill School; B, M
1913 Henry H. Ketcham '14; New York City; Hotchkiss; B
1914 Nelson S. Talbot '15; Dayton OH; Hotchkiss; B, M
1915 Alexander Wilson; Binghamton NY; Exeter; B, M
1916 Clinton R. Black, Jr. '17; New York City; Exeter; B, M
1917 No team
1918 No team
1919 John T. Callahan '18; Lawrence MA; Andover; L, M
1920 John T. Callahan '18

1921 Malcolm P. Aldrich; Fall River MA; Durfee HS; B, M
1922 Ralph E. Jordan '23; Bangor; Exeter; B, M
1923 William N. Mallory '24; Memphis; Pomfret; B, M
1924 Winslow M. Lovejoy '25; Montclair NJ; Exeter; L
1925 John H. Joss '26; Indianapolis; Taft; L, PS
1926 Philip W. Bunnell '27; Scranton; Central HS; B, M
1927 William A. Webster '28; Shelton CT; Hotchkiss; B
1928 Maxon H. Eddy '29; Middlebury VT; Exeter; Med, M
1929 Waldo W. Greene '30; Huntington PA; Lawrenceville; B, M
1930 Francis T. Vincent '31; Torrington CT; Hotchkiss; B

1931 Albert J. Booth; New Haven; Hillhouse HS/Milford Academy; B, C
1932 John S. Wilbur '33; Cleveland; Loomis; B, M
1933 Robert Lassiter, Jr. '34; Charlotte NC; Woodbury Forest School; L, PS
1934 Francis C. Curtin '35; North Abington MA; Exeter; E

1935 Mather K. Whitehead '36; Westfield NY; Andover; B, M

1936 Lawrence M. Kelley '37; Williamsport PA; Peddie; E, B, C

1937 Clinton E. Frank '38; Evanston IL; Lawrenceville; B, M

1938 William V. Platt '39; Rye NY; Andover; B

1939 J. William Stack, Jr. '40; E. Lansing MI; E. Lansing HS; B, M

1940 Harold B. Whiteman, Jr. '41; Nashville; Taft; E (college president), M

1941 Alan E. Bartholemy '42; Portland; Jefferson HS; B, M

1942 Spencer D. Mosely '43; Highland Park IL; Oak Park HS; B, C, P, M

1943 Townsend W. Hoopes '44; Derby NY; Andover; PS

1944 Macauley Whiting '45; Detroit; Mountain Valley School; B, M

1945 Paul F. Walker '46; Oak Park IL; Oak Park HS; B, C, P, M

1946 Richard M. Hollingshead III '47; River NJ; Lawrenceville; B, M

1947 Endicott Davison '45; Locust Valley NY; Groton; L, M

1948 William E. Conway '49; Cleveland; University School; B, C

1949 Levi A. Jackson '50; New Haven; Hillhouse HS; B, M

1950 Bradford H. Quackenbush '51; Aurora IL: W. Aurora HS; B

1951 Robert S. Spears '52; Minneapolis; Staunton Military Academy; B

1952 Joseph B. Mitinger '53; Greensburg PA; Kiskiminetas; L, M

1953 S. Joseph Fortunato '54; Montclair NJ; Montclair HS; L

1954 Thorne Shugart '55; Los Angeles; Hamilton HS; B, M

1955 Philip S. Tarasovic '56; Bridgeport CT; Warren Harding HS; B, M

1956 John P. Owseichik '57; Greenfield MA; Greenfield HS; B

1957 John F. Embersits '58; Pittsburgh; North Catholic HS; B

1958 Paul A. Lynch '59; Brookline MA; Brookline HS; L

1959 Richard A. Winkler '60; LaGrange Park IL; Hinsdale HS; L

1960 Michael Pyle '61; Winnetka IL; New Trier HS; P

1961 Paul Bursiek '62; Des Plaines IL; Maine Township HS

1962 Henry Higdon '63; Greenwich CT; Andover

1963 George Humphrey '64; Chagrin Falls OH; Hotchkiss

1964 H. Abbot Lawrence '65; N. Caldwell NJ; Naperville HS

1965 F. David Laidley '65; Glenville IL; Glenville HS

1966 Robert Greenlee '67; Daytona Beach FL; Asheville School

1967 Rodney Watson '68; Bangor; Bangor HS

1968 Brian Dowling '69; Cleveland Hts. OH; St. Ignatius HS

1969 Andy Coe '70; Wilmette IL; New Trier HS

1970 Tom Neville '71; Shaker Hts. OH; University HS

1971 Richard Maher '72; Akron; Hoban HS

1972 Robert Perschel '73; Milford CT; Jonathan Law HS

1973 Gary Wilhelm '74; Ithaca; Ithaca HS

1974 Rudolph Green '75; Fort Worth; St. Stephen's HS

1975 John Smoot '76; Dorchester MA; Boston College HS

1976 Victor Staffieri '77; Lynbrook NY; Malverne HS

1977 Robert Rizzo '78; Livingston NJ; Livingston HS

1978 William Crowley '79; New Kensington PA; Livingston HS

1979 Tim Tumpane '80; Midlothian IL; Mt. Carmel HS

1980 John Nitti '81; Westbury NY; Westbury HS

1981 Frederick Leone '82; E. Northport NY; John Glenn HS

1982 Patrick Ruwe '83; Decatur IL; Eisenhower HS

1983 Thomas Giella; East Meadow NY; Chaminade HS

Contemplation of these roll calls of honor invites comparison and arouses the statistical urge. Yielding to temptation, one is bound to remark on some differences. For example, of the 102 Harvard captains, 62 (60 percent) hail from Massachusetts, with New York a very poor second (10), while the Yale count is much more evenly distributed: New York leads with 26 names (25 percent) but with Connecticut and Illinois (11 each) making a respectable showing. Nor can one fail to note that captains from the Middle West loom large, with 26 representatives (the same as New York). However, in numbers of high school graduates as against prep school boys the count is strikingly similar: 34 for Harvard and 35 for Yale.*

These figures become more interesting if we divide our listings into three chronological layers. The first, from 1875 through 1916, which we may call the Ancien Régime, has a social-cultural personality distinct from the time span between 1919 and 1942, which in its turn is of a texture quite different from that of the years following World War II. We may call the first of these two latter eras the Middle Years and the sec-

*I classify Boston Latin and Roxbury Latin as high schools, although they were not publicly supported until early in our century.

ond the Nuclear Age. All historians of culture would readily recognize that each of these strata has its own color. In the Ancien Régime the domination of Massachusetts in the Crimson roll call is impressive. The Bay State has 31 out of the 38 captaincies (80 percent). The second age sees a notable shrinkage to a mere 50 percent. One would expect the trend to continue but in fact the third period shows a resurgence to 60 percent.

For Yale the changes are not quite so spectacular but they too have a story to tell. In Age I New York has 14 out of 38 captaincies, very close to 40 percent; perhaps it should be noted that the runner-up is Ohio, with 6. In Age II the New York figure has shrunk to 2, lower than Massachusetts and Connecticut (3 each); 14 states are represented in the captaincies. But the figures for Age III are even more arresting: primacy has now gone to Illinois with 9 captaincies to New York's 7. And from the Middle West come no fewer than 15 out of the total of 41 (better than 36 percent).

In the social sector, chronology is also illuminating. At Harvard in Age I, 9 out of 38 captains are high school graduates, while at Yale the figure is 2 out of 38. Before giving Harvard credit for precocious democracy we must remember that in the environs of Cambridge some excellent high schools could be found, notably Boston Latin,* which supplied the Crimson with 4 leaders; Yale had only Hillhouse. And generally speaking high school boys did not travel far in those days. In our second era Yale has 5 high school captains against Harvard's 3, and a real social revolution is revealed by the figures for the third period, with high school recruits taking charge to the tune of 60 percent for both schools.

Captains, of course, compose only a small minority of the Blue and Crimson soldiery. Ideally a study should be made of the complete muster. For Yale, in fact, A. B. Crawford in three successive monographs has documented every Yale player from 1872 to 1960. I know of no comparable study on the Harvard side and I have not had the facilities to undertake such a task. But we can take some useful specimens. Let us choose a decade from each of our three strata, with some confidence that even such a limited harvesting may be fruitful. For the Ancien Régime let us look at the classes of 1891 through 1900; this is the high tide of nineteenth-century football. For these years I have the dossiers of 61 Harvard players and 95 wearers of the Blue.† The disparity in numbers is not the result of faulty research; all records show that in the early years

Yale squads were regularly larger than Harvard's. (As we noted in our narrative, football was simply more popular at Yale than it was by the banks of the Charles; many good Harvard athletes preferred to save their efforts for crew.)‡ In this period high school boys make up 15 percent of Harvard teams and 11 percent of Yale's task forces. Following the figures for the captaincies, 62 percent of Harvard's players are from Massachusetts. For Yale, New York leads in contributions with 28 percent followed by Connecticut with 16 percent. And already the Middle West looms large in the Bulldog roster, contributing 22 percent of the troops. Yale has a wider range of states, too, with seventeen represented plus one man from Nova Scotia. Harvard's range runs only to ten states but her register also includes one Canadian and two Englishmen.

For Age II let us scrutinize the third decade of our century, canvassing the classes from 1921 through 1930. Squads are growing larger and the numbers approach parity; the count runs to a Harvard total of 133 players and a Yale total of 138. Again high school boys do better at Harvard (28 percent) than at Yale (14 percent). The Bay State still predominates in Crimson lineups (50 percent), followed by New York with 13 percent. An interesting novelty is that 5 of Harvard's players in this time span are from California. Twenty-one states are represented in the Crimson roll call as well as 2 Canadians and one Alaskan. For Yale the three major contributors are fairly evenly matched, with 18 each (14 percent) from New York and Connecticut and 15 from New Jersey. The Middle West, though still strong, has dropped a little (16 percent).

Finally, for the atomic age I have chosen the sixth decade (classes from 1951 to 1960). Once more Yale's numbers are higher (Harvard went through a few discouraging years in the fifties): I count 193 Yale names as against 166 for Harvard. (Both are higher than the figures for the twenties; in part because the rules permitted freer substitution). High school quotas are notably higher: 50 percent for Harvard and 54 percent for Yale. Massachusetts with 76 is still the *patrie* of the majority of Harvard players but the percentage has slipped to

---

†Data on the Harvard side were compiled by Melville Smith of Cambridge.

‡My census takes account only of undergraduates. However, in these years the Harvard roster included 7 Law School students and 2 from the Medical School. Yale had a contribution of 3 from the Graduate School and 2 each from the Law School and the Medical School.

40 percent. New York and Pennsylvania are runners-up with 14 each, but a significant figure is the rise in the Middle West contribution: 35 warriors (21 percent). New York's 30 (15 percent) is the largest contribution of any one state to the Blue cause; the Middle West provides an astonishing 50 recruits (25 percent). Twenty-two states are represented in the Harvard total; 28 (plus England) in Yale's. Both teams have widened their bases over the years, but the core of a Harvard squad remains Massachusetts; Yale has no one state of dominance. But it has consistently drawn healthy percentages from New York and collectively the Middle West.

In the category of careers I shall include the captains of each decade of my census. Of course for all three decades and for both schools the largest category will be my catchall of "business". This is, incidentally, true for the classes as a whole, not merely the football segment. The contributions to the professions, however, are not insignificant. In the years 1891 through 1900 Harvard's football corps turned out 13 lawyers, 2 doctors, and 1 public servant; 2 went into education, 1 became an engineer, 2 were architects, and 1 became not only a successful financier but also a notable coach (Percy Haughton). The Blue harvest yields law 17, medicine 7, public service 3, engineering 4, education 1 (George Cutten, president of Colgate, who was concurrently an ordained minister), and 1 writer of some repute, Ralph Paine, '94. For both Yale and Harvard the business percentage is 60 percent.

For the twenties, although the business category for both school runs to well over 60 percent, yet the numbers entering the professions are substantial. Fifteen Harvard players went into education, 7 into law, and 4 into medicine. The Crimson count also shows 3 engineers, 2 ministers, and 3 scientists as well as Captain Kane of '22, who served the Federal government. For Yale the figures are law 12, medicine 13, education 6. The Blue roll call also includes 1 architect, 1 professional singer, and 1 Catholic priest.

The yield for the sixth decade is as follows: for Harvard, law 11, medicine 23, education 7, public service 5 (including two senators, Culver of Iowa and Kennedy of Massachusetts), and 1 architect. For Yale the census runs law 31, medicine 11, education 13, public service 5; 2 scientists, 1 architect, and 1 who entered the Marine Corps. The grand total of 786 records of both Blue and Crimson players thus includes 93 in law, 60 in medicine, and 59 in education and public service combined. It is a record to be proud of.

Crawford's survey also includes the undergraduate achievements or distinctions of his Y men. Football players are inevitably prominent campus figures, and it is not surprising that most of them win election to College councils or fraternities or societies. As to their academic performance, the compilation of detailed documentation in that sector daunts even Crawford; he reports, however, that "football players regularly have a somewhat less than average total class representation at the *highest* academic levels . . . but likewise many fewer men at the lower (unsatisfactory) levels." And he notes that less than 3 percent have failed to graduate. One may suspect that the same statement would hold true for Harvard players, at least with regard to dropouts: of all the Crimson players I have cited in my narrative only a handful failed to complete their course. The popular notion that football players are not as bright as their classmates simply does not hold true for Harvard and Yale.

DIRECTORS OF ATHLETICS*

Harvard

1926–1951	William J. Bingham
1951–1962	Thomas D. Bolles
1962–1970	Adolph Samborski
1970–1977	Robert B. Watson
1977–	John P. Reardon

Yale

1940	Clarence W. Mendell
1941–1946	Ogden Dayton Miller
1946–1950	Robert Kiphuth
1950–1953	Robert A. Hall
1953–1954	Clarence W. Mendell
1954–1976	DeLaney Kiphuth
1976–1977	Carmen Cozza (Acting)
1977–	Frank Ryan

COACHES†

Harvard

1874–1880 Team captains served as coaches
1881 Lucius N. Littauer
1882–1884 Team captains served as coaches
1885 Harvard did not field a team
1886 Frank A. Mason
1887–1889 Team captains served as coaches
1890–1892 Co-coaches: George A. Stewart and George C. Adams
1893 George A. Stewart and Everett G. Lake
1894 William A. Brooks
1895 Robert W. Emmons
1896 Bertram G. Waters
1897–1898 W. Cameron Forbes
1899–1900 Benjamin H. Dibblee
1901 William T. Reid
1902 John W. Farley
1903 John S. Cranston
1904 Edgar N. Wrightington
1905–1906 William T. Reid
1907 Joshua Crane
1908–1916 Percy Haughton (first professional coach). Assistants: C. Bagden, D. Campbell, C. Daly, E. Graves, F. Nesmith, H. von Kersburg
1919–1925 Robert Fisher. Assistants: C. Coolidge, H. Dadmun, H. Gardner, H. Hardwick, D. Parmenter, W. Snow, D. Watson, P. Wendell, R. Wigglesworth, P. Withington
1926–1930 Arnold Horween. Assistants: J. Brader, E. Casey, C. Carney, E. Clark, R. Horween
1931–1934 Edward Casey. Assistants: W. Fesler, M. Lane, A. Walsh
1935–1942; 1945–1947 Richard Harlow (first non-Harvard coach). Assistants: R. Crowther, 1935–42; J. Dunn, 1935–42; W. Fesler, 1935–42; H. Jacunski, 1946–47; H. Kopp, 1946–47; H. Lamar, 1945; H. Margarita, 1946–47; A. McCoy, 1945; M. Palm, 1935–42; F. Stahl, 1945
1948–1949 Arthur Valpey. Assistants: F. Jordan, H. Lamar, E. Maden, B. McCabe, S. Sebo
1950–1956 Lloyd Jordan. Assistants: H. Lamar, J. Maras, T. Schmitt, N. Shepard, J. Williams, all 1950–56; B. Margarita, 1951–56
1957–1970 John Yovicsin. Assistants: A. Bell, 1958–59; E. Dickie, 1969–70; F. Fazio, 1968; J. Feula, 1961–70; R. Gongola, 1962–64; R. Jelic, 1968–70;

---

*Before the creation of directorships in both institutions supervision of athletics was in the hands of a faculty committee, with alumni playing a prominent role in policy making.
†I am indebted to the Sports Information Offices of Harvard and Yale for supplying data on coaches.

H. Lamar, 1957–58, 1967–68; R. Lasse, 1969–70; J. Lentz, 1957–67; P. McKee, 1960–63; T. Modrach, 1970; S. Novick, 1964–67; C. O'Neill, 1970; L. Park, 1965–69; R. Pickett, 1958; R. Robinson, 1957–62; T. Schmitt, 1957–60; N. Shepard, 1958, 1965–67; P. Stark, 1963–68, T. Stephenson, 1967–70; B. Yates, 1968–70

1971– Joseph Restic. Assistants: A. Bruno, 1971–81; G. Clemens, 1976–83; R. Corbin, 1979–83; L. Fanning, 1982–83; L. Glueck, 1973–83; R. Goldston, 1971; R. Horan, 1971–78; G. Karras, 1971–78; J. Kubacki, 1981–83; R. McCarthy, 1979–83; A. Nahijian, 1972–81; C. O'Neill, 1971–78; L. Park, 1976; C. Schuette, 1971–75; M. Singleton, 1978–83; W. White, 1982–83

Yale

1872–1887 Team captains served as coaches

1888 Walter Camp. Mrs. Walter Camp served as co-coach.

1889–1892 Walter Camp. In 1892 William T. Bull served as assistant.

1893–1894 William C. Rhodes. In 1893 Frederick W. Wallace and Wyllys Terry served as assistants.

1895 John A. Hartwell. Assistant: Laurence T. Bliss

1896 Samuel B. Thorne

1897–1898 Frank S. Butterworth

1899 James O. Rodgers

1900 Malcolm L. McBride

1901 George S. Stillman

1902 No head coach. J. R. Swan served as line coach and Walter Camp as advisor.

1903 George B. Chadwick

1904 Charles D. Rafferty. Assistant: W. Ledyard Mitchell

1905 John E. Owsley. Assistant: Foster

H. Rockwell. Walter Camp served as advisor.

1906 Foster H. Rockwell. Assistant: Lydig Hoyt. Advisor: Walter Camp

1907 William F. Knox. Assistant: Carl S. Flanders

1908 L. Horatio Biglow 2d. Assistant: T. A. D. Jones. Advisory Coach: Walter Camp

1909 Howard H. Jones. Assistant: Henry M. Wheaton

1910 Edward H. Coy. Assistant: Henry G. Holt

1911 John W. Field. Assistant: Effingham B. Morris

1912 Arthur Howe. Assistants: Elmer W. McDevitt, James W. Scully

1913 Howard H. Jones (Yale's first paid coach). Assistant: Henry M. Wheaton

1914–1915 Frank A. Hinkey. Assistants: P. G. Cornish, 1914–15; Henry A. Marting, 1914; Maurice R. Brann, 1915. For the last two weeks of the 1915 season Thomas Shevlin directed the team.

1916 T. A. D. Jones. Assistants: Clarence F. Alcott, Dr. William T. Bull, Dr. Arthur E. Brides

1917 Informal season. Dr. Arthur E. Brides and Johnny Mack, trainer, were in charge.

1918 No games played.

1919 Dr. Albert H. Sharpe. Assistants: Dr. Arthur E. Brides, Dr. William T. Bull, John M. Cates, Herman P. Olcott

1920–1927 T. A. D. Jones. Assistants: M. Aldrich, 1922; D. Allen, 1926; G. Becket, 1923–25; E. Blair, 1925–26; A. Brides, 1920; W. Bull, 1920–23; P. Bunnell, 1927; B. Chamberlin, 1923–24; C. Comerford, 1921–27; J. Cutler, 1924–25; T. Dickens, 1921; R. Dilworth, 1924–25; C. Esselstyn, 1924–25; J. Field, 1920; M. Fuller, 1922–27; S. Gill, 1926; N. Guernsey, 1923;

G. Hutchinson, 1920; E. Jacques, 1921; R. Jordan, 1923; C. LaRoche, 1920; W. Lovejoy, 1925–27; W. Mallory, 1924; C. Milst; C. Milstead, 1924; G. Moseley, 1920; S. Osborne, 1926; C. Osbourn, 1922–27; J. Owsley, 1923–24; R. Pond, 1925; Maj. W. Pritchard, 1927; D. Saunders, 1922; M. Stevens, 1925–27; C. Taft, 1921; H. Vaughan, 1920

1928–1932 Marvin A. Stevens. Assistants: E. Blair, 1928; A. Booth, 1932; C. Comerford, 1928–32; J. Diller, 1928; B. Friedman, 1931; J. Godman, 1930–31; W. Greene, 1930–31; R. Hall, 1931; W. Lovejoy, 1928; C. Milstead, 1929–30; L. Noble, 1929; C. Osbourn, 1928–32; R. Pond, 1929–32; Maj. M. Pritchard, 1928; R. Root, 1931; S. Scott, 1928, 1931; F. Vincent, 1931; A. Walsh, 1929–32; W. Webster, 1928–29

1933 Reginald Root. Assistants: H. Barres, A. Booth, C. Comerford, D. Ferris, P. O'Connor, A. Palmer, R. Pond, S. Scott, M. Stevens, P. Sullivan, A. Walsh

1934–1940 Raymond W. Pond. Assistants: T. Avery, 1935–36; D. Colwell, 1940; J. DeAngelis, 1936, 1938–40; G. Ford, 1937–40; M. Franklin, 1939–40; A. Hessberg, 1939–40; R. Humaston, 1938; W. Levering, 1936–37; F. Loeser, 1934; C. Milstead, 1934; R. Mulligan, 1938; D. Myers, 1934, 1935–37; A. Neale, 1934–40; W. Neale, 1934–36, 1938–40; E. Nelson, 1939–40; B. Rankin, 1939; W. Renner, 1936–40; R. Root, 1934–40; S. Scott, 1934; M. Wells, 1936–38; I. Williamson, 1934–40

1941 Emerson W. Nelson (first non-Yale head coach). Assistants: D. Colwell, G. Ford, M. Franklin, E. Howell, W. Renner, R. Root, J. Sabo, W. Voights, I. Williamson

1942–1947 Howard Odell. Assistants: A. Booth, 1945–47; C. Caldwell, 1943; S. Clancy, 1946–47; D. Colwell, 1942; F. Coyle, 1943; J. DeAngelis, 1946–47; R. Farabaugh, 1944; J. Ferguson, 1947; M. Franklin, 1947; J. Glassford, 1942; E. Hirschberg, 1942; D. Hoopes, 1946; D. Kiphuth, 1946–47; C. Miller, 1945; P. Moonves, 1944–47; R. Odell, 1946–47; R. Root, 1942–47; A. Seccombe, 1942; T. Smith, 1946–47; J. Timm, 1942–44; B. Walker, 1946; P. Walker, 1946; I. Williamson, 1946; E. Zeigler, 1945–47

1948–1951 Herman Hickman. Assistants: F. Barzilauskas, 1950; S. Clancy, 1948–51; W. Conway, 1949; J. Dunn, 1949–51; J. Ferguson, 1948–49; M. Franklin, 1948; D. Greenwood, 1949; J. Holgate, 1949–51; H. Jacunski, 1948–51; N. Katys, 1949–51; A. Kelley, 1950; H. Kopp, 1948–49; H. LaBonte, 1951; S. Lenzi, 1949–51; H. Margarita, 1948; W. Posey, 1950; J. Prendergast, 1948; J. Robertson, 1950; W. Simon, 1949, 1951; D. C. Walker, 1951; E. Zeigler, 1948

1952–1962 Jordan Olivar. Assistants: F. Barzilauskas, 1954–62; A. Bertelli, 1952–53; E. Bryant, 1954–56; T. Carta, 1953, 1955–62; S. Clancy, 1952–62; W. Dudley, 1952; V. Frank, 1952; O. Henkel, 1962; J. Holgate, 1952–62; H. Jacunski, 1952–62; J. Lyon, 1954–55; J. Neri, 1952–62; J. Prendergast, 1952–62; A. Puryear, 1959; A. Raimo, 1954–62; R. Raines, 1952; W. Shanahan, 1952; W. Simon, 1952–62; R. Stoviak, 1958–62; G. VanGaleder, 1959–62; A. Young, 1953; J. Younger, 1961–62

1963–64 John Pont. Assistants: C. F. Barzilauskas, 1963–64; T. Carta, 1963–1964; C. Cozza, 1963–64; H. Fairfield, 1963–64; J. Fry, 1963–64; J. Holgate, 1963–64; W. Irons, 1964; H. Jacunski, 1963–64; E. Plank, 1963–64; J. Van Schoyck, 1963–64

1965– Carmen Cozza. Assistants: B. Amendola, 1965–81; P. Amodio 1968–74; F. Barzilauskas, 1971–74; James Benanto, 1980–83; Joseph Benanto, 1981–83; R. Blanchard, 1965; S. Burrell, 1972–83; R. Caivano, 1967; L. Calhoun, 1970–71; A. Capraro, 1968; T. Carta, 1965–68; 1980; T. Chase, 1978; W. Crowley, 1983; V. DeVito, 1973–74, 1977–82; G. Dubinetz, 1977; R. Feryok, 1976; A. Fitzgerald, 1973; M. E. Franklin, 1970; J. Galat, 1970–71; J. R. Gallagher, 1971–72; C. Getman, 1970; R. Green, 1976; D. Herbert, 1968; D. Holahan, 1972; W. Irons, 1965–68; H. Jacunski, 1967–83; J. Kaplan, 1971–72; D. Kelley, 1972–83; R. Krause, 1982–83; S. LaSpina, 1965–83; P. Lata, 1982; W. Mallory, 1965; D. Martin, 1981–83; J. Massey, 1971; B. McDermott, 1981; L. McElreavy, 1975–80; R. McHenry, 1973–74, 1979; D. Melina, 1978, 1983; W. Narduzzi, 1966–71; D. Nelson, 1958; J. Pagliaro, 1981; F. Payne, 1970; T. Piccolo, 1982–83; A. Pinkston, 1983; R. Pont, 1968–83; N. Putnam, 1965–70; R. Riggio, 1974–79; R. Rizzo, 1978–79; J. Roberti, 1975; A. Roberts, 1970; J. Rogan, 1983; J. Root, 1965–67; W. Samko, 1982–83; W. Simon, 1974–80; C. Sizemore, 1972; W. Story, 1975–77, 1981–83; M. Waldvogel, 1980–83; T. Weigel, 1967–68; R. Wickerham, 1972–74; R. Wiedl, 1980; R. Williams, 1965; M. Yoho, 1966–67

Total Games Played 100

Games Won	Yale 54	Harvard 38	Tied 8
Total Points Scored	Yale 1,192	Harvard 980	
Average Points Per Game	Yale 11.92	Harvard 9.8	
Shutouts For	Yale 28	Harvard 18	
Shutout Ties	Yale 6	Harvard 6	
Team Scoring First Has Won	Yale 45	Harvard 34	

Outstanding Harvard Football Performances vs. Yale

Most Touchdowns	Eddie Mahan	4	1915
Longest Scoring Run	Ted DeMars	86 yards	1972
Longest Scoring Pass	Chet Boulris to Hank Koehane	85 yards	1959
Longest Punt	Percy Haughton	86 yards	1897
Longest Field Goal	Ralph Horween	42 yards	1919
	Jim Villanueva	42 yards	1982
Longest Score on Pass Interception	Russ Savage	74 yards	1976
Longest Score on Punt Return	Fran Lee	78 yards	1940
Longest Score on Blocked Kick	Jack Neal	0 yards*	1971
Longest Score on Kickoff Return	Fergie Locke	90 yards	1933
Best Rushing Performance	Ted DeMars	153 yards (16 attempts)	1972
Best Passing Performance	Larry Brown	301 yards (19 of 27 attempts)	1978
Best Total Offense Performance	Larry Brown	306 yards (5 rush/301 pass)	1978
Most Forward Passes Caught	Carter Lord	9 (188 yards)	1967
Team First Downs		23	1982
Team Rushing		286 yards	1982
Team Passing		301 yards	1978
Team Total Offense		457 yards	1982
Team Points		(Harvard 45−7)	1982

*Scored on blocked kick in Yale end zone.

Most Points, One Team, One Game

1.	45	Harvard (45−7)	1982
2.	41	Harvard (41−0)	1915
3.	36	Harvard (36−0)	1914
4.	35	Harvard (35−6)	1959
	35	Harvard (35−16)	1971
5.	29	Harvard (29−29)	1968
1.	54	Yale (54−0)	1957
2.	52	Yale (52−0)	1884
3.	42	Yale (42−14)	1956
4.	41	Yale (41−14)	1952
5.	39	Yale (39−6)	1960

Most Points, Both Teams, One Game

1.	63	Yale	35	Harvard	28	1978
2.	58	Harvard	29	Yale	29	1968
3.	56	Yale	42	Harvard	14	1956
4.	55	Yale	41	Harvard	14	1952
5.	54	Yale	54	Harvard	0	1957
6.	52	Harvard	45	Yale	7	1982

Most Consecutive Victories Each Team

Harvard		PF−PA
4	1912−1915	112− 5
4	1919−1922	39− 9
3	1928−1930	40− 6
3	1964−1966	48−14

Yale		PF−PA
8	1880−1889	129−14
6	1902−1907	75− 0
4	1891−1894	34− 4
4	1942−1947	93−38

Outstanding Yale Football Performances vs. Harvard

Most Touchdowns	Alex Coxe	3	1884
	Thomas Bayne	3	1884
	Art Fitzgerald	3	1945
	Robert Furse	3	1947
	Ed Woodsum	3	1952
	Herb Hallas	3	1957
Longest Scoring Run	Henry Flanders	100 yards	1884
Longest Scoring Pass	John Spagnola to	77 yards	1978
	Bob Krystyniak		
Longest Punt	Herb Pruett	54 yards	1951
Longest Field Goal	Jim Braden	52 yards	1919
Longest Score on Pass Interception	John Hutcherson	50 yards	1960
Longest Score on Punt Return	William Finche	65 yards	1900
Longest Score on Blocked Kick	None		
Longest Score on Kickoff Return	Robert Watson	100 yards	1880
Best Rushing Performance	Dick Jauron	183 yards	1972
		(28 attempts)	
Best Passing Performance	Tom Doyle	237 yards	1974
		(16 of 25 attempts)	
Best Total Offense Performance	Tom Doyle	268 yards	1974
		(31 rush/237 pass)	
Most Forward Passes Caught	Gary Fencik	11 (187 yards)	1974
Team First Downs		28	1973
		28	1978
Team Rushing		395 yards	1973
Team Passing		240 yards	1957
Team Total Offense		539 yards	1978
Team Points		(Yale 54−0)	1957

I wish to express my thanks to Mr. John H. Norton of Concord, Massachusetts, who has generously permitted me to use material in his "Harvard–Yale Football Series Records, 1875–1983," which are published in his booklet *Harvard–Yale Football 1984*, Concord, Mass. I have added the items on Fumbles and Penalties. The statistics for the category Most Fumbles date from 1908. Those for Fewest Penalties date from 1907. It is notable that only one team, Harvard 1927, has a spotless record of no fumbles and no penalties.

Most Consecutive Games Without Defeat

Harvard		PF−PA
6	1910−1915 (4−0−2)	112− 5
4	1919−1922 (4−0−0)	39− 9
3	1928−1930 (3−0−0)	40− 6
3	1963−1966 (3−0−0)	48−14

Yale		PF−PA
11	1876−1889 (10−0−1)	131−14
6	1902−1907 (6−0−0)	75− 0
5	1890−1897 (4−0−1)	34− 4
5	1923−1927 (4−0−1)	58−13

Most Consecutive Game Scoring Streaks

			W−L−T	PF−PA
17	Yale	1967−83	9−7−1	317−271
11	Yale	1882−94	10−1−0	167− 30
11	Harvard	1946−56	3−7−1	149−242
11	Harvard	1958−68	7−3−1	213−138

Fumbles: Fewest

Harvard	0	1927, 1929, 1930, 1933, 1959, 1963
Yale	0	1909, 1922, 1929, 1939, 1941, 1942, 1952, 1981

Fumbles: Most

Harvard	8	1909, 1923
Yale	11	1912

Fumbles: Most Lost

Harvard	5	1923
Yale	6	1968

Penalties: Fewest

Harvard	0	1926, 1927, 1954
Yale	0	1919, 1938, 1965, 1966, 1971, 1975

Penalties: Most

Harvard	12	(for 130 yards)	1908
Yale	10	(for 89 yards)	1978

Chapter 1. Incunabula, 1875–1885

1. Samuel Eliot Morison, *Three Centuries of Harvard: 1636–1936*, p. 323.

2. Allison Danzig, *The History of American Football*, p. 10.

3. Edward Byrne, "The Yale–Harvard Series," p. 48, comments: "The admission price was fifty cents to insure the cost of entertaining the Harvard team and giving them $70.00 previously agreed upon as expenses." Fifty cents was not cheap in an era when the cost of tuition at Yale was $50.00 a term.

4. From the account in the *Crimson*, quoted in Morris A. Bealle, *The History of Football at Harvard, 1874–1948*, p. 27.

5. *New Haven Register*, November 15, 1875.

6. Bealle, *Football at Harvard*, p. 28.

7. *New Haven Register*, November 15, 1875.

8. *Harvard Advocate*, November 24, 1876.

9. Bealle, *Football at Harvard*, pp. 30–31.

10. *Field and Stream*, November 23, 1876.

11. Parke H. Davis, *Football, The American Intercollegiate Game*, p. 253.

12. Quotes from the *Advocate* are from Bealle, *Football at Harvard*, p. 37.

13. Ibid., p. 40.

14. Ibid., p. 42.

15. *New York Times*, November 13, 1881.

16. *Advocate* quotations from Bealle, *Football at Harvard*, p. 46.

17. Ibid.

18. Ibid., p. 49.

19. Ibid., p. 52.

20. Ibid., p. 53.

21. L. H. Baker, *Notebook, 1825–1902*, p. 174.

22. Bealle, *Football at Harvard*, p. 57.

23. *Touchdown! As told by Amos Alonzo Stagg to Wesley Winans Stout*, p. 84. Although he quotes the effusion of the *Yale Daily News*, Stagg was not much impressed by the new field; he writes, "Many a high school would blush today for that field. It looked like a village ball park. There was no covered grandstand, but the bleachers seated perhaps 600. Most of us preferred to stand on the sidelines."

24. Bealle, *Football at Harvard*, pp. 58–60.

Chapter 2. The Blue Express to the Nineties, 1886–1894

1. Morison, *Three Centuries of Harvard*, pp. 362–63.

2. Bealle, *Football at Harvard*, p. 65.

3. *Touchdown!* pp. 93–94.

4. Tim Cohane, *The Yale Football Story*, p. 61.

5. The development of equipment is discussed in Danzig, *History of American Football*, pp. 88–89.

6. Harford Powel, Jr., *Walter Camp, The Father of American Football*, p. 61.

7. Bealle, *Football at Harvard*, pp. 77–78.

8. Quoted by John D. McCallum, *Ivy League Football Since 1872*, p. 29.

9. Baker, *Notebook, 1825–1902*, p. 345. Baker adds: "After he [Stickney] was ordered out of the game, he deliberately struck Rhodes on the face before leaving the field."

10. *Yale Daily News*, November 25, 1889.

11. For details on Handsome Dan I, see Cohane, *Yale Football Story*, pp. 72–73.

12. Thomas C. Thacher, "Football in the Eighties," in *The H Book of Harvard Athletics*, p. 384.

13. Bealle, *Football at Harvard*, p. 83.

14. McCallum, *Ivy League Football*, p. 43.

15. Bealle, *Football at Harvard*, p. 81.

16. Quotes from *The Globe* are from ibid.

17. Thacher, "Football in the Eighties," p. 388, on Cumnock's invention and Conant's innovation. Stagg's claim is stated on p. 109 of *Touchdown!*

18. Bealle, *Football at Harvard*, p. 87.

19. *Boston Globe*, quoted in ibid. pp. 86–87.

20. Cohane, *Yale Football Story*, p. 92. V-shaped wedges, with players dropped back from the line to form the sides of the V and the ballcarrier in the angle, had become standard practice since mass plays came into being. Deland added momentum to the V.

21. Bealle, *Football at Harvard*, p. 89.

22. Baker, *Notebook, 1825–1902*, p. 451.

23. James L. Knox, "The Transition Period: From 1891 to the World War," in *The H Book of Harvard Athletics*, p. 402.

24. Quoted by Bealle, *Football at Harvard*, p. 92.

25. *New York Times*, November 25, 1894.

26. Bealle, *Football at Harvard*, p. 101.

27. Knox, "Transition Period," p. 404.

28. *New York Times*, November 25, 1894.

29. Davis, *Football*, p. 98.

Chapter 3. A New Century, A New Game, 1895–1907

1. Morison, *Three Centuries of Harvard*, p. 384.

2. George Wilson Pierson, *Yale College, 1871–1921* (New Haven, 1952), pp. 5–9. Among other things, the philosopher reported that the Yale character "is a boyish type of character, earnest and quick

in things practical, hasty and frivolous in things intellectual. But the boyish ideal is a healthy one, and in a young man, as in a young nation, it is perfection to have only the faults of youth. . . . No wonder that all America loves Yale, where American traditions are vigorous, American instincts are unchecked and young men are trained and made eager for the keen struggles of American life."

3. Baker, *Notebook, 1825–1902*, p. 574.

4. Bealle, *Football at Harvard*, p. 117.

5. Knox, "The Transition Period," p. 410.

6. Bealle, *Football at Harvard*, p. 132.

7. Baker, *Notebook, 1825–1902*, p. 655.

8. Bealle, *Football at Harvard*, p. 136.

9. Ibid., p. 137.

10. Knox, "The Transition Period," p. 412.

11. Quoted in Brooks Mather Kelley, *Yale: A History* (New Haven, 1974), p. 320. Teddy may have been thinking of two Bulldog pigskin chasers, Reginald Ronalds, '86S, and John Greenway, '95S, who had served with his Rough Riders in Cuba.

12. Quoted by Bealle, *Football at Harvard*, p. 140.

13. Details of the Cutts affair are engagingly set forth in Cohane, *Yale Football Story*, pp. 123–25.

14. Bealle, *Football at Harvard*, p. 145.

15. Cohane, *Yale Football Story*, p. 128.

16. Davis, *Football*, pp. 108–10. Actually it took two years to carry the stripes from goal line to goal line. The rule effective in 1903 gave the quarterback license to initiate his run only between the twenty-five yard lines, so that for that year the longitudinal markings were necessary only in that zone. In 1904 the entire field was open to a running quar-

terback, though the lateral restriction remained, Hence it was in 1904 that the whole field became a checkerboard. With the abrogation of the five-yard rule in 1910 the checkerboard was no longer necessary.

17. Bealle, *Football at Harvard*, p. 150.

18. Cohane, *Yale Football Story*, p. 136.

19. *New York Times*, November 20, 1904.

20. Baker, *Notebook, 1902–1919*, pp. 812–13.

21. Harold W. Turner, "The Reason Y," unpublished memoir.

22. S. B. Sutton, *Cambridge Reconsidered* (Cambridge, Mass., 1976), p. 99.

23. J. C. Furnas, *Great Times, 1914–1929* (New York, 1974), p. 385.

24. Stagg, *Touchdown!* p. 253.

25. Bealle, *Football at Harvard*, pp. 164–65.

26. Harry von Kersburg, "Coaches and Coaching," in Bealle, *Football at Harvard*, pp. 411–13, quotes Reid on the subject.

27. Bealle, *Football at Harvard*, p. 171.

28. Knox, "The Transition Period," p. 420.

Chapter 4. With Crimson in Triumph Flashing, 1908–1922

1. Bealle, *Football at Harvard*, p. 179.

2. On the Haughton system, Lothrop Withington, captain of the Harvard 1910 team and later a member of Haughton's staff, comments:

Men who have risen to coaching heights have asked what was the "Haughton system." It is today somewhat hard to explain that in 1907 coaching was mostly a one-man job. Except for Yale, where there were many who thoroughly understood and could teach line, backfield or

end play, good coaches were few and hard to get. Haughton established the idea of a complete coaching staff—a backfield, a line and an end coach, all coordinated under the head coach, with specialists for expert instruction in kicking and passing, and a scouting system that covered each opponent.
The military precision and discipline which Haughton established in his first years, with Majors Daly and Graves as his backfield and line coaches, were never relaxed throughout his regime. Each season was regarded as a race against time, each minute of practice was carefully allotted to individual offensive and defensive instruction, followed by team evolution and then scrimmage with the jayvees or freshmen. ("Percy Haughton and Harvard's Golden Era," in Allison Danzig, Oh, How They Played the Game, p. 222)

For Haughton's own comments on his methods, see his *Football and How to Watch It* (Boston, 1922).

3. These and other details may be found in von Kersburg, "Coaches and Coaching," pp. 442–47. It has been said that Haughton "made the game a science," which may account for Morison's verdict: "Haughton was the first of the modern 'big-time coaches,' and he certainly 'delivered the goods'; but it may be questioned whether his talent for picturesque profanity made the game more enjoyable, or whether his strategical and tactical developments turned football in the right direction" (*Three Centuries of Harvard*, p. 414).

4. Von Kersburg, "Coaches and Coaching," p. 443.

5. Bealle, *Football at Harvard*, p. 184.

6. Bealle, ibid, p. 186, comments:

"For Harvard, Fish and Minot were All-America, and McKay and Fisher made it the next year. Yale had Goebel, a guard, who made it a year earlier, and Howe, a quarterback, who made it the following year, added to the six—Coy, Philbin, Hobbs, Kilpatrick, Andrus and Cooney—who were on Camp's first All-America in 1909. . . . This made a total of twelve All-America players on the two teams, which has never been approached."

7. *New Haven Register*, November 19, 1909.

8. Cohane, *Yale Football Story*, p. 177.

9. *New York Times*, November 21, 1909.

10. Baker, *Notebook 1902–1919*, p. 976.

11. Davis, *Football*, p. 116.

12. Withington, "Percy Haughton," p. 221.

13. Powel, *Walter Camp*, p. 128. Powel goes on to quote some exultant verses from the *Harvard Lampoon* a few years later, addressed to Dean Briggs, asserting that Yale supremacy is dead and buried and joyously concluding:

Gabriel's Trump could not awake her,
    she will never reappear
Undefeated as we knew her, when she
    held her title clear
To the great blue-bosomed triumph
    stretching on from year to year.

In those years of Yale's abundance ere
    she loosed her iron clamp,
Who prepared her gaudy conquests, who
    around the evening lamp
Coached the coaches at New Haven? We
    remember Walter Camp—

Cool, resourceful, cunning, patient. Dimly
    might we then discern
Any hope to break the shackles; still you
    bade us live and learn

Never doubting right would triumph, or
    the longest worm would turn.

After thirty years of glory, full of honor
    and renown,
Camp went back to making clockworks
    and the star of Yale went down!
Princeton beat her soft elevens, so did
    Colgate, so did Brown.

Wash. and Jeff. harpooned her freely;
    Boston knocked her for a goal;
Harvard's annual performance must have
    warmed your iron soul
When the frog-like chorus faltered in
    their horror-haunted Bowl.

14. Bealle, *Football at Harvard*, p. 204.

15. Ibid., p. 211.

16. Furnas, *Great Times*, p. 383.

17. Crimson and Blue chauvinists have occasionally debated the advantages of the Stadium over the Bowl and vice versa. The latter is certainly much more comfortable and easier of access. But a good seat in the Stadium can bring the spectator very close to the action on the field—a bad seat is hardly worth paying for. In the Bowl, as a Harvard alumnus observed, "you cannot get a bad seat—nor a good one either." With regard to location, the Stadium and adjacent practice fields are certainly more useful to the armed forces than the Bowl and its playing fields. Young Bulldogs must spend at least forty minutes commuting to practice sessions; Harvard gladiators have only to walk across the bridge. An old Blue once remarked to me that by the time of the annual clash Harvard teams have had at least twenty hours more of practice than Yale teams.

On the other hand, a prominent Yale administrator maintains that in placing such temples of Hercules (he would include the baseball park) far from the campus Yale is tacitly making a significant statement. Almost everywhere else arrogant stadiums overshadow classrooms, labs, and libraries. Not at Yale.

18. The dire fate of his cohorts that sad day in the Bowl has obscured Talbot's own distinction. His election to the captaincy was a rare honor, for at that time he had had but one year of combat experience. (The ruling barring first-year men from varsity competition meant that "Sheff" undergraduates had only two years of eligibility, for at that time "Sheff" was a three-year course. Consequently, between 1907 and 1920 "Sheff" men were at a disadvantage in the competition for captaincy. Oddly enough, "Cupie" Black two years later duplicated Talbot's achievement.) Talbot went on to a very successful career in after years; a successful financier, he became also a generous philanthropist and served in both world wars, retiring from the Army Reserve as a brigadier general.

19. Haughton's comment is worthy of quotation. In *Football and How to Watch It*, p. 84, he writes:

Good coaches are content to perfect the known qualities of offense and defense, rather than attempt to "upset the apple-cart" by some untried method of attack. . . . The most radical departure from the beaten path occurred during 1914 at Yale, when an adaptation of the Canadian or Rugby principle of the lateral pass was introduced. Until the final game was played, this system of attack swept the defense off their feet, but Harvard devised a defense wherein only four men were stationed on the line of scrimmage, the other seven being so placed as to cope not only with the lateral but forward passes which had baffled Yale's other opponents. In spite of suffering a 36−0 defeat Yale on two occasions had the ball within Harvard's five-yard line, proving the unusual ground-gaining qualities of this scheme of attack.

20. Bealle, *Football at Harvard*, p. 220.

21. Cohane, *Yale Football Story*, p. 198.

22. *Yale Alumni Weekly*, November 26, 1915, pp. 307, 319−20.

23. James L. Knox, *The H Book of Harvard Athletics*, p. 432.

24. Cohane, *Yale Football Story*, p. 205.

25. Sixty-six years later Ralph Horween writes: "I have nightmares over the Yale game of 1916. Eddie Casey ran eighty yards for a touchdown but was called back for 'tripping' by Colcott Caner, who threw a block (he was a tackle and it was a line-around play) horizontally and his lower leg hit his man. Later, when Yale had the ball on about our 35-yard line, LeGore, coming through tackle on my side (I was playing wing back), fumbled just as I was going to tackle him. The ball hit his knee and rolled fast, going by everyone without being touched, and rolled out of bounds on about our 16-yard line. Yale's ball—and they scored." Letter to author, September 26, 1982.

26. Could he have read the future, perhaps P.D. would have chosen to return to his alma mater. He had little time left to him. Of his last years Harry von Kersburg writes (Bealle, *Football at Harvard* pp. 427−28):

After the war, P.D. again entered the financial field, where he remained until 1923 when he accepted the position of head coach at Columbia. He was building up football at Columbia as he had built it up at Harvard when he died suddenly on October 27, 1924, two hours after he had sent his squad through its daily practice. . . .

Two days prior to his death his team scored a fine victory over one of the strongest elevens that ever represented Williams. On that particular Saturday afternoon, a decidedly Harvard group was brought together in the Columbia−Williams game. When I returned to the locker building at Baker Field after the final whistle, Percy sent word by one of the football managers that he wanted to see me in the head coach's room. . . . We sat there for several hours and rehashed things that had taken place earlier in our careers, particularly in that never-to-be-forgotten Fall of 1908.

On Monday evening, October 27, just two days later, I was attending the weekly meeting of the Football Officials Association. Shortly after it had started, one of our members, a former coach at Columbia, joined us. I can still see him standing there saying, "Fellows, I have some very bad news. Percy Haughton died an hour ago!" The meeting was adjourned immediately by mutual consent. Most of us were too broken up to continue.

Of the many tributes paid him, Haughton would assuredly have most appreciated the words of Walter Camp, who had but a few months to live himself, when he wrote: "[Percy Haughton] was a commanding figure in the football world. He was a sportsman of the highest type. . . . He took life as he took sport, full of intense enthusiasm, which he communicated to all about him. And the remembrance of him will remain as an inspiration, not only to us who knew, admired, and loved him but to a succeeding generation of the university world (quoted in Danzig, *History of American Football*, p. 271).

27. Quoted by Bealle, *Football at Harvard*, p. 233.

28. Ibid., p. 247. Harvard's coach Fisher comments (*The H Book of Harvard Athletics*, p. 422): "As a sporting event the Harvard−Yale game of 1921 will never be forgotten. It was the kind of football we all like to see and undoubtedly satisfactory to those who are trying to reform the game." Like Horween, Aldrich has vivid memories of a bouncing ball. He recalls a Harvard fumble on the Crimson 20-yard line: hotly pursued by three Bulldogs, the oval capriciously nestled in the arms of the one Harvard defender in the area, who was totally surprised by Fortune's gift. Aldrich finds consolation in the statistical evidence that shows Yale outplayed her rival. Incidentally, he denies that his team was "overconfident." Letter to author, April 15, 1982.

Chapter 5. Toward Parity through Boom and Bust, 1923−1942

1. *New York Herald Tribune*, November 25, 1923, III, 1.

2. Ibid.

3. Bealle, *Football at Harvard*, p. 257.

4. *New York Times*, November 25, 1924.

5. Ibid.

6. Cohane, *Yale Football Story*, p. 238. Parke H. Davis's summary of Camp's career, published in the *Football Guide* for 1925, reminds us of Camp's amazing versatility as an athlete:

Walter Camp was a leader in sports afield and on the water. His were the fleetest feet in the schools of all New Haven. His arm was among the first and the best to master the new art of pitching a curve with a baseball. He was an adept in the water sports upon the Sound, powerful and versatile as a swimmer and diver, and able to bend and to feather an oar with the best of the watermen of the har-

bor. In Yale he made every varsity team that existed in that period. He was pitcher and captain of the nine. He was halfback and captain of the eleven. He ran the hurdles and is credited at Yale with having invented the present hurdle step. In swimming he repeatedly won races from short distances up to five miles. He rowed upon his class crew. (in Danzig, History of American Football, p. 126)

But Camp's versatility extended beyond the area of athletics. He was a more than competent writer, as is attested by his many journalistic pieces and the wide success of his wartime manual on exercise, *The Daily Dozen.* Nor did he lack the creative spark; his story *The Substitute,* written for a youthful public, shows a talent for managing narrative and characterization as well as a lean and lucid style. Among his undergraduate honors he had been chosen class poet by his classmates.

7. Funds for the memorial were raised by two committees, one representing the NCAA and the other Yale alumni. The gateway was formally dedicated on November 3, 1938, in a ceremony preceding the Dartmouth game. The *Yale Alumni Weekly* for November 9, 1928, p. 219, describes the memorial as "a lofty ornamental structure of brick and stone, seventy feet wide and fifty feet high, flanked by a low wall which extends on either side to a distance of about four hundred feet. . . . Over the arched entrance is carved 'Walter Camp Field,' and upon the walls are tablets which bear the names of the 224 other colleges and universities and the 279 preparatory and high schools which shared in the cost of the Memorial." It stands at the southern side of the Bowl enclosure, where of old the yellow trolley cars would discharge their passen-

gers. The structure was designed by John W. Cross, 1900. The roll call is impressive; it is truly a national tribute.

8. Will Cloney, in *The Second H Book of Harvard Athletics,* p. 62.

9. Bealle, *Football at Harvard,* p. 264.

10. Baker, *Notebook, 1920–1939,* p. 1904.

11. *New York Herald Tribune,* November 25, 1928.

12. Ibid., November 24, 1929.

13. The chronology might suggest that, as it sometimes happened, Yale had followed a Harvard initiative. But such was not the case. The notion of creating small residential units had been shared by Lowell and Angell, but it was Yale that made the first approach to Mr. Harkness and received his approval in principle (this was in the fall of 1929). But the endowment was contingent on the presentation of a definite plan, and for a complex of reasons Yale was slow in preparing one. In the interim the impatient Harkness took his offer to Harvard, where Lowell had his plan ready and waiting. Later, Harkness relented and generously funded the Yale colleges too. The tale, which reads like a novel of suspense, is told at length in George Wilson Pierson, *Yale, The University College, 1921–1937* (New Haven, 1955), pp. 207–45.

14. Morison, *Three Centuries of Harvard,* p. 269.

15. George C. Carens, *Boston Evening Transcript,* November 24, 1930, p. 4.

16. Harry Cross, *New York Herald Tribune,* November 23, 1930, III, 2.

17. Cloney, in *The Second H Book,* p. 77.

18. Cohane, *Yale Football Story,* p. 269.

19. Carens, *Boston Evening Transcript,* November 21, 1931.

20. Barry Wood was the scholar–athlete

par excellence. For three successive years he won his varsity letter in football, baseball, and hockey. He was also awarded a letter in tennis. He was captain of the football team and president of the student council. And he was elected to Phi Beta Kappa and graduated summa cum laude. It is a record unsurpassed by any athlete at Harvard and probably anywhere else. One cannot readily think of anyone who has matched it.

21. Cohane, *Yale Football Story,* p. 276

22. Harvard readers will pardon and Blue followers may fairly expect a little further comment on the Bulldogs of 1934, a rather unusual company. It was a team without stars—until Kelley flashed forth. Only two players, Captain Curtin and DeAngelis, had been starters in '33; it was a team of "unknowns." By the time of the Harvard game, however, it had become formidable on defense. "Choo-choo" Train at left end reminded some old-timers of Hinkey; Wright and Scott were an outstanding pair of tackles; Curtin, Grosscup, and DeAngelis (who distinguished himself in the Harvard game) were of like caliber. On offense Roscoe developed into a very good quarterback. Thirty-four was not a spectacular team (save for Kelley) but it was smart and strong. Three games were lost, to be sure, but none by the margin of more than one touchdown—and Curtin's warriors held both old rivals scoreless in the big games—an achievement not matched since.

23. *New Haven Register,* November 20, 1937, p. 1

24. Daniel Mulvey, *New Haven Register,* November 21, 1937.

25. *New Haven Register,* November 24, 1940.

26. Ibid.

27. Cohane, *Yale Football Story*, p. 303.

28. *Yale Alumni Magazine*, November 26, 1941, p. 10.

Chapter 6. Sailing to Ivyland, with Ollie at the Wheel, 1945–1956

1. Cloney, in *The Second H Book*, p. 27. Apparently it was about this time that the term *ivy* in the sense that we now use it came into being. "The term *Ivy League* was coined by the *New York Herald Tribune* sportswriter Caswell Adams in the 1930s to describe the older, prestigious men's colleges like Yale and Harvard. . . . His sports editor Stanley Woodward has also been credited with inventing the term *Ivy League*, which he probably took from Adams. Originating as a phrase of football jargon . . . it quickly became a popular term to describe many aspects of life associated with a small group of scholastically and socially prestigious Eastern schools." (Judith Ann Schiff, Chief Research Archivist, Yale University Library)

2. Cloney, in *The Second H Book*, p. 28.

3. Ibid., p. 200.

4. Daniel F. Mulvey, *New Haven Register*, November 24, 1946, II, 2.

5. *New York Times*, November 23, 1946.

6. Cloney, in *The Second H Book* p. 102.

7. Ibid., p. 103.

8. In the world of the forties the election of a black to an Ivy League team captaincy was a notable event. Jackson was not only Yale's first black captain but also her first black player. Perhaps concern for Harvard's primacy in this area of integration moved Wilbur Wood, sports editor of the *New York Sun*, to report (in the *Sun* of November 24, 1948, reprinted in Bealle, *Football at Harvard*, pp. 534–35) that on Thanksgiving Day of 1893, William H. Lewis, "a Negro," had been chosen Harvard's captain for the game with the University of Pennsylvania, since Waters, the regular captain, had been injured and could not play. Jurists may debate whether this gives Harvard a true primacy in this special sector. For statisticians of such matters it may be noted that, leaving Lewis aside, Yale has now had two black captains and Harvard one.

9. Cloney, in *The Second H Book*, p. 111. It is good to know that the William J. Bingham Award "awarded to that member of the graduating class of Harvard College who, because of his integrity, courage, leadership and ability on the athletic field, has best served the high purposes of Harvard as exemplified by former Athletic Director William J. Bingham," first given in 1954, is the most coveted honor that a Harvard athlete can receive. (Ibid., p. 37)

10. Ibid., p. 114.

11. Allison Danzig, *New York Times*, November 21, 1953.

12. Cloney, in *The Second H Book*, p. 115.

13. *New York Times*, November 21, 1954.

14. *New Haven Register*, November 20, 1955.

15. McCallum, *Ivy League Football*, p. 182.

16. Cloney, in *The Second H Book*, p. 122.

17. Randall Beach, Harvard, '71, in the Special Supplement to the *Journal Courier* and the *New Haven Register*, November 18, 1983. Nor has the tailgate lacked its bard. An anonymous Eli sings:

In the season of the pigskin
we foregather at the tailgate.
Thither, from their lairs in Woodbridge
and Strathcona come the Yale greats,
thither come the lordly Masters
with their gracious debonair dames,
lawyers too and doctors, bankers
and full many a grizzled late great—
some in shining brand new Lincolns
some in dented out of date crates
differing in style and status
all to mingle with their playmates . . .

Chapter 7. The Yovicsin Years, 1957–1970

1. *The Second H Book*, p. 124.

2. Ibid., pp. 124–25.

3. Letter to author, July 31, 1972.

4. Olivar had opposed the innovation. He writes (in the letter cited above): "The extra point by kicking had been bad enough but henceforth all coaches would be put on the spot; no matter what choice they made second-guessers would fault them."

5. *The Second H Book*, p. 132.

6. "Just so the crowd could see them one more time—and the crowd responded beautifully." Jordan Olivar to author, August 14, 1972.

7. *The Second H Book*, p. 139.

8. *News and Views: Harvard Sports Review*, November 29, 1962, p. 3.

9. McCallum, *Ivy League Football*, p. 207.

10. Ibid., pp. 208–09.

11. "The Last of Football," *The New Yorker*, Nov. 2, 1946, pp. 35–36.

12. McCallum, *Ivy League Football*, p. 213

13. *News and Views*, November 28, 1967.

14. Ibid., p. 3.

15. Contemplation of these lofty peaks

of rarely shared eminence leads inevitably to comparisons, some of which illuminate the progress—or at least the changes—in the sport as well as in the country over a period of six decades. With regard to the personnel the differences are truly noteworthy. First of all, in 1909 the combined total of warriors engaged was thirty-four (eighteen for Yale and sixteen for Harvard); in 1968 no fewer than eighty-five make up the combined total (thirty-nine for Yale and forty-six for Harvard). For the twenty-two starters in 1909 the average weight was 190 pounds and the average height 5 11¾. Figures for the twenty-four starters (i.e., the offensive and defensive lineups) for 1968 are 202 pounds and 6 ⅝. Yet, though lighter and shorter than the '68 delegations, those of '09 played two halves of forty-five minutes each as compared to the four fifteen-minute quarters of today. Although the forward pass was legal in '09, only four attempts were made, two by each team; none was complete. In 1968 a total of forty-three passes was thrown, with twenty-one completed. In 1909 the punt total was twenty-seven, in 1968 only fourteen.

Moving to the social-demographic department, we may note that in 1909 only four high school graduates were in the starting lineup; three for Yale and one for Harvard. Of the forty-four starters of '68, twenty-eight were high school graduates; eighteen for Yale and ten for Harvard. As for provenience, six states are represented in the Harvard team of '09 plus one member hailing from Paris, France; Yale had representatives of nine states. For both teams Massachusetts was the leading supplier; 27 percent of the Harvards and 10 percent of the Elis hailed from the Bay State. In 1968 both roll calls included

representatives of ten states; for Harvard the largest single contributor was again Massachusetts and for Yale it was Ohio. Attendance had gone up a little but not much: 38,000 in '09, 40,000 in '68 (there would have been more had the game been played in the Bowl).

16. *Harvard Alumni Bulletin*, December 2, 1968, p. 7.

17. Steve Cady, *New York Times*, November 24, 1968, V, p. 1.

18. *New Haven Register*, November 24, 1968.

19. Some disappointed followers of the Blue faulted Cozza for not inserting Dowling and Hill on defense in those last frenzied seconds. But Carm felt—and still feels—that defense was better left to those who had been trained for it.

20. *News and Views*, November 27, 1968.

21. Sutton, *Cambridge Reconsidered*, p. 113.

22. The account of Bobby Seale weekend is covered in "May Day at Yale: A Chronicle of Events," a special section of the *Yale Alumni Magazine* for May 1970.

23. *News and Views*, December 1, 1970, p. 2.

24. *Yale Daily News*, November 23, 1970, p. 1.

Chapter 8. The Ballad of Carm and Joe, 1971–1983

1. *News and Views*, November 28, 1972, p. 4.

2. *Football Y News*, November 30, 1973, p. 5.

3. Integrationists may note that the replacement of Gesicki by Gordon gave the Bulldog almost an all-black backfield; only Tommy Doyle was white.

4. *News and Views*, November 27, 1974, p. 4.

5. Ibid.

6. *News and Views*, November 25, 1975, p. 4. Jon Judge added: "It's a pleasure to play a team like that. They're real sportsmen." In the same column Dave Matthews notes that Jiggetts "was the first person to captain Harvard in an indisputed championship year."

7. *Football Y News*, November 16, 1976, p. 4.

8. After the game, Cordova spoke with admiration of Spagnola's feat: "If one man made the difference, he did" (quoted by Joe Concannon, *Boston Globe*, November 19, 1978, p. 41).

9. *Football Y News*, November 21, 1978, p. 5.

10. Ibid., p. 4.

11. *Football Y News*, November 20, 1979, p. 3. The *Yale Alumni Magazine*, seeing in the tragedy the operation of an eternal law, headed its account of The Game with the caption "Fama vitrea est; tum, cum splendet, frangitur."

12. *Football Y News*, November 25, 1980, p. 6.

13. Cloney, *News and Views*, November 23, 1982, p. 1.

14. *Football Y News*, November 23, 1982, p. 1.

15. Since it seems unlikely that such a glittering company will assemble again in our lifetime, it is only fitting that the roll should be called here (names are followed by years of their captaincies). For Harvard the muster runs: Hamilton Fish, 1909, John H. Dean, 1933, Herman W. Gundlach, Jr., 1934, C. Russell Allen, 1937, Joseph W. Gardella, 1940, Francis M. Lee, 1941, Donald Forte, 1942, Lloyd M. Anderson, 1943, Walter H. Trumbull, Jr., 1944, Robert Cowan II, 1945, Cleo A. O'Donnell, Jr., 1946, Philip L. Isenberg, 1950, Carroll M. Lowenstein, 1951, War-

ren D. Wylie, 1951, John D. Nichols,
1952, Richard J. Clasby, 1953, William W.
Meigs, 1955, Robert T. Shaunessy, 1958,
Harold J. Keohane, 1959, William South-
mayd, 1963, John F. O'Brien, 1964, Ken-
neth L. Boyda, 1965, Justin Hughes, 1966,
Donald J. Chiofaro, 1967, Victor E. Gatto,
Jr., 1968, John F. Cramer, 1969, David P.
St. Pierre, 1973, Brian P. Hehir, 1974,
Steven J. Kaseta, 1977, Michael G.
Brown, 1979, Charles F. Durst, 1980,
Peter M. Coppinger, 1981. For Yale the
veterans present were: Henry H. Ket-
cham, 1913, Malcolm P. Aldrich, 1921,
Winslow M. Lovejoy, 1924, Philip W.
Bunnell, 1926, Waldo W. Greene, 1929,
Francis T. Vincent, 1930, Mather K.
Whitehead, 1935, Lawrence M. Kelley,
1936, Clinton E. Frank, 1937, J. William
Stack, Jr., 1939, Harold B. Whiteman, Jr.,
1940, Spencer D. Mosely, 1942, Town-
send W. Hoopes, 1943, Macauley Whit-
ing, 1944, Endicott Davison, 1947, William E. Conway, 1948, Robert S. Spears,
1951, Joseph B. Mitinger, 1952, S. Joseph
Fortunato, 1953, Philip S. Tarasovic,
1955, John F. Embersits, 1957, Michael
Pyle, 1960, George Humphrey, 1963, H.
Abbott Lawrence, 1964, Brian Dowling,
1968, Robert Perschel, 1972, Gary Wilhelm, 1973, John Smoot, 1975, William
Crowley, 1978, Timothy Tumpane, 1979,
Frederick Leone, 1981, Patrick Ruwe,
1982.

Books

Baker, L. H. *Notebooks*. Three bound volumes of typescript containing descriptions of games, with lineups and commentary, played between 1875 and 1939. In archives of the Yale Department of Athletics.

Bealle, Morris A. *The History of Football at Harvard, 1874–1948*. Washington, D.C.: Columbia, 1948.

Cohane, Tim. *The Yale Football Story*. New York: Putnam's, 1950.

Danzig, Allison. *The History of American Football*. Englewood Cliffs: Prentice-Hall, 1956.

———. *Oh, How They Played the Game*. New York: Macmillan, 1971.

Davis, Parke H. *Football: The American Intercollegiate Game*. New York: Scribner's, 1911.

Football Y Men, 1872–1919. Edited by Albert Beecher Crawford. Men of Yale Series. Volume 1. Yale University, 1962.

Football Y Men, 1920–1939. Men of Yale Series. Volume 2. Yale University, 1963.

Football Y Men, 1940–1960. Edited by Albert B. Crawford. Men of Yale Series. Volume 3. Yale University, 1963.

Furnas, J. C. *Great Times: An Informal Social History of the United States, 1914–1929*. New York: Putnam's, 1974.

The H Book of Harvard Athletics. Edited by John A. Blanchard, '91. Published by the Harvard Varsity Club. Printed at the Harvard University Press, Cambridge, Mass., 1923.

Haughton, Percy D. *Football and How to Watch It*. Boston: Marshall Jones, 1922.

Kelley, Brooks Mather. *Yale: A History*. New Haven and London: Yale University Press, 1974.

McCallum, John. *Ivy League Football since 1872*. New York: Stein and Day, 1977.

Morison, Samuel Eliot. *Three Centuries of Harvard, 1636–1936*. Cambridge, Mass.: The Belknap Press of Harvard University Press, 1936.

Pierson, George Wilson. *Yale College and University, 1871–1937*. Volume 1, *Yale College: An Educational History, 1871–1921*. New Haven: Yale University Press, 1952. Volume 2, *Yale: The University College, 1921–1937*. New Haven: Yale University Press, 1955.

Powel, Harford, Jr. *Walter Camp, The Father of American Football: An Authorized Biography*. Boston: Little, Brown, 1926.

The Second H Book of Harvard Athletics, 1923–1963. Edited by Geoffrey H. Movius, '62. Published by The Harvard Varsity Club. Cambridge, Mass., 1964.

Stagg, Amos Alonzo, as told to Wesley Winans Stout. *Touchdown!* New York: Longmans, Green, 1927.

Sutton, S. B. S. *Cambridge Reconsidered. 3½ Centuries on the Charles*. Cambridge, Mass.: The MIT Press, 1976.

Periodicals

I have not listed newspapers and magazines cited since all are self-identifying. However, three items call for special definition:

Edward Byrne, "The Yale–Harvard Series," was published in the program for the 1959 game.

The Football Y News is published weekly during the football season by the Sports Information Office of the Yale Department of Athletics. It is sponsored by the Football Y Association.

News and Views: Harvard Sports Review is published by the Harvard Varsity Club. It appears weekly throughout the academic year.